Bobby Kennedy

THE MAKING
OF A FOLK HERO

Also by Lester David

THE LONELY LADY OF SAN CLEMENTE:
THE STORY OF PAT NIXON

SECOND SIGHT

TED KENNEDY: TRIUMPHS AND TRAGEDIES

JOAN, THE RELUCTANT KENNEDY

ETHEL: THE STORY OF MRS. ROBERT F. KENNEDY

JACKIE AND ARI (WITH JHAN ROBBINS)

RICHARD AND ELIZABETH (WITH JHAN ROBBINS)

IKE AND MAMIE:
THE STORY OF THE GENERAL AND HIS LADY
(WITH IRENE DAVID)

THE SHIRLEY TEMPLE STORY
(WITH IRENE DAVID)

Bobby Kennedy

THE MAKING OF A FOLK HERO

Lester David
and
Irene David

DODD, MEAD & COMPANY • NEW YORK

To

Baran and Robert and Sarah Nan
and the others who may yet come.

All photographs not credited were provided through the courtesy of the John F. Kennedy Library.

Copyright © 1986 by Lester David and Irene David

Published by Dodd, Mead & Company, Inc.
79 Madison Avenue, New York, N.Y. 10016

Distributed in Canada by
McClelland and Stewart Limited, Toronto

Manufactured in the United States of America

Designed by Jeremiah B. Lighter

First Edition

1   2   3   4   5   6   7   8   9   10

Library of Congress Cataloging-in-Publication Data

Lester.
  Bobby Kennedy: the making of a folk hero.
  Bibliography: p.
  Includes index.
  1. Kennedy, Robert F., 1925–1968. 2. Legislators—
United States—Biography. 3. United States. Congress.
Senate—Biography. I. David, Irene. II. Title.

E840.8.K4D38   1986   973.922'092'4 [B]   86-8902
ISBN 0-396-08501-6

Contents

Acknowledgments

The authors express grateful appreciation to all those who contributed information for this book, including members of the Kennedy family, political associates as well as foes, classmates, teachers, neighbors, friends, newspersons, and archivists in the United States and England.

It is not possible to list all those who gave so graciously of their time—their contributions are cited in the text—but we owe a special debt of gratitude to a number, and we thank them herewith for their kind and considerable assistance:

We thank Ramsey Clark, Pierre Salinger, former Senators Eugene McCarthy, George Smathers, Fred Harris, and Jacob Javits, Cesar Chavez and his staff at the United Farm Workers Organizing Committee, James H. Meredith, Edwin Guthman, John Seigenthaler, Donald Wilson, Harris Wofford, John English, John Burns, Jennie Littlefield (formerly Mrs. Allard Lowenstein), Pete Hamill, Kristi Witker, Roger Rosenblatt, LaDonna Harris, José Torres, Gene Schoor, Joe McCarthy, Willard Edwards, and Ronnie Eldridge.

Also David Hackett, Samuel Adams, Nicholas Rodis, Don Dowd, Luella Hennessey Donovan, E. Gerald Tremblay, and Endicott Peabody Davison. Invaluable was the cooperation of the staff of Portsmouth Priory and the teachers, former classmates, and others at Milton Academy, especially Herbert G. Stokinger, Adams Carter, Emily Perry, Mrs. Albert Norris, and Thomas and Charlotte Cleveland.

Grateful appreciation is also extended to the staff of the John F. Kennedy Library at Columbia Point, in Boston, for their patience and assistance during the many months of research there, particularly Dr. Henry Gwiazda, curator of the RFK Collection; E. William Johnson, chief archivist; Ronald E. Whealan, librarian; Barbara Anderson, archivist; Allan Goodrich, audiovisual archivist; Michael Desmond, research assistant; and Joan Carey, librarian. They were most helpful (and extraordinarily patient) in providing access to the numerous oral histories collected there in both the RFK and JFK Oral History programs, to the vast political and personal RFK files, and to new archival accessions and openings previously unavailable to researchers. Thanks are also due to Antoinette W. Roades for research in Charlottesville.

Special thanks, too, are offered to the staff of the Press Association on Fleet Street in London, which, through the courtesy of David Chipp, editor in chief, allowed us to consult the mines of information in its files.

Extensive personal files kept by the authors for more than two decades, including hundreds of interviews, have been drawn upon for this book, although most of the content is based on new research and interviews with those whose lives touched that of Robert Kennedy. The authors have had conversations over the years with Senator Edward Kennedy at Hyannis Port and Washington; with Joan Kennedy, his former wife; and with Rose Kennedy. Considerable unpublished material obtained in interviews with the late Kenneth P. O'Donnell, Lemoyne K. Billings, and Marvella Bayh are also included, and acknowledgment is hereby made. The authors talked frequently with Lem Billings over the years but refrained from printing his more pungent comments during his lifetime; his passing has liberated us from that self-imposed restriction, as it has for Kenny O'Donnell's often uninhibited observations.

To Lewis W. Gillenson, friend for many years, we offer deepest appreciation for encouragement and wise counsel. And we extend our sincerest gratitude to Cynthia Vartan for her guidance and superb editorial skills over the long, long haul.

Lester David and Irene David

PART
ONE

Chrysalis[*]

[*] The state into which the larva of most insects passes
before becoming an imago (the final and perfect form
of an insect after its metamorphosis). In the chrysalis
state, it is wrapped in a hard sheath.
—*The Oxford Universal Dictionary*

"There was a kind of mystical aura about him something that was electrifying and almost religious in its intensity."

Cesar Chevaz

RFK
A Prologue

*A*FTER SUNDOWN on an unseasonably hot day in spring, Robert Kennedy ended a five-hour tour of a Manhattan neighborhood. Perspiration pasted his white shirt to his back as, head sunk almost to his chest, he crossed Park Avenue—not the broad boulevard of exclusive apartment buildings, but where it narrows into the Spanish Harlem of dirt and decay.

Kennedy's guide through the mean streets that day in 1968 had been José Torres, the former world's light-heavyweight boxing champion, who knew them well. The two men walked in silence toward Bobby's automobile, parked beyond the heavy, grime-caked arches supporting elevated tracks where commuter trains rattle past the rotting tenements, heading for affluent Westchester and Connecticut suburbs.

Ever since Bobby had announced his candidacy for the Presidency, Torres had wondered why the rich man's son came to the ghettos on quick trips back east; why, in fact, he was working so hard and so long, often sixteen hours every day, for a goal that seemed so distant for him. At the car, Torres asked, "Why are you doing this? Why are you running?"

Bobby replied in a voice so low José had to lean close to catch the words.

"Because I found out something I never knew," Kennedy told him. "I found out that my world was not the real world."[1]

3

The answer, ingenuous in its simplicity and directness, encapsuled the transformation of Robert Francis Kennedy from a self-admitted social problems illiterate into a passionate crusader for the deprived.

This century has not seen a more remarkable reversal made by a public figure.

As the twentieth anniversary of his murder draws near, Robert emerges as the Kennedy who felt the deepest, cared the most, and fought the hardest for humanity—crying out against America's involvement in the Vietnam War, championing the causes of blacks, Hispanics, and Mexican-Americans, and crusading against the suffering of children, the elderly, and anyone else hurt or bypassed by social and economic progress.

Strangely, this legacy was created only in his final seven years. In the first thirty-five, his public persona was considerably less than admirable.

Bobby grew up knowing in his head that there were untold millions of people outside the Hyannis Port compound and the gates of his family's succession of fine suburban homes who were less fortunate than the Kennedys, but he did not know it emotionally. Joe Kennedy told his children at those much-reported dinner/quiz/lecture periods that underprivileged people existed in America, and that they were—somehow—expected to do something about it all.

But Bobby was not touched. "You don't know," he told José Torres one day in the barrios, "unless you *see*." Since he did not see until maturity, little wonder that when asked how Joe Kennedy's offspring felt about the condition of the Negroes in the United States, he responded, "We didn't lie awake thinking about it. . . . I don't think it was a matter we were extra concerned about."

He added, "As we were growing up, there wasn't any great problem."[2]

The naive comment was one that only a cloistered son of wealth could make. In the America of the Twenties to the Forties—the years of his "growing up"—the problem was monstrously large and scarcely hidden. "The Negro in the South," wrote John Gunther in 1946, the year Bobby turned twenty-one, "has to be seen to be believed."[3] But for the next fifteen years, young Kennedy did not see the sad story being played out.

In the South, the policy of segregation was unwavering and absolute in the schools, recreation areas, and all public places, but it barely existed for Bobby. He grew to manhood "unconcerned" that blacks were not permitted to argue with white people over anything or shake their hands or, even if they were eminent doctors, professors, or scientists, enter the homes of whites by the front door. If there was no gas, water, or electricity in southern communities because utility lines stopped at the edge of white neighborhoods, he was unaffected. Thousands of lynchings were estimated to be occurring every year, yet even up to 1952, the year his brother ran for his first political office, Bobby could not recall a single occasion when the condition of the Negro in Boston or anywhere else constituted an issue for the Kennedys.

By then he was a grown man of twenty-seven, a lawyer and campaign manager for John, who was seeking a congressional seat from the Eleventh District, which encompassed the north and east ends of Boston. Bobby's interest was focused only on electing John.

"We weren't thinking of the Negroes in Mississippi or Alabama, or what could be done for them," he said. "We were concerned only with what could be done [for the candidate] in Massachusetts."[4]

Since there were not many blacks either in Massachusetts or the district in which John was running, Bobby paid scant attention to them or their problems. When he went into the wards where they clustered, he was there for a very practical reason: "[We] were simply looking at how many votes we would receive, rather than what [we] were going to do afterward particularly," he said. When John was elected to Congress, he did nothing "particularly," and Bobby never urged him to act otherwise.

Even up to the time of his brother's election to the Presidency and his own appointment to the Cabinet, Bobby Kennedy was candidly admitting that he "wasn't thinking about them [blacks] much . . . I didn't know about all the injustice."[5]

The process of growth and change started soon after he was named United States Attorney General in 1961, at the age of thirty-six. By the time he was gunned down in that grease-spattered Los Angeles pantry, he had metamorphosed utterly—not in his intense emotionalism, his capacity to rage against enemies, his moralism or his ferocious, near-obsessive drive to achieve goals, but in the nature of the goals themselves.

"I never saw a change in his character," said Harris Wofford, the college professor who worked closely with Bobby as special assistant to President Kennedy for civil rights. "But I did see a great change in his view of the world."[6]

Because he stirred people up, he was hated with a frightening intensity by many and, at the same time, loved with a near fanatic devotion by others.

Right-wingers called for his blood, quite literally.

One day in the spring of 1968, William Sullivan, the number-three man in the FBI at the time, was at headquarters talking with J. Edgar Hoover, the director, and Clyde Tolson, his second in command. Sullivan was shocked to hear Tolson utter this venomous comment about Bobby: "I hope that someone shoots and kills the son of a bitch."[7]

A few years earlier, Tolson, Hoover's close friend and companion for decades, had burst out after the assassination of JFK: "Goddamn the Kennedys! First there was Jack, now there's Bobby, and then Teddy. We'll have them on our necks until the year 2000.'' Hoover, who hated them, too, had nodded his head in agreement.[8]

Hating Bobby became faddish in places as diverse as saloons in the rural South, swank northern country clubs, and reform Democratic clubhouses, where, as Jack Newfield says, his very name was the equivalent of an epithet.

But when Bobby came to visit Cesar Chavez, with whom he had formed an almost mystical relationship, hundreds of members of Chavez's United Farm Workers Organizing Committee rushed at him, just to touch his hand. When Kennedy finally disentangled himself, his hands were scratched and bleeding.

Chavez called him ''my brother''; the NAACP said, ''Robert Kennedy was the best Attorney General on civil rights in the whole history of the United States.''[9] By 1968, he aroused liberals to a frenzy of excitement wherever he appeared, particularly the young. He was mobbed by girls, who gave him the wild reception they reserve for superstar sex symbols, but boys, too, cheered him worshipfully.

Bobby knew he was hated. ''I am so well aware of being disliked,'' he said, ''that it no longer surprises or disturbs me. I no longer care.'' He understood the reasons, too: ''I have been too closely involved in too many struggles.''

But he also understood that he had the affection of others. ''They elected me, did they not?'' he said. ''The poorer people like me. They are for me, I know.''[10]

The contradictions in his character and behavior throughout his brief life were as startling as the love-hate he engendered.

He was, indeed (the word must resurface after nearly twenty years), ruthless, despite his own and his followers' denials. ''We're a young group, and we're going to take over America,'' he announced before a state caucus that had not made up its mind whom to nominate in Los Angeles in 1960. After Jack became the candidate, Bobby barged through the campaign with tunnel-vision determination to elect him, regardless of who would be hurt. With index finger outthrust, he made his views clear to New York City reform leaders during his brother's Presidential campaign: ''Gentlemen,'' he said, ''I don't give a damn if the State and County organizations survive after November, and I don't give a damn if you survive. I want to elect John F. Kennedy.''[11]

Time and again, the older brother had to apologize for Bobby's actions, promising to ''talk'' to him. Bobby didn't care what other people thought of him. His brother could smooth their feathers, if he wished, but he would not. ''If they aren't getting off their asses, how do you say that nicely?'' he asked.[12]

After Jack's assassination, Marvin Belli, defense counsel for Jack Ruby, summed up a widely prevailing view in caustic terms: "He's arrogant, rude, and even ignorant of the law. He's the moneyed Little Lord Fauntleroy of Government. Every newspaperman knows he is, and even [President Lyndon] Johnson can't stand him, but everybody's too scared of the son of a bitch."[13]

But that same year, Bobby heard that a black National Guardsman named Cooper, a resident of the District of Columbia, was ambushed and killed while on duty in Georgia. Kennedy called in Wes Barthelmes, his press aide, and told him to make sure Cooper's widow and four children received adequate financial help from his personal funds. Soon after, the mother died of natural causes. Bobby put all work aside to find out who would care for the orphaned children. He and Barthelmes traced the family to an aunt in Syracuse. He called her and made arrangements to provide for the children. "I don't want it to get out," he told Barthelmes.[14] It never did, until now, when the death of the press aide ended the restriction he had placed on publication of the oral history he had made for the Kennedy Library.

He was in the world of politics all his adult life, as an investigator and prosecutor for congressional committees, as a Cabinet member, and in elected office, yet he did not like politicians. He once said, "There aren't ten politicians in the whole state [of New York] I like and trust."

He was a sharp-taloned hawk in the early years of the Vietnam War, voting for appropriations to fuel America's involvement, and ended up as one of the most powerful opponents of the conflict in the U.S. Senate.

He was an ardent McCarthyite in the days when the liberals called the Communist-hunting junior senator from Wisconsin every contemptuous name in their lexicons; when the President's own brother, Arthur Eisenhower, described Joseph R. McCarthy as a "throwback to the Spanish Inquisition"; when the cartoonist Herblock continually caricatured him as an ape and the political writer Richard Rovere assailed him as a "bully" and a "fraud." Yet the Bobby who defended this man ended up more liberal than the must vituperative McCarthy critic.

Only family members and close friends ever called him Bobby. To others who worked for and with him, he was Bob. He himself always introduced himself as Bob Kennedy. The childish nickname didn't fit the mature man with the deepening lines in his face and graying hair, yet the nation and the world knew him as Bobby. In Paris, beneath the front page of *France Soir* announcing his death, which was displayed outside the newspaper's office, someone had written, "Good Bye Bobby."

He had simple tastes in food and clothes—he rarely carried money, never wore a watch, and always had to borrow a pen—but his world vision

7

was grand and lofty. Once David Frost asked him in a television interview what he would like the first line of his obituary to read. Kennedy answered with a quotation from the French author Albert Camus:

Perhaps we cannot prevent this world from being a world in which children are tortured. But we can prevent the number of tortured children.

Kennedy told Frost he wanted to be remembered "as one who tried to lessen that suffering."

He lived by the code of a stern moralist, bred into him by a variety of elements: partly his devout Catholicism; partly his early experiences in battling corruption, which truly shocked him as he came up close to the seaminess in society; partly a sensitivity honed to an extra-keenness by his own painful experiences; and partly by who knows what. Those who seek answers to human behavior can trace just so deeply, then get lost in the labyrinths of the human mind.

He is remembered as he wished to be—by the world and, what would be far more important to him, by his children. His oldest daughter, Kathleen, is an attorney and social activist who worked as a public defender, has specialized in environmental law, and says, "I am committed to social change, equal justice, equal economic rights."[15] His oldest son, Joseph P. Kennedy III, is the founder and head of a nonprofit company selling heating oil to the needy at costs far below market prices. Both have embarked on political careers.

As for his two youngest children:

On December 6, 1984, seventeen-year-old Douglas Harriman and his sister Rory, sixteen, left their home in McLean, Virginia, and went by car to the South African embassy on Massachusetts Avenue in Washington.

In Douglas's pocket was a folded sheet of paper. The evening before, he had torn it from a school notebook and copied some sentences from a book in his family's library. He and Rory joined a demonstration that was already in progress at the embassy. College students, clad in jeans, many with the names of their schools on their sweaters, massed on the sidewalk and spilled out into the streets, chanting, "Free South Africa! Free Namibia! Free the slums! Free the ghettos! All people must be free!"

The demonstration was part of a protest movement against South Africa's racial policies of apartheid that was spreading across the nation. Protesters, who were nonviolent, were being arrested in Boston, New York, and Chicago. Young Kennedy mounted a makeshift rostrum and, reading from his sheet of notebook paper, said, "I feel my presence here and the presence of so many other students symbolizes the fact that my father's ideals for the world are still alive."

He paused as Rory Elizabeth took her place beside him. The pretty blond teenager had never known her father; she was born six months and a week after he died. Douglas read:

> Each time a man stands up for an ideal or acts to improve the lot of others or strikes out against injustice, he sends forth a tiny ripple of hope, and crossing each other from a million different centers of energy and daring, those ripples build a current which can sweep down the mightiest walls of oppression and resistance.

His father had written those words and, exactly two years before he died, spoke them in the great hall of the University of Capetown in South Africa.

After Douglas finished, he and Rory went to the embassy, where police barricades had been erected. They crossed the lines and, at the very door, linked arms and began singing "We Shall Overcome."

Two burly policemen arrested the young Kennedys along with a friend and took them to the station house, where they were charged as juveniles with the misdemeanor of congregating within 500 feet of an embassy with intent to demonstrate.

"My whole family has been concerned with this issue for a long time," Douglas said as he was led away.

Bobby Kennedy would have loved it.

1

His Father's Son

A STIFF October wind cut the faces but not the spirits of several hundred students and their parents watching a football game at Milton Academy, south of Boston, one afternoon in 1943. On the tawny grass beneath the embankment where the spectators sat, the school's team was on its way to its second straight undefeated season, a fact that had everyone in a state bordering on delirium.

Milton defeated Thayer Academy in the closing minutes by a score of 7 to 6, the victory due in large measure to the hard-charging efforts of its slim blocking back, listed in the lineup as Robert F. Kennedy. It was Kennedy, too, who caught the ball and held it as his lifelong friend, Dave Hackett, kicked the winning point after the tying touchdown.*

After more than four decades, Coach Herbert Stokinger—"Stokie" to generations of Miltonians—has vivid recollections of that game, that season, and the 150-pound team member. At the age of eighteen, Bobby Kennedy was a regular on Stokie's eleven, a good performer though never a star, with one characteristic that marked his style of play.

"Bob loved to crunch," said Stokie, who retired a few years ago as Milton's director of physical education and athletics. (Now the playing field, on the northern edge of the campus, is named after him.)

"When Bob was blocking, he cast all caution to the winds and really *blocked*. When he tackled, he cast all caution to the winds and *tackled!*

"He loved to hit his man. And when he hit, he seemed to come alive."[1]

* The following week, the team journeyed to Groton, where it lost.

10

Bobby's intense, lifelong need to battle fiercely, and when necessary to "crunch," demonstrated early in life by his behavior at Milton, has been attributed to his standing as the seventh of nine children of Rose and Joseph P. Kennedy. He himself said, "When you come from that far down, you have to struggle to survive."

Yet Edward Moore (Teddy) was even further down in the birth order, last of the nine, and he grew up plump, cheerful, and uncomplaining, with the best disposition of any of his brothers and little need to "prove" himself. Teddy never had any desire to "crunch." His nurse, Luella Hennessey Donovan, who was hired in 1937 when Teddy was five, said, "He was the sweetest and kindest of all the boys."[2]

Bobby was different. But the source of his temperament was not his runt-of-the-litter status in the family circle, as has been commonly assumed, but the patriarch who dominated much of his life.

By the time Bobby was born on November 20, 1925,* Joe Kennedy was already worth more than a million dollars, a vast fortune in those pre-inflation years, with much more to come. But he had failed to achieve a lifelong ambition to cross the invisible barrier erected by the Boston Brahmins against Irish Catholics.

Joe's story was not a Horatio Alger tale. Born September 6, 1888, he, too, was a wealthy man's son. His father, P. J. Kennedy, was a powerful politician who had served five terms in the Massachusetts state legislature. It was Bobby's great-grandfather whose blood had boiled when, arriving from County Wexford, Ireland, after the potato famine of 1848, he had heard himself and his fellow immigrants scorned as the "scum of creation" by the Yankees and was met with "No Irish Need Apply" signs when he looked for work. That Patrick Kennedy found a job as a cooper, but died only fourteen years later.

Young Pat, Joe's father, orphaned at four and raised by his mother and older sisters, held a variety of jobs on the Boston docks, eventually putting together enough money to buy a tavern. The taverns served as clubs for the Irish immigrants, a place where they could swap tips on jobs, housing, and politics, as well as get help. P. J. was kind and influential. He soon developed his own political organization, becoming one of the strongest ward bosses in East Boston, and acquired a second tavern. Later, he sold them, became a wholesale liquor dealer, and moved into banking, organizing the Columbia Trust Company and the Sumner Savings Bank.

The family lived in a big house on Webster Street, and, unlike many of

---

* Each time Rose presented Joe with a child, he gave her a gift, increasingly expensive as his fortunes improved. After Jean, Bobby's younger sister, arrived, Rose received an exquisite diamond bracelet. When a friend of the family asked Joe what he could think of to give his wife if she had another baby, he replied, "A black eye." Teddy was the next one born.[3]

his peers, Joe did not need summer and afterschool jobs for pocket money, although he invariably managed to find or create some. P. J. sent him to the prestigious Boston Latin School, where Protestant Boston sent its progeny, and to Harvard, where few Irish Catholics were enrolled at the time. Joe was popular, did spectacularly well in extracurricular activities, but was never admitted to the top echelon of the schools' social groups. He made the Hasty Pudding Dramatic Club but was turned down for the most elite of institutions, the Porcellian and the Fly clubs, rebuffs he felt keenly all his life.

Joe had met Rose Fitzgerald, the beautiful, dark-haired daughter of another old Boston politician, John "Honey Fitz" Fitzgerald, when they were both children vacationing with their families at Orchard Beach, Maine. The oldest of the young Fitzgeralds, Rose dated Joe often in their growing-up years, dismaying her ambitious father, who thought his daughter could do better.

Upon his graduation from Harvard in 1912, Kennedy took a job in the counting rooms of the Columbia Trust, which he soon left to become an assistant bank examiner for the Commonwealth of Massachusetts. He spent the next eighteen months mastering the intricacies of banking and finance, and when Columbia Trust was up for sale, Joe borrowed the money to get a controlling share of stock. At twenty-five, he became its president, the youngest bank president in the United States.

Honey Fitz, master of the art of political strategy, failed to keep his daughter and Joe Kennedy apart, though he tried every trick he knew. He arranged long trips for Rose during Joe's vacation periods at Harvard. Once he sent her to study abroad for an entire year with her sister Agnes. Rose went dutifully, but carried a photograph of Joe in her suitcase.

At length, Honey Fitz had to yield, his objections vanishing with Joe's rapid, and surprising, rise in the world of banking and finance. On October 7, 1914, he gave his twenty-four-year-old daughter in marriage to twenty-six-year-old Joe Kennedy at a small wedding in the private chapel of William Cardinal O'Donnell, the Archbishop of Boston. After a short honeymoon, the young people set up housekeeping in a three-story gray frame house at 83 Beals Street, Brookline. Their first child, Joseph P. Kennedy, Jr., was born exactly nine months and twenty days after the marriage in his grandfather Honey Fitz's summer mansion at Hull across Boston Harbor.

The Beals Street home, now a national historic shrine, was the birthplace of the future president, John Fitzgerald Kennedy. All the older children were born on its upper floor, where Rose had placed the bed near a large window to give the doctors more light.

At the outset of World War I, Kennedy took a defense job as assistant general manager in the Bethlehem Steel shipyard at Quincy, Massachusetts.

When the war ended, he went into a brokerage house, where he learned how to manipulate the market. In the booming Twenties, he launched his career as a "majestic speculator,"[4] daring and almost psychic in his ability to predict future financial trends. Prescient enough to foresee the coming disaster, he sold all his holdings before the stock market collapse in October 1929, sitting with his million while others moaned and leaped from tall buildings.

In 1926, Kennedy applied for membership in the Cohasset Country Club and once again was blackballed from a social asset he coveted. "Boston," he raged, "is no place to bring up Irish children." By then, he had his seventh Irish child, Bobby, who was born in a twelve-room house in Brookline, at the juncture of Naples Road and Abbotsford.

Joe rented a private railroad car and moved his family to Riverdale in New York City. A year later, he took them a few miles north to a $250,000 Georgian mansion set in five acres of lawn and gardens in the elegant suburb of Bronxville.

From his earliest years, Robert idolized his father. He did all he could to please him in every way, was upset when he thought he might not, and even permitted his father to dictate to him the jobs he accepted in public life. The events of his life clearly show that in political ideology, Robert Kennedy as a young man was a clone of Joseph P. Kennedy.

If nature gave Bobby his father's pale blue eyes, nurture bred in him Joe Kennedy's tenaciousness in the pursuit of self-defined goals and the willingness to use raw power when necessary without thinking twice about the effects. If Joe could, and often did, drive business competitors into bankruptcy without pity or regret, Bobby could, and often did, destroy egos and bruise people's lives in his first thirty-five years.

Noting his son's direct-action approach to matters, the father once said, "Bobby resembles me more than any of the other children," an estimate with which his friend Arthur Krock, who watched Bobby grow, completely agreed. "He had the same capacity for likes and dislikes, for love and hate."

Unlike Jack, Bobby was never known to have argued with Joe, or to have criticized him, and he went to great lengths to carry out his wishes. Joe had an inflexible rule: everyone must come to meals on time—even one minute late was too late. Jack and his older brother, Joe junior, sometimes got in under the deadline, but often they ambled in beyond it, prompting long lectures from their father on the virtues of punctuality.

Young Robert was never late. When mealtime approached, he was there. Once his wish to be an obedient child landed him in a doctor's office for treatment of multiple lacerations.

13

He was playing in the living room of the Bronxville house when the dinner bell sounded. Bobby jumped up and ran. A large sliding glass partition separated the living and dining rooms. This evening, it was in the closed position, which Bobby, intent on making the deadline, did not notice. He ran squarely into the heavy glass, splintering it. Bleeding profusely, he fell among the shards. "Even at the age of five," Rose observed, "he was already working hard at being dutiful."

Fifteen years later, a Harvard senior and proudly wearing the big "H" he won on the football field, Bobby was still rushing to be at the table by Joe's deadline. Sailing on Nantucket Sound one summer morning in 1948, he suddenly realized that lunchtime was nearer than he thought. Joe had returned from a business trip the evening before, and the deadline was in force.

Bobby turned the tiller, and the Wianno class sailboat caught the breeze, heading for the compound's private dock. Minutes were flying now. Mooring the craft would make him late. So Bobby leaped overboard, shouting to his sailing companion, James Noonan, to fasten the boat. He swam to shore, raced up the beach, and made lunch.

Noonan, who was a sailing neophyte, barely made port. "In desperation," he said, "I tried to hail any passing boat. Finally a power boat came alongside and helped me to a safe mooring."

Bobby's early education, a kaleidoscope of shifting scenes, school standards, and teachers, always remained unclear in his mind. Not bothering to count, or perhaps unable to, he said he had gone to ten different elementary and secondary schools, a reasonable estimate. Ted once counted his and came up with an equal number, including two in England and the others divided between New England and Palm Beach.

Rose changed her children's schools frequently, alternating among private, public, and parochial institutions. She preferred religious schools because, she said, "Children respect their parents and their parents' opinions, but religious education helps buttress stability, reinforces their faith." Her husband went along with this theory so far as the girls were concerned but, sexist as he was, balked when it came to the boys. For them, he wanted more broadly based schooling, because they needed hard, practical training to equip them for doing combat with the world.

Bobby went to public and private schools in Hyannis Port, the public schools in Bronxville (which Kathleen, Eunice, Patricia, and later Ted also attended), and the private Riverdale Country Day School. He was quiet and well-behaved, ordinary enough to be barely remembered by most of his teachers. One who did call him to mind said that, at age ten, he was "a nice freckle-faced little kid, his hair some shade of brown, a regular boy. He needed no special handling."[5] Lemoyne K. Billings, John's roommate at the Choate School in Wallingford, Connecticut, and a family go-fer ever after, met Bobby for the first time when he was eighteen and Bobby twelve and knew him well until he was killed. "He was just a nice kid," Billings said. "We barely noticed him in the early days, but that's because he didn't bother anybody."[6]

As with most children who behave well in school, he was somewhat less self-effacing at home, though not much.

There were times when he would get himself injured but would not let anyone know because he took seriously his father's admonition that Kennedys don't cry. One day, when he was eight, he was exploring in the basement of the Bronxville house, where a large cast-iron radiator had been stored. Bobby pulled and tugged at it until the radiator, unconnected to the heating system, toppled. He failed to leap back in time, and it crushed his toe. His brother Joe came running and asked if he was hurt. Despite severe pain, Bobby shook his head. Hours later, when the toe had swollen so that he could no longer hide the injury, the family discovered that it had been broken.

He and Ethel would bring up their own children the same way, offering little sympathy for bruised knees and elbows and cuts suffered at vigorous play. The children were expected to pick themselves up, clean themselves off, and get back into action. So, too, were adults invited to play at Kennedy games. Once the singer Andy Williams limped into their home, where he had been scheduled to play tennis, with a broken toe in a large cast. Ethel told him, "Don't look for any sympathy from us. You're not going to let a little old broken toe stop you—we need a fourth." Williams saw that the other three weren't being coddled either. Ted Kennedy, whose back had been broken in an air crash two years before, was wearing a heavy metal brace. Mountain climber James Whittaker had undergone an operation on his veins and still had his leg in bandages. Ethel herself was obviously in the last trimester of another pregnancy. He joined them on the court.

With the best of intentions, Rose and Joe played down the importance of money as their children grew. All received tiny allowances (a dime a week at age seven, increasing by small increments as they got older), and the subject was never discussed openly at mealtime or other family gatherings. "It wasn't a forbidden subject," Rose said, "but simply didn't meet the criterion that if you want to talk, have something interesting to others to talk about."

The result was that the boys grew up with little personal knowledge of this important commodity. None ever took any serious interest in the family fortune, either in understanding its size and diversity or in handling the many millions Joe left. Steve Smith, Jean's husband, ended up running the Kennedy enterprises, which he does with considerable efficiency, and the surviving offspring are happy to have him do it.

Most of Bobby's vacations were spent in the much-publicized seafront acreage at Hyannis Port, where Joe bought the big, gabled house that would eventually become the centerpiece of the famous "compound." Bobby was a year old when his father paid $25,000 for the fifteen-room home that had been built at the turn of the century.

The many thousands of words that have been written about life at the Cape have stressed the fun and games, the family traditions of huge birthday parties, wedding anniversary celebrations, and Christmas and Thanksgiving Day dinners, all of them warm and festive. But there was also a regimentation, to which the Kennedy children and their numerous cousins were expected to conform, that was almost militaristic. Joe delegated Eunice to be activities counselor. She drew up a schedule and posted it on the porch of the main house. Breakfast at eight, followed by an hour each of tennis, touch football, and basketball. Then lunch, rest, and, at 2:30, sailing, then the swim period. Indoor games were planned if the weather was inclement.

Later, Eunice's duties were taken over by a live-in sports instructor, who was hired by Joe to supervise the activities and help the children improve their skills. The younger ones were under the care of Alice Cahill, a trained governess, and a registered nurse took care of the infants and toddlers.

Everyone had to be out of bed by seven for calisthenics on the broad lawn and, depending on age, in bedrooms by nine or ten at night. If an older boy or girl overstayed curfew, Rose, who kept close tabs, would climb into her little blue coupe and drive up and down Scudder Avenue alongside the Kennedy property, looking for them and shooing them home.

Rose encouraged promptness (lunch, 1:15; dinner, 7:30) by placing large electric clocks in every room, and reading, by putting lamps near almost every chair. Bobby developed his lifelong preference for cold milk, clam chowder, and ice cream at Rose's table. The food she served was simple and hearty—"sturdy New England fare," she called it, including five gallons of milk each day.

Joe was away a great deal, making money,* but daily phone calls came from wherever he was. To make certain the family could reach him at all times in emergencies or just to chat, he set up a telephone central in his office in New York City that would relay calls to him at any hour to any place.

---

* Soon after Bobby was born, Joe went to Hollywood to challenge the "pants-pressers," his contemptuous term for the existing movie moguls. In less than three years, during which he produced some of the worst trash that ever emerged from the film capital (*A Poor Girl's Romance, Red Hot Hoofs*), he earned an estimated $5,000,000.[7]

Christmas and Easter vacations were spent in yet another grand house, the neo-Spanish villa Joe bought on Millionaire's Row in Palm Beach for $100,000. The sixteen-room stucco home on North Ocean Boulevard, still owned by the Kennedys, has a pool and tennis court on its two acres and, of course, is prime beachfront property. Rules were just as ironclad there: the lunch and dinner hours were signaled by a large bell, which scarcely endeared the rambunctious Kennedys to their posh neighbors on North Ocean.

Bobby was a thin boy, not so ruddy-cheeked healthy as Ted nor as sickly as Jack, but something in between. He suffered from almost the entire range of childhood illnesses; the chart Rose kept faithfully of everything from shoe sizes to inoculations shows that he had chicken pox, mumps on both sides, scarlet fever, whooping cough, measles, and that his tonsils and adenoids had been removed. He had his teeth straightened, suffered from bad colds, and, when he was eleven, came down with pneumonia. Rose had a theory about the contagious diseases: when a child comes down with one, put him or her in close contact with the others, so that they could all catch it and hence get it all over with at once.

Bobby spent most of his early years trying to catch up to the others. He was the poorest sailor and, although he came to love the sea, never mastered the art of sailing to windward. There is no record that he ever won a regatta. In 1942, he was at the helm of the *Victura*, John Kennedy's boat, which is now on permanent exhibit at the Kennedy Library, south of Boston; of the fifteen craft in the race, Bobby outraced only two. He climbed trees with his brothers and sisters and managed to fall out of the branches, while they scrambled up like squirrels. Jean said, "She [Rose] worried about him because there were four girls ahead of him, so much competition from the older brothers, and he was accident prone."[8]

All through Bobby's adolescence and early manhood, he was over-shadowed and often ignored. Once, in his mid-teens, he came to the Cape during school recess. Jack, back from Harvard, was in the living room with several friends, talking and laughing. No one greeted Bobby, who paused a moment, then began walking up the stairs to his room. Midway, he turned and called to Jack in a plaintive voice, "Aren't you glad to see me?"

Another time, when he was a few years older, he returned from Harvard to find friends of Kathleen, then twenty-four, snitching some of Joe's liquor. Knowing his father disapproved and well aware of Joe's wrath if he found out, Bobby told them they were running a big risk and urged them to replace the booze. Kathleen paid no attention to him. "Get lost," she said, and he obligingly did.

Shy about speaking out, he even had trouble making himself heard at the dinner-table discussions. When he was fourteen, the question of America's involvement in the war in Europe was hotly debated: Jack took the position that the United States must enter the conflict; Joe junior and their father were heatedly opposed. Bobby, who had been taken to Europe and had seen something of life in the Third Reich, including the masses of uniformed, booted soldiers chanting "Heil Hitler," agreed with his father and oldest brother, wanted to say so, but was drowned out by the others.

Before his forty-fifth birthday, Joe Kennedy had amassed a huge fortune and, having been denied social acceptance, sought the prestige that only high government office could bestow.

He had contributed heavily to Franklin D. Roosevelt's Presidential campaign in 1932, served on the Democratic Party's finance committee, and in 1934, he got his reward. He was appointed to head the newly created Securities and Exchange Commission, charged with policing Wall Street. He served one year, from July to the following summer, often playing host to the President at a magnificent twenty-five-room mansion he had rented across the Potomac in Maryland.

Joe wasn't shy about asking favors from the President. Time and again, he requested him to send his children signed photographs and letters. Once, after Bobby had begun to collect stamps, Joe asked Roosevelt—the nation's number-one philatelist—to write a note of encouragement to the boy.

Roosevelt obliged. Early in 1935, he wrote the following personal letter to Bobby:

Dear Bob,
      I understand we share an interest in stamps. The next time you journey to Washington with your father, you must stop at the White House and inspect my stamp collection. Meanwhile I am enclosing some interesting new stamp issues to add to your own album.

FDR also sent Bobby a book of advice to young hobbyists. On July 19, on stationery headed Hyannis Port, Massachusetts, young Kennedy replied:

Dear Mr. President,
      I liked the stamps you sent me very much and the book is very useful. I am just starting my collection and it would be great fun to see yours which mother says you have had for a long time.
      I am going to frame your letter and I am going to keep it always in my room.
      Daddy, mother and all my brothers and sisters want to be remembered to you.
               Bobby Kennedy
               Son of Joseph P. Kennedy

Bobby kept Roosevelt's letter all his life. Ethel obtained a photostatic copy of Bobby's reply, and the two letters, framed, are still on the wall of her late husband's bedroom in their Virginia home.*

Kennedy aimed high. The post he coveted was Secretary of the Treasury, but Roosevelt, convinced Joe would run the department "contrary to my plans and views,"[9] rejected the idea. Kennedy bided his time. In 1936, he worked hard for Roosevelt's reelection, again pouring money into the party's coffers, again serving on its finance committee, and this time seeking to cement his claim on a top job by signing his name to an adulatory book, *I'm for Roosevelt*. When FDR read it, he sent Joe a note: "I'm for Kennedy. The book is grand."[10]

In light of what would be disclosed about Joe Kennedy's ambitions for his sons, the most remarkable (and perhaps funniest) part of the book was a single line that appeared on page three: "I have no political ambitions for myself or for my children."

In the spring of 1937, Roosevelt named Kennedy chairman of the Maritime Commission, which he would later call "the toughest job I ever handled in my life." Considering the ferocious clashes between the seamen's and longshoremen's unions and the country's merchant fleet at the time, he was plunged into a hornet's nest and happily retired from the job the following year.

When the United States ambassador to Britain, Robert W. Bingham, became gravely ill, Kennedy lobbied for the post. Ambassador to the Court of St. James—this would finally give him the social recognition he had been denied. Let the Boston Brahmins top this.

The novel notion of sending an Irish Catholic to the British court, particularly one with rough edges and a breezy, direct manner, who could shake up the slow-moving diplomatic set and get things done, appealed to Roosevelt. In less than two years, the President and Kennedy himself were to reap the whirlwind: the decision was one of FDR's worst.

The appointment, though, was made with good cheer and high hopes on December 9, 1937. Rose and Joe made plans to sail for England. One evening, however, Rose awoke with a sharp pain in her abdomen. She was rushed to a hospital, where an emergency appendectomy was performed. Joe waited as she was recuperating, and then, on February 23 of the following year, sailed to England aboard the U.S.S. *Manhattan* without his family.

---

* The letters came to light in 1970, when National Archives researchers were assembling material for their journal *Prologue* on Roosevelt's many hobbies.

2

Little Altar Boy

OR THE FIRST time in their lives, the exuberant Kennedy children and their equally active mother lost their zest for nonstop activity. Six of them, en route to join Joe Kennedy in England, lay white-faced and miserably seasick as the liner *Washington* pitched and tossed in a furious storm that lasted three days. Only Luella Hennessey, a young nurse hired a few months before to care for the children, was unaffected; she bustled from one to another to ease their distress.

Luella was to become an important member of the Kennedy household through the years. At first a nurse, she became nursemaid, companion, and finally friend, not only to the children but also their wives and husbands in later years. She assisted at the births of all but one of the twenty-nine Kennedy grandchildren.

On March 15, 1938, the great ship steamed into Plymouth Harbor, where Joe, who had journeyed down from London, was waiting, surrounded by a crowd of British newsmen. Kennedy's breezy Yankee manner, a sharp contrast to his dignified and often stuffy predecessors, as well as his large family, had delighted the British press. One headline welcomed him with: "Nine Children and Nine Million Dollars"; another called him "the *father* of his country."

Accompanying Rose were Bobby, who was thirteen; Teddy, six, and three girls—Kathleen, eighteen, Pat, fourteen, and Jean, ten. Eunice, seventeen, and Rosemary, twenty, were to arrive in a few months after completing their school years. Joe junior and Jack, who were at Harvard, would

20

follow in early summer. Joe was planning to give his eldest son a post as a junior secretary and later to send him on special missions to European nations as an unofficial observer.

Joe installed his family in the official residence, a six-story stone house that still stands at number 14 Prince's Gate, a short street in fashionable Knightsbridge, overlooking Kensington Gardens. Rose, then forty-seven years old, black-haired, small-figured, and extraordinarily youthful-looking, pronounced it "a nice location" but wondered how she would divide her nine children into the eight bedrooms, considering that she and Joe would occupy one and that several had to be left open for distinguished visitors. Wandering into the two upper floors, usually reserved as servants' quarters, she found thirteen other bedrooms, a number of which she appropriated. One by one, she spoke to the staff of twenty-three, not including the three chauffeurs, and life in London began.

In the next months, the Kennedys were settled in: Eunice, Pat, and Jean were sent to a convent school; Kathleen took special courses at the University of London; and Rosemary, who was showing increasing signs of mental retardation, was kept close to the family, her condition hidden from the public. Today, it is easy to forget that in the Thirties retardation was considered a stigma reflecting upon the parents and, as such, an affliction not ever to be disclosed. "I used to think it was something to hide,"[1] Joe said later, after he learned differently. Back then, he gave out the story that she was studying to be a kindergarten instructor. Although she was becoming prone to violent outbursts of rage followed by periods of brooding silence, he was determined to have her presented at court; and she was.*

In London, Bobby was a quiet and serious teenager, making a few few friends and doing only middling well at the day schools he and Teddy attended: first, the Sloane Street School for Boys in Chelsea and, later, the smaller and more fashionable Gibbs. Just as he was the poorest athlete of the bunch back home, he was baffled by cricket, never getting the hang of Britain's national sport, and, for years after the London experience, he wondered what the English saw in the game. His mind was sharp, though, when he wanted to apply himself, and if he couldn't beat the others at athletic games, he could—and did—at checkers and back-

---

* Two years after her arrival in England, Rosemary was returned to the United States, where her rages, compounded now by convulsions, worsened. Her parents consented to have her undergo an operation, disclosed by Rose for the first time in 1974. She called it "a certain form of neurosurgery."[2] According to several later accounts, Rosemary underwent a prefrontal lobotomy, but the family has not confirmed this. Steve Smith told Dr. Herbert Parmet, "In any discussion of the matter, never have I heard that choice of words to describe the operation. It is my impression that, very definitely, that was not the nature of it."[3] The violence and the seizures ended for Rosemary, but the surgery left her permanently incapacitated.[4] She has spent the years since the 1940s at St. Coletta's in Jefferson, Wisconsin, a convent and school where she lives in her own home, with a car and chauffeur at her disposal. Ted and her sisters visit regularly.

gammon. When the entire family organized a tournament, Bobby came out first.

On balance, Bobby's British experience was not a happy one. Unlike young Joe and Jack, who were old enough to be involved in the glittering social world and even more involved with the pretty English girls, Bobby had little to do and never caught on to the British ways. David Ormsby-Gore, the former British ambassador to the United States who became Lord Harlech, recalled that Bobby "loathed" his schools, where, among other things, he was made to wear the tiny skullcaps he felt made him appear ridiculous. When his father, noting his dissatisfaction, suggested he join the English Boy Scouts, he said he would not—belonging meant he would have to swear allegiance to the King. Joe understood, wrote letters to America, and soon Bobby became a Tenderfoot in the ranks of the Boy Scouts of America. He was then allowed to attend British scout meetings and activities as a visiting member.

Never a part of the life abroad, Bobby was content to spend free hours playing with Teddy. They would toss baseballs and footballs in Hyde Park beyond Alexandra Gate, race along Rotten Row, tumble in the grass on nice days, and ride their bikes on the long marble terrace at the rear of the mansion. Luella, young and peppy, had her own bicycle and would ride along with them.

Both boys were invited to perform ceremonial functions as sons of the American ambassador. Bobby read with grave intonation a speech prepared for him by the embassy staff at the laying of a foundation stone for a youth temple in Camberwell, and Teddy babbled away to reporters at the opening of a children's zoo.

Bobby was present at the private audience the family had with Pope Pius XII after his succession in March 1939. While he was not quite fourteen, religion had taken firm hold in his life. The stern moralism by which he lived and acted throughout his career had its roots in the conscience bred into him early by the teachings of the church, a conscience that was at once unyielding, prickly, and driving.

The story of Jesus came to be a central influence in everything he undertook. One associate asserted, "Bobby had a Christ complex. As the Christians would say, 'Take up my cross and follow me,' he said it too, and he truly believed that.

"Bobby was a little altar boy all his life."[5]

In London, his piety was clearly displayed. Luella has some vivid recollections. On nice days, she would be waiting outside the school at five o'clock to walk the boys the three-quarters of a mile back to the embassy residence. Bobby and Teddy would emerge, pudgy Teddy skipping, Bob walking sedately, each dressed like English schoolboys in maroon jackets, gray flannel pants, and their tiny round caps. Their route home along Brompton Road took them past the famous Brompton Oratory, a magnificent church built in the 1880s, where the Kennedys worshipped.

As they approached the building, Bobby would say, "Let's go in and pay a visit to the Lord."[6] His mother had impressed upon the children the importance of stopping at a church when going by, not just waiting until Sunday. Luella would take the two boys into the ornate, Italian Renaissance interior, and the three would kneel in prayer for a few minutes before continuing their walk home.

One Sunday, after a service at the Oratory, Bobby heard from a church employee that the rooms in which the priests lived were heated by wood-burning fireplaces, for which the fathers were expected to purchase their own logs.

"And so when they don't have any money," he told Joe on their way home, "they don't have any fire, and they have to stay in the cold room."

The next day Joe Kennedy arranged for a year's supply of wood to be sent to the church for use by the priests.

Incidents such as this made Luella feel that one day Bobby would enter a seminary and follow the religious life. Rose thought so, too, and harbored the wish, common among Catholic families, that one child would have the call to the church.

A time did come when Bobby indeed considered entering the priesthood. A family friend recalled that his earliest ambition was to be a fire chief or conductor of a trolley car. "Then he wondered about being a priest," said the friend.

The brothers had differing feelings about their religion. John looked upon religion "like everything else, with detachment."[7] Joe junior, despite his irreverent attitude toward life in general, absorbed a good deal of his mother's training. He was president of the Holy Name Society at the naval air station in Jacksonville, kneeled in prayer every night, and, on a trip to Rome, climbed up the famous Scala Sana or Holy Stairs opposite the Lateran Palace on his knees, an act performed by devout pilgrims.

Bobby accepted his religion totally, without speculating or analyzing. His faith was absolute. He became an altar boy at St. Joseph's Roman Catholic Church in Bronxville, the Kennedys' home parish, where he received his first communion on April 30, 1933.

"He worked hard at it," his sister Pat remarked. "I used to go into his room to hear his Latin. Then mother would come in, too, so he could show her how much he learned."[8]

It was Rose, the daily communicant whose piety has been underscored in all accounts written about the family, who was the wellspring of Bobby's devotion to his church. "Pope Rose," as some irreverent parishioners at St. Francis Xavier in Hyannis Port called her, worked hard to instill religious faith in all her children and succeeded better with Robert than any of her other sons. He, more than the others, would open the Bible Rose had packed into his luggage when he went away to school, and he, more than the others, would pray the rosary with the beads his mother left on all her children's beds when they were at home.

Robert's father was less devout than his wife and, even though he cultivated high Church officials as personal friends, was considerably less knowledgeable about Catholic ritual. Once he asked his friend Francis Cardinal Spellman to offer a requiem mass for his late mother in the living room of his Palm Beach house. At the suggestion of Arthur Krock, he also invited Governor Frank Murphy, who was staying in the area.

As the mass progressed, it became obvious to Krock that Kennedy was making mistakes. "So I followed Murphy, who was letter perfect," Krock said. Afterward, Krock told Joe he had blundered several times, but Murphy had not. Kennedy, though overcome with emotion by the ritual, was still able to reply pungently: "That character [he used a much stronger word] ought to have been a priest." Unknown to either, Spellman had returned to the room to pick up something he had forgotten and heard the expletive. Kennedy and Krock froze, but the Cardinal pretended he hadn't heard.[9]

Late in September 1939, after Hitler's panzers had rolled into Poland, igniting World War II, Kennedy sent his family back to Bronxville aboard the liner *Washington*, this time crammed with refugees who slept on the decks, in the lounges, and even in passageways.

Joe remained in England another year, his enormous early popularity plummeting, as the tensions with Germany heightened and his isolationism, muted at the beginning of his tenure, emerged more clearly. In cables to Roosevelt, Kennedy warned again and again that Britain would surely lose a war, should it come, pleading with him to do everything possible to avoid a collision with Germany. Publicly, he urged the British to reconcile their differences with Hitler and adopt a policy of coexistence with dictatorships.[10]

Britain's declaration of war at 11:00 A.M. on September 3 devastated him. Kennedy woke Roosevelt in Washington, where it was four in the morning and, barely able to speak through his sobs, said, "It's the end of the world, the end of everything." These were not words Roosevelt or the British cared to hear, yet Kennedy pursued his theme of isolationism more vigorously than ever. He was especially vitriolic when he returned to the United States in February 1940 for talks in Washington, proclaiming in an astonishing performance at the State Department that Germany would win, that France and England would "go to hell," and that his one interest was to save money for his children.*

In November he returned to the United States again and, once more firing from the hip, finally shot himself in the foot. In a ninety-minute wide-ranging interview with *The Boston Globe*, he gave his views on Britain, America, the Queen, the British Cabinet, and everything else he could think of. The remark that infuriated the British: "Democracy is finished in England." A close second: "She [the Queen] has more brains than they [Churchill's Cabinet] have."[12]

Joe's efforts to explain that the interview was off the record were laughed off. He had resigned as ambassador four days before, on November 6, 1940, but if the story did not actually end his career as ambassador, it left a legacy he did not want. The British never forgave him.

He returned to America to fulfill the overarching purpose he now had in life—to make one of his sons President of the United States. "For the Kennedys," he told Arthur Krock, "it's either the shithouse or the castle—nothing in between."[13]

* Harold L. Ickes, FDR's Secretary of the Interior, reported that William Bullitt, ambassador to France, was being interviewed by J. J. Patterson, publisher of the New York *Daily News* and Doris Fleeson, its Washington correspondent. Kennedy barged into the conversation, Ickes said Bullitt told him, and asserted his views. "He began to criticize the President very sharply," Ickes said, "whereupon Bill took issue with him. The altercation became so violent that Patterson finally remarked that he suspected he was intruding, and he and Doris Fleeson left, but Joe continued to berate the President. Bill told him that he was disloyal and that he had no right to say what he had before Patterson and Fleeson. Joe said that he would say what he Goddamned pleased before whom he Goddamned pleased—or words to that effect. Joe's language is very lurid when it is unrestrained, as it was on this occasion."[11]

3

Preppie

ROBERT KENNEDY passed through three fine preparatory schools in the next four and one-half years, and, after he left, almost nobody remembered he had even been there.

He was like one of those nameless, faceless, undistinguished classmates everyone has in early life, a student who comes to class, plays on athletic teams with indifferent success, and is seen around the premises every day, but is totally forgotten once school days are over.

Emily Perry, widow of headmaster Arthur B. Perry at Milton Academy, said of Bobby, "He was a very intelligent boy, quiet and shy, but not outstanding, and he left no special mark on Milton." Thomas G. Cleveland, now head of the religious department, who knew Bob when he was a student there himself, declared, "He came and he went."[1]

Only because of his later accomplishments is Robert Kennedy called to mind by those whose lives touched his in those days, but it is difficult for them to bring him out of the mists with any great clarity. Said one, "I know he was there because he's in the yearbook, but for the life of me I can't recall a blessed thing about the guy." The story of his school days must be reconstructed from the records and the memories of the few friends he did make, almost all of whom remained close to him for the remainder of his life.

Following his return from England, Bobby was enrolled in St. Paul's, a famous and fashionable Protestant prep school near Concord, New Hampshire, the choice made by Joe Kennedy from London. Soon, though, Bobby

26

began writing home that he was compelled to attend chapel every day—
Protestant chapel—and that the *Protestant* Bible was read a number of times
daily as well.

Urgent letters came from Rose via diplomatic pouch, complaining that
Bobby was getting too strong a dose of Protestantism and demanding that a
change be made. Joe backed down and told Rose to put him back in the
Riverdale Country Day School.

Instead, Rose selected a Catholic boarding school for boys that had been
built only fourteen years before on 120 acres fronting on Narragansett Bay
in Portsmouth, Rhode Island. Then called Portsmouth Priory (later
Portsmouth Abbey School), it is run by Benedictine monks, who daily lead
the full monastic life enjoined by the rule of Saint Benedict and teach most
of the classes.

Appealing most to Rose were the Priory's twin aims, as stated in its
catalogue: "The first . . . is to give Catholic boys a thorough training in the
knowledge and practice of their religion. The second is to give them a liberal
education, at least as good as that given in the best non-Catholic schools, but
from a sound Catholic viewpoint."[2]

Robert Kennedy arrived at the school in the winter of 1939 and was
assigned to St. Benet's House, a large Gothic building of red brick, which
housed forty lower-school students. His room, which he shared with another
student, was Spartan—less than fifteen feet square, it contained two single,
iron-frame beds, two scarred wooden chests, and two initial-carved desks.
A small rug covered the bare wooden floor.

While the school has been greatly enlarged since Kennedy's day, St.
Benet's still looks much the same. At one end of the long marble corridor
on the main floor is an austere library with only a few new books among
the old volumes on its shelves. Ironically, one of the recent additions is the
novel *Lincoln*, by Gore Vidal, one of Bobby's most implacable foes. At the
other end is an equally severe common room. Here Bobby played board
games or read; now boys cluster around a large television screen, watching
football games.

The Priory did not coddle its students.

Bobby was jolted from sleep by a bell at 6:30 A.M. and twice a week had
only twenty minutes to wash, dress, and make it to the chapel for mass. Next
year, when he entered the upper school, mass would be a thrice-weekly
requirement.

A 7:30 breakfast was followed by six solid hours of classes, with a
fifteen-minute recess at half-past ten. After dinner at noon and a brief "quiet
time," he was expected to be on the athletic fields for two hours. A short tea
break and a forty-five-minute study period came next, then nightly prayers,
required of all students. There would be another hour and three-quarters of

study and reading after supper, and lights were ordered out at 9:45, a half hour later in the upper school.

Religious instruction was heavily stressed. Each year, Bobby studied Christian doctrine. He was trained in the liturgy of the church. He attended weekly sermons and frequent conferences on spiritual and moral subjects. He was required to go to an annual retreat during Holy Week from Wednesday through Saturday.

The two and one-half years he spent there built a strong superstructure upon the religious foundation that Rose had laid down for him at home. The Priory intended that its instruction in Catholic faith and practices should be at the center of—and exert its influence upon—the whole life of the boys. For Bobby, it was and they did.

It was here that Bobby's moralistic view of the world was shaped and hardened. The code by which he lived and judged people and actions, the battles he waged against the forces of Evil and on behalf of the armies of the Good, his sense of service to mankind, his intense devotion to family and its traditions, even his fervent embrace of McCarthyism, which would become evident in a little more than a decade—all these were forged in the crucible of the Priory.

He met all the religious requirements faithfully. Once he spent three hours praying in chapel and wrote home that "I feel like a saint."

But he didn't apply himself to studies, and so his grades were nothing to write home about. The school did, though, and got him in trouble with his parents.

Rose couldn't understand how he could possibly have gotten such a low mark in Christian Doctrine of all subjects—only 64—and barely scraped by in the others. Joe grumbled, "The boy is spending far too much time on religious subjects and not enough on academics. That's what will get him into Harvard, the religion won't."

Joe was programming all his sons for his alma mater. His oldest boy had graduated in 1938, Jack in 1940, and Teddy, though still in grade school, had already been told he would go to Harvard (and, of course, he eventually did).

Bobby's best achievements at the Priory were extracurricular, and these were not of high order either. He was manager of the hockey team and vice commodore of the yacht club. Still quiet and retiring, he stoutly (and successfully) resisted Rose's efforts to get him to attend dancing classes in Providence, twenty-two miles away. He hated dancing then and always did, going out on a floor only when absolutely necessary.

Rose worried that he wouldn't acquire social polish. Joe junior and Jack could dance, make small talk, and were even then highly successful with girls—just how successful Rose surely did not know, though she may have

28

suspected—but Bobby gave no sign he would emerge from his shell. In Palm Beach for Christmas vacation from the Priory one year, she asked him to go to the Bath and Tennis Club and meet the young people from the best families who would be there. He flatly refused.

Rose sighed. "He is very unsociable," she said.

The transcript of his grades for the 1941–42 school year, his last at the Priory, showed the following:

Grammar..................76
Latin......................71
French....................65
Arithmetic 80
Social Studies 82

Francis I. Brady, the assistant headmaster, wrote this comment on the report:

> Robert Kennedy has good intelligence and a keen, sharp mind. When he is under pressure, he is quite industrious, but very often, if the pressure has relaxed, he lets up. He has, in general, made normal adjustments to all the requirements of the school life, but he has not shown much sense of social responsibility.[3]

On the morning of All Souls' Day, early in November, a visitor to the school, seeking to learn what impression young Robert Kennedy made on the school, drives past the rolling farmlands of its greatly expanded grounds (now 500 acres) to the Manor House, which houses the library.

The young librarian is astonished. "Did he really come here?" she asks. So are all the others questioned on the campus. The dons, who teach the students, are at mass, but a spokesperson who has made inquiries earlier assures the visitor none remembers him. At noon, the students emerge from the redwood fieldstone chapel. They, too, are questioned. They look at one another blankly.

No stories about Bobby have been handed down through the generations of students. He left the school at the end of the 1941–42 year, never returned, and was soon forgotten.

In September 1942, the family limousine deposited Bobby at Milton Academy just south of Boston. The chauffeur helped him lug his bags to his room at Forbes House, a three-story red brick building with Corinthian columns in front, one of the four boys' dormitories on the 125-acre campus.

The room, which was even more stark than his quarters at the Priory, was furnished only with an iron bed with a plain spring and mattress, one chair, a small desk, a square bureau, and an overhead light. Desk lamps and curtains could be provided by the students, if they wanted them. The room had once been occupied by T. S. Eliot, who would win a Nobel Prize for Literature six years later. Afterward, Kennedy told friends, "He didn't leave any of his literary talent for me."

Nor, it seems, any of his academic abilities. Bobby drew a low C in English the first year and a D the second. His other grades hovered between passing and failure. Only two months after the start of his senior year, Albert Norris, his housemaster at Forbes, was compelled to write Rose and Joe that Bobby's examinations were "weak indeed" and indicated that he was perilously close to being held back a grade.

Besides the English D, he scored an E-minus in French and flunked Latin. Because of this abysmal showing, Norris felt he wouldn't be able to handle the usual five courses next semester and suggested he limit himself to four.

Even this lightened program could prove too much, Norris thought. "It is quite possible," he told the Kennedys, "that Bob may need tutorial assistance, and I should therefore like your permission to have him work along with a private tutor if and when he finds his courses too difficult."[4]

Joe put off a trip to California to drive to Milton, where Norris, who had a formidable reputation for fairness and frankness, jolted him. Bobby's problem, he said bluntly, stemmed from the peripatetic nature of his education.

"He no sooner gets in a school situation," Norris told Kennedy, "than he is pulled out, put into a new school situation, with different methods of teaching, different rules and regulations. He has no roots. He is always on the move. It's no wonder his grades are so low."

Kennedy, accustomed to making tycoons quail, who had told Franklin Roosevelt the year before, "You will either go down as the greatest President in history or the greatest horse's ass," had no answer to this. For the first time, he was being told that his arbitrary rule of his sons' education was a failure. Joe had spent much time studying the schools, rejecting those he felt were not up to his standards and choosing the "right" ones. Yet none had worked out because of his son's educational rootlessness, something he hadn't reckoned with.

Of the four boys, only Joe overcame this disadvantage. At the Choate School in Wallingford, Connecticut, he had won the Harvard Trophy, awarded to a graduating senior for excellence in scholarship and sportsmanship. Jack, who had followed Joe at Choate in 1931, remaining until 1935, skirted academic failure most of those years. Declared Hubert S. Packard, his French teacher: "He was frequently unprepared, and his homework was sloppy and badly done. He just squeezed through with a 65 in his sophomore year.'' In Latin, according to Owen Morgan, he did hardly better with a 69. Eventually, Jack graduated with a C average, sixty-fifth in his class.*

Teddy, who came to Milton in 1946, had never spent more than a year in any school either and, like Bob, barely squeaked through. Arthur Hall, the dean of students during Ted's years, remarked, ''He was a straight C student—with help.''

The help came from one Kernel Holloway, famed at Milton for hammering knowledge into the heads of academically deficient students with his tutorial techniques. Ted had to visit Holloway for an hour every evening during most of his school years. ''He was the favorite customer of Holloway, an extraordinarily good tutor who got Teddy through,'' Hall remarked.[5]

Bobby's Milton years were the least happy of his adolescence, made tolerable by two close friends. There were few others. Having entered as a junior, he was unable to break through the boy-bonding relationships formed by his classmates, nearly all of whom had known each other since lower school days. Moreover, he was one of a handful of Catholics in a predominantly Protestant student body. His family's wealth and father's high position were no help. ''Nobody cared who he was,'' Tom Cleveland remarked. ''He was just another guy.''

The two boys who accepted him were David Hackett, then a tenth grader, and Samuel Adams, who was in his class. Bobby was closest to Hackett, a boy from a modest background who was to attain a near-legendary status at school. Hackett was a brilliant student, a superb all-around athlete, and extraordinarily popular. Years later, Hackett was asked if he went to school with Robert Kennedy. His reply: ''In those days, the Attorney General went to school with *me*.''

Shy though Bobby was, a quiet sense of fun broke through from time to time. Emily Perry, the headmaster's widow, recalled that in his second year, after he had become more comfortable with his surroundings, he put up a hand-lettered sign on the bulletin board at the beginning of November: ''Eighteen days to Robert Kennedy's birthday.'' Next morning there was a new sign: ''Seventeen days . . . ,'' and every day after that the days were recorded in large letters. Finally, on November 20, he got his presents and, of course, a big cake at dinner.

---

* Jack's room, too, flunked all inspections. His housemasters called it a ''pig sty.'' In February 1967, Bob Kennedy visited Choate and asked to see his brother's room. Headmaster Seymour St. John took him to the first floor of East Cottage, a white clapboard house, which was still used as a dormitory. Mr. St. John opened the door to the room, which was in a state of shambles; books, clothing, records were strewn all over. Snapping to attention inside was a young man, still dripping from the shower he had taken in the bathroom twenty feet down the hall. Said Bobby, ''I see it hasn't changed much. The place looks just like it did when my brother was here.''

31

It was also during his senior year that Kennedy and Hackett fought their hilarious War of the Rooms. Sam Adams recalled the prank:

It began when Dave borrowed one of Kennedy's ties from his room without telling him. Bobby retaliated by slipping into Hackett's room, in Robbins House, next to Forbes, and taking one of his jackets. Dave waited a day or two, then hauled Bobby's desk into the hall while he was in class. So, when Dave was in class, Bobby moved both his bureau and a chair outside.

It escalated fast. Hackett came back to his room to find his bed, neatly made, but standing in the corridor. Next day, two of Kennedy's jackets, a coat and some linens were on the lawn. Each day they evicted more and more of the other's things and brought their own stuff back. Finally, nearly all of Dave's furniture and much of his belongings were stacked outside, and everything Bobby owned was in his suitcases at the side of the house. At this point, Al Norris, the housemaster, stepped in and called it a draw.

Soon after, Bobby, Sam Adams, and two other seniors pulled the Great Shredded Wheat Caper, which had the dietician bewildered for a week. One night, the four slipped from their rooms after lights out and stole silently to the kitchen, which had been closed off against nocturnal marauders by a ten-foot-high wire fence. It was a daunting barricade, but Bobby climbed it with little trouble, helped the others over, and searched the pantry for food. They found some boxes of shredded wheat and containers of cream, which they ate.

Next morning the dietician, a Mrs. Shane, wondered where the cereal and cream had gone. The raiding party repeated the operation several times more, removing nothing but shredded wheat and cream and putting Mrs. Shane in a state of increasing anxiety. When it became clear that her next step would be to inform the housemaster, the boys stopped. Mrs. Shane never found out where the boxes and the cream went.

While Bobby carefully avoided all conflict with authority at prep school, John Kennedy brazenly sought it out, once so rebelliously he was almost expelled. Dr. Seymour St. John, who was headmaster at Choate for twenty-six years following the death of his father George, tells the story.

With his roommate, Lemoyne K. Billings, Jack organized the Muckers Club, mocking George St. John's dictum that any student who fell below the behavioral standards of Choate was a mucker—a "rough, coarse person." They enlisted a dozen boys and had little gold charms made for themselves inscribed "Choate Muckers Club."

Furious, St. John wrote to Joe Kennedy in Washington: "I think you and Jack and I ought to have a three-cornered talk. Could you come up here?" Joe Kennedy went at once. The scene that afternoon in the headmaster's study was memorable. Joe ripped into his son. And when he let up, St. John began. Neither man, St. John was to admit afterward, "held anything back."

Recalls Seymour St. John, "My father laid it on the line to Jack Kennedy: If he didn't respond, if he didn't shape up, he faced expulsion from school. The choice was made crystal clear to him—if he was to stay on at Choate, he would have to change his ways. Jack knew it and his father knew it. Jack Kennedy promised to dissolve the Muckers, and did."

Both brothers had a common problem in prep school: the inability to live up to their father's expectations of athletic success because of small stature. Dr. St. John said, "Jack wanted terribly to make his mark. He had an overwhelming ambition and drive, but his size and strength were insurmountable handicaps. He was too small for any varsity team. Nor could he make it in student government in a popular election for office. Boys choose strong, confident persons, the very opposite of what Jack was."[6]

Bobby was never elected to anything either. When his graduating class was asked to choose the student "most likely to succeed" and "class executive," he received no votes. Nor did he garner any as class "most argumentative" or "ladies' man." He did, however, get four votes for being "most humorous." The yearbook, *Orange and Blue*, where these distinctions were listed, noted that Bobby's nickname was "Fella,"[7] which in itself connotes a kind of nobodyness.

Like Jack, Bobby won no gridiron laurels, though he was on the field practicing doggedly every free moment. In his senior year, he made the second backfield and saw action from time to time as a substitute. "Not even athletics came easily for him," Hackett remarked. One classmate offered a devastating comment: "He was no good at small talk, he was no good at social amenities, he was no great lover."

At Milton, Bobby's piety deepened. Mrs. Norris, who drove the boys to church on Sundays, noted he never missed a day: "He was always downstairs, neatly dressed, ready to go." He also went to all the special holiday masses, as Rose had instructed. He would ask permission to leave the grounds and, with Sam Adams, would walk to the nearest Catholic church, a mile and a half away in Dorchester.

His lifelong dislike of scatological humor and a prudish attitude toward sex became clearly evident at Milton. "He was very intolerant of smutty jokes," Adams declared. "He wouldn't laugh at them, wouldn't even listen. It may have been part of his religious approach to purity and cleanliness."

A touching story revealing the depth of Bobby's faith was recounted by Adams. Two weeks before the 1942 Christmas break, Housemaster Norris took young Adams aside and, as gently as he could, told him bad news: Sam's father had been killed in an automobile accident in Chicago. In tears, Sam went to his room to pack for the sad trip home.

Ten minutes later Bobby, who had heard, came up. "We sat on the bed," Adams recalled, "and talked about faith. I said to him, 'I wish I had your acceptance, your conviction. I wish I could believe that it's not all over when you die, and that I would see my father again.'

"Bobby was very sure. He believed that very surely. He told me that faith would get me over this great burden. Not his faith, but mine. Even though I had no particular religious belief, and he knew it, he said that I *can* find faith, and that I could find comfort in it."

The boys sat together a long time, then Bobby left. Sam never forgot the episode.

At Milton, Bobby discovered girls. He was not as painfully shy with them as accounts have depicted him, but he was a long way from being the campus heartthrob. He had at least two big crushes at school, one on a beautiful blond girl named Ann Appleton but, in competition with at least half his class who were similarly smitten, got nowhere with her.

Later he turned his attention to a lovely English girl named Jane, who, like Ann, was a student at Milton's girls school. His friend Sam Adams had also discovered her. One Sunday afternoon, each wanted to see her but, heavily burdened with homework, agreed to suspend their rivalry. Neither, they decided, would see Jane. Besides, it was raining hard.

Just before dinner chapel that day, Sam saw Bobby come in dripping wet. "Where have you been?" Sam demanded.

Bobby, glowing, replied, "Walking in the rain with Jane." He had completed his assignments and slipped out to meet her. All is fair . . .

Bobby attended the heavily chaperoned dances held three times during the school year, but rarely ventured out on the floor. He never improved. Years later, a report appeared in a gossip column that he had done the frug until 3 A.M. at the Peppermint Lounge, a popular New York café. "I not only don't do the mashed potato and the monkey," he commented, "but I really don't dance."[8]

On occasion, he would invite a girl to spend a weekend at Hyannis Port. Charlotte Cleveland, a student who later married Tom, recalled the time she went to the big house on the bluff and was enormously impressed by the Kennedy lifestyle. "Imagine having your own movie theater in your own home! They had one downstairs in the playroom."* It seemed to her that at dinner a butler was standing behind every guest. "Mrs. Kennedy would

---

* With twenty-seven comfortable seats, it was the first private talking-picture theater installed in New England.

flick her hand, and your dish would be whisked away and something else would come swiftly."[9]

Bobby's sexual stirrings, powerful at seventeen, were suppressed rigorously. He would never exceed what he considered proper behavior with a girl. Sam explained: "To Bobby, women were supposed to be as much Catholic, and as much beyond reproach, as he was."

His brother John placed no such restrictions on himself. He lost his virginity during his Choate years with a prostitute in New York's Harlem, where he went with his roommate. During the time he and his brother Joe spent in Europe when their father was ambassador, they competed with one another for feminine conquests. Tex McCrary, the publicist and former radio personality, who knew them during the war, said, "They were the best swordsmen in the ETO."

In August 1943, John Kennedy became an authentic war hero. Bobby's pride was enormous. His father, who had received a message from the Navy Department that Jack was missing in action, kept the news from the family until he learned that Jack was safe on a tiny Pacific isle after his PT boat was sliced in half by a Japanese destroyer. He had swum five hours to land, towing the boat's injured engineer behind him.

Earlier that year, a little-known incident occurred that had all but cemented Bobby's determination to be a Navy man, like his brothers, and a pilot, like Joe. Young Joe, a junior grade lieutenant in naval aviation, was stationed in Norfolk, Virginia, where he was flying PBM Mariners on patrol missions out into the Atlantic, hunting for U-boats. One day, Bobby received a call from Joe. Could he come to Norfolk for a visit?

Bobby received special permission from school and went. At the base, Joe astounded him by asking, "How would you like to go out on a mission with me?"

Defying regulations, Joe smuggled Bobby aboard the bulky flying boat and let him sit in the copilot's seat. Once out over the ocean, Joe said, "Now take the controls."

Bobby, startled, shrank back. Joe told him it would be all right, to do exactly what he was told. Bobby did—and for a heady half-hour, actually flew a U.S. Navy plane on a search mission.[10]

Joe's squadron soon left for Dunkeswell Airdrome at Cornwall in England, from where he continued the patrol missions he found increasingly boring. In the fall, just before his eighteenth birthday, Bobby and Sam went to the Office of Naval Officer Procurement in Boston to enlist. They chose the V-12A program, which called for a year of college, followed by preflight training and, eventually, a commission. They would be released from active duty until the completion of the year at Milton.

"We went through the physical," Sam recalled, "both of us wearing these big cards around our necks with our names printed on them. Even though his father had been ambassador and his grandfather the mayor of Boston, Kennedy got no attention at all.

"When we reached a corpsman who was taking blood samples, he ignored Bobby and read out my name. 'Samuel Adams, eh?' he said. He jammed that big needle into my vein and said: 'O.K., Sam, let's see if it's blue.' ''

If the corpsman was not impressed by the Kennedy name, Boston newspapers were. When photographs of his younger brother being sworn in reached Jack in the Pacific, he sent him a letter, noting that Bobby was wearing the prized houndstooth jacket Jack had purchased in London.

"I'd like to know what the hell I'm doing out here, while you go stroking around in my drape coat," Jack wrote, "but I suppose that what we are out here for, or so they tell us, is so that our sisters and younger brothers will be safe and secure—frankly I don't see it quite that way—at least if you're going to be safe and secure, that's fine with me, but not in my coat brother, not in my coat. In that picture you looked as if you were going to step outside the room, grab your gun, and knock off several of the houseboys before lunch. After reading Dad's letter, I gathered that cold vicious look in your eye was due to the thought of that big blocking back from Groton . . .''

Five months later, Bobby exchanged Jack's coat for the uniform of a naval officer candidate and went to Cambridge to report for active duty with a Navy training unit.

4

Turn in the Road

O N AN OPPRESSIVELY humid day in August 1944, Bobby came home to Hyannis on leave. Jack, pale and scarecrow-thin, was already there on a weekend pass from Chelsea Naval Hospital near Boston. Invalided home because of malaria and severe spinal injuries suffered in the Solomons, the war was over for him. Also at the Cape were Eunice and Jean, and Kathleen, now married to a young British nobleman and working for the American Red Cross in London.

On days such as this, the family would always have lunch on the broad shaded veranda of the house, which looked down over the lawns and the blue-gray sea. Today, there had been roast chicken with hot biscuits, blueberries picked from the Kennedys' own bushes, and ice cream. A sailing race had been scheduled for later in the afternoon, and Jack was looking forward to trying the helm of his Wianno class boat.

About two in the afternoon, Joe, who had been reading the Sunday newspapers, told Rose, "I'm going upstairs for a nap," and went inside. Only the faintest breeze from the Sound reached the porch, so moments later the others moved inside to the large living room and spread themselves out on the comfortable chairs to talk quietly and read.

About 2:30, the Reverend Francis O'Leary, a short and heavyset Navy chaplain, and another priest arrived at the house and knocked on the front door. Father O'Leary was the senior Catholic chaplain of the First Naval District, which encompasses the Northeast; he had been assigned the duty of informing Ambassador Kennedy that his son was missing in action. The two priests flew to the Naval Ordnance Depot in Hyannis and drove to the Kennedy home.

Rose, believing they represented some charitable drive, asked them to join the family in the living room until Joe awakened. Father O'Leary said his message was urgent. In the hallway, he told her: the oldest Kennedy son was missing and presumed lost.[1]

Racing upstairs, she woke her husband and blurted out the news.

Bobby, Jack, and the girls had gathered at the foot of the steps, aware that something momentous had happened but not knowing what. Joe, followed by Rose, came down. He asked them all to come out on the veranda.

There he read them the Navy dispatch, which said that Joe had been lost while flying a mission and that no hope could be held out. Soon they would learn that he had volunteered to fly a drone Liberator bomber loaded with 21,000 pounds of high explosives and bail out with his copilot over the English Channel. The plane would then crash-land on its target, a V-2 rocket launching site in Normandy from which the Germans were attacking British cities. Something had gone wrong; the PB4Y had exploded over the channel, killing both pilots.*

Here, in a catastrophic time, the influence of the father upon his two remaining older sons differed significantly.

"I want you all to go ahead with the sailing race," Joe told his children.

John Kennedy would not race. Instead, he went down to the beach and walked alone for hours before returning to his room. But Bobby, obediently, went to the dock, boarded the Kennedy craft, and sailed it until nearly sunset.

This first of the Kennedy tragedies came at the most vulnerable time in young Robert's life so far. He was struggling against a sense of failure, troubled by his ineptitude, his shyness, his poor showing in studies, and a growing sense of isolation. "He'd have been happier if he'd had more friends," a classmate said of him; but he was unable to make more friends and to keep them.

He was, moreover, confused and hurt by the way his older brothers and sisters felt toward him. No kid brother likes to be known as a prig, yet he was so considered, and he knew it. Jack, whom he idolized, had a kind of hearty big-brother attitude but was impatient with Bobby's puritanical views.

He and Jack had clashed over Jack's passionate involvement with Inga Arvad, a beautiful woman four years older than Jack, a former Miss Denmark.[2] Inga was John Kennedy's first serious attachment. A friend of his sister Kathleen, she had met him when she worked on the *Washington*

---

* Years after the war ended, the discovery was made that Joe's mission was in vain. The Nazis had moved the launching site to another location.

Times-Herald, and by the fall of 1941, when he was stationed in Washington in the Office of Naval Intelligence, she was living with him in the capital. Because of Inga's close former ties with high Nazi officials, Kennedy was transferred out of Naval Intelligence that year. Until he met Inga, Jack Kennedy had rarely slept with the same woman twice; now, however, he was in a relationship that was intensely sexual but also a warm and loving one. For a time, he considered the possibility of marriage. Joe Kennedy was furious with his son when that was brought up, exclaiming, "Damn it, Jack, she's already married!" (Inga had been divorced, then married again to a Hungarian named Paul Fejos.) Newspapers were speculating that Joe would contribute a large sum to the Church, thereby paving the way for an annulment so that she and Jack could wed.

By 1942 the romance had ended, but while it was blazing openly, Robert was shocked at his brother's flagrant disregard of the moral code he himself prized.

Talking to Jack did no good; he was brushed off as a kid who had to grow up. This argument over Jack's sexual practices would continue all their lives.

Another problem was burdening Bobby, this one even more heavily than Jack's lack of sexual restraint.

In March, while he was at Harvard, the family had received word that Kathleen, his attractive but headstrong older sister, was planning to marry outside her faith. In London, the romance of "Kick" Kennedy, who had become the darling of British society, with William Cavendish, Marquess of Hartington, had been the subject of much gossip. Rose and Joe read the newspapers and heard the talk from their friends, but hoped that soon Kathleen would flutter on to someone else.

She did not. In spring, Kick wrote home that she had decided to marry Billy, one of England's wealthiest men, who was an Anglican. The Kennedys and the Cavendishes disapproved strongly. Neither the Catholic Church nor the Church of England would sanctify such a union. But Kathleen was adamant, and on May 6, 1944, she and Billy were wed at a simple civil ceremony before a few witnesses at the Chelsea Registry Office in London.

Neither Rose nor Joe attended. The only member of the family present was young Joe, who gave his sister away. Kathleen's action, which Evelyn Waugh later called "the final insult of apostasy," hurt Bobby deeply. He could never look upon her in the same way again, his friends said.

Only three months later came the news about Joe's death.

Lem Billings, Jack's Choate roommate who came frequently to Hyannis Port, declared, "With Kathleen's marriage followed by Joe's death, the kid was absolutely crushed. He idolized Jack, but Joe had been a god." Marie

39

Green, a close friend of Rose since their childhood days who remained a confidante through the years, recalled, in her Brookline apartment, that Bobby looked bewildered days afterward. Rose told Marie, "Of all the children, Bobby is taking it hardest."[3]

"It was ironic," said Sam Adams, "that only a short time after Bobby had talked to me about my own tragedy came the test for himself. Because he had faith, the burden for him was eased."

A permanent wall was built between Bobby and Kathleen by her defection from their religion.

Seven years later, Bobby named his first child Kathleen Hartington, remembering his sister's name and place in the family, but he set down a firm condition: she would never be called by the nickname "Kick," and she never was.

Nor did friends ever hear Bobby talk about his sister. He kept a vow he made four years after her marriage.

Just one month after the quiet ceremony in London, Billy's Coldstream Guards regiment was called up to fight in the Allied invasion of Normandy. In mid-August, two weeks after Joe junior's death, Kathleen received word that Billy had been killed by a sniper.

Then, in 1948, at the age of twenty-eight, Kathleen, too, met her death in an air crash in southern France, where she was flying with a new lover, Earl Fitzwilliam, a Protestant and a married man. Bobby went to England to find out all he could about Kathleen's last years from Ilony Solymossy, her housekeeper. When he left, he said, "We will not mention her again."[4]

That August day when he learned of Joe's death was a watershed in Robert Kennedy's life. Everything began changing. Looking back, he himself called the death of Joe a "crucial" turn in the road for him, though he did not recognize it as such at the time. The direction he would take in the coming years, his position in the family hierarchy, even the way Jack and his sisters looked upon him underwent a gradual process of mutation. He had become second in line, but nobody had designated him as such, though a mythology has arisen over how it came about.

The story has circulated so often that it is now widely accepted as fact: that some sort of family conclave was called by the father at which there were exhortations of the torch being passed; that the mantle of succession must now be draped around Jack Kennedy, with Robert as Hotspur; and that the entire family, like medieval nobles closing ranks around a new leader, pledged their fealty.[5]

The succession was established, but there were no such dramatic scenes. John tried another career, journalism, for a year before he agreed to run for Congress the first time, and Robert had no idea what would be expected of him. Joe knew what *he* wanted, hoped to persuade his son, believed he could—but there was time.

As the war progressed, Bobby spent a total of twenty-three frustrated months on college campuses, often angry, sometimes wearily resigned, seldom happy.

He was at Harvard for eight months, Bates College in Lewiston, Maine, for seven, and back at Cambridge for another eight. He wrote countless letters to his father, to Jack, to Dave Hackett, and to others in his family, telling them all how much he ached to get into some kind of action. "If I don't get the hell out of here soon," he wrote Hackett from Maine, "I'll die."

Joe knew that, eventually, this third son would go to war but hoped the day could be postponed as long as possible. Jack had gone to war and almost died. Joe had gone and was dead. There had been sacrifice enough.

While Bobby was going through his training in the Naval Reserve Officer Candidate program, Joe kept up a flow of correspondence, imparting fatherly solicitude for his son's welfare along with long and strong doses of his own conservative political ideology.

Once Robert wrote, "I wish, Dad, that you will write me a letter as you used to Joe & Jack about what you think about the different political events and the war as I'd like to understand what's going on better than I do now."

Kennedy, in a lengthy reply, told his son that when the war ended the country would see massive unemployment, with all its attendant problems. In a passage that was typical of the ideas he was infusing into Bobby in these impressionable years, he warned, "There will be a cry that the only way to solve all these problems is to let the Government do it, and that will be the beginning of some form of socialism in this country. . . . I can't see anything but the Government mixing itself more and more into everybody's lives."

Bobby thanked him. "The letter is just what I wanted," he wrote back.[6]

His letters home alternated between wry humor and self-analysis. Thus, from Harvard he wrote his parents: "We haven't really had too much action here in Harvard Square, but we're on the alert at every moment for an attack."

And from Bates: "My usual moody self. I get very sad at times."

Finally, in late autumn of 1945, there was jubilation in a letter to Jack: "Pappy has got some angle of getting me out of college."[7]

Joe's angle soon became clear. He had talked to his good friend, Secretary of the Navy James Forrestal, and had Bobby transferred to a newly commissioned 2,200-ton destroyer. Bobby, however, would have to give up his chance to become an officer and come aboard in the lowest rank of seaman apprentice.

The ship Joe had chosen for Bobby's active duty was the U.S.S. *Joseph P. Kennedy Jr.*, named for his eldest son. It had been put into service officially in December 1945 at the Quincy, Massachusetts, shipyard of the Bethlehem Steel Company. Bobby had been there in his naval uniform, standing alongside his father, his brother Ted, and his grandfather Honey Fitz, then nearing his eighty-second birthday and ebullient as ever. Joe could not control his tears during the ceremony. Jack, feeling miserable, had gone to their Palm Beach home to rest in the sun.

On February 1, 1946, the war now over, Robert Kennedy sailed to the Caribbean, where he hosed decks, painted, scrubbed, chipped, and stood watches for four months, becoming increasingly bored and frustrated.

Two decades later, he recalled how he felt. "There I was," he said, "on a ship named for my brother, sailing the placid waters, and watching beautiful sunsets. Jack had been a hero. Joe had died a hero. Okay, I didn't especially want to be a hero, but it was galling not to have seen any action at all."[8]

On May 30, he received an honorable discharge in Boston. He had been promoted to seaman second class and was awarded two medals, the Victory Medal, which every serviceman got, and a medal for having served in the American Theatre of War. After a short trip to South America, he hung up his sailor suit and went back to Harvard as a student.

Harvard was an extension of Milton—poor to middling grades, efforts to overcome athletic mediocrity by incessant practice, and continuing sexual inexperience.

He was brusque, sullen, and altogether unfriendly except in his own small circle of football players, most of them huge and muscular. He was intolerant of other students who went out to have good times. "Nobody who ever went to parties and gatherings made any real contribution," he told Kenny O'Donnell. "What's the good of going to those things and drinking. I'd rather do something else." The prim and proper posture, however sincere, alienated many.

"He was looked upon as a kind of nasty, brutal, humorless little fellow," said Dr. John H. Knowles, a classmate who later became director of Massachusetts General Hospital in Boston. "But I don't think you could fault him for hard work or his moral commitment. He was a wry, feisty little guy, tough on himself, tougher than hell."[9]

Joe junior, Jack, and later Teddy chased after girls as much and perhaps more than most Harvardians. Bobby ran after footballs.

"He had very few dates," declared Nicholas Rodis, who was in Bobby's circle of friends and later athletic director at Brandeis University for many years. "He wasn't a party boy."

Sam Adams, who had also gone to Harvard after the war, said, "He never joined in the sexual escapades of the other boys. Once in a while, the other fellows would make a trip to the local red light districts in the Boston area. Bobby never went along. I didn't either, though I wasn't as pure as he was. I was inhibited for social reasons."[10]

By contrast, Teddy's lack of inhibition was well-known at Harvard and extraordinarily well-publicized thereafter. It is interesting to compare his behavior at Harvard with that of Bob.

With a classmate, Ted kept a list of girls who were rated from A (top quality) to E (only in an emergency). Classmates agree he dated mostly A's and B's. And when he did, he made his intentions known almost at once. If the dates indicated they would not go to bed with him, he would be too polite to ditch them, but they never got another call.

When Ted was initiated into Pi Eta, one of Harvard's exclusive social clubs, he was told to go to Scollay Square, Boston's rambunctious entertainment area, and return with a prostitute. He went and fulfilled the challenge.

With the family's fixation on football, it is understandable that all five Kennedy males roomed at Harvard with football stars: Joe senior with Bobby Fisher, captain of the team; Joe junior with quarterback Bob Downes and T. J. Reardon, a guard, both first stringers; Jack with Torbert (Torby) H. MacDonald, all-American halfback; and Ted with Richard Clasby, team captain, and William Frate, tackle and guard. Bobby teamed up with Kenneth P. O'Donnell, who also captained Harvard's eleven and would later become special assistant to President Kennedy. All the Kennedys lived in Winthrop House, the red brick residence hall facing the Charles River, which was known as the university's jock house.[11]

Bobby's concentration on football was frightening in its intensity. Consumed by a desire to perform well, he arrived early on the field and stayed late, as at Milton, wearing out far bigger and more experienced players. Watching him rising again and again after being flung down, often brutally, by 200-pounders, Henry Lamar, the freshman coach, observed, "You'd have to kill him to make him quit." Classmate William J. Brady, Jr., believed, "He didn't give a darn about anything else."[12]

Later, he would be able to joke about his football days. "I was a short end at Harvard in 1947," he said at ceremonies awarding the Heisman Trophy to Oregon State quarterback Terry Baker in 1962. None of the other Kennedys was much good either, he declared and jokingly added, "A little bit of research has revealed that there was a Kennedy who was a head coach of Oregon State, but that was in 1894."

As a student, though, he attached the highest importance to getting his

Harvard letter, awarded to a varsity player who, if only for a few moments, plays in the traditional game with Yale. He knew what winning the big red "H" meant to his father, who had been in the stands a few years before when Joe junior sat on the bench at the Yale-Harvard match. The game ended, but Joe, then in his final year, was not sent in. Shaking with rage, Joe senior had raced to the Harvard locker room and berated Coach Harlow for not giving his boy a chance to play. Harlow was stunned and Joe junior embarrassed by the outburst.

Only 155 pounds, slow of foot, unable to dodge and dart well, Bobby was relegated by the assistant coaches to the sixth or seventh squads, which as Kenny O'Donnell pointed out, usually means exile in college football. "The varsity coaches," Kenny said, "never see you again." It was, Kenny believed, quite fair. "He had no right to make the varsity."[13]

Yet, in his senior year, he did, although he played only in two games, the first and the last. He was sent into the lineup against Western Maryland, a low-rated opponent, and caught a pass thrown by O'Donnell, carrying the ball thirty yards to a touchdown. An injury to his leg sidelined him after that until the Yale game—ironically, on November 22, the day his brother John was murdered in Dallas seventeen years later.

The Yale-Harvard game was in its final moments of the fourth quarter when Dick Harlow, perhaps remembering the patriarch's torrential outburst when Joe was kept on the bench, waved Bobby into the game as right end. Yale was ahead by ten points, 31 to 21, and there was little chance of a reversal.

Despite Robert's low marks, the distinguished Dr. Arthur N. Holcombe, Eaton Professor of the Science of Government at Harvard, considered his intelligence to be the equal of his two older brothers. Dr. Holcombe was the only professor at Harvard who taught all five Kennedy males—the father and his four sons.

"My relations with the three older brothers were on an intimate basis in my course," Dr. Holcombe declared, "and I know personally that they were students of superior ability. Robert had a keen mind, grasped material well, and retained it. His trouble was that he had athletic interests, which occupied too much of his time and energies.

"Jack was brilliant, but a B student, because he, too, did not apply himself completely. Jack became very much interested in the research work done in my government classes. As for Ted, he was thinking about athletic and social activities mostly, and academics came third."[14]

Ted, Dr. Holcombe recalled, was in great demand by socially ambitious mothers in Boston society to attend functions, and he accepted most invitations. Bobby received some and accepted very few.

"At Harvard," Bobby admitted, "I wasn't interested in my studies. I didn't press too hard. I was much more interested in playing varsity football and arguing with my roommates about sports."[15]

With his grades, he had no chance of being admitted to Harvard Law School, knew it, and applied instead to the University of Virginia Law School, in Charlottesville. He was accepted with the warning that, unless he did markedly better than in undergraduate school, he wouldn't be there long.

5

Bobby and Ethel—The Early Years

*B*OBBY'S MARRIAGE to Ethel Skakel was one of the most remarkable in Washington's recent history.

At a time when more political marriages than ever before were unraveling, reflecting swiftly changing moral standards and the raising of consciousness by women, theirs grew stronger.* All around them, friends and colleagues who would not divorce for religious reasons were pursuing separate lives, wed in name only. Bobby and Ethel remained together, establishing a reputation as Washington's happiest, though at the same time one of its most eccentric, couples.

Lem Billings put it this way: "It was a love match, but they led absolutely crazy lives." Leland Hayward, the producer, after a day spent with the family, said, "Their lifestyle would make the damnedest musical comedy the Broadway stage has ever seen."

In an era of rapid change, Ethel and Bobby stood out as an old-fashioned couple, he the worker, she the homemaker. Ethel never wanted to be liberated from anything.

As career horizons widened for more and more women, Ethel had no

---

* A few examples of marriages that could not survive the pressures: Ted Kennedy's law school classmate, former Senator John V. Tunney of California and his wife, Mieke, were divorced after thirteen years. Mieke "couldn't take the life," Tunney admitted. Senator Robert Dole of Kansas, now majority leader, and his wife of twenty-three years, Phyllis, ended their marriage. "He got so involved with his job that he let his family fall into the background," Phyllis said. Nancy Riegle, who was divorced from Representative Don Riegle, stated the problem candidly: "These guys think they're being unselfish worrying about the kids in Vietnam and the poor in ghettos, but that's a bunch of crap. . . . It's all for their own aggrandizement. When it comes to being a daddy or a husband, there is no time."

ambition for any job outside her home. Declared Fred Dutton, a former White House assistant and RFK's personal aide during his Presidential campaign, "She had no interest in center stage. She didn't want to write a book or study law or teach school. All she wanted was to be Bob's wife and the mother of his children."[1]

Defining her role, she said, "A politician's wife should work at making her home a nice place for her husband to come home to." And she worked hard at it, all through their married life, becoming widely known as supermom and superwife. She had no time for, understanding of, or sympathy with, the women's movement.

Her sister-in-law Joan, raised like Ethel as a rich girl in a Catholic family, was similarly uninformed about feminism when she first arrived in Washington in 1962, but she grew. "I have yet to meet a women's lib member or enthusiast," she said then and, even ten years later, admitted she "didn't know very much" about it all. Missing the point of the movement, she said it would not be fair for her to comment on it because she had "certain freedoms," such as "help at home and no need to go out and make a living." The breakup of her marriage was the catalyst that made her realize that even women with "help" and plenty of money need personal fulfillment. After diligent study, she received a master's degree in music education from Lesley College and now spends much of her time teaching and being involved in Boston's music and arts world.

Jackie, too, has found that work outside the home was essential to her life, even though she is reported to be worth more than $40 million. "Of course women should work if they want to," she declared. "A definition of happiness is complete use of one's faculties along lines leading to excellence in life. . . . It applies to women as well as men. We can't all reach it, but we can try to reach it to some degree." And so, the twice-widowed Jackie works a four-day week at Doubleday & Company, a New York City publishing house, where she is a senior editor earning between $40,000 and $45,000 a year. She arrives between 9:30 and 10:00 in the morning and leaves about four, but she always takes home a briefcase bulging with manuscripts.

Ethel subsumed her own identity into Bobby's, making his career, his ambition, his drives her own, rejoicing in his successes and suffering in his defeats. She had no selfness and wanted none.

"There never was anyone else but Bobby," she once said. And he said, "The best thing I ever did was marrying Ethel." They merged into an extraordinarily happy marriage, something neither Joan nor Jackie ever had.

"He called her at least ten times a day from wherever he was," said John Burns, the New York State Democratic chairman when Bobby ran for the Senate. "I have never seen a couple that close."

Declared Ramsey Clark, "Somebody once said that happiness is being married to your best friend. They were just that. They teased each other, thought of each other, and shared passionate devotion to their children."[2]

When Robert Kennedy traveled abroad, he wrote her a letter every day, telling her how much he loved her in the language of the country where he was at the time.

Despite her well-publicized boisterous, offbeat behavior, Ethel was rigidly puritanical. Dirty stories, sexual innuendos, and obscenities of any kind shocked her. She was more innocent, and for much longer, than wide-eyed Joan, who once asked Jackie why Truman Capote spoke in that effeminate manner. "Is he," Joan whispered, "well—queer? You know, gay?" Jackie, helpless with laughter, managed to affirm that Capote was "gay as paint" and added, "Joan, you're hopeless. We'll never corrupt you."

On campaign trips with Bobby, unmarried couples either would not risk pairing up in hotel rooms, or did it with great care, when Ethel was present. Washington hostesses knew she would not stand for even mildly risque humor. One time she and Bobby were invited to a dinner party by a hostess who usually paired partners by handing men guests bolts and women nuts, and letting them circulate to find a fit. When Bobby and Ethel accepted, she ordered place cards instead.

No unmarried men and women living together were ever invited to her home. In Washington, hostesses reportedly were asked by Ethel to remove couples having live-in relationships from a guest list before she and Bobby would agree to come. "In a town like Washington," said Nicholas von Hoffman, "which seems to have a higher than expected number of screwy living and loving arrangements, Ethel's puritan perversities are a recurring source of exasperated amusement."[3]

Both Bobby and Ethel were intensely competitive, sometimes to the point where onlookers shook their heads in disbelief long afterward. Note twin examples:

In the summer of 1965, Senator Fred R. Harris of Oklahoma, weekending at Hyannis Port, was drafted into a softball game.

"Everybody played," Harris said, "down to the littlest children. All through the game the young ones would get the easy treatment, very slow balls lobbed up to them.

"Well, came the end of the ninth inning, with the score tied, two men on base and two out. Kerry Kennedy came to bat. Bobby was pitching for the other side. He wound up and threw her a hard fastball, which she missed of course. Then another and a third, striking her out and retiring the side with the score still tied." Kerry was just a month short of her sixth birthday.

At dinner that night, Harris told the story to Rose, who said, "Oh Bobby, you didn't!"

"Can I help it if Kerry is a sucker for an inside fastball?" he said innocently.[4]

The same year Ethel was teamed in tennis doubles with William vanden Heuvel, a special assistant on Bobby's Justice Department staff. Vanden Heuvel, feeling the heat of the day, slowly walked to the rear of the court to serve. Ethel, watching from the baseline, trotted up to him and whispered her strategy: "Bill," she said, "what you've got to do is *run* to your position between games. The other side is tired and if they see you run they'll be demoralized."

They were markedly different in one fundamental personality trait: he was shy and introverted, she outgoing. He was self-conscious, given to feelings of inferiority, spells of moodiness, and tended to keep in the background on social occasions. She leaped atop tables and tap-danced if someone asked her, and often when nobody did. All of this was good; when he wrapped himself in thoughts and buried himself in work, she could tease him out of it and snap the stresses.

Her religious faith was equally deep. Reared by a mother as devout as Rose, Ethel has gone to mass every day of her life, taking with her all children who had been "church broke," usually about age five, when they could sit without squirming or squealing. In the library of her mother's home, there had been a font of holy water and four or five prie-dieux, upholstered kneeling stools for praying. They were used daily.

She is a graduate of the Manhattanville College of the Sacred Heart,* then located on Morningside Heights in New York City, where the teachers were nuns in long black habits and the curriculum was heavy with courses in religion. Sister Florence Weston, the academic dean, recalled Ethel as a "pious girl." For a time, she thought seriously of becoming a nun.

From her mother and her education, she developed a lifelong fundamentalist concept of her faith, at one time becoming angry because the Catholic schools to which she sent her children were teaching that the story of Noah was a form of myth rather than actual fact. Another time she argued with Chief Justice Earl Warren that prayers in school should be permitted because "God is everywhere."

In a personal communication to the author, the former Father Abbot of the Abbey Gethsemane, a Trappist monastery, who was a close friend of the Skakels, explained that Ethel's faith was not merely an intellectual acceptance of Catholic dogma. "Rather," he wrote, "it is a faith which penetrates her entire being—and which motivates her everyday rounds of duties, of sorrows, and of joys."

The media have always regarded Ethel with considerable affection.

* Manhattanville, now in Purchase, New York, has dropped the "Sacred Heart" from its name and, though its roots are still Roman Catholic, it is nonsectarian and coeducational.

Through the years, her often outrageous prankishness, which would earn disapproval for others, was Teflon-like for Ethel: nothing stuck to diminish the regard in which she was held.

When she pushed Washington's elite into the swimming pool fully clothed during the Camelot years, she was applauded for dampening egos and shrinking them to size. When she threw the contents of a glass of wine in the face of men who began telling smutty stories, she was hailed as a guardian of virtue. Once, at the swank "21" Club in New York, Governor Hugh Carey of New York was attending a small party in a private dining room with Ethel and some friends.

Ethel, offended at something Carey said, made no allowances for rank. He got a glass of wine in his face.

Jack Paar, who tells the story, regards it as hilarious. "It was just our Ethel being playful," he said. She was also being playful when, sailing on a family yacht, she overturned a bowl of cole slaw on the head of historian Arthur Schlesinger, Jr., spilling some of it on Mrs. Schlesinger, who "was picking celery out of her bosom for minutes." Said Mr. Paar, "It goes with the territory."[5]

One has to wonder how the governor of New York, and other celebrated persons, truly felt about Ethel's playfulness.

If she had inhibitions, they were never apparent. When Robert Frost, who had won the Pulitzer Prize for poetry four times, was a dinner guest, she passed paper and pencil among the guests and asked them all to write poems. Frost also got a pencil and paper.

She has been called scatterbrained, with some justification. In perfect seriousness, she could ask her Tokyo hosts if it were true that Japanese cats do not have tails, and later ask in wonderment why she could not visit Egypt and see all its ancient glories. Astounded, Andrew Glass, then a reporter for *The New York Herald-Tribune*, explained that as the wife of a New York senator, whose constituency was one-third Jewish, a journey to the country then dominated by Israel's implacable enemy, Gamal Abdal Nasser, would not be politically wise. "Oh," Ethel said.

"She did appear to be scatterbrained sometimes," said Senator Harris. "Once my former wife, LaDonna, and I were at her home for dinner and Ethel said grace. Afterward, Art Buchwald asked her: 'Ethel, why don't you call on me?'

"She looked surprised. 'But what God will you pray to?' she asked Art, a Jew.

" 'The same as yours,' he replied. 'Only He's been around longer.' "[6]

Their homologous relationship was also due to a significant extent to the almost eerie similarity of their origins. Like the Kennedys, Ethel's family was large, very rich, rambunctious, geared to go-go athleticism, and, as the years went on, they were also victims of multiple tragedies.

George Skakel, Ethel's father, a stocky, taciturn man with a dry wit, was single-minded in his pursuit of wealth. At a dinner in Washington in the early Fifties, the wife of a State Department official tried to draw him into conversation with no success. Trying gamely, she asked, "Do you have any hobbies?" Skakel perked up.

"Sure," he replied. "Old and new money."[7]

He made plenty of both. Beginning in the coal and coke business in 1919, he later formed the Great Lakes Carbon Corporation, one of the country's largest privately owned companies, with holdings in many areas. Skakel, who married Ann Brannack, brought up his family in Chicago, where Ethel was born on April 11, 1928. In 1936, the Skakels moved to Westchester and, the following year, settled in a three-story mansion on a large wooded estate off Lake Avenue in Greenwich, Connecticut.

There were seven children in the Skakel family, Ethel the next to youngest. Two of her three older brothers, James and George junior, considerably wilder than Joe and Jack Kennedy, unglued Greenwich and environs by driving cars at breakneck speeds over the narrow roads and galloping horses like charging cavalrymen.

Ethel's must-win personality was a hand-me-down from her father and older brothers. Rushton, the third brother, described George senior in the very words said repeatedly about the elder Kennedy: "He hates to lose." George junior was the same. He was a handsome man, strong-chinned, with close-cropped dark hair, a long face, and piercing eyes beneath bushy brows. He rammed his way through football seasons at Amherst, inflicting considerable damage on opponents and himself, and played polo at the Blind Brook Polo Club in Purchase like a drunken cowboy on an unbroken mustang.

Ethel, devoted to her father, grew up imitating him. "She walked like him, adopted his mannerisms and even the way he talked," Rushton recalled. George Skakel was a highly moral man, prim to the point of embarrassment when anyone told even a slightly off-color story. Like Joe Kennedy, Skakel was not as religious as his wife. His marriage crossed religious lines: he was a Dutch Protestant but, late in his life, began taking instruction in the Catholic faith.

Within a dozen years, four members of Ethel's family died violently. On October 4, 1955, the Skakel company plane, a converted twin-engine Martin Marauder, crashed after taking off from Tulsa, killing George and Ann. Eleven years later, in the fall of 1965, George junior and four others were killed when his single-engine Cessna 185 was trapped by the nearly vertical walls of Crooked Creek Canyon in a primitive area of Idaho. Skakel, who was not at the controls, was only forty-four. Less than eight months later, his wife Patricia died when a piece of meat became lodged in her throat during dinner in her Greenwich home.

Bobby met Ethel through that time-honored method, a fixup by a sister. Jean Kennedy and Ethel were roommates at Manhattanville. Jean felt that the high-spirited, extroverted Ethel would be just right for her shy, moody brother. So, in the winter of 1944, she invited a group of boys and girls to a skiing party in the Laurentian Mountains of Quebec, including, of course, Ethel and Bobby.

They met, and Ethel promptly fell in love. Unhappily for her, Bobby did not. Back home, they dated a few times, but Bobby became totally disinterested when he met Ethel's sister Pat, three years older, at a dance.

Far less bouncy than Ethel, much more serious-minded, Pat was the first real love of Bobby's life. He pursued her with ardor, calling daily, dating her as frequently as she would accept his invitations.

"Bobby fell in love with my sister Pat," Ethel remembered, "and he went with her for two years."[8]

The romance, however, was one-sided.

"He was very pleasant, and very funny, and very good-looking," Pat recalled. "He wasn't any of the things then that he turned out to be. He was magnificent in the latter part of his career, but when I knew him he was just a teenager practically."[9]

Bobby wanted to marry Pat, but she had met an Irish architectural student, Luan Peter Cuffe, who was in Boston studying for his master's degree at Harvard. Cuffe was nine years older than Bobby. Pat dropped Bobby and, soon after, married Cuffe and went to live with him in Dublin. Rushton Skakel declared that Pat was as devout as Ethel. "I thought she would become a nun," he said. "She surprised us and married an Irishman."

Bobby didn't begin dating Ethel again until four years later, after both had gotten their first taste of political activity in John Kennedy's first campaign, the 1946 race for the Democratic nomination in the 11th Congressional District. This was where Honey Fitz had launched his career. It would become known as the spawning ground for young Kennedys embarking on political careers.

Newly discharged from the Navy, Bobby clamored to help Jack. Kennedy's backers were not overwhelmed by his offer. At Kennedy's headquarters, someone suggested that Bobby be assigned to East Cambridge, an area nobody had the slightest hope of carrying. That was Mike Neville country. Neville, a former mayor and popular state legislator, was also running for the vacant congressional seat. "The kid can't do any harm there," said a Kennedy strategist.

Bobby moved into a three-room apartment Jack had rented at 122 Bowdoin Street (which would remain JFK's voting address) and tackled his beat with his customary intensity.

Day after day, he rose before dawn and slogged until 9 or 10 P.M. through the Italian-American area, walking up and down stairs, knocking on doors, entering shops. "I'm Bobby Kennedy," he told them all, and earnestly talked about his brother.

East Cambridge comprises three wards, and Bobby covered almost every house in each with Lawrence deGuglielmo, brother of Joseph Austin deGuglielmo, an important political figure in Cambridge.

"What they did," said deGug, "they went around and met the kids, and played a lot of touch football with them. It had the effect of proving the Kennedys weren't snobs—that Bobby was willing to pal around with them. And Bobby made a lot of friends in East Cambridge."

He made so many that, on June 18, primary day, he pulled off a minor political miracle. John Kennedy had expected to lose by a five-to-one vote in East Cambridge; Bobby cut the loss to two and a half to one. Jack's victory was a landslide, 42 percent of all votes cast in the 11th District, and in November he overwhelmingly defeated the Republican candidate, Lester Bowen.

Ethel had been active in the campaign, too, helping to organize the famous Kennedy tea and coffee parties in neighborhoods. She asked women to invite their friends to their homes, then rushed around and helped deliver paper cups, napkins, and cookies, all bearing the slogan: "Coffee with the Kennedys." The candidate would race from one to another, charming the ladies and winning votes. (The innovation was so successful, the parties were repeated at every election. When Jack defeated Henry Cabot Lodge for the Senate in 1952, Lodge said, "It was those damn tea parties!")

Both Bobby and Ethel returned to school, and he began calling her again. This time he, too, fell in love.

They were married on June 17, 1950, at St. Mary's Roman Catholic Church on Greenwich Avenue. Pat Cuffe flew in from Dublin to be matron of honor. The groom's best man was John Kennedy, and among the ushers was George Skakel junior. Skakel, in fine form, saw Lem Billings bending over to pick up something and gave him such a thrusting kick that Lem hurtled at least twenty feet down the aisle.

George had begun celebrating the evening before at a bachelor party for Robert at the Harvard Club on West Forty-fourth Street in Manhattan. He started a donnybrook there that almost wrecked one of the banquet rooms on the third floor, an event still remembered by old-timers.[10] Jack Kennedy, who was there, taking note of Bobby's roistering jock friends, said, "I've never seen such a bunch of outrageous, irreverent characters in my whole life.''

Bobby had invited most of the Harvard football team, all of them heavy-weights and all of them too poor to afford the morning suits the occasion called for. Kenny O'Donnell told this to Bobby, saying, ''To hell with it. We're going back to Boston.'' Said Bobby, ''Hold on. I'll pay for the suits.'' And he did.

The year Bobby took Ethel to live in Charlottesville was special in a number of ways.

They were, to begin, newlyweds rapturously in love. Each was to re-member the months spent in the gently rolling hills of middle Virginia as perhaps the most idyllic of their lives. ''It was pretty near perfect,'' Bobby told Lem Billings afterward. Thirty-three years later, Ethel showed up un-expectedly one Sunday morning at the door of the house in which they had lived, accompanied by Robert junior. George Rodeheaver, who lives there now, said Ethel asked if she could show her son where she and his father had lived. For almost a half hour, Ethel walked through the rooms, talking as much to herself as to her son, as she described the way it was back then.[11]

The winter had a kind of Camelot quality. It was milder than usual, with a number of snowfalls from late November through January. The Kennedys would awaken to a fantasy world of white lace outside their windows; then, as the day promptly warmed up, the snow would disappear as though in obedience to King Arthur's ''legal laws.''

It was followed by a uniquely lush spring, even for that part of Virginia. From every room in the house, Bobby and Ethel looked out on a landscape of pink and white dogwood trees in fullest bloom, hot pink azaleas, chrome yellow forsythia, daffodils, and jonquils of every shade and design.

Throughout law school, Bobby's cars, like his clothes, were old, well-worn, and often in need of repair. At one time, they had been of excellent quality and make, but were long since past their prime, and looked it.

''He had a preference for convertible automobiles,'' said Judge Gerald Tremblay, a law school classmate who remained friendly with Robert throughout his life. ''He drove some good Joe Kennedy hand-me-downs, but he took no care of them, and they reflected their lack of care. He had one light-blue 1941 Chrysler convertible with a top that was always down in all kinds of weather. The reason it stayed down was because it would not go up.''

Mrs. Phillip Sommer, Bobby's landlady during his second (pre-Ethel) year, said that his clothing style as a bachelor student was even worse than most—''the sloppiest.'' After his marriage, Judge Tremblay noted, he changed, not unusual when a wife begins to exert influence. He began showing up in class in khaki pants, socks, scuffed shoes, and jacket. "Ethel," observed Judge Tremblay, "kept him coordinated."

She also had considerable influence on his home behavior.

The year before he was married, Bobby and George Terrien, who married Ethel's oldest sister Georgeann after graduation, had rented the large white-shingled house at 2421 Jefferson Park Avenue from the Sommers. Terrien lived upstairs, Kennedy downstairs, in identical five-room apartments.

"There were no girls, no wild parties, nothing even like them," Mrs. Sommer stated. "Bobby went to mass regularly at Holy Comforter Catholic Church."

That, said Mrs. Sommer, whose husband was an engineering professor at the university, was the good part.

Not so good was that, unhappily, "they didn't take care of anything." She declared, "Bobby had an arrogant rich-boy's attitude, a feeling that 'I pay such a high rent I can do anything.' "

He gouged her beautiful wooden floors with golf cleats, permitted friends to let their cigarettes burn down and scorch the mantel, put his muddy feet atop her furniture, and was always leaving doors and windows open in winter, pushing up heating costs.

In later years, Bobby Kennedy had considerable difficulty deciding whether to run for the Senate and, later, whether to seek the Presidential nomination. But in law school, he rushed to judgments swiftly—much too fast, his friend Endicott Peabody Davison recalled.

"He would read *Time* magazine," Cottie said, "and come to instant conclusions about what was right and what was wrong. He would stubbornly insist he was right and, once he made up his mind, it was impossible to shake him from his convictions.

"I'd ask him, 'Now Bobby, how do you know all these facts? Aren't you making too many assumptions?' He'd just answer stubbornly: 'I'm right. I know I'm right.' "

He still had few friends and made no effort to make more. He was a loner, joined almost no organizations. His puritanical views had become even more rigid.

"At law school," Cottie said, "the students would work very hard and then there would be a big party. Some of the women there were pretty loose. He was disgusted with them and would say so. And this was before he was married."[12]

After Ethel came down in September 1950, things changed. "She made Robert more aware of the people around him and more sensitive to their lives and feelings," Judge Tremblay declared. Specifically, she modified his behavior at their home, which began to look less like an animal house and more like a honeymoon cottage.

Not that Ethel was, then or ever, a perfect homemaker. When the children and their pets began arriving, she gave up the battle to keep the house they occupied uncluttered. Her wooden floors were scratched, not by cleats, but by charging children, and, on too frequent occasions, peed upon by the family's dogs. But here, in her very first, she made a valiant effort at neatness, and succeeded to a degree.

She was a good deal less efficient in the kitchen, where, to put it bluntly, she was totally helpless and hopeless. Nothing she tried ever came out even marginally palatable, surprising because her mother was an excellent cook who supervised her kitchen staff carefully and, when she was without servants, could take on the duties of feeding her large family with ease and excellent results.

Ethel's morning bacon was invariably burned or underdone, her scrambled eggs were too hard or too soft, and the hamburgers never came out as she intended they should. After several months of culinary disasters, she gave up and hired a cook.

In 1958, she was named Homemaker of the Year by the Home Fashion League of Washington. By that time the Kennedys were living at Hickory Hill, where Ethel could find her way to the kitchen but, once there, would be hard put to tell where things were or what to do once she found them. Bobby advised Ethel to hurry on down and pick up her award, "before they change their minds."

In Virginia, he worked harder than he ever had at a school, reading his cases, writing his reports, and struggling along, with no better grades than he had always received. John Ritchie, one of his professors, called him a "competent" student, but offered no higher praise. In between classes and study, Bobby worried a great deal about his future, which seemed as hazy as a large patch of fog in the road ahead.

He was graduated in June 1951, midway in his class, fifty-sixth of 125 students. He never made *Law Review*. His one accomplishment—which has received less attention than it deserves, because of what it portended for the future—was his work with the Student Legal Forum, his sole extracurricular activity.

The forum had been established several years before, as a talk and discussion series that brought prominent persons to the Virginia grounds, but interest had declined and it was now moving along listlessly, attracting little attention and less important speakers. Bobby perceived the forum as a paving block in his own personal road, joined the organization committee and, in his final year, was elected president.

It wasn't much of a committee, but it did make a big stir, giving the forum an upward boost. Davison recalled, "Actually, Bobby and I and another fellow were the whole committee."

But with his father's connections, Bobby lined up star attractions: Supreme Court Justice William O. Douglas; Thurman Arnold, FDR's trust-busting assistant attorney general and Yale law professor; former President Herbert Hoover; James M. Landis, the New Deal brain truster; and the junior senator from Wisconsin, Joseph R. McCarthy, who had just launched his anti-Communist crusade. On his own, Bobby invited his brother, Representative John F. Kennedy.

McCarthy, Joe Kennedy's good friend, received a lukewarm reception, despite the earthquakes he was causing elsewhere. The audience was unusually quiet, asking only a few questions. But, when Joe came down on December 12, 1950, he sparked a spirited and sometimes angry response to his isolationist views.

Kennedy assailed the Truman Doctrine, which called for aiding countries threatened by the spread of Communism, and urged the United States to pull in its horns, its troops, and its influence from global matters. His remarks were greeted with delight in Russia, where *Pravda* reprinted them in full.

"Robert Kennedy did not agree with his father's views," said Judge Tremblay, "but he did not press the point. He did not argue with his father."

"One day in spring," Cottie Davison remembered, "Bobby and I were sitting around, wondering who we would bring down in the fall. 'Hey,' Bobby said, 'why not Ralph Bunche?' "[13]

Dr. Bunche, the Under Secretary of the United Nations, was a respected world figure, soon to be the first black awarded the Nobel Peace Prize. Cottie was enthusiastic, and the next day they went to law school dean Hardy Dillard, who agreed. Bobby wrote to Bunche, who accepted with one condition—the audience must be integrated. In early fall, Bobby and Cottie were summoned to the dean's office. He looked frustrated.

"He told us that under Virginia law, the mixing of blacks and whites was prohibited in public places, such as movie theaters, concert halls and auditoriums," Cottie Davison remembers. "Still, he said he wouldn't oppose Bunche's appearance if we could get the leadership of the student body, the student government council, to back us and, in addition, could get the approval of the Board of Visitors, the university's governing body.

"So we went to the student council and they all thought it was a great idea until it came to sign a resolution saying so. Then many balked. They were for the most part southerners, some of whom were interested in political careers, and they didn't want their names tainted with the possibility that they had cooperated in bringing a black to the University of Virginia."

Bobby was livid. "You're all gutless," he bellowed at the student leaders. "You're willing to go ahead with this idea but you're afraid to let anyone know you're backing it!" He continued to berate them, but his rage strangled his voice and he became inarticulate. He sat down.

After a moment of tense silence, the board took up the question and decided that, while it would not officially approve the resolution, it would not interfere either.

"We're going to win," Bobby told Cottie. "We're going to beat this thing."

The next step was approval of the Board of Visitors, more difficult to obtain. For this, Bobby and Cottie obtained the help of Dean Dillard and Professor Charles O. Gregory, who gave them a legal basis for their fight. Not long before, in the case of *Sweatt* v. *Painter*, the University of Texas Law School had been ordered by the U.S. Supreme Court to enroll a black. Ergo, since Ralph Bunche's address would be of an educational nature, and educational institutions by high court edict could not be segregated, the Virginia statute would not apply.

The argument carried the day. Bunche arrived and gave his talk before a packed, unsegregated hall.

Clearly, in his first real defense of civil rights for blacks, Bobby Kennedy won an important victory. But was the fight he waged a matter of principle, or was his finely honed competitive nature aroused by the challenge? Was he committed—or did he just hate to lose?

One must take note of the fact that, a short distance from his house, was the Farmington Country Club, whose red-brick main building was designed by Thomas Jefferson and built in 1803. It was, and is, a beautiful, gracious private establishment with excellent facilities. Bobby and Ethel joined the club and went there frequently to play golf and tennis and to swim.

In those days, the club did not accept blacks as either members or guests. Apparently, then, Bobby Kennedy had no problem with helping to break down the university's color barrier by inviting a black man to speak, then going off to a club that would exclude him.[14]

His years at Charlottesville were a period of flux in the development of his social conscience.

6

"A Royal Pain"

A FTER HIS graduation from law school, Bobby and Ethel spent the summer in Hyannis Port, where, on July 4, 1951, their first child, Kathleen Hartington, was born. The entire family attended the baptism ceremonies, along with a number of close friends, several of whom flew up from Washington.

One of these was Joe McCarthy, the junior senator from Wisconsin, whose four-year firestorm had already started. Bobby had asked him to be his daughter's godfather. If the parents were unable for any reason to rear the child in the Catholic faith, it would be Joe McCarthy's responsibility under Church law to do so.

As summer waned and the nights grew chill at the Cape, Bobby pondered his future.

He held a law degree but never considered entering the legal profession. "I'll be glad to open a law office for you anywhere you like," his father told him. "Washington, New York, Boston, Hollywood, anywhere." Bobby wasn't interested. Neither would he accept his father's offer to call his friends and find a job for his son as an associate in a major law firm.[1]

During law school days, Bobby had thought briefly of entering business school and of teaching, but abandoned both notions. He confided his indecision about a lifework to Charles Spalding during long walks on the Cape at vacation time. Spalding, who had known the Kennedy brothers well since 1940, believed that despite casting around, Bobby had known all along where he would go. "It was quite clear it [his choice] would be government

59

work," Spalding asserted.[2] With Jack already there, not to mention the family conditioning, there was little chance he would do anything else.

Still, he did make an effort in another direction. He had a career in journalism, one of the briefest on record, with the old *Boston Post*, where he had worked for a short time during summer vacations as a Harvard undergraduate. He started in September 1951, covered the signing of the peace treaty with Japan in San Francisco, and resigned in October, after he got a telephone call from Jack.

"How would you like to come with me on a trip around the world?" Jack asked. Bobby knew Jack did not have a long vacation in mind. "The prime purpose of the trip," Bobby said later, "was to prepare Jack for the 1952 campaign, so that he could talk about foreign policy."[3]

Family training—that the ones behind must help the one ahead—was strong. Bobby put his own career on hold, and the brothers, accompanied by their sister Pat, set off on a 25,000-mile globe-girdling journey. The trip was notable for the distinct lack of interest that officials of foreign countries had in either of the Kennedy brothers.

"We went to the Middle East for a short period," Bobby said, "and met Franklin D. Roosevelt* there, who received all the attention. It was almost as if we weren't there particularly. Congressman Kennedy, they didn't care about him. They cared just about Congressman Roosevelt, who was the major figure and sort of led us around."

In a letter home, Bobby with wry humor wrote from Israel that he had finally discovered why the Jewish people have not accepted Christ.

"FDR junior is what they have been waiting for," he said.[4]

Afterward, the three went to meet with Jawaharlal Nehru, the prime minister. The Kennedy brothers were no more popular with him than they were with Israeli leaders.

"He didn't pay the slightest attention to my brother," Bobby said, "but was just destroyed by my sister Pat. He wouldn't talk to him [Jack] at all . . . just to Pat and directed everything to her. My brother always remembered that. It was very funny, you know, and we really laughed about it.

"President Kennedy never liked Nehru. He didn't like him much then, not just because of that, but because he was so superior, and his personality was rather offensive. He really disliked Nehru when he came to the United States in 1962. Everybody thought that they got along so well, but he really disliked him as a personality."

A week later, on October 19, the brothers were in Vietnam, which, with Cambodia and Laos, was still French Indochina, the fast-crumbling remnants of an empire. France's 280,000-man army, mostly volunteers, supported

* Young Roosevelt was then a newly elected representative from New York City.

by American money and materiel that had begun to flow the year before, was battling Ho Chi Minh and his 300,000 trained jungle fighters of the Communist Vietminh.

Here, on the first journey either had taken to the land that would throw the United States into one of its worst convulsions in history, the Kennedy brothers became convinced that America's policy was on a course headed for ultimate disaster.

Bobby saw that the French were despised by the Vietnamese. He believed that, if a vote were taken, the entire country—then divided into Cochin China or Southern Vietnam, Annam, the central portion, and Tonkin in the north—would vote overwhelmingly for Ho Chi Minh. Prophetically, he wrote to Joe senior, "As it stands now, we are becoming more and more involved in the war to a point where we can't back out."[5]

John Kennedy, too, disagreed totally with French policy in Indochina. "He thought it was a disaster," Robert said later, "that we didn't have the right policy and that we were going to get into a great deal of difficulty." Moreover, Bobby declared, his brother had little use for the U.S. Foreign Service representation in Vietnam. "He felt it was very second rate, [our] people associated themselves just with the leaders and not with the people or the aspirations of the people." In addition, they had little knowledge of what was going on.[6]

The brothers flew up to Hanoi, accompanied by the French commander, General Jean de Lattre de Tassigny. The city greeted them with wild enthusiasm.

"They had a big parade welcoming us into the city," Bobby asserted, "with all of the children of Hanoi coming out and waving flags."

Then he added a word filled with meaning: "Ironic."[7]

The irony was that, despite JFK's strong belief in 1951 that the United States was headed for tragedy in Southeast Asia, despite his total mistrust of the Foreign Service, ten years later he had begun to step up America's involvement in the Vietnam conflict. By October 1963, the U.S. military presence was numbering 16,732, with more personnel en route, and men were already dying in the jungles.

Bobby never could explain the paradox. "I don't know which would be best," he admitted later, "to say that he didn't spend much time thinking about Vietnam; or to say that he did and messed it up." Pointing heavenward, Bobby cried out, "Which, brother, which?"[8]

A frightening episode occurred after the brothers had concluded their visit to Vietnam.

"He was going to Korea," Bobby said, "and I went to Japan. He was a little sick at the time, but then he got really sick."

"Really sick" meant a temperature so high doctors did not think he could survive. When Bobby got word in Japan, he made arrangements to fly his brother to a military hospital in Okinawa and rushed to the bedside.

Soon after his arrival, Jack's temperature shot up to 107 and Bobby was told to prepare for the worst.

Bobby knew then what the world was not to learn until years later—Jack had a severe illness, which was adroitly hidden by the Kennedys. Four years before, he had been told he had Addison's disease and had been given a year to live. Addison's is a withering away of the adrenal glands, sometimes from tuberculosis but more often from unknown causes, which reduces hormonal secretions. In 1947, hormonal replacement by cortisone therapy brought about a dramatic improvement.

The illness was denied then and is still being played down in some accounts. Dr. Janet Travell, the White House physician during JFK's administration, has stated that he did have the disease as it was then defined. Her statement is in the oral history she made for the Kennedy Library. Yet as recently as 1960, when Kennedy and Lyndon Johnson were rivals for the nomination, Bobby Kennedy burst out at Bobby Baker, Johnson's aide, after Lyndon had talked to the media about Jack's Addison problem. "You've got your nerve," Bobby said to Baker, his voice almost a scream. "Lyndon Johnson . . . lied by saying my brother was dying of Addison's disease. You Johnson people are running a stinking damned campaign."

But Bobby knew; he knew back then, in 1951, when Jack was once again close to death. Addison patients are prone to infections. He had no way of knowing if the burning fever was caused by Jack's adrenal problem or the malaria and jaundice he had suffered while in the Navy.

It was a long night for Bobby, who was halfway around the world, away from family and close friends.

"They thought he would die," he remembered. "Everybody just expected him to die."

But John Kennedy lived through the night. By morning, his fever broke, and he improved rapidly.

"We stayed a few days there," Bobby said, "and then he flew back [home.]"

In November, after several weeks of serious contemplation about his future, Bobby went where he had known he would. His father called a friend who called a friend: Senator Joe McCarthy telephoned Frank Parker, the angular, thinning-haired United States Attorney for Eastern New York, and asked him to give Bobby a job.

One month later, Bobby went down to the old courthouse on Washington Street near the Brooklyn Bridge, where Parker and his staff worked. It was a block-square stone structure that also served as the main post office in

Brooklyn, a landmark with a bell tower, where criminals were still being hanged for capital crimes as the nineteenth century drew to a close. Across the street were the offices of the *Brooklyn Eagle*, now defunct, and on the other side of a broad plaza, Sonsire's Cafeteria, where he would sometimes go for lunch.

Bobby's salary was $4,200 a year, about $800 more than the other assistants on Parker's staff were receiving.

"The fellow didn't even have an office," recalled Nathan Borock, one of the eighteen assistants, who himself earned $3,400. "The rest of us had two-room suites on the fifth floor, with our names on the door, and a secretary, but Bobby worked wherever he could, in the library or at any vacant desk. He came and he went, and nobody paid much attention to him."[9]

He spent only three months there, but those all-but-forgotten times set his feet on the road he would travel most of his life. It was in that building and in Washington, where he traveled often, that he learned about the seamy underside of life in America, the existence of corruption on a massive scale.

Assigned to the Internal Security Division, he began scratching into charges against a number of former high officials in Harry S. Truman's Administration, unearthing evidence that helped convict Joseph D. Nunan, former Commissioner of Internal Revenue, of evading $100,000 in income taxes and former Assistant Commissioner Daniel P. Bolich of trying to fix a tax case.

"It was an education," Bobby said of his first look into the functionings of the criminal justice system. "There's a lot of red tape in this business," he said naively, "and I'd like to see it cut. And there's quite a spread between indictment and conviction. It's one thing to accuse a man; it's another to convince a jury of the guilt."[10]

Still, once into the work, he found it fascinating and wanted to pursue it. But family obligation summoned him elsewhere.

While Bobby was working in Brooklyn, Jack had been crisscrossing Massachusetts, speaking in American Legion halls, before church groups, in bowling alleys, anywhere he could find an audience in preparation for a new campaign that fall. He wasn't certain if he would run for the Senate, where he would face the formidable Henry Lodge, or the governor's chair, then occupied by the popular Paul A. Dever, a Democrat whom he'd have to beat in the primary.

Each weekend, Bobby journeyed up to Boston to meet with Jack and travel with him, to thrash out the dilemma. Said Bobby, "The problem was that he had to not only beat a Democrat in the primary, which would be unpleasant and have a major effect on the party and his relationship with the party in the future, but secondly it took him out of what he enjoyed most, which was Washington.''

As they talked, Jack's attention turned increasingly toward the governorship. ''He very, very seriously considered it,'' Bobby said. But Joe Kennedy changed his mind.

''My father was in favor of him running against Lodge because he thought that, first, you haven't got much even if you became Governor, and he [Jack] wouldn't like it as much. But, secondly, that Lodge was the major figure in the State, and perhaps in the country, and when you beat him, you beat the number one person, and it [would make] John Kennedy a major, significant figure overnight.''[11]

As soon as the decision was reached, Bobby resigned his job, hating to leave but explaining, ''I owe it to my brother Jack to return to Massachusetts and do my part before the Democratic primary in September.''

Unskilled in politics and, except for a brief period, with no experience in the tough Massachusetts brand, Bobby was brought in as his brother's campaign chairman. Kenny O'Donnell had spoken urgently to him, saying Jack's organization was in the same kind of dreadful mess his rooms had been at Harvard, only this was much more important. Joe called, too, so Bobby went to Boston.

''People didn't like me,'' Bobby said of his experience there. ''But it never bothered me, and I never cared. I mean, it wasn't at all important to me.''

His remark was an understatement. One old Boston pol put it succinctly: ''He was a royal pain in the ass.'' He bulled his way through the organization much as he had through an opponent's line on the football field. He didn't know the veterans there and paid them little respect, once ordering a powerful figure out of the office. He even managed to enrage Governor Dever, when he barged into his office at the State House and lectured him. Annoyed at a speech Dever had made, Bobby told him, ''You're hurting Jack's campaign. You want to watch what you say. You ought to read your speeches before you deliver them.''

Dever, almost apoplectic with rage, called Joe Kennedy on the phone and hollered at him, ''I know you're an important man around here, but I'm telling you this and I mean it. Keep that fresh kid of yours out of my sight from now on.''[12]

Bobby was everywhere. Once he heard that campaign workers were having trouble hanging a huge ''Elect John F. Kennedy'' poster on a high point on the Charlestown Bridge where thousands of commuters would see it daily. No ladder tall enough could be found.

Bobby drove there, climbed the ladder, and standing on tiptoes, hung the sign himself. Dave Powers, one of JFK's earliest political friends and now a curator of the Kennedy Library, stood at the base of the ladder, holding it tightly and wondering, "How could I explain it to the ambassador and Jack when Bobby fell and broke his neck?"

He shook up the organization until it rattled. He tossed overboard the wisdom of the experienced pols who told him political campaigns shouldn't get started before Labor Day. "We had to work in the summer if we wanted to win," he said and astounded everybody when he told them to give up their days and weekends at the beaches and get down to business.

"We spent all summer building the machine," Bobby asserted. Nobody worked harder than Bobby, who went everywhere and did almost everything, even inspecting automobiles at factories, to see if cars had Jack Kennedy bumper stickers.[13]

His tactics worked. Jack's organization was straightened out, and—with vast infusions of cash and effort from Joe Kennedy—the campaign turned out to be one of the most detailed, intricate, and smoothly working in the state's history.

Bobby made few mistakes, although he was witness to a monumental gaffe at an election eve rally in the overwhelmingly Jewish community of Mattapan. Robert Murphy, the state's lieutenant governor, was introducing John Kennedy, who was seated on the rostrum with Bob and Ted. In his peroration, Murphy told the crowd, many of whom wore yarmulkes, "I'm telling you that if you go out and bring home the Democratic Party tomorrow, the Democratic Party is going to bring home the bacon for you for the next four years."[14]

The audience was silent. On the dais, Jack gulped and Bobby hid his face in his hands.

It didn't hurt. Jack Kennedy went on to beat Lodge by more than 70,000 votes. The tally was barely counted when Kenny O'Donnell overheard Joe, who turned to a jubilant Bobby at campaign headquarters and said, "What are you going to do now? Are you going to sit on your tail end and do nothing now for the rest of your life? You'd better go out and get a job."

7

McCarthyite

*J*OE DID NOT leave the job-seeking to his son. Aware that the young man, at this stage, needed a post that provided high public visibility, he got word to James McInerney, a former FBI agent and assistant attorney general under President Truman, that he would like to have Bobby placed on Senator Joe McCarthy's investigative staff as chief counsel.

McInerney made the recommendation to McCarthy, who had just been reelected for a second term on the strength of his anti-Communist crusade. Robert A. Taft, majority leader, slotted McCarthy into the chairmanship of the Senate Subcommittee on Investigations, part of the Committee on Government Operations, where, he hoped, the nettlesome senator would devote his time to watchdogging the General Services Administration's accounting practices and spending and forget about hunting for Communists.

Taft blundered badly. McCarthy made it plain he had just begun. Small wonder—the voters had told him unmistakably that he had their support. By that time, McCarthy had become the best-known figure in the Republican Party, powerful enough to bring about the defeat of Millard Tydings when he went to Maryland to campaign. Tydings, considered unbeatable, lost by 40,000 votes.

McCarthy could have gone into Massachusetts, too, hurting, and in all probability, helping to defeat John Kennedy. But Joe made a special plea to him to stay out of the state, and since Kennedy had made a generous contribution to his campaign, McCarthy obliged.

He was a frequent visitor to Hyannis Port and Palm Beach and dated the eligible Pat for a while. In 1961, Joe senior made their relationship very clear: "In case there is any question in your mind, I liked Joe McCarthy. I always liked him."

When McCarthy heard that Joe Kennedy wanted the chief counsel job for Bobby, he scratched his head in perplexity. He had already found the man he wanted—Roy M. Cohn, then only twenty-five, who had been attracting attention on the staff of the United States Attorney's office in the Southern New York district. Cohn was something of a prodigy, a Columbia Law School graduate before he was twenty-one and not yet eligible for a license. His law school diploma was neatly framed on the wall of his Park Avenue apartment, but he had to wait six months before formal admission to the bar.

Cohn had impressed McCarthy with his work in 1951 on the prosecution team in the trial of Julius and Ethel Rosenberg and Morton Sobell. In early December 1952, shortly after Joe's reelection, he asked Roy to meet him in New York. In a crowded suite at the Hotel Astor, which reminded Cohn of a scene from a Marx Brothers movie, McCarthy, yelling over the din, told Cohn about the glowing reports he had heard and asked him to serve on his staff.[1]

Then came Joe Kennedy's request for a job for Bobby. McCarthy telephoned Joe and told him he would certainly place Bobby. Considering Kennedy's hefty contribution, he could scarcely say less. Still, he did not want to leave himself open to a charge that he was paying off a valuable donor. With his genius for creating chaos, McCarthy hit upon a solution that not only threw the committee into turmoil but helped fire a feud between Cohn and Bobby Kennedy that would endure for years.

"Bobby just doesn't have enough legal experience to be chief counsel," McCarthy told Joe Kennedy a few days later, "but I've got a good spot for him."

He would name Bobby assistant to Francis D. ("Frip") Flanagan, a former G-man who was then general counsel to the committee. And Roy Cohn would be appointed chief counsel.

The problem was that nobody, least of all Joe McCarthy, knew the difference between general and chief counsel.

"Who is superior to whom on the committee?" McCarthy was asked by a reporter when the staff changes were announced. "What does each title mean?"

McCarthy had to admit he didn't know. Cohn, watching as his new boss confessed with a broad smile that he could not tell, had a foreboding of what was to come. "I had my first hint of the chaos that was to prevail," he said later.[2] (In a few months, Flanagan got another job, and Cohn took over.)

John Kennedy, busy with his own senatorial work, heard what was being planned for Bobby and didn't like the idea one bit. In Washington and in their parents' Palm Beach home, he tried to dissuade his younger brother from joining McCarthy's team.

Jack's arguments fell on deaf ears, because Robert had become a true believer—"passionately devoted" to McCarthy's anti-Communist crusade, Arthur Krock recalled.[3] Jack, though, knew in his gut McCarthy was wrong. In 1960, he would write a favorable review of Richard Rovere's devastating book about McCarthy. But Jack was all but silenced by two potent factors— his father and his own constituency.

When Bobby stubbornly insisted on accepting the job with McCarthy, Jack threw up his hands. "Oh hell," he said resignedly, "you can't fight the old man."[4] Jack loved his father but had no use for his views and attitudes. During his campaign for the Presidency, he said of old Joe, "There isn't a motive in him which I respect except love of family, and sometimes I think that's just pride."[5]

But Jack found that not even he, with his ability to kid Joe when nobody else could, was able to thwart his father's wishes. Even after he became President, he would bow, though reluctantly, to Joe's demands on key appointments.

As for his constituency, Jack admitted, "Hell, half my voters in Massachusetts look on McCarthy as a hero."

Frank Parker, too, had tried to persuade Bobby not to link up with McCarthy. After he received McCarthy's offer, Bobby lunched with Parker at the Hotel Astor and told him, "I'm thinking of going with McCarthy. What do you think?"

"I'm against it," Parker told him flatly. Prophetically, the United States Attorney said, "He's making a lot of fuss now, but if you ally yourself with the man, it won't help your reputation one bit in later years."[6]

Nevertheless, Bobby accepted the job, and a jubilant Joe placed a call to Flanagan. "Joe Kennedy here," he announced. "I understand Bobby's gonna work for you, and I just want you to know that, by God, you won't have any trouble with him."

Joe gave Flanagan his private telephone number, saying that, if Bobby did present any problems, "just give me a call." The implication cannot be missed: If Bobby got out of line, Dad would straighten him out.

In January 1953, Bobby, Ethel, and their growing family moved to Washington. There were two children now: Kathleen was a year and a half old; and Joseph Patrick III, born September 24, 1952, was four months. By spring, Ethel would be pregnant again.

Bobby was tight with money. Even in Milton days, David Hackett recalled, he would always total up a restaurant check with consummate care to make sure he wasn't overcharged. "Sometimes he would be," Hackett said, "and he would insist on a correction. Occasionally, he'd stage a kind of mini-scene, his voice rising as he insisted on a correct count."

He installed Ethel and the children in a medium-priced hotel apartment and instructed her to find them a suitable house. "But make sure you don't pay more than $400 a month rent," he told her.

He had, of course, ample funds. His father had given him a million dollars when he turned twenty-one, the same sum Joe gave each of his children so that, he said, "They could tell me to go to hell." Invested conservatively, Bobby's million generated between $40,000 and $50,000 annually. Ethel's father, too, was many times a millionaire.

Bobby's money-mindedness manifested itself on pay days during his work for the McCarthy committee. He was always first in line to collect his salary, waiting impatiently for the envelopes to be handed out, as a line of secretaries, file clerks, and other committee employees formed behind him. He earned $4,200 a year.[7]

With her friend, Dickie Mann, Ethel bypassed the real estate agencies and went on a street-by-street hunt for a home in the Georgetown section, a quaint neighborhood of hundred-year-old homes, small but elegant shops, and quiet, tree-lined lanes. They saw a number of vacant places, but the only ones in the rental range Bobby had stipulated were either tiny, in need of extensive repairs, or both.

After days of fruitless searching, she complained to Bobby that there simply wasn't anything to be had for the price. He replied that they would not spend more and that he was sure she would eventually find something within that price range.

Finally, by sheer good fortune, Ethel found a four-bedroom house on S Street with decent-sized living and dining rooms and a lovely postage-stamp garden in the rear. Ethel charmed its owner, an Army colonel who was being transferred out of Washington, into renting it for $400. Within a week, the Kennedys moved in.

Bobby attacked his first McCarthy assignment with typical zeal.

In terms of actual accomplishment, what he did made scarcely a blip in the history of the era. But the story deserves elaboration, because it taught Bobby that father did indeed know best. Joe had told him that he would be in a highly visible job that in all probability would earn him national attention.

Assigned to find out how many Allied ships continued to trade with Red China during the Korean War, he made some startling discoveries. By May, he had dug into the files of Naval Intelligence and found that, in 1952 and so far that year, at least 355 vessels owned by nineteen shipping firms of Allied nations had been delivering cargoes to the Communists and that two

British-owned ships had transported Chinese Communist soldiers along the coast of China.

Testifying before the subcommittee on May 5, Bobby caused a sensation with his revelations. Said Senator McCarthy, "We should keep in mind the American boys who had their hands wired behind their backs and their faces shot off with [Communist] machine guns . . . supplied by those flag vessels of our allies." Continuing the attack, McCarthy demanded, "Let's sink every accursed ship carrying materiel to our enemy!" Illinois's Senator Everett Dirksen, a Republican member of the committee, asked with withering sarcasm, "Is it a fair assumption that we are trying not to win the war?"

Hot denials came swiftly from Britain. The ships carried "no goods of strategic importance," said the official British information agency, and in London the owners of the vessels charged with transporting Chinese Communist troops blasted the accusation as "a horrible lie—it just did not happen."

Nonetheless, McCarthy, from his bed in Bethesda Naval Hospital, where he had gone for treatment of a knee injury, instructed Kennedy to draft a letter on committee stationery to President Eisenhower, assailing the practice and demanding action.

Bobby wrote it and rushed to the hospital to show it to McCarthy. Joe signed it in his hospital room. Then Bobby went to the White House to deliver it personally. A copy was also given to Vice President Richard Nixon, who immediately telephoned McCarthy and urged him to withdraw it, arguing that the letter would prove a "tremendous bonanza" for the Democrats.

McCarthy grudgingly accepted the logic of the argument. Telling Nixon he trusted him but not "those other bastards in the Administration," he agreed to withdraw the letter and asked the Vice President to intercept Ike's copy before it went to the Oval Office.

When Bobby heard that the letter was withdrawn, he was embarrassed and morally outraged. In a sense, he was silenced. Nothing was done about the question of Allied trade with Red China, but the episode, now all but forgotten in terms of historical importance, was significant in one major respect. Joe Kennedy was proven dead right.

Bobby's revelations were in headlines in every newspaper in the United States, just as Joe had predicted.

Involved as he was, Bobby was still giving football a high priority. While he was preparing his explosive report, Teddy telephoned from Cambridge with an urgent plea. Winthrop House, where he was rooming, was scheduled to play a jock house from Yale that afternoon but lacked an eleventh good player. Alumni were eligible; was Bobby available? He was.

Bobby put his report on hold, raced to the airport, and arrived in Boston in time for the game. Winthrop House won by scoring the only touchdown of the game.

Bobby remained with the subcommittee only seven months, resigning in late July. While he was there, Joe Kennedy, from Hyannis Port, Palm Beach, and New York, called him and McCarthy constantly for reports and to offer advice. Roy Cohn recalled that, each day, Kennedy would harangue McCarthy long distance.

On one occasion, Cohn watched as McCarthy, his eyes glazing over, held the receiver to his ear and punctuated the cracklings coming through with, "Sure, Joe," and, "That's a good point." Tiring of listening, McCarthy put the telephone down, rose, and walked behind his desk for a few moments. Kennedy, unaware he had completely lost his audience, talked on. Back at the phone, McCarthy continued his "Sure, Joes" and wrote a note on a pad, which he handed to Roy.

"Remind me to re-check the size of his campaign contribution. I'm not sure it's worth it."[8]

Bobby won few admirers during his brief service with the subcommittee. Truculent and abrasive, he was angry most of the time and alienated most people with whom he worked. The Bobby of those days, recalled Theodore Sorensen, who met both brothers that year, was "militant, aggressive, intolerant, opinionated, somewhat shallow in his convictions . . . more like his father than his brother."[9]

Lem Billings, who had journeyed with him to South America two years before, was less elegant in his assessment: "A lot of people thought he was an asshole." In 1972, in the course of a lengthy conversation with the authors in his Fifth Avenue apartment, Billings said candidly, "You would have hated Bobby then. Most people did."

After he left the McCarthy committee, Bobby moped around Hyannis Port with Ethel and the children, out of work. He remained jobless only two weeks. One evening, after a day of sailing, Joe Kennedy asked him, "How would you like to come to work for me?"

Joe had been reappointed to the Hoover Commission on Reorganization of the Executive Branch. A member of the first commission from 1947 to 1949, he had been renamed by Eisenhower to the second commission to continue the work.

Bob jumped at the chance to be his father's executive assistant but soon regretted it. The job was excruciatingly dull; moreover, Herbert Hoover, then eighty years old, ran the committee with a stubborn willfulness and was bickering continually with the other old men on the commission.

Bored, irritated, worried about his future, Bobby sank into a period of "bad doldrums," Lem Billings said. "He was filled with so many things he wanted to do, but he felt he wasn't accomplishing anything."

One day he took out his frustrations in a bloody fistfight with a hulking student near the Georgetown University campus in Washington. Bobby, Ted, and some friends, playing touch football, were annoyed by the boys who kept batting baseballs in the middle of their field. When they wouldn't stop on request, Bobby waded into the largest, who was more than thirty pounds heavier, and the two slugged it out until both became too weary to battle any longer. At dinner that evening, Ethel wondered where Bobby acquired the puffy lips and cut cheek. He didn't tell her.

Early next year, Bobby was offered the post of counsel to the three-member Democratic minority of the McCarthy subcommittee and grabbed it. Hoover, accepting his resignation, showed he had been more observant than Bobby thought. "There is little to do until the task forces have reported," the former President wrote. "I realize a restless soul like you wants to work."

Bobby was plunged into more exciting work than he had ever imagined, for the curtain soon rose on one of the most extraordinary dramas of the times, the Army-McCarthy hearings, which enthralled the nation for thirty-six days. The hearings centered around the Army's charges that McCarthy and Cohn had sought preferential treatment by improper means for a young private, G. David Schine, a former committee consultant before he was drafted into the armed forces, and countercharges by McCarthy and Cohn, embodied in a forty-six-point bill of particulars, that the Army had improperly attempted to stop the subcommittee's investigation of the Army.

Each day, 20 million Americans, an incredible number for those days of television's infancy, saw the spectacle being played out in the marble-columned, seventy-four-foot-long Senate Caucus Room. Stores across the country reported sharp rises in the sales of TV sets, while other retail purchases nosedived, absenteeism from work skyrocketed, and housewives neglected their chores as they watched.

McCarthy's high-pitched "point of order, Mr. Chairman, point of order" became a catchword; the sixty-two-year-old Joseph P. Welch, the courtly Boston lawyer for the Army, became a national figure overnight; and Americans finally got a good look at the senator who was turning the country inside out.

"Ethel never had to ask Bobby in the evening, 'What happened at the hearings today?' She would know," said Dickie Mann. Ethel attended every one of the thirty-six sessions, driving Bobby to the Senate Office Building each morning, returning to Georgetown to have lunch with the children, then hurrying back until the gavel fell.

In the supercharged atmosphere of the hearings, a feud began between

Bobby Kennedy and Roy Cohn that was to continue long after the hearings ended. The cause may have been rooted in bad chemistry between the two bright young men, as George Smathers believes, or it may have been job jealousy: Cohn had the position Bobby coveted. Whatever the reason, Bobby made known his intention of "getting Roy" in a bizarre manner and place.

Just before the hearings opened, Bobby went looking for Mary Driscoll, Senator McCarthy's quietly efficient secretary. He had a message he wanted her to deliver to the senator. She was not at her desk. Clerks in the office told Bobby she had gone to the beauty parlor in the basement of the Senate Office Building. Bobby went downstairs, found the beauty shop, and went in.

Mary Driscoll was there, among the hair dryers. He told her he wanted her to tell Senator McCarthy that he was behind him 100 percent—all the way—but that he hated Roy Cohn and would try to go after him during the forthcoming hearings. Would she tell the senator? Mary wanted to know why Bobby wouldn't give McCarthy the message himself. It would not be wise, Bobby insisted; he preferred it be done this way.

And it was done. Mary duly reported Bobby's declaration of war to McCarthy, who relayed it to Cohn.

On June 11, shortly before the hearing ended, Kennedy and Cohn became embroiled in a shouting match that almost came to blows. None was launched because onlookers intervened, which was fortunate for Bobby, who would have had to live down a fistfight at a congressional hearing. Later, Cohn said, "I probably was the gainer in the stopping of the fight," because "touch football and mountain climbing were not my long suit."

The verdict of the Army-McCarthy hearings, when it was announced August 31, was along party lines: the GOP majority absolved the senator of charges of improper influence, while the Democratic minority charged McCarthy and Cohn with "inexcusable actions."

In preparing his report, Kennedy told Ed Welch, an aide to Democratic Senator Stuart Symington of Missouri, "At least we can say that Senator Joe is one of the greatest senators we've ever had."

Welch, who later was to head the U.S. space program, did not agree. He told Kennedy, "Well, if you can find that in the transcript, we'll put it in." Nowhere in the 2 million words of the 7,424 pages of transcript could such an assessment be found. It was not included.

To those who revere his memory, Bobby's association with McCarthy is still the most painful episode of his career, and over the years has been the hardest to live down.

"Because of it," said Edwin Guthman, who served with Bobby in the Justice Department, "many persons never fully trusted him." The stain enabled Kenneth Keating, the incumbent New York senator, to cut deeply into Bobby's vote in the 1964 Senate race, and it was visable enough in 1968 to alienate liberal Californians in the Presidential primary.

For Bobby, McCarthyism was not a brief flirtation with an ideology that intrigued him, nor could his allegiance be ascribed to youth and inexperience. "Hell," asserted George Smathers, "he was no kid when he went to work for McCarthy. It was 1953, and Bobby was already twenty-eight."[10]

In his lovely townhouse not far from Washington's Union Station, Willard Edwards, the *Chicago Tribune* reporter who covered the McCarthy era from its beginnings, asserted, "Bobby Kennedy was convinced that a serious risk existed domestically, that the Pentagon, the State Department, and other sensitive areas of government were an absolute paradise for Communist spies, and that many had infiltrated those departments."[11]

Those were the charges that Joe McCarthy was trumpeting around the country, and the remarkable thing about it all was that Bobby believed in them more than the senator did himself.

McCarthy was an opportunist who foresaw big political fallout from a battle against communism and was at no time sincerely committed to his own cause. "He was bewildering because he was a semi-sociopath utterly indifferent to the truth," points out George Will, the conservative journalist and commentator.[12] Wrote Richard Rovere, "His talents as a demagogue were great but he lacked the most necessary and awesome of demagogic gifts—a belief in the sacredness of his own mission."[13] And William Manchester said, "If he had a creed it was nihilism, a belief in nothing, or next to nothing."[14]

Bobby stood at the other pole, a moralist devoted to what he perceived as the truth. "I thought there was a serious internal security threat to the U.S.," he said afterward. "I felt at the time that Joe McCarthy seemed to be the only one who was doing anything about it."[15]

To this stunning admission, Bobby added, "I was wrong." But redemption did not come until some years later.

Bobby had liked McCarthy from the time they first met at the student forum in Charlottesville. "He was always so nice to me. I never had any personal dispute with him," he said. And at no time during the next six years of McCarthy's life did Bobby renounce him.

He was not neutral, ever. Even after he left the subcommittee, he remained on close friendly terms with McCarthy and became viscerally angry when anyone attacked him. Some examples:

In 1955, the Jaycees—Junior Chamber of Commerce—named Bobby in its list of ten outstanding young men of the year. He journeyed to Louisville, Kentucky, for the dinner at which he and the others would be honored. Edward R. Murrow, the journalist who the year before had denounced McCarthy in a memorable "See It Now" broadcast, was the principal speaker. When Murrow again assailed McCarthy in his talk, Bobby rose and left the room.

He visited McCarthy at Bethesda Naval Hospital several times during his final illness.

He kept a framed photograph of the senator on his office wall during the senator's lifetime and for years afterward.

In 1963, Gore Vidal reported an angry confrontation between Kennedy and actor Paul Newman on the subject of McCarthy. The year before, negotiations were in progress on a screen adaptation of Bobby's 1960 book, *The Enemy Within*, the story of his investigations into labor union corruption. Budd Schulberg had written the script, and after many consultations, Bobby chose Paul Newman to act his role. He was surprised to hear that the star turned down the part.

Bobby met with Newman to find out why and accepted the explanation that, since Bobby's chief enemy, Teamster boss James Riddle Hoffa, had disappeared, the story could not have a satisfactory ending. Then Kennedy asked Newman about his next film.

The star replied that he was planning to narrate a documentary about Joe McCarthy. Bobby bristled.

"You shouldn't allow your name to be associated with that," he said sharply.

Newman wanted to know why not. After all, the story would not be fictionalized but would offer only actual events in the form of film clips. Newman added, Vidal said, that he didn't like McCarthy and that the project would be useful in reminding Americans of McCarthy's divisive methods.

"Bobby exploded," Vidal reported. "Newman wasn't qualified to judge. He knew nothing about McCarthy. Newman said he had followed McCarthy's career at the time; he had also read Richard Rovere's book on the subject. 'Well, Rovere didn't know anything about it either,' said Bobby."

Newman ended the conversation with: "According to you, I'm not qualified to vote since I can never know enough about any issue to form a proper opinion."[16]

Even the circumstances under which Bobby left the McCarthy subcommittee remain unclear. Four years later, he wrote, "I told McCarthy that I disagreed with the way the committee was being run, except for the work that Flanagan had done, and that the way they were proceeding I thought it was headed for disaster."[17]

However, that was not what he wrote to McCarthy in his letter of resignation, dated July 29, 1953:

> With the filing in the Senate of the Subcommittee report on Trade With the Soviet Bloc, the task to which I have devoted my time since coming

with the Subcommittee has been completed. I am submitting my resignation at this time as it is my intention to enter the private practice of law at an early date.

I have enjoyed my work and association on the Subcommittee, and I wish to express to you my appreciation for the opportunity of having served with your group.

Please accept my sincere thanks for the many courtesies and kindnesses you have extended to me during these past seven months.

Two days, later, Senator McCarthy acknowledged receipt of the letter. "I know it is needless to tell you that I very much regret seeing you leave the Committee," he wrote. "In accordance with our conversation, I sincerely hope that you will consider coming back later on in the summer to complete the project with Mr. Flanagan and the full Committee.

"From discussing your work with the other members of the Committee, I can tell you that it was the unanimous feeling on the part of the Senators that you were a great credit to the Committee and did a tremendous job."

The senator offered his kindest regards and signed the letter, "Joe."[18]

Early in the evening of May 2, 1957, Robert Kennedy received a telephone call at his office, where, as usual, he had been working late. Joe McCarthy was dead.

Bobby put down the phone and wept.

He was then chief counsel to the Senate Select Committee on Improper Activities in the Labor and Management Field, heading a staff of sixty-five persons. Many had already left for the day. Bobby rang for a secretary and told her to send those who remained home.

He sat alone for a long time, then went home himself. That night, he wrote in a journal he kept from time to time, "It was all very difficult for me as I felt that I had lost an important part of my life."

McCarthy was given a state funeral in the chamber where, three years before, sixty-seven of his colleagues had voted to censure him for unethical behavior toward the United States Senate. Among those who attended was Robert Kennedy. That day he had also gone to services at St. Matthew's Cathedral in Washington, McCarthy's parish church.

On May 7, Bobby flew up for services with a planeload of about twenty others from Washington, landing at the Green Bay airport thirty-one miles northwest of Appleton. Edwin R. Bayley, a political reporter for the *Milwaukee Journal* assigned to cover the arriving delegation, watched from his Cadillac convertible as the plane door opened. He wrote down the names as they deplaned.

"After all the others had come out, Bobby appeared at the exit door," Bayley recalled. "He came down the ramp all alone. The others had disappeared into the terminal.

"Bobby spotted me and came over to the car. He asked if he could ride into town with me. It was about ten in the morning, and the church services and burial were scheduled for the afternoon.

"I said, 'Sure, hop in,' and he did.

"I suspected that Bobby didn't want anybody to see him, which was soon confirmed.

"We reached Appleton and, since it was still early, had lunch together. He was in a somber mood."

That afternoon, the body of the late senator was lowered into a grave on a bluff above the Fox River near Appleton after a funeral mass at St. Mary's Catholic Church. Bobby stood at the graveside, apart from the others, as a squad of Marines and veterans fired a volley across the river.

"Afterward," Bayley said, "he came over to me and said that if it didn't make any difference, he would prefer that I didn't say anything about his being there.

"I did not report his presence. After all, I reasoned, he was just one of several hundred persons. It really made no difference if his name was reported or it wasn't."[19]

Bobby Kennedy's McCarthy connection, even in later years, remains puzzling, a part of the enigma of the man himself.

He knew McCarthy's methods were wrong and said so, yet he never disavowed him and, in his next job as a rackets investigator, used many of the same McCarthy-type baiting tactics himself. He believed that "one of McCarthy's greatest mistakes was that he was loyal beyond reason to Roy Cohn and G. David Schine."[20] Yet he regarded McCarthy as more sinned against than sinning and remained loyal beyond reason and logic to him.

He liked the senator personally, yet he felt so strongly about the way he ran his subcommittee that he would have stood up against his father and voted to censure McCarthy, something Jack Kennedy couldn't bring himself to do. As everyone knows, Jack remained silent on the censure of McCarthy. Although he was seriously ill at the time, after undergoing double spinal surgery, he could have gone on record or paired with another senator. He did neither, because McCarthy was a family friend and because his brother had been on the staff in 1953.

Neither of these considerations would have deterred Bobby, had he been in the Senate when Senate Resolution 301 was put to a vote on December 2, 1954. "I thought he had brought the Senate and the United States into disrepute by his operation of the committee," he said.[21]

Ed Guthman, who became a loyal aide and friend after being initially "deeply troubled" by the McCarthy issue, cast the brightest light yet on this dark corner.

Bobby Kennedy, he said, lived by a special code: a man does not abandon a friend, no matter how much or how strongly he may oppose his views. "That's the way relationships between men ought to be," Bobby said. The remark was made in 1964 at St. John Fisher College in Rochester, when a student wondered how he could support a machine politician like the controversial Representative Charles Buckley, the Bronx Democratic leader, and at the same time put himself forward as a reform leader.

Friends mattered. "Regardless of the passage of time or a change in circumstances, he would go to great lengths to help friends or acquaintances, particularly if they were in trouble," Guthman said.

It is as much as we are ever likely to know about Robert Kennedy and Joe McCarthy.

8

First There Was Beck . . .

*T*HEY MADE AN odd couple—the stern-visaged, sepulchral-voiced Mc-Clellan, who looked like a preacher warning of hellfire awaiting disbelievers, and Kennedy, thirty years younger, who could be (and often was) mistaken for a New England preppie.

Together, the Arkansas senator and Bobby were never far from center stage in Washington for five years. Beginning in 1954, they led the largest and most efficient investigative organization then operating on Capitol Hill, the Senate's probe of labor and management. McClellan ran the committee, but Bobby was in total charge of the investigations and prosecutions.

Their origins could not have been more different. John S. McClellan's father was a tenant farmer in Grant County, one of the poorest in the state, who studied law while he worked his fields and eventually became an attorney. John, like his father, had no formal education; he, too, read law books between chores and, at the age of seventeen, became a member of the bar, after the Arkansas legislature passed a special statute permitting him to practice.

Once a district attorney himself, McClellan could spot a man with prosecutorial instincts. He, like Bobby, believed that a Communist threat to America's internal security did exist, and he was drawn to the younger man for yet another reason. Often the former Arkansas farmboy would describe himself this way: "I am an uneducated man, but I know right from wrong." Bobby, he felt, stood foursquare for honesty and integrity and against venality, corruption, and greed.

When the dour McClellan asked Bobby to take the post of chief counsel to his Senate Select Committee on Improper Activities in the Labor and Management Field, Bobby could only gulp and stammer, "I'll have to talk to Ethel."

But he went home elated. A new cause was being offered to him: the chance to bring to justice wrongdoers who were preying on poor, hardworking wage-earners. As the recently concluded battle against communism had done, this, too, appealed to his deepening moralism.

"The hours are going to be long, and I'll be away from home a lot," he told Ethel. "But it's the most exciting thing yet." He was right on both counts. Much of the time for the next few years, he was chasing down evidence all over the United States. And when he was in Washington, he rarely came home before 10 P.M., when he and Ethel would have dinner.

"They say the later the hour, the more fashionable the dinner," he once said ruefully, "so I guess we're pretty fashionable. Luckily, Ethel has a big appetite, and eats with the children first."

By then, he and Ethel had outgrown their tiny house on S Street and, seeking larger quarters, were offered a 140-year-old white brick Georgian home in McLean, Virginia, a suburb of Washington. Jack and Jackie Kennedy had bought the house, which stood on six and one-half acres of rolling countryside, several years before. Expecting her first baby, Jackie had decorated a large, beautiful nursery. But in August 1956, the baby was born dead. After that, she no longer wished to live in the house. She and Jack sold the estate to Bobby and Ethel for the same price they had paid, $125,000, and moved to a furnished home in Georgetown.

There were now five little Kennedys. In a little more than three years, Ethel had given birth to three more children: on January 17, 1954, to Robert Francis, Jr.; on June 15 the following year, to David Anthony; and on September 9, 1956, to Mary Courtney.

Ethel did, in fact, have two dinners nightly, plus a large breakfast and a more than adequate lunch. By 7 A.M. Ruby, their housekeeper, would have hot cereal, eggs with bacon or ham, a batch of hot biscuits or rolls, and cocoa and milk ready for the family. Along with millions of other mothers who had moved out to rapidly expanding suburbia, Ethel put herself on the car-pool roster, faithfully taking her turn at driving and picking up when the children reached school age. Her first dinner (and it wasn't picked at either) was at six; the second, to which she gave equal justice, when Bobby came home.

The McClellan-Kennedy team worked well together. McClellan, busy with other senatorial duties, let Bobby run the whole show, then was briefed on findings at informal meetings before committee sessions. Bobby handpicked forty-five accountants and thirty-five investigators skilled in ferreting out fraud; with twenty secretaries and clerks, the force jammed every available inch of space in its basement offices, Room 101 of the old Senate Office Building.

From late 1954 until the fall of 1956, conflict of interest cases absorbed Bobby's attention.

His reputation as a tenacious, hard-driving prosecutor was ratcheted up several notches when he brought about the resignation of Harold E. Talbott, Secretary of the Air Force in Eisenhower's Cabinet. After a lengthy investigation, Bobby confronted Talbott with charges that he had solicited Air Force business for the engineering firm of Paul Mulligan & Company, in which he had retained an interest before moving to his government post. Talbott hotly denied any wrongdoing, but several days later *The New York Times* published a number of letters from him on his official stationery to businessmen, suggesting they retain the Mulligan firm. Eisenhower asked Talbott to resign, and he did.

Another investigation, which involved kickbacks to government officials in the purchase of military uniforms, resulted in a half-dozen convictions for fraud.

All this was heady stuff for Bobby. "He was doing something important," said Lem Billings. "You could see on his face the deep satisfaction he was getting from the work. It was a happy period for him."[1]

As summer recess approached, Justice Douglas called him at home one night to say that his five-year effort to get Soviet permission to tour central Asia had finally borne fruit. Back in Charlottesville, when he addressed the student legal forum, Douglas had asked Bobby, "Would you like to travel through Marco Polo country with me?" Bobby, of course, had leaped at the chance. Finally, after years of battering against the stone wall of the Soviet Embassy in Washington, clearances arrived.

When Congress adjourned, Bobby set off on his three-month tour, joining Mr. and Mrs. Douglas, who had left earlier, in Tehran. The trip was magnificent. After meeting with the Shah of Iran, who knew all about Bobby's work with the McClellan committee, they duplicated part of Marco Polo's exotic route across Afghanistan, Pakistan, India, and Tibet, entering Russia from the northern Iranian border.

In Baku, Russian officialdom proved no match for American ingenuity. Without warning or explanation, the guides who had been assigned to the travelers were withdrawn, despite an agreement that they would accompany them for the entire trip. The three were told they had to find their own places to stay and the means of getting there.

Dismayed, Kennedy and the Douglases talked over the situation in their hotel room, which—they quickly discovered—was bugged with easily detected hidden microphones. Bobby began talking, as loudly as he could, about the distressing turn of events, knowing he'd be overheard. Douglas caught on at once.[2]

"This must be a mistake," Bobby said. "Yes," Douglas replied loudly, "a bad mistake."

The only way out of the dilemma, they agreed, was to telephone the Kremlin and report the entire story, no detail omitted, to the Premier of the Soviet Union, Nikita Khrushchev.

A short time later, a Soviet official was at the door, bowing as he explained that a terrible mistake had been made and assuring the visitors they would have a guide at their disposal at once.

For a man never known to be venturesome when it came to food, the exotic fare in some of the countries presented insuperable problems. "We got tired of dishes like lamb's ear, scrambled lamb's brains, or passing the head of a lamb around, so you could take a bite," he wrote home.[3]

As for water, even though they popped pills into it to kill off the bacteria, for Bobby, "It still tasted as though you had drunk from a swimming pool." When he came home in the fall, Ethel was startled by his appearance. He had lost seventeen pounds.

"The McClellan committee got into the labor racket investigation because it didn't have anything else to do," said Edwin Guthman, the tall, husky editor of the *Philadelphia Inquirer*, with a slight smile.[4] Guthman joined the committee as an investigator in 1956 and worked closely thereafter with Bobby for years.

It was quite true. The conflict-of-interest cases had dried up. Bobby, once again restless, was wondering what to do with himself, not to mention the large staff he was building up.

Meanwhile, a small group of brilliant investigative journalists, working independently, was uncovering the biggest crime story of the decade—unbelievable corruption and brutality within the largest and most powerful labor organization in the world, the International Brotherhood of Teamsters. At the *San Francisco Chronicle* and later at *Collier's Magazine*, stocky, young Pierre Salinger was writing articles about the mess; Ed Guthman and Paul Staples of the *Seattle Times*, Wallace Turner and William Lambert of the *Portland Oregonian*, Don Irwin of *The New York Herald-Tribune*, and Paul F. Healy of the New York *Daily News* were digging into it, too.

So, too, was Clark Mollenhoff of the *Des Moines Register-Tribune*, who was talking to Bobby one day in Washington and suggested he take a long, hard look at the Teamsters.

Bobby was dubious. There had been two other investigations of the Teamsters, he said, and each had gone nowhere. Besides, he wasn't sure his committee had jurisdiction over the union.

Mollenhoff's answer was brief and pointed. "These other two investigations were fixed because of political pressure," he told Bobby, "and you do have jurisdiction, because these unions are tax exempt and are misusing their funds."

Bobby finally agreed. When he told his father the direction in which he planned to move, Joe Kennedy was genuinely frightened for one of the few times in his life. It was one thing to tackle white collar crime, quite another to wade into gangsters who have their own unpleasant ways of dealing with those who oppose them. This was risky business for Bobby, Joe knew, and he wanted no part of it for his son.

"It's not the sort of thing or the sort of people to mess around with," Lem Billings reported him as saying.[5] Joe felt that Bobby just didn't know what he was getting into. He called Justice Douglas and pleaded with him, as a good friend, to talk Bobby out of it.

Douglas tried, but Bobby wouldn't budge. The chance, he told the justice, was too great to pass up.

The work of the McClellan committee, spearheaded by Bobby Kennedy, was a watershed, establishing beyond any doubt that racketeers were operating in America on a scale hitherto unimagined.

In the 1930s, Thomas E. Dewey had dug into organized crime and, while his probing had bagged Charles (Lucky) Luciano, it had carried no forward momentum. In 1950 and 1951, the rangy Estes Kefauver of Tennessee had taken a Senate committee around the country to look into the problem. Poking beneath the crust, he uncovered enough to give the nation an uneasy feeling that something was indeed wrong, if not rotten, in American life. Kefauver's investigation resulted in an eighteen-month jail term for Frank Costello, Luciano's lieutenant and a kingpin of organized crime, for perjury.

In the three years from September 1956 until late 1959, the "rackets committee," as it became known, called more witnesses (1,525), held more sessions (over 500), and took more words of testimony than any other group of investigators in history.

The cast of characters Kennedy encountered or brought to the witness stand were straight out of an Edward G. Robinson or James Cagney gangster movie. One had been Al Capone's personal bodyguard, another, a lieutenant of the racketeer Frank Costello, still another, a member of Brooklyn's infamous Murder-for-Money gang of the 1930s.

Bobby was at the controls all the way. It was important work, he told Jack, the most important he had ever done. There was evil abroad in the land, and it had to be surgically removed. No other course was possible, he felt, "When there is corruption at the top and a close association with the underworld—this kind of power is a threat to every decent person."

He went out himself to find his evidence, crisscrossing the country with Carmine Bellino, his chief accountant-consultant, and other lieutenants. With them, he tracked down witnesses, pored over subpoenaed records, and followed leads that took him to seedy hotel rooms, nightclub hangouts, and dead-of-night meetings in alleyways with informers.

Only a month after the committee began looking into labor racketeering, Bobby got a firsthand initiation into how the practitioners worked. He and Carmine had gone to Los Angeles, where they uncovered evidence of shakedowns and beatings by rival unionists, capped by the experience of one labor representative who had gone to San Diego to organize jukebox operators.

The man was given a blunt warning, which carried an unmistakable "or else": "Stay out of San Diego!" He didn't heed. After going to Los Angeles, he went back to San Diego to resume organizing.

A few days later, he awoke, groggy, bleeding profusely, and with a sharp pain in his lower abdomen. A blow from behind had knocked him unconscious. As he tried to clean himself off, the pain in his stomach grew worse. Limping to his car, he began the drive back to Los Angeles, but the pains intensified, and he went to the nearest hospital.

There, X-rays revealed that a large cucumber had been thrust into his rectum and was lodged in his colon. Emergency surgery had to be performed to remove it.

Until that winter, Bobby had had no notion that Dave Beck was anything but an upstanding union leader, the Teamsters Union head who had his picture taken with President Eisenhower and was on the board of trustees of a university. He learned differently just before Christmas in 1956, in his suite at the Palmer House on State Street in Chicago.

There he and Carmine Bellino opened the record books they had obtained through subpoena of Nathan Shefferman, a labor-management consultant and a Beck associate.

It took Bobby and Carmine only one hour to discover that America's most powerful labor leader had another face.

Beck was a product of the Pacific Northwest, born only a year after the Klondike gold rush and reared in Seattle, where he learned firsthand about prospectors who made fortunes and about the others who died of cold and fever. In this frontier atmosphere, Dave Beck grew up tough. Now he was a battle-seasoned Goliath, sixty years old, fighting a puny-looking David.

Kennedy did not dislike Beck, as he did most others he summoned to the witness table. Certainly, he never developed the venomous hatred of Beck that he did for his successor in the Teamsters, Jimmy Hoffa. Beck was a heavy man who kept in trim by regular exercise, running on the open road long before jogging came in style. He was not a drinking man, nor did he smoke. Bobby liked that.

Beck did not rise to lead the great Teamsters Union by snapping under pressure. He fought back, heaving and threshing like a huge fish caught in a trawler net, beginning with his first meeting with Bobby on a bitingly cold evening in 1957.

On that January 5, at 9 P.M., Bobby and Carmine were ushered into Beck's suite at the Waldorf-Astoria Hotel in New York. They had come to tell him that the rackets committee was planning to look into charges that gangsters had infiltrated his union.

Beck listened impassively. He expressed concern, which escalated to shock: he, too, he told his visitors, wanted nothing more than to clean up his union, if indeed undesirable elements were in there.

"He warmed to the task of convincing us," Bobby recalled. "His face grew red and florid, and his voice began to climb to a higher pitch until he was almost shouting."[6]

Bobby and Carmine were neither cowed nor fooled. On March 27, after the groundwork had been laid with other witnesses, they called Beck to testify in the colonnaded Caucus Room.

Throughout the questioning, on that day and afterward, Bobby was in single-tracked pursuit of Beck, his antenna tuned at all times for slips, shreds of evidence, and leads. Beck and Frank Brewster, the president of the Western Conference of Teamsters, would relax during recess periods and let down their guards. Bobby did not, even while wisecracking with them in the corridor.

On one occasion, Kennedy was trying to find out about a loan of $270,000, alleged to have been made by the union to Beck. During a recess, Brewster casually mentioned that the loan probably had been listed in the books of the union.

Bobby perked up. Moments later he was in a telephone booth away from the Caucus Room, talking to the Teamsters Union bookkeeper in Seattle. Was this money recorded on the books as a loan?

Minutes later: no, it was not. When the hearing was resumed, Bobby had another piece of evidence to lay before the committee.[7]

At the hearings, Beck began like a lion but soon began his ritualistic responses invoking the Fifth Amendment to question after question, a total of 140 times.

He even refused to reply when he was asked if he knew his son. ("I decline to answer because it might open up avenues of questioning which might tend to incriminate me.") The following testimony had the hearing room rocking with laughter:

Kennedy: Do you feel that if you gave a truthful answer to this committee on your taking of $320,000 of union funds that might intend to incriminate you?

Beck: It might.

Kennedy: Is that right?

Beck: It might.

Kennedy: You feel that yourself?

Beck: It might.

Kennedy: I feel the same way.

Chairman: We will have order, please.

Kennedy: I want to know, breaking that money down, Mr. Beck, did you use Union funds to purchase five dozen diapers for some of your friends at $9.68?

Beck declined to answer, citing the Fourth and Fifth Amendments.

As the inquiry progressed and the country became increasingly fascinated with the combatants, Ethel and her sister-in-law, Pat Skakel, pulled off a bubble-headed prank that earned a stinging rebuke on the front page of Stamford newspapers.

In August, George and Pat Skakel sent out invitations to a big party in honor of the Kennedys. Ethel happily went along with a plan to inform the press that Dave Beck and his son would come to pay tribute to Kennedy, an item that naturally attracted considerable attention. A man who vaguely resembled the younger Beck and a woman were recruited to pose as the Becks when photographers arrived. The father, they would explain, had been present but was suddenly called away.

The day of the party, the fake Becks posed in a group photograph that was published around the country, with an accompanying story by the Associated Press, in which "Beck" was quoted as saying, "Although our policies differ, socially we get along famously."

The roof fell in when someone discovered that the younger Beck was not married and that his father had been on the West Coast all the time. Ethel, contrite, confessed it had been a "crazy" idea.

The Stamford *Advocate*, agreeing it certainly was, published the following story on its front page:

An apology to the Dave Becks Sr. and Jr.: This is an apology. If you will just read along you'll understand why an apology is coming out of the blue Connecticut sky on Aug. 13, 1957.

They had a real big do on the palatial estate of the George Skakels Jr. in Greenwich on Saturday night. George's sister married Bob Kennedy, that

86

fellow with the Senate committee, and she was there and they had a great crowd. . . .

It appears they had more fun than you fellows ever had at a Teamsters' clambake. Somebody had the gay idea that two of the guests would be named Dave Beck Sr. and Dave Beck Jr.

And so Mrs. Skakel reported to representatives of this newspaper as early as 6 P.M. on Saturday and several times as the evening wore on towards Sunday. And then on Monday morning from his New York office Mr. Skakel solemnly confirmed that you two fellows had been his house guests on Saturday night.

Well, of course, you fellows know that when the kin of The Kennedys are reported entertaining The Becks of Oregon (The Becks live in Washington State, Ed.) during this session of the Senate, that's BIG NEWS.

Within a few hours, after the news broke Mr. and Mrs. Skakel were the objectives of several score reporters and after a time Mrs. Skakel said the whole thing was a prank and hoped she hadn't caused any inconvenience.

Frankly, we believed the Skakels on Saturday night and Monday morning and we suppose we've got to go along with their latest story.

Outside of this incident, things have been pretty quiet up this way. Some poor fellow lost all his money at the racetrack the other day and reported to police that he was held up and robbed in order to have an excuse for the wife. The cops discovered it was a prank and they hauled him off to the can. That happened in Greenwich, too, so you can see it's not such a dull summer.

Hope you are both well. If you have any thoughts on adult delinquency I wish you would drop me a note.

Sincerely,
E. R. McCullough
Managing Editor

During the hearings, Bobby faced the gangster types fearlessly, but lost his cool when he queried the fat madam of a bawdy house in Oregon when she took her place at the witness table.

He did not flinch when Joey Gallo, with his record of seventeen arrests and four convictions, came to Room 101 dressed entirely in black, like George Raft, and insolently asked one of the secretaries if she wanted to come to work for him. Salary: "Take as much as you want from the till." He grinned.

He showed no emotion when a jukebox distributor, who had objected to signing with a Teamsters local, testified that his head had been split open by a steel bar one dark night. Or when another said he signed up in desperation after being so savagely beaten that blood poured from his ears and nose.

But the madam, who looked like a middle-aged schoolteacher, cracked him up. She had described in a sworn affidavit how she operated her business.

Bobby began reading from the document, which opened with an explanation of the distinctions that existed in the business of prostitution.

"A 'call house' is distinguished from a regular house of ill fame," he read, "which is sometimes known as a 'walk-in,' by the fact that the clientele is a select one."

By the time he completed that first sentence, a blush had crept up Bobby's neck and into his face, and he was having difficulty controlling his customarily flat, unemotional voice. But, bravely, he went on.

"By that I mean, unless a person is known or is referred, he cannot gain access to the house. It may fairly be termed an 'exclusive clientele' operation. A house of ill fame, or 'walk-in,' will accept anyone who comes to . . . to . . . the prem . . . the premises." Bobby was clearly on the verge of a crackup.

A moment later, he started a passage beginning "Another feature of the 'call house' is . . . " but broke down and, convulsed with laughter, sat down and buried his head in his hands. The hearing room rocked with guffaws. McClellan, allowing himself the barest suggestion of a smile, intoned, "Does counsel desire that the chair take over the reading of the affidavit?" Bobby, composing himself, replied, "No, sir," and was able to finish.

His name and fame spread, though not always in ways he preferred. Once he entered a taxicab in New York City and told the driver to take him to LaGuardia Airport. On the way, the cabbie, aware he looked familiar yet unable to identify him, kept peering in the rearview mirror.

Finally he got it—or thought he did. Stopping for a light, he turned around and said triumphantly: "I know who you are. You're Roy Cohn!"

He was a tough boss. "Get off your butt" sprang easily to his lips when he felt any of his people weren't working hard enough or producing the evidence he sought. Nobody ever left before 9 or 10 P.M. Yet he could be extraordinarily thoughtful, professionally as well as personally.

Knowing that credentials are crucial for advancement, he insisted that investigators receive due credit for their contributions. He issued a directive that the name of the staff member responsible for an investigation be placed beside his own in the final report of each case that was made public and filed with the Senate.

Nightly, Ethel would pick up Bobby in their ancient, scarred station wagon and, almost every evening, give La Vern J. Duffy, a part-time junior staff member, a lift to his law school, where he was attending evening classes.

Late one summer, Duffy became ill at the office. He told Ruth Watt, the committee's chief clerk, that he'd better visit the congressional clinic. There, a staff physician examined him and told him to go home and get into bed.

"I managed to get to my hot furnished room," Duffy said. "A few minutes later, there was a knock at the door. Bob Kennedy was there, telling me to get dressed and come along. He drove me to his house in Georgetown.

"Ethel was at the Cape and the house was empty, but Bobby saw to it that I went to bed in an air-conditioned room, and within an hour his personal physician was attending me."[8]

Some of Rose Kennedy's dinner-table instruction and quizzing in American history had stuck to Bobby. Often when he traveled on official business, he would slip off to visit local shrines. Once, on a trip to Nashville, he drove twelve miles east of the city for a fifteen-minute tour of the Hermitage, the home of President Andrew Jackson, before flying back to Washington.

"He was so enthralled," reported John Jay Hooker, Jr., a Nashville attorney who accompanied him, "that after a few minutes he called Ethel and said he wanted to make a later plane." Bobby spent four hours examining the stately colonial mansion and walking over its extensive grounds.

Afterward Hooker thought: "Bob Kennedy has a real feeling that he and his family are going to be a part of future American history, and that he was spending the time at the Hermitage for the purpose of gathering from the past some of the spirit of America."[9]

What happened to Beck was an anticlimax.

Ultimately, he was convicted in 1959 on a total of six counts—four charges of evading income taxes and two for filing false tax returns for the Teamsters Joint Council 28 Building Association, and was sentenced to serve five years in prison. After a three-year legal battle, the Supreme Court, on appeal, overturned the conviction on the four counts but refused to review his appeal on the filing of false returns for the building association. The three-year statute of limitations having expired, local prosecutors were unable to press charges of misappropriation of union funds, except for a single one of selling a Cadillac owned by the union and embezzling the $1,900 obtained from the sale. For this, he was sentenced to a two-to-fifteen-year term, to run concurrently with the other.

Prison doors finally slammed on Beck in June 1962. After serving eighteen months, he was freed on parole on December 10, 1964, and retired to Seattle. In May 1975, then eighty years old, he was given a "full and unconditional" pardon by President Gerald Ford, which wiped out his conviction and restored his voting rights as well as other civil rights.

The crucial point was that his power as America's biggest labor boss was broken. A stocky, forty-four-year-old coal miner's son was elected president of the Teamsters and moved into Beck's office in the $5 million marble palace that was union headquarters in Washington. He was James Riddle Hoffa.

The Man He Became

These were his greatest years, the most exciting years, the years when Bobby came into his own.

—Ramsey Clark

9

When Two Strong Men Meet Face to Face

*K*ENNEDY VERSUS HOFFA has been called a battle between a tough rich kid and a tough poor one. Hoffa began poor, but by the time he and Bobby tangled, he lived richer than Kennedy.

During the years of their square-off, Hoffa's French chef served him his favorite luncheon, cold crab and lobster, in the private dining room of his magnificent third-floor executive suite. He was driven to work in a chauffeured limousine and wore custom-tailored suits.

If Bobby had a private movie theater at Hickory Hill, Hoffa had one, too, at the union headquarters building, a Washington showplace that was completed in 1955. The landscaped terrace of the penthouse had a breathtaking panoramic view of the city. A private elevator took Jimmy to his large walnut-paneled office with its inch-thick carpeting, richly carved furniture, and elegant window drapes. On his desk were forty-eight buttons set into an interoffice communications system that put him in instant touch with all Teamster officials. Along one wall was a custom-designed television and high fidelity system and a fully equipped bar.

Often told is the story of Hoffa's one-upmanship gambit on the subject of pushups: when Hoffa and Bobby met at the district courthouse in Washington following Hoffa's arrest in March 1957, the forty-four-year-old union leader, five-five but 180 pounds of well-toned muscle, asked Bobby how many he could do, boasting that he could manage twenty-seven. Bobby, unimpressed, boasted back that he could do fifty.

Not discussed in the stories of that confrontation was the fact that Hoffa maintained his state of physical fitness by working out regularly in a private gymnasium he had built in the basement of Teamster headquarters, equipped with the latest in gleaming exercise machines, a steam bath, and showers. On hand, too, was his own masseur to work out the kinks after a session. At home, he spent part of his vacation chopping wood in northern Michigan.

Despite their obvious differences, there were a number of curious similarities between Hoffa and Kennedy. Each was capable of hard, grinding, night-and-day work without apparent fatigue; each had a trigger temper, which exploded in public on numerous occasions; each made physical fitness a virtual religion. Hoffa did not smoke or drink, opening his bar only for high-ranking guests; Kennedy did not use tobacco and would sip wine only occasionally. Each had a tough veneer but a soft core that could bring tears at stories of individuals in distress.

Two economists who studied Hoffa at close range for months, Ralph and Estelle James, found that, like Bobby, loyalty to family and friends was central to his personality. Pursuing the strange resemblances, Hoffa, too, was a master at using his family for career advantage. Just as the Kennedy women, led by the indefatigable Rose, would race around neighborhoods and to cities canvassing for votes and speaking at luncheons and teas, Jimmy Hoffa's wife, Josephine, was recruited to help strengthen his popularity among the rank and file and, when he was caught in Kennedy's net, to rouse them to battle against those who would "wreck the union."[1]

During the years of the Kennedy assault, Hoffa left Washington at about six-week intervals to whoop up support around the country. The Teamsters' political division planned each stop carefully in advance: when his plane touched down at the airport, he would be greeted by a uniformed brass band playing the Teamster anthem, "America the Beautiful," and Sousa marches, local officials would make welcoming addresses, and Jimmy would step into the back seat of a limousine and lead a motorcade down main street, ticker tape showering upon him.

At each stop there would be "Jo Hoffa" luncheons, as close to "coffee with the Kennedys" as one could get. After the "Star Spangled Banner," which always brought the teamsters roaring with patriotic fervor to their feet, there would be songs and dances by prominent entertainers, followed by speeches stressing the importance of a united front. Finally, Jo Hoffa would be introduced.

In a brief speech, she would tell the teamsters, "I have had to sit in silence on the receiving end of the slurs of McClellan and the Kennedys. I am glad to have the opportunity to help through DRIVE." (The Democratic

Republican Independent Voter Education program organized by the Teamsters to help preserve the union.) Her little talk would always receive a standing ovation.

"Hoffa's scheme of bringing his wife into the act has proved a great hit," the Jameses found, "especially with the wives who feel she is truly one of them." Hoffa's own talk, in which he accused Kennedy of conducting a vendetta and warned of antilabor legislation if Bobby should be successful, would be almost an anticlimax. After the speeches, Jo Hoffa would meet privately with the women, give them each a perfume atomizer, chat warmly about home and children, and be off with her husband for the next city.

As Beck's power in the Teamsters Union was declining precipitously, even though his arrest and imprisonment were still years off, Jimmy Hoffa was rising rapidly. He began his labor career at the age of eighteen in a Detroit warehouse, where he led a small corps of workers in a strike for higher pay for shipping strawberries. Soon he organized them into Local 674 of the city's Teamsters, which in that Depression year of 1933 had just one dollar in its treasury for each enrolled member, or a total of $400. By the time World War II ended, Hoffa was the undisputed Teamster czar in Detroit, having increased its membership to 5,000 and the treasury to well over $50,000.

Quietly, he extended his influence into union management around the country until, a decade later, he emerged as heir apparent to Dave Beck. By then, Bobby, and everyone else, knew it was only a matter of time, and little time at that, before Jimmy would move into the marble palace.

Seven months before Jimmy formally assumed control, a telephone call came into Bobby's messy office suite from New York City, and the Kennedy-Hoffa battle was joined.

It was Valentine's Day of 1957, Hoffa's forty-fourth birthday. A forty-nine-year-old lawyer-investigator named John Cye Cheasty got through to Bobby and said in a whispery voice, "I've got news that will make your hair stand on end." But it was too hot to be transmitted by phone.

"Then get the hell down here!" Bobby snapped.

Before lunchtime next day, a frosty Thursday, John Cheasty walked into Kennedy's warren. Bobby swept a pile of papers and ledgers from a chair so he could sit down and tell his story. He had not exaggerated.

Cheasty said Hoffa had hired him as a spy to work his way into a job with the McClellan committee and obtain whatever information or evidence he could get his hands on. He had been promised an $18,000 fee, and, to prove it, he produced the $700 that remained of a $1,000 check he had been given.[2] (Later Cheasty, a former Naval Intelligence officer, explained why he betrayed Hoffa. "All my life I have regarded good as something to work for, and evil as something to be fought." He believed, he said, in right and wrong, and that "I must answer to God for my conduct.")[3]

That February 14 at noon, Cheasty became a double agent, and an exciting drama unfolded. The FBI was informed, and Bobby, with a picked squad of agents, set a trap for Jimmy Hoffa. Cheasty was given a batch of committee documents and told to arrange a meeting at which he would hand the papers to Jimmy and receive a packet of bribe money in return, all done under FBI surveillance.

Before the trap was sprung, Kennedy and the Teamster boss met face to face for the first time at, of all places, a quiet little dinner party in a white split-level home in a Washington suburb.

It was arranged by Edward T. Cheyfitz, a lawyer and former public relations director of the union, who hoped that he could help iron out some misunderstandings. Kennedy was dubious but at the same time intensely curious to meet Jimmy. Hoffa was even less enthusiastic but equally curious. He agreed to fly in from Detroit.

The dinner was hardly a conventional one in the hare-and-hounds race that was starting. Considering that, before he left for the Cheyfitz home, Bobby had been told by the FBI that their double agent had arranged to meet Hoffa to turn over documents, the legal ethics were at best questionable. Later Edward Bennett Williams, Hoffa's counsel, stated that since the trap had already been set, "the ethics of decency should have required that Kennedy at least stay away from the dinner."[4]

Despite the attitude of fearlessness he had been displaying, Bobby was jittery at the prospect of meeting the union boss. He had not told John McClellan or anyone in the FBI about the planned encounter. Hoffa, after all, had a reputation for doing away with his enemies. Should he have protected himself? All he had done was ask Ethel to telephone him at 9:30, to make sure he was still there and all right.

At 7:45 on February 19, he rang the bell of Cheyfitz's house. Hoffa had already arrived. They shook hands.

"From what I heard about you," Kennedy said, "I probably should have worn a bullet-proof vest."[5]

Hoffa only smiled slightly.

Mrs. Cheyfitz had prepared a dinner of roast beef, which they ate while conducting a wary conversation revolving around the Teamsters' alleged abuses of power, Hoffa's association with underworld characters, and Hoffa's chartering of so-called "paper locals," memberless organizations that could nonetheless "vote" and thus strengthen his power.

As a dinner party, the evening was a flop. As a getting-to-know-you meeting, it only confirmed the opinions the antagonists already had of each other. To Hoffa, Kennedy's attitude toward him seemed patronizing. Bobby, interested in knowing more about trade unionism, asked searching questions, which Hoffa misinterpreted as put-downs. "It was as though he was asking, with my limited education, what right did I have running a union like this?" he said. Hoffa had left school in the seventh grade and was always sensitive about the gap in his formal education. He came to the conclusion that Kennedy was "a damned spoiled jerk."

For his part, Kennedy was unimpressed by Hoffa's macho boasting. "He talked so much about how tough he was I had difficulty believing he really was tough," he told Clark Mollenhoff afterward. "By the time he left," Mollenhoff said, "Kennedy had already decided that Hoffa was not the little superman he was supposed to be."[6]

Back at Hickory Hill, Ethel was looking at her watch every few minutes. At 9:30, as she had been instructed, she called the Cheyfitz home. When Bobby was told his wife was on the line, Hoffa caught the precaution quickly.

"She probably called to see if you're still alive," he said. At the phone, Bobby said in a deliberately loud voice, "I'm still alive, dear. If you hear a big explosion, I probably won't be."

As Kennedy left, Hoffa told him, "Tell your wife I'm not as bad as everyone thinks I am." Bobby went home and told Ethel that Hoffa was even worse. "This is a selfish, cynical, and power-hungry man," he said.

That dinner cemented Bobby's determination to devote himself totally to Hoffa's destruction.

Looking back, it is little short of amazing that a wary man like Hoffa, who had successfully climbed a path of power booby-trapped by his enemies within the union, should have walked innocently into a hoary snare such as the one planned for him by Bobby and the FBI. Yet four weeks later, having been softened up by Cheasty, who was playing his double agent role masterfully by slipping him FBI-vetted documents, Hoffa walked into the Dupont Plaza Hotel a half-mile from the White House and into the arms of a half-dozen G-men.

On Wednesday, March 13, Cheasty was given an especially hefty manila envelope to give to Hoffa. He called Jimmy and arranged to meet him shortly before midnight for the exchange—papers for cash. At dinner that evening, Bobby told Ethel, "Get on the phone and call the press. Tell them to be down at the federal courthouse at midnight. Then you come along, too, and watch the fun." He didn't tell her the subject of the fun.

Comfortable after a good dinner at the Sheraton-Carleton Hotel, Hoffa made an excuse to leave his companions, the Republican House delegation from his home state, and approached the Dupont Plaza entrance. Cheasty was waiting. He gave Jimmy the envelope and, in return, received a roll of bills amounting to $2,000. Hoffa proceeded into the hotel, where he was surrounded, arrested, and hustled down to the district courthouse.

Ethel had carried out her assignment well, rousing even Ed Guthman from sleep. Dozens of reporters and cameramen were jamming the corridors as Hoffa entered. Two hours later, he was arraigned before a United States marshal, and next day he was indicted on bribery and conspiracy charges.

Before the arraignment Hoffa paced the floor. Clark Mollenhoff, one of the journalists who had sparked the probe, called to him, ''Well, Jimmy, so you finally slipped and slipped good. I was beginning to wonder if anyone could catch up with you.'' Hoffa, cold hate in his face, did not respond with a customary flip remark. He had never been arrested before by the FBI, never had to face a federal court. Mollenhoff saw fear in his face, too.[7]

Kennedy was certain now that he had Hoffa. His case seemed all but buttoned up. Ed Troxell, an assistant United States attorney who was in charge of the prosecution, exuded confidence. ''It is just a matter of putting the case in the record, and of avoiding reversible error,'' he said.

Underestimating Hoffa, and particularly the thirty-six-year-old, curly-haired Edward Bennett Williams, his defense counsel, Kennedy gave an airy reply to a shouted question.

''Hey, Bobby, what will you do if Hoffa is acquitted?''

Bobby smiled, and Ethel giggled, as he yelled back, ''I'll jump off the Capitol dome.''

Four months later, as the capital sweltered in midsummer heat, Williams had a package delivered to Bobby's office. It was a small parachute.

Bobby had been in the hearing room when John Cheasty telephoned. ''You wouldn't believe this,'' Cheasty told Angie Novello, Bobby's secretary. ''But Hoffa was acquitted.'' The jury had deliberated only three and one-half hours.

''We were all sick,'' Angie said. She sent Bobby a note. When he read it, he sucked in his breath audibly, and his face took on a deathly pallor. Watching, Clark Mollenhoff, who hadn't expected a quick verdict and had gone to watch the Textile Workers Union hearing, didn't have to be told what the yellow slip of paper said.

It had been a classic case of snatching defeat from the jaws of victory. Government lawyers, never dreaming Hoffa would take the stand in his own defense, were unprepared to cross-examine him carefully. But Eddie Cheyfitz had gone to the records and discovered that almost all defendants who failed to take the stand had been convicted. When Mollenhoff tried to convince the prosecution that Hoffa would indeed try to talk his way out of his charges, his views were unheeded.

Hoffa was one of the first called when the defense began its case. Smoothly, he explained that he had hired Cheasty to do some legal work for him, completely unaware that he also worked for the McClellan committee. Had he received papers from Cheasty? Of course, but he hadn't checked them. He had turned them over to his staff. Besides, aren't lawyers supposed to give papers to their clients?

The prosecution was weak. For only thirty-two minutes, Troxell questioned Hoffa, failing to elicit facts about his two criminal convictions or the inadequate financial records of the union. Watching, Mollenhoff was so shocked he felt ill.

Joe Louis, the enormously popular retired heavyweight champion, had also delivered a roundhouse blow that sent the prosecution reeling. One day he appeared in the courtroom and sat with Hoffa's supporters. The jurors, eight blacks and four whites, recognized him at once and watched him intently. (Louis's visit had been arranged by Robert [Barney] Baker, a 350-pound ex-pug who worked for the Teamsters, and Paul [Red] Dorfman, described as being well-connected throughout the underworld.)

After the afternoon recess, Hoffa went over to where Joe Louis was sitting. He put his hand on the Brown Bomber's shoulder and smiled at him. Louis half-turned and reached for Hoffa's arm. They talked for a while.

The jurors watched every move.

Learning of this at the hearings, where the investigation of the Textile Workers Union was in progress, Bobby raged impotently, knowing there was little he could do. He had not been able to do anything either about a black newspaper that had published a front-page article a few weeks earlier under the headline, "The Facts Behind the Hoffa Trial," that lauded Jimmy as a defender of civil rights and the "hardest hitting champion" of the Teamsters, in whose ranks were enrolled 167,000 black truck drivers.[8]

When stories surfaced that the paper had been delivered to the homes of the Hoffa jurors, Judge Burnita Matthews was outraged and had the panel sequestered. But the damage to the prosecution's case had been done.

It had looked too quick and easy, but now years of combat followed. In the two years after his acquittal, Hoffa was questioned longer and more often by a congressional committee than anyone else in history to that time. He was by turns cockey, belligerent, defiant, and proud. Unlike the parade of hoodlums Bobby called to the stand, he never took the Fifth Amendment.

He was fearless and told Kennedy so. In one exchange, Bobby asked him if he refused to fire five teamsters convicted of selling out union members for fear of being exposed by them.

Hoffa leaned forward at the witness table, and, staring full into Kennedy's face, he barely moved his lips to say, "I'm not afraid of anybody."

Bobby could make little dent in Hoffa, though he hurled charges of financial malpractice, gross misuse of Teamster funds, pocketing payoffs from employees, violence, and racketeering. Bobby and McClellan called him a thief, a liar, and a cheat. Recessing the hearings in September 1958, McClellan charged Hoffa with "willful perjury" and "arrogant disrespect for members of the union, the general public and the United States Government."

Nothing seemed to stick. When Hoffa was tried on perjury and wiretap charges in late 1958, a federal court jury in New York City could not agree and was dismissed. Two years were to elapse before another charge was brought.

Bobby refused to let Hoffa get even the smallest edge. Frequently recounted was the story of the time he and his aides left their office late in the evening after a long day's work. A short distance away, Bobby could see the lights burning on Hoffa's floor. "If he could work late," he told his people, "so can we. I'm not going home any earlier than that bastard."

What Bobby never found out was that Hoffa knew Kennedy would do precisely that. Thus, when he finished work for the day, often at a reasonable hour, he would order the lights in his office to be kept burning. As Murray Kempton observed, "They had a passion for the other's discomfort."[9]

Hoffa became a national celebrity and reveled in the role. He was stared at in public, asked for his autograph, was the subject of a *Playboy* magazine interview, and appeared on television shows. On *David Brinkley's Journal* he declared, "Kennedy is just a spoiled young millionaire that never had to go out and find a way to live by his own efforts, and he cannot understand resistance to what he wants." When he traveled, crews of airlines would leave their cockpits to gaze at him in fascination. Bobby Kennedy was not nearly so well recognized.

Furious and frustrated, Bobby drove himself and his staff to the limits of exhaustion and beyond. There were times when he would come home so tired he fell asleep at dinner.

"Even during lunch hours you gobbled a hamburger and kept going," said Walter Sheridan. One lunchtime was interrupted by Bobby, who told Sheridan, between bites, "Go and call this guy from the trucking company." Information had been received that a firm was making payments to Barney Baker,* who was being questioned at the time. Baker was a Team-

---

* The six-four Baker convulsed the hearing room during his testimony when Bobby asked him about a New York waterfront shakedown operation. Denying any personal link with the setup, Baker said he knew of some individuals who were connected with it.
Kennedy: Who were the people who did?
Baker: A Mr. Dunn.
Kennedy: Cockeyed Dunn?
Baker: I don't know him as Cockeyed Dunn. I knew him as John Dunn.
Kennedy: Where is he now?
Baker: He has met his Maker.

ster organizer and twice-convicted hoodlum who could eat forty dollars' worth of food (at 1950s prices) at one sitting, then use Teamster funds for hospital costs to lose some of his 350 pounds.

Sheridan called the company head, identified himself, and asked if he had made any payoffs to ensure labor peace. Caught unaware by the phone call, he replied, "Yes, I did."

At the afternoon session, Kennedy confronted Baker with the new evidence. Later that week, the company president also testified he had paid money to work out labor problems. Baker was subsequently indicted for taking payoff money, convicted, and sentenced to serve two years.

Victories such as this were balanced by more than an equal number of defeats, some of them humiliating. Once Bobby got a tip from a prison inmate that a woman investigative reporter who had written a series of articles exposing union racketeers had been murdered and her body buried in a field near Joliet, Illinois.

Kennedy, accompanied by James P. McShane, one of his inner circle of aides, flew to Joliet and questioned the prisoner who told a long and, apparently, convincing story of the slaying and burial. He even pinpointed the area for them. Elated, Bobby got the warden to release the man to act as a guide.

He led them to the spot, where Bobby and McShane, a portly man, shucked their jackets and began moving the earth. They hadn't dug far when a farmer appeared, demanding to know what they were doing.

McShane, who would later be named United States Marshal for the District of Columbia, sweating profusely as he leaned on his shovel, said with a straight face, "We're state officials doing a survey on metallurgical ores." The farmer nodded and left.

After they had dug several feet, Bobby and Jim turned inquiringly to the inmate, who shook his head and reckoned he may have erred on the location. He took them a few hundred feet off, where they dug again. The farmer approached again, but this time he had several strapping youths with him, ready to deal with trespassers.

Finally, Bobby and Jim realized they'd been taken in by the prisoner, whose sole purpose in concocting the tale was to get a day out of prison.

Hoffa toppled slowly, like a giant statue whose supporting base had been weakened over the years.

Across the country, thirteen grand juries were called to hear evidence that could lead to indictments. In 1960, he was indicted for mail fraud in Florida in connection with a real estate deal, but the charges were dropped

Kennedy: How did he do that?
Baker: I believe through electrocution in the city of New York or the state of NewYork.

when another, larger case developed in Chicago. There, a grand jury charged him with defrauding the trustees of a Teamsters pension fund.

Meanwhile, in Nashville, Tennessee, another panel charged him with violating the Taft-Hartley Labor Act, the labor-management relations law that bars payments by employers to union officials.

In October 1962, Hoffa went on trial in Nashville, but the jury was unable to agree and was dismissed. When Bobby heard the news, he reportedly held his head and moaned aloud. In May 1963, Hoffa was indicted for tampering with the jury that could not reach a verdict and trial was set for the following January. Meanwhile the Chicago case was docketed for April that year.

At long last, in March 1964, exactly seven years after he began the chase, Kennedy got news he had been waiting for: Hoffa had been convicted in Chattanooga and sentenced to eight years in prison. In midsummer, more good news: Hoffa was found guilty in Chicago on charges of mishandling pension fund loans. For this, he received a five-year term, to be served after the other eight, for a total of thirteen years in jail.

Between the trials, President Kennedy had been assassinated in Dallas. Hoffa reacted bitterly. When Teamster officials closed the Washington head-quarters building, sent the employees home for the day, and had the flag lowered to half-mast as a sign of mourning, Jimmy, in Miami, was informed of the action by telephone.

"He flew into a rage," Walter Sheridan reported, "and became very abusive. He told them he was not going to be a hypocrite and that they should not have done what they had. He also yelled at his secretary for crying. When he was finished they hung up and left the building."[10]

In Nashville, he told reporters, "Bobby Kennedy is just another lawyer now." Later, in Utica, New York, where he went to attend a dinner celebrating the thirtieth anniversary of the founding of Local 182, he told journalists, "Bobby Kennedy is out. He will no longer have [the] veto power of the Presidency behind him. . . . He is just one of nine men in President Johnson's cabinet."

Finally, on December 12, 1967, the U.S. Supreme Court denied the last of Jimmy Hoffa's appeals. The following March, a small group of union officials gathered in a Baltimore hotel room, where Hoffa turned to Frank Fitzsimmons, saying, "Fitz, I'm going to jail and I want you to take over my duties."[11]

At 9 A.M. on Tuesday, March 7, Hoffa drove to the United States marshal's office in Washington and surrendered himself. That afternoon, he became No. 33298 in the Lewisburg Penitentiary, where his prison assignment was to stuff and repair mattresses.

*   *   *

102

It was over.

The following year, when Robert Kennedy was campaigning for the Presidential nomination in 1968, his staff was approached by a representative of the Teamsters. If the union would support Kennedy's candidacy, would he talk to the Attorney General, then Ramsey Clark, and have Hoffa transferred from the mattress shop to the farm, so that he could get outdoors?

The story of the offer was told by David Burke, then administrative assistant to Senator Edward Kennedy.

"A day or two later," Burke declared, "Robert Kennedy arrived in Indianapolis. I remember he was taking a bath. Edward Kennedy went into the bathroom, and I went in with him and related to him this conversation."

"Robert Kennedy said, 'Well, I will tell you. What you can do is, you go back to your fellow from the Teamsters and you tell him that I will not speak to Ramsey Clark. As far as I am concerned, Jimmy Hoffa can stay in the mattress factory forever. And if I am ever elected President of the United States, he has a darn slim chance of ever getting out of jail.'"[12]

But Robert Kennedy was not elected President; Richard Nixon was. On December 23, 1971, Nixon ordered Hoffa's sentence commuted from thirteen years to six years and six months under an executive grant of clemency, even though four months earlier, the parole board had turned down his third bid to be freed. Hoffa was one of forty-nine prison inmates on the list. The order stipulated that Hoffa must not be involved in "direct or indirect management of any labor organization" until March 6, 1980.

The crucial point involved in the commutation was that, since he had already served four years of his new term, under federal law he could be freed at once.

And he was.

Commented *The New York Times* in an editorial, "It is a bit difficult to avoid the suspicion that imminence of the 1972 election [in which Nixon would seek a second term] was a factor in Mr. Nixon's decision to release him." *The Times* noted the "strange love affair" between the Administration and the two-million-member union.[13]

Jimmy Hoffa was grateful. On February 13 of the following year, appearing on the nationally telecast *Issues and Answers* program on ABC, he was asked about his preference among the candidates for the Presidency that year. "I would say President Nixon is the best qualified man at the present time for the Presidency of the United States, in my personal opinion."

Hoffa received a $1.7 million pension settlement from the Teamsters and enjoyed three and one-half years of freedom. In 1975, he and Josephine were spending the hot summer months at their cottage at Lake Orion, a few miles north of Detroit. On Wednesday, July 30, shortly before 1 P.M., he left, telling Josephine he would return after lunch. He never came back.

Police found his car, a green 1974 Pontiac, in the parking lot of a restaurant not far away. His disappearance remains unsolved. Authorities believe, but cannot yet prove, that he was abducted and executed by warring crime factions in a power struggle for control of the union. Josephine died in 1980. In 1982, the courts declared Hoffa legally dead.

Bobby's conduct as a labor rackets investigator has received mixed reviews.

Arthur Goldberg, whose legal and labor credentials are impeccable, wrote to Bobby in 1960: ''I followed your work throughout and am aware of no instance where any legitimate, honest labor leader or labor organization had any cause for complaint because of your conduct as counsel of the committee's affairs.''[14]

Ed Guthman was profoundly impressed. ''Bobby was the first person I ever encountered who took responsibility for what his witnesses would say. He would get information but he would not present it until he knew it was accurate,'' Guthman declared.

''At the very start,'' said Guthman, ''Kennedy told us how he would run the committee, that he would be thorough, that he would take responsibility for his witnesses, that he would protect his sources. We decided to trust him and he kept his word.''[15]

In his Manhattan law office, Ramsey Clark, who watched it all from the inside as an assistant attorney general, summed up Bobby's behavior dispassionately. ''There was disagreement within the department on the merits of some of the cases, but there was no naked use of power such as you would see in a lawless government. Watching it as I did, I believe there was extensive deliberation on the cases. You don't deliberate when you do something arbitrary or authoritarian.''

At the same time Clark, who later served as Attorney General from 1967 to 1969, asserted, ''In an ideal situation, an Attorney General would not have become so closely identified with one criminal investigation as Bobby was. There were too many other cases to oversee. In those years, we filed more than 30,000 criminal indictments in one year alone. Spending too much time on one creates an inequality. Yet you talk about equal justice under the law.''

Clark cited another problem: ''When an AG becomes so personally involved, as Bobby was, it can affect the judgment of others in the department, even if they don't want it to. Ambitions are keen in the higher levels of the Justice Department.

''Here was one man, Robert Kennedy, who had the power of making a career by a single appointment to a key post. So some people might say 'yes' to a leader in the belief that it may enhance their careers.''[16]

Some members of the McClellan committee sharply disapproved of the manner in which he ran the hearings. *Time* magazine quoted a Republican member as saying, "The Senators don't have the slightest idea who is to be called, but we can read the witness lists in the newspapers. The witnesses are gangsters, and you can't defend them. Even so, a lot of the things that are done are unfair. For example, staff investigators will be put on the stand and will make statements without any proof. These statements become part of the record, but often they are nothing more than the investigator's belief. There is no effective rebuttal. The effect is that some witnesses who might testify if they get a fairer chance take the Fifth Amendment."[17]

Alexander Bickel, professor of law at Yale University, deplored Bobby's lack of "civility" in the conduct of the hearings. "He seemed to engage in punitive expeditions," Bickel said. "In more than one instance, the purpose of calling witnesses and the manner of questioning them gave fairly blatant evidence of purposeful punishment by publicity rather than fulfillment of the function of informing Congress."[18]

Under the broad canopy of a congressional investigation, Kennedy was entirely within the law when he interrogated witnesses and ticked off, by question after question, all the crimes he believed they had committed. Did they receive kickbacks from the union, run extortion rackets, even have affairs financed with union funds? Weren't they selfish, yellow? Didn't they consort with crime figures? All and much more were spread on the record, unanswered of course because the witnesses took the Fifth. Said Bickel, "Mr. Kennedy's exercise of the power to destroy or damage individuals was not subject to such safeguards as the right to cross-examination and the right to an impartial judge who is not at the same time also the prosecutor. . . . No one since the late Joseph P. McCarthy has done more than Mr. Kennedy to foster the impression that the plea of self-incrimination is tantamount to a confession of guilt."[19]

In his passion-driven efforts to punish evildoers, Bobby showed little concern for their civil rights. Paul Jacobs, then a staff member of the Center for the Study of Democratic Institutions in Santa Barbara, surgically dissected the way the hearings were conducted, concluding with this stunning observation: "It is a cliché and a truism that the most important civil rights are those of our enemies—of the people with whom we disagree. And so, although I have nothing in common with Hoffa, the union leader, Hoffa, the citizen, is me. His rights are the same as mine and required the same protection."

Jacobs cites the following instance: "The committee was raising a great row about the spectre of an alliance between the Teamsters and the International Longshoremen and Warehousemen's Union under Harry Bridges. Louis Goldblatt, secretary-treasurer of Bridges's union, was confronted at the hearings with evidence of his Communist youth in 1934, and Hoffa was questioned at length about the alliance. To further cinch this case against Hoffa, Kennedy pointed out that the ILWU had been expelled from the CIO for following the Communist Party line and that in contrast to the Teamsters, the East Coast longshoremen had indignantly refused to be part of any deal with Bridges. However, Kennedy neglected, at the time, to also point out to the committee that the East Coast longshoremen he used as an example of political virtue had been expelled from the AFL-CIO for being dominated by racketeers at the very time they were expressing their righteous horror at the idea of being associated with Communists.''

David Previant, a Teamster lawyer, compiled a list of ways in which the McClellan committee abused its powers. ''We had guilt by association, guilt by marriage, guilt by eating in the same chop house, guilt by the general counsel's amazement, guilt by somebody else taking the Fifth Amendment, guilt by somebody else refusing to testify. But we think the 'doozer' was the one that happened when the committee was taking testimony concerning a criminal case in which eight defendants were tried for eleven weeks; the jury was out only eight minutes and came in with the verdict of 'not guilty.' The police detective who helped prepare the case said the prosecution felt it was not a fair trial. The committee nodded in sympathy and agreement. This is guilt by acquittal.''[20]

In the fall of 1958, Clark Mollenhoff asked Hoffa, ''Jimmy, are you worried about the McClellan committee?''

Hoffa laughed. ''You know me better than that, Clark,'' he replied. ''That committee isn't going to be around forever. They'll be going for another nine months, and Bob Kennedy will be running off to elect his brother President.''

Mollenhoff knew Hoffa's mind. Jimmy was convinced he would beat the charges and be rid of Bobby forever.

He was right, and he was wrong.

Exactly nine months later—after writing a best-selling personal account of his rackets probing, *The Enemy Within*—Bobby left to head Jack's Presidential campaign.

But Jimmy had not been rid of him at all.

10

Electing Jack

*B*OBBY WAS THE SPINE of the Kennedy-for-President race, and the legs, nerves, and guts, too. He left the McClellan committee in the fall of 1958, when its mandate ran out and, on April 1 of the following year, sat at the head of Joe Kennedy's dining room table in Palm Beach, chairing the first organizational meeting of the campaign. Joe had ordered a lunch of roast turkey with stuffing and a choice of pies for the inner circle that, that afternoon, carved up the chores as the cook had carved the bird. Theodore C. Sorensen, until then temporary chairman, moved over for Bobby to become national policy chief.

The meeting lasted until late afternoon, and when they left for the airport to board the Kennedy plane, the *Caroline,* for the flight to New York, each knew who would be responsible for what and that Bobby would be responsible for everything. Although Jack would not announce his candidacy officially until January 2 of the following year, the campaign had begun.

A year later, during the West Virginia primary race, the two brothers met at the airport near Charleston, the capital city.

"Hi, Johnny," Bobby said, "how are you?"

Jack Kennedy shook his head. "Man," he said, "I'm tired."

"What the hell are you tired for?" Bobby replied. "I'm doing all the work!"

It was, of course, a fraternal jest, but there was much truth in it.

Bobby brought in most of the organizers, key people who had talent, loyalty, and drive, and let them know he expected full measure of all three qualities all the time. Before the nominating convention opened, he assigned one person to each state delegation who would report at a meeting of the entire group every morning. One day, a man was missing. When he was located at Disneyland, Bobby "read him the riot act," said Joseph F. Dolan, who later became administrative assistant to Kennedy at the Justice Department. "I don't know who he was, but that guy was looking for a hole in the floor. . . . Bob can make a fellow feel more guilty than the occasion demands. Then everybody works harder so that they don't get themselves in that position at any time in the future," Dolan asserted.[1]

When John Kennedy was nominated for President on the first ballot on July 13 at the Los Angeles Sports Arena, his exhausted staff whooped it up in their Biltmore Hotel rooms, many getting pleasantly plastered, and looked forward to a spell of rest and relaxation at the Cape. They felt they had earned some beach and sailing time after the hard months of the primary campaigns.

Bobby thought otherwise. The day after they arrived at Hyannis Port, he roused them early and summoned them to his home on Irving Avenue inside the compound. Shuffling papers, Bobby gave the general outlines of an action plan for the coming four months. The staff, red-eyed from lack of sleep, listened in amazement. Someone called out, "Hey, Bob, let's taste this for a little bit. We're bushed."

Kennedy stared at him coldly. "You can rest in November," he said curtly and gave out their assignments.

That night at the Cape he was up until 2 A.M. with his glassy-eyed strategists, studying the most recent polls. They were disheartening: Richard Nixon was leading by a 50 to 44 percent margin.

"That's going to be cut and damn soon," Bobby told the staff. He slept a few hours, then shortly after dawn he was up again, walking across the rear lawn of his own house to his brother's smaller one, where he had told the staff to meet him. One by one, they sleepily arrived to listen to an animated Bobby outline more organizational plans.

When the nominee flew to Palm Beach to rest at poolside, Bobby went to Washington to check on the working efficiency of the Democratic National Committee. He found it top-heavy with chiefs but no Indians: there were more than one hundred specialists but only one secretary capable of taking dictation.

Bobby changed that in a hurry. In a month, the staff was balanced, and bulletins, press releases, memos, and all the rest were flowing from dozens of newly rented offices. Often—nobody knew when—he would show up to oversee operations from a tiny office on Connecticut Avenue.

Bobby trusted nobody but family and a few—a very few—friends and political allies. He didn't suspect the loyalty of others; he just did not believe

108

they would work hard enough, "hard" being defined in his lexicon as the other side of exhaustion.

Around him he gathered Lawrence F. O'Brien to head the organization committee; Kenny O'Donnell to act as coordinator of scheduling; Pierre Salinger, who had worked as a McClellan committee investigator, as press adviser; brothers-in-law Steve Smith, who would be the money man, and Sargent Shriver, who would work with black leaders, along with Harris Wofford; Byron (Whizzer) White, a Rhodes scholar who had been an All-American halfback, to head the Citizens for Kennedy committees; Luther Hodges was to be chairman of the businessmen's group; and a few dozen other intimates.

Teddy, twenty-eight years old and just back from a belated South American honeymoon with beautiful Joan Bennett, was made Rocky Mountain coordinator, an impressive-sounding assignment, the duties of which were to bring the western states into the Kennedy column.* He dashed off, flying between Arizona, Idaho, Nevada, Washington, and Oregon, riding bucking broncos, dancing Irish jigs, making many friends. Once at a rally in Wyoming, a delegate to the forthcoming convention called out, "I wish you were running!"

Teddy made up in energy and derring-do what he lacked in political savvy, risking his neck on an unbroken bronco and an 180-foot ski jump for votes. He had never been on either in his entire life. Shortly after the leap, he got a call from his brother.

"Jack called to say he had just talked with the state chairman in Wyoming who told him I was coming there," Teddy said. "They were arranging to have a sharpshooter shoot a cigarette out of my mouth at twenty yards. Jack said casually that he didn't think I had to go through with that if I didn't want to, but . . ."

In New Mexico, Ted pulled a college-style practical joke that might have backfired, but instead won a key Democrat's support.

Philip Muhic, the Pueblo County Democratic chairman in Colorado, who liked Jack personally but wasn't entirely sold on his candidacy, had arrived late in Santa Fe for a meeting of the National Committee. Every hotel was jammed, and Muhic, known as "Tiger," was bushed. At 2 A.M., Ted told him, "The senator isn't coming in until sometime tomorrow. Why don't you take his room?" Tiger gratefully accepted and went to sleep in Jack Kennedy's bed. Ted, however, had known Jack was coming in at 5 A.M. Meeting him at the airport, he explained the joke.

* Nobody expected Teddy to win any of the States, which were heavily Republican, and he didn't. After the returns were in on Election Day, Bobby looked dejected. When Kenny O'Donnell asked what was wrong, Bobby replied, "I'm worried about Teddy. We've lost every State that he worked in out west. Jack will kid him, and that may hurt Teddy's feelings."

At the hotel, Jack woke Tiger and, affecting sternness, demanded to know what he was doing in his bed. It took Tiger a while to catch on, but after that, he was sold on Kennedy.

"From then on, we never had any trouble with Tiger," Joe Dolan asserted. "He'd say, 'What do you mean am I for Jack Kennedy? I slept in his bed down in Santa Fe.' "[2]

Bobby worked harder than any of them.

"I saw him get up in a snowstorm at six in the morning and thumb his way to a meeting of twenty-five people," his cousin, Polly Fitzgerald, recalled.[3] At airline terminals, when there was no time for lunch or dinner, she would plug coins into vending machines and bring him hot soup; he would stock up on candy bars at newsstands and stuff them in his pockets.

From July to November, Bobby rarely slept more than five hours a night. His eyes became red-rimmed and hollow, his normal stoop so pronounced with fatigue, he resembled a walking open parenthesis. John J. Hooker, Jr., the Tennessee attorney who worked with him on the campaign, reported that during July and August he "was like a prizefighter who was unconscious of the fact that he was being hit and hurt, and unconscious of whether or not he would be able to defeat his opponent. He was simply fighting with his total energy."[4]

Jack was able to separate himself from the problem. Once, in Chicago, he left orders not to be disturbed and slept around the clock. He worried about Bobby, saying, "He's living on his nerves."

Ethel worried about him, too, flying to his side as often as she could, ordering him to eat properly (which he did not) and pleading with him to rest (which he could not).

"A fire wouldn't divert Bobby from a problem," one aide said. Neither did a police chase.

In Nebraska, the campaign was bogging down in early fall. The Democratic organization was dragging its feet, failing to give the candidate sufficient support. Bobby, who had gone to the state to find out why, was driving toward the capital city, Lincoln, with the party's nominee for the Senate, Robert Conrad, and Helen Abdouch, executive secretary of the JFK organization in Nebraska.

"What's *wrong*?" Bobby was asking. "Aren't your volunteers working hard enough?" Conrad, at the wheel, replied angrily, "Bob, it's not as simple as that." He was about to explain when he heard the blast of a siren and saw flashing lights in the rearview mirror. A patrolman was flagging him down.

Taking no notice, Bobby talked on, asking if it would be possible to enlist the county organization to work with the local faction. When Conrad left the car to discuss the matter with the highway cop, Bobby turned

110

to Miss Abdouch, pressing for a solution. Conrad returned, started the car, and drove on. Bobby, still on the subject, did not ask if they had been ticketed; it was even doubtful if he knew why they had been stopped.

Bobby seemed to be everywhere and often was, prompting campaign staffs around the country to whisper to each other, "Little brother is watching." After he told reform Democrats in New York that he didn't give a damn if they survived, as long as John F. Kennedy won, the cry of ruthlessness was raised, never to subside.

Joe Kennedy heard it and, explaining that he spoke as one to whom the term had been applied for a half-century, said, "Anybody who is controversial is called ruthless. Any man of action is always called ruthless. It's ridiculous." Bobby, he added, was not ruthless at all, but dedicated.

All through the campaign, he insisted on doing things his way. "We had a lot of trouble with Bobby," said George Smathers, then senator from Florida, who was an old friend of Jack Kennedy, "a *lot* of trouble. He didn't want Pierre Salinger or anybody else to make the decisions. He wanted to run the campaign himself."

Bobby was told off by leading southern Democrats when he invaded their territory and tried to cancel their plans for a train journey that would carry Lyndon Johnson, the vice presidential candidate, across the entire tier of southern States.

Smathers explained what happened. "Jack needed Lyndon because he needed Texas with its twenty-four electoral votes, and he needed the South. Down comes Bobby, and he was trying to tell us how to run the South, but he knew nothing about it. He had been to Palm Beach, but he had never been to Alabama, never been through South Carolina, Georgia, or Louisiana, where Kennedy was virtually unknown.

"We, on the other hand, knew how to make the most of Lyndon's presence on the ticket. We had planned the train journey to carry him into every area, and also to link up with Jack at major centers like New Orleans and Birmingham for joint appearances.

"We had a meeting, a big blowup in an Atlanta hotel. Bobby had come down with a friend, a hell of a nice guy who had gone to Harvard Law School but hadn't been elected to anything. They wanted to change things all around. Bobby didn't want the train trip, he wanted to do something different. Well, we had a real knockdown drag-out affair. We told Bobby to shut up and get the hell out of the way. It ended up when we picked up the phone and called Jack Kennedy, who told Bobby to back off, get out of there, and leave it to us.

"He was an arrogant guy, Bobby was. He didn't have respect for anyone's views but his own. He was just like the old man."[5]

111

The circumstances under which Johnson landed on the ticket are still as murky as the day it happened.

Nobody, not even the candidate for President, could figure out how it came about. After the convention, John Kennedy tried to piece the confusing fragments together for Pierre Salinger, his press secretary, then stopped suddenly. "The whole story will never be known," he said. "And it's just as well that it won't be."[6]

Salinger was unable to understand or explain that mysterious statement.

The selection of Lyndon Johnson, whom Bobby hated and Jack feared would antagonize the liberals, had an Alice-in-Wonderland quality about it from start to nomination. A series of weird events, involving secret meetings in hallways, hotel suites, and locked bathrooms, ensued and shortly took on a life of their own, which neither the candidate nor his principal adviser was able to control.

The possibility exists that John Kennedy began the move to put Johnson on the ticket, then changed his mind but was unable to stop it once it gathered momentum.

A telegram started it all.

Johnson had been mentioned as a possibility for second place well before the convention, but nobody—least at all John Kennedy—took the reports seriously. Lyndon's name headed the list of six choices Ted Sorensen had presented to Jack. Because of his position as Senate majority leader, and because he came from a large state securely lodged in the Kennedy doubtful column, Johnson should be given the right of "first refusal," Sorensen argued.

Kennedy believed Lyndon's virtually Shermanesque statement during the primaries, that under no circumstances would he yield his powerful position in the Senate for the relatively impotent position of Vice President.

Then the wire arrived. After Jack's triumph in the Sports Arena, Johnson sent a message so full of heartfelt congratulations, so obviously sincere, that Kennedy wondered, "Would Lyndon want the job after all?" He respected Johnson's talents enormously, having observed during the primaries that, if he lost, the big Texan was the man best qualified to be President.

He called Johnson's suite at the Biltmore to thank him and perhaps to find out. However, it was then about 3 A.M., and Johnson had gone to bed, leaving orders that he did not want to be disturbed. According to Evelyn Lincoln, Kennedy's secretary, the nominee left word with a Johnson aide to telephone him when he rose.

Soon after, the telephone jangled Sargent Shriver awake in the same hotel. Johnson, the caller said, would accept the vice presidential nomination.

Shriver was dumbfounded. He could not remember the caller's name

112

nor, of course, understand what the message meant. He repeated it to Kennedy at 8 A.M.

At ten that morning, Kennedy paid a personal visit to Johnson. To avoid the journalists who were swarming around the hotel, he quietly left his suite, number 9333, and slipped down a rear staircase to Lyndon's seventh-floor suite, number 7334. A conversation ensued, but nobody knows exactly what was said. Lady Bird Johnson was there, along with a number of aides, but Kennedy, LBJ, and Sam Rayburn, Speaker of the House, locked themselves in the bathroom, where they remained for ten minutes.

Later, Johnson said he had been asked to run, but he had "more or less" said no. At the same time, he said he asked for time to think it through and consult with advisers.

Kennedy, however, had a different version. When he returned to Bobby's suite on the eighth floor, Bobby remembered that he said, "You just wouldn't believe it. He wants it."

Bobby's response was short and crisp: "Oh, my God!"

This exchange was recalled by Bobby four years later in an oral history he made for the the JFK Library.

But there was a third version of that bathroom conference.

A few weeks after the July convention, Kennedy said that he had gone to Lyndon's room only to take soundings on his availability and that Johnson had astonished him by replying that he was indeed available.

After Kennedy had gone, Rayburn, Hale Boggs, *Washington Post* and *Newsweek* publisher Philip Graham, and Lady Bird conferred with Johnson on the "offer." And in JFK's suite, the candidate was being lectured sharply by a labor delegation, aghast when Kennedy said he might turn to Johnson.

Walter Reuther, the UAW president, Jack Conway, his administrative assistant, and Arthur Goldberg, then a prominent labor lawyer, pushed for Hubert Humphrey or Stuart Symington. But Johnson? They threatened a floor fight if the man who backed the hated, union-restricting Landrum-Griffin Bill only the year before was shoved down their throats.

At the door, Jack Conway turned to Bobby and said, "We've come a long way. If you do this, you're going to fuck everything up."[7]

When the labor leaders left, Kennedy had another bathroom conference, this time with Arthur Goldberg. He asked the lawyer to tick off the problems that could result if LBJ were chosen. Labor would not be happy, Goldberg replied. George Meany, the AFL-CIO president, might even stage a floor rebellion. Kennedy asked Goldberg to try to calm him down.

Kennedy still had to convince himself and win over his close aides. Kenny O'Donnell, for one, was jarred to his back teeth. "The idea churned my stomach," said the strongly liberal-leaning Kenny. "I tell you, I never was so pissed off in my life."

JFK, who knew Kenny's value and wanted his support, held yet another bathroom parley. Kenny said, "I really lit into him. I guess I called him all sorts of things, telling him he was being false to himself and to all liberals."

Jack argued persuasively, saying that, while Johnson still had not accepted, the move was a shrewd one, designed to appease Johnson and Rayburn and clear the way for Mike Mansfield to take LBJ's place as majority leader. Besides, he said, a resentful Johnson, wielding strong power in the Senate, might well stymie the social program Kennedy was planning. "If Johnson and Rayburn leave here mad at me," Kennedy said, "they'll ruin me in Congress in a month. Then I'll be the laughingstock of the country."

Now Bobby had to be convinced, and that was a lot harder. He recalled later, "I pointed out to my brother that this was going to be very hard to explain to many of our supporters. Johnson had tried to block us, to fight us all the way, and the fight had gotten personal in the final stages."

During the afternoon Bobby even went to Johnson's suite, probably to ask him not to take it, but never got to see him. Wisely, Lady Bird had advised her husband to talk only to Jack.

The conferences continued on the eighth foor. By then, Jack Kennedy himself wasn't too certain. "We just vacillated back and forth as to whether we wanted him or didn't want him," Bobby said.[8] Upstairs, Philip Graham, aware of the pulling and tugging going on downstairs, called Jack and told him it was too late to change his mind.

Johnson still had not responded, mostly because he wasn't at all certain by that time that he was really wanted. Bobby again barged into Johnson's suite, saw the majority leader this time, and asked him point-blank to remove himself from consideration, citing the rebellion which his selection would spark. Instead, Bobby said, Johnson could become chairman of the Democratic National Committee, a post in which he would have vast influence in the party.

On the ninth floor, Kennedy aides and other high political figures were freely offering predictions. "Lyndon isn't going to take it," Smathers told Jack. "He'll never do it," agreed Adlai Stevenson.

But, finally, he did. Graham telephoned the Kennedy suite, got through to Jack, and said, "Lyndon will accept."

Now there was no turning back. Kennedy was caught in a bind of his own making. The arguments of his liberal supporters that Johnson would hurt him grievously had been effective. Would a loss there balance the strength he would gain in the South? He still had not made up his mind.

Johnson's acceptance ended his indecision. He could not say no at that critical juncture. For better or worse, he had a running mate, who was nominated by acclamation that day.

A few hours later, Kennedy and Bobby were sitting around the pool on the Marion Davies estate, still uncertain if the right choice had been made. Joe Kennedy reassured them: "Don't worry, Jack. In two weeks everyone will say that this was the smartest thing you ever did."

Four months later, the day after the election, both Kennedys were saying it, too. Without the Texas electoral vote and those of two or three other southern states, JFK would have lost the Presidency.

The linchpin of the carefully constructed campaign was television. The Kennedy women, who went everywhere, provided the pull of glamour, chic, and sophistication that played to the fantasies of voters who led mundane lives; polls pinpointed areas of weakness, clever advertising techniques supplied the needed strength, and money made much of this possible. But it was television, which reached millions, that turned the trick for John Kennedy.

Bobby remembered what he had seen and learned four years before when he had been detached from Jack's senatorial campaign to travel with Adlai Stevenson and observe him as he ran against Dwight D. Eisenhower. Bobby watched closely, taking copious notes. Stevenson, he saw, was trying to capture votes old style, by playing to the crowds lining the streets and filling the auditoriums and town squares. Once he watched in amazement as Stevenson delivered a long and complex speech on world affairs to some two dozen coal miners on a railroad siding in West Virginia. At one point during the tour, he told Newton Minow, who had been Stevenson's law partner, that the candidate was ignoring television, with its vast audience, and Minow "quickly and painfully agreed."[9]

In 1960, all this was in Bobby's notebook, and in his head. Knowing his brother with his looks, charm, and easy grace was perfect for television, he insisted that considerable time and money must be spent on commercials and telecast speeches and that TV stations be given top priority in the coverage of Jack's appearances. He would not permit press conferences to begin or speeches to start until the television crews had arrived and were in place.

The campaign organization even scrutinized the TV listings carefully before buying speech time, to make sure that commercial programs with large followings were not preempted, thus angering audiences who watched them.

The quartet of television debates—on September 25 and October 7, 13, and 21—was the turning point of the campaign, particularly the first, in which John Kennedy's coolness and composure contrasted sharply with Richard Nixon's pallid, haggard look. Bobby may have played a role in that famous initial encounter in Chicago when 65 million viewers saw a sick-looking Nixon on their TV screens.

Nixon had refused to wear makeup, applying only a light pancake covering to hide his normally heavy beard. According to one story, a Nixon aide, apparently aware that Bobby was better versed in the medium than most, ingenuously asked him what he thought of the candidate's appearance.

"Terrific! Terrific!" Bobby is said to have replied. "I wouldn't change a thing."[10]

Unfortunately for Nixon, the television camera, unlike one that takes still photographs, works electronically and, somewhat like an X-ray, can penetrate beneath the skin. Since the outer layer of facial skin, the epidermis and dermis, are naturally thin, the camera can go through this outer surface and reveal lines and hollows not apparent to the naked eye. Makeup, however, can counteract the effect.

Bobby may have suspected this and contributed to the appearance that was devastating to Nixon.

He was all business, at least most of the time. But his sense of humor remained. During the campaign, he received a note from Joey Gallo, the notorious underworld figure, who wrote that he had the power and resources to help get JFK elected.

"What can I do?" Joey asked.

Kennedy wrote back: "Just tell everybody you're voting for Nixon."

Once he had barely concluded a speech from the rear platform of a train when it suddenly started to move away. A large throng of newspersons in front, who were traveling with him, were left stranded. Bobby gave them a big smile and called out, "Be sure to write!"

Jack, too, kept his humor intact. Before the convention opened, Bobby had appeared on Jack Paar's late-night television program. He made such an excellent impression that an attorney on the West Coast wrote to John Kennedy suggesting that Bobby would be a better candidate for the Presidency. His plan: let Jack yield his Senate seat to Bobby to give his younger brother a clear field for the race. Jack responded to the letter.

"This is to acknowledge your letter and to tell you that I am taking your recommendation under advisement. I have consulted Bobby about it, and, to my dismay, your idea appealed to him."

Both Kennedy brothers were annoyed at Jacqueline during the campaign. With the women's vote, particularly in so-called Middle America, crucial, they noted with dismay the contrast between the candidates' wives.

Pat Nixon was meatloaf, Jackie Kennedy, pheasant under glass. Pat gave interviews in inexpensive off-the-rack dresses, talking about homemaking, sewing dresses for her children, and standing behind her husband, personifying the Average American Housewife. Jackie wore purple Pucci slacks, as she lounged on the floor of her Georgetown house during an interview. When *Women's Wear Daily* claimed she spent $30,000 a year in Paris on her wardrobe and that women hated her for it, she quipped, "I couldn't spend that much unless I wore sable underwear."

When the remark made headlines, Jack hit the ceiling. "That's the last time that that woman will give an interview until after the election!" he shouted.

Bobby, aware it wasn't his place to speak to his sister-in-law, pleaded with Jack to talk to her. The candidate did. He told her to confine her remarks to uncontroversial matters. "Just smile a lot and talk about Caroline," he said. "And don't smoke in public."

"Jack appreciated Jackie's qualities," said Smathers, "appreciating her for what she was and didn't really want to change her, but there were times when he thought she looked too uptown for the occasion."

"A candidate's wife," Jack told Smathers, "must be like the wife of a defendant at a trial. How she looks, dresses, and behaves is important in helping to influence the jury."[11]

Both wives hated politics, but Pat, adept at the art, was able to hide her feelings while Jackie was not.[12] Jackie's boredom showed during interviews, by her open dislike of political types surrounding her husband ("jackals and imbeciles," she called them), by the relief she expressed when she became pregnant during the primaries ("Thank God, I get out of those dreadful chicken dinners"). She was "driven up the wall by gassy old windbags" at political functions, she said.

Oddly, though she campaigned minimally, the little she did carried a long way. They loved her in ethnic neighborhoods, where she would greet voters in fluent, perfectly accented French, Spanish, and Italian.

However, when Bobby heard about one incident, he grimaced. In Kenosha, Wisconsin, Jackie was asked to warm up the crowd before the candidate appeared. As she walked out on the stage, someone said in a loud whisper, "Get 'em singing." Jackie thereupon asked the Kenoshans to join her in a chorus of "Southie is My Home Town," a song famous in Boston and almost nowhere else. The bewildered Kenoshans sat silently as Jackie sang alone.

At 4:40 A.M. on November 9, the day after the election, John Kennedy went to bed after eating a sandwich and grousing because there was no more milk in Bobby's refrigerator. Bobby's house had been turned into a vote-tabulating and analysis headquarters. On the sunporch, fourteen girls were at the telephones receiving the vote count, as precincts closed around the country, and transmitting them to the tabulators in the dining room, who in turn sent them upstairs, where pollster Lou Harris and his staff analyzed their meaning.

Six hours earlier, a major Kennedy swing appeared in the making, and Jackie had turned to her husband and said, "Oh, Bunny, you're President now!" Jack knew better. "It's too early yet," he told her. An hour later, Jackie, in her ninth month of pregnancy, went to bed.

The tide swung toward Nixon around midnight, then steadied at an almost dead heat. By 3 A.M., Kennedy had 261 electoral votes but needed another eight. A few minutes after three, Eastern Time, Nixon, with Pat at his side, appeared in the ballroom of the Ambassador Hotel in Los Angeles and said, "While there are still some results to come in, if the present trend continues, Senator Kennedy will be the next President of the United States." Pat's face was contorted; she ground her teeth and tears started to roll down her cheeks. Still, Nixon did not concede defeat, and Kennedy, three thousand miles away, would not claim victory.

One by one, the staff drifted off to bed. The control-room operators shut down their equipment and boarded buses for their hotels. Staff people drifted off.

Bobby Kennedy sat alone in the command post, tieless, sleeves rolled halfway up his forearm, calling around the country on the one remaining telephone.

At 5:30, Michigan went to Kennedy, giving him 285 electoral votes, a majority of the 537. It was enough for the Secret Service to send sixteen agents to the compound to guard the President-elect of the United States. By 7 A.M., a ring of security had been forged around Kennedy.

The candidate still slept. Bobby, finally satisfied, went upstairs and, taking off only his shoes and trousers, fell asleep.

Joe Kennedy, the man who started it all, who wanted it desperately, and whose money made it all happen, had exiled himself for the entire year and a half it took to elect Jack. He made no public appearances, granted few interviews. With his own political views spread so clearly and fully on the record, he knew that coming out as his son's booster would scarcely enhance Jack's progressive image.

Ducking attention, he had traveled in secret to Los Angeles, slipping into Marion Davies's palatial home, where he had a battery of telephones installed at poolside. He used them constantly to advise Jack at the Hotel Biltmore, about ten miles away. Rose went to the convention, but Joe did not, telling her he'd rather be away from the crowds and the photographers. He was conspicuously absent from the platform when the delegates cheered their candidate.

Next day, Joe flew east as secretly as he had come and vanished and was seen rarely during the Presidential campaign, when the chant arose: "Jack and Bobby will run the show, while Ted's in charge of hiding Joe."

After Jack was elected, Joe emerged from his self-imposed exile only on rare occasions, but he always had plenty of advice to offer behind the scenes. Several days after the victory, for example, he butted into a conversation the new President was having with Bobby at the Cape over the need to make drastic changes in the State Department and the Foreign Service.

Peter Lisagor, the late syndicated columnist, recalled this incident: "Ambassador Kennedy was sitting in a corner presumably reading a newspaper or a magazine and not paying much attention, but he was, in fact, eavesdropping. He heard the two boys say that they were going to really overhaul this thing, they were going to get all this tired, dead wood out of there and going to put in some new, lively young people, fresh, with a lot of get up and go about them.

"He listened until his patience ran thin, and then he said, 'Sons, I want to tell you that I once went to see Franklin D. Roosevelt who made much the same kind of talk that you're making now. He lamented the State Department. He talked about razing the whole thing (that is, burning it down) and starting from scratch. He didn't do a damn thing about it, and neither are you.' "[13]

Still, Joe was wise enough to remain out of sight, much as he would have liked to savor the fruits of his accomplishment in public. The day after the election, Jack and his entourage prepared to leave for the U.S. Armory in Hyannis to address the nation on television. Joe watched from the shadows of his porch as the motorcade formed in front of his house.

"Jack suddenly realized what was happening," Pat Lawford recalled. "He got out of the car, went back up to the porch, and told Dad to come along and hear his speech. Jack insisted on it. And finally he talked Daddy into getting into the car."

Joe also went to the Inaugural Ball. Twenty-three years before, as he and Rose were dressing to be presented at court following his appointment as United States ambassador, he had turned to his wife and said, "Rose, this is a helluva long way from East Boston, isn't it?"[14] On January 20, 1961, he put on the same white tie and tails he had worn then, and Rose, slender as ever, was also able to wear the same Molyneux dress with its gold and silver embroidered pailettes and silver lamé train. It was an even longer way from South Boston.

Three days after the election Jack went off to Palm Beach to sit in the sun, swim in the ocean, and hold meetings with major Democrats over the shape of his Administration. Just before he left, he turned to Bobby and asked what he wanted to do.

"He asked me if I wanted to be Attorney General," Bobby remembered. "I said I didn't want to be Attorney General."

That, it appeared, was that.

Bobby feared the charge of nepotism would be raised immediately. Besides: "I had been chasing bad men for three years, and I didn't want to spend my life doing that," he said.

He had been too busy to think about his own future, but now that the battle was over and Jack would soon be in the White House, he looked inward and saw nothing. Ticking off his options, he discarded everything but a role, somewhere and someplace, in public life. He had no interest in practicing law, heading a business, or dealing in the world of finance. Perhaps the presidency of a college or university or the presidency of a foundation endowed to make a contribution to the public good were closer, but even these, he felt, could not equal the stimulation, challenges, and satisfactions of a career in government.*

He hated being idle, and the abrupt letdown after more than eighteen months of frantic activity made matters worse. The loneliness and uncertainties he knew were around the corner were palpable this morning after the election, when his brother was acknowledging cheers as the victorious candidate. Nobody noticed Bobby as he stood at the far end of the platform, hands thrust deeply into his pants pockets, staring glumly at the shouting, applauding audience.

He was back once again at the point where he was after graduation from law school, no career path ahead. Before he made up his mind, he had vague notions that he would "travel, read, something. I didn't know."[15]

Joe Kennedy, however, did know where Bobby should go.

George Smathers tells the story of an afternoon he spent with the President-elect at Palm Beach.

It was in mid-November, and the two men were talking about the makeup of the new Cabinet. After listing a number of possible choices, Kennedy paused, then turned to Smathers and said, "I don't know what to do with Bobby. I've got to do *something* about Bobby."

"Why don't you suggest to him that he be named Assistant Secretary of Defense," Smathers said. "It's a big job. Defense has the biggest budget of all the Government departments, and in time he'll be made secretary.

"It seems a very appropriate position for him. After all, he will still be close to you, which I'm sure he wants to be."

Jack was silent for a moment. "That's a very sound idea," he said to Smathers. "Look, Father's coming down in about a half hour to sun with us here. You take it up with him."

Shortly, Joe Kennedy, whom Smathers had known for many years, arrived. After the customary amenities, the Florida senator made the sug-

* Bobby bared his dilemma in a frank talk with his old friend Justice Douglas in the latter's chambers. Douglas recalled the conversation in *That Shining Hour*, page 47.

gestion. "Mr. Ambassador," he said, "don't you think it would be a good idea if Jack made Bobby Assistant Secretary of Defense? It's got this enormous budget, billions of dollars to spend, and it's an enormously important post."

Joe looked at Smathers as he spoke—"disdainfully, very much down his nose," the senator remembered. Nor did the patriarch reply to him. Instead, he turned to the President-elect and said, "I want Bobby to be Attorney General.

"He is your blood brother. Nobody has sacrificed more of his time and energy in your behalf than your brother Bobby, and I don't want to hear any further thing about it." He turned away and lay back on his chaise.

Now it became apparent why John Kennedy, a few weeks earlier in Hyannis Port, had asked his brother if he wanted the Attorney Generalship: Joe Kennedy had made his preference known to his son, the President.

"And that was it," Smathers said, as he concluded his account of the astonishing scene.[16]

Bobby himself confirmed that there was no place for him but his brother's Cabinet, but told a somewhat different version of Joe's attitude toward the Defense Department job.

"He felt, if I was there, I should be involved in all the major discussions that were made, and that if you had a position lower than anybody else's position it made it difficult," Bobby asserted.

"He said he was willing, if I could become Secretary of Defense in a year—he was willing to listen to that as long as it was understood that the person who was going to be appointed would be out in a year. Second, he felt that the President should have somebody that was close to him and had been close to him for a long period of time, and he wanted me in this job."[17]

While his own future was being decided, Bobby was in charge of filling more than one thousand key subordinate jobs in the new Administration. People had to be found, convinced to leave their present positions, and hired in less than two months, a formidable assignment.

Bobby carried it out methodically, breaking down the jobs into categories, then writing in the names of possible choices in each classification. The names were supplied by teams of talent hunters, headed by Sargent Shriver, Lawrence F. O'Brien, Ralph Dungan, Dick Donahue, and others. Long lists flowed in, to Kenny O'Donnell who, working with the FBI and the Secret Service, checked each for security clearance.

If it hadn't been for Bobby's opposition, J. William Fulbright would have been Secretary of State in the Kennedy Cabinet instead of Dean Rusk. In the last three or four days before the final decision, the choice had narrowed down to the senator from Arkansas.

Jack had already invited Fulbright to Palm Beach and played a round of golf, while they discussed the appointment. The media, sensing a major selection was near, gave the story intense coverage.

Bobby flew to Palm Beach to talk his brother out of offering the job. "The President was quite taken with him," he said, "but I really stopped Fulbright."[18]

It took days of persuasion. Jack, holding firm, said he admired Fulbright's brains and judgment, and had high regard for the firm, diplomatic way he had chaired the Senate Foreign Relations Committee, whose deliberations were often stormy.

Bobby was equally insistent. "You will never get over the fact that you had selected a senator from Arkansas who had signed the Manifesto and had been tied up on all segregation votes," he said. (On May 17, 1954, the Warren Supreme Court, in a landmark ruling, had struck down segregation in schools as unconstitutional. Two years later, 101 senators and representatives signed the Southern Manifesto, denouncing the decision and calling for a reversal. Fulbright was one of the signers.)

Wasn't it clear to Jack, Bobby asked him, that a man with that kind of record would be a liability when dealing with the newly developed countries, who were acutely sensitive on racial matters?

The debate continued en route to the airport, aboard the plane to Washington, and even inside Georgetown Hospital, where the Kennedys went for the christening of Jack's new baby boy, John junior, who had been born November 25.

Back in Palm Beach, after Joe Kennedy sided with Bobby, Fulbright—never too enthusiastic about the appointment in the first place—finally asked to be dropped from consideration. On December 12, the choice of Dean Rusk was announced.

Bobby approved. Rusk, he felt, had the requisite toughness the Kennedys wanted in a front-line cabinet officer. As president of the prestigious Rockefeller Foundation, he had been involved with the Third World countries and was respected by them. Finally, "even though he was from Georgia, he wasn't so pointedly identified with the South" as was Fulbright.

Adlai Stevenson, who had run against Eisenhower twice and had sought his third nomination at Los Angeles, was never considered, though he lobbied hard for the post. "Jack never really enjoyed his company, never took much stock in his advice, and felt he was not really much help," Bobby declared.

Jack Kennedy never forgot a visit Stevenson, a former Illinois governor, had made to Chicago's Mayor Richard Daley during the Los Angeles convention. Illinois had sixty-nine delegate votes, and Dick Daley controlled fifty-five of them.

"Stevenson had gone to Daley after Daley had come out for Kennedy and asked him to switch on the first ballot," Bobby asserted. "Adlai had said, 'You've got to have a favorite son, and I come from Illinois. You've got to be with me because it would be embarrassing if I didn't have Illinois.'

"Dick Daley almost threw him out of the office."

Kennedy offered Stevenson the post of United Nations ambassador. Deeply disappointed, Stevenson accepted on December 10. Privately, Jack Kennedy told Bobby he thought Adlai would be effective in the job—"as long as he stayed away from him [JFK]."

Bobby's future still was not settled. Jack, independent though he was, saw the validity of his father's argument. Besides, the question of family loyalty to his brother and his father could not be ignored. Bobby did indeed deserve a high appointment, and his father did have the right to cash in chips after all he had done (and spent) to help make Jack Kennedy President.

However, after the initial offer to Bobby at the Cape and talks with advisers in Palm Beach, he had a change of heart. Bobby, he reasoned, didn't want the job. The best candidate was Governor Abraham A. Ribicoff of Connecticut, the staunch liberal who, Kennedy acknowledged, was "the first public official in the United States to support my campaign for the Presidency."[19]

But Ribicoff said no. "I don't want a Jew putting Negroes in Protestant schools in the South," he told Kennedy. He preferred an appointment to the Supreme Court. "If he took Attorney General," Bobby said, "[he felt] he'd make so many enemies, create so much controversy about himself that he'd never get approved." Shortly after, Ribicoff became Secretary of Health, Education and Welfare.

"So actually," Bobby added, "I was second choice."[20]

Bobby and Ethel went to Mexico for a brief vacation, and the discussions of his future resumed. He refused flatly to fill his brother's Senate seat, to which he could have been appointed by the Massachusetts governor. He wanted to be elected on his own or nothing. Neither would he take a job on the White House staff.

Meanwhile, a trial balloon sent up by John Kennedy was shot down at once. After he leaked the possibility of Bobby's appointment to *The New York Times,* an editorial was published warning that the position must be kept "out of the political arena." The Republicans gleefully reminded him of his own statement, made just before the elections, that "nepotism is dangerous to the public interest."

Fed by an outburst of criticism from the press, eyebrows were raised around the country and fingers were dug into ribs: there go the ambitious

Kennedys, handing the plums around to each other. This very young man, who had never even tried a single case in a real courtroom, whose only legal experience had been in the freewheeling atmosphere of a congressional investigation, would be named to be the chief legal officer of the United States?

He was a Galahad with the strength of ten because his heart was pure, a Boy Scout, a "Savonarola in short pants."[21] He would be "a bad appointment," Sam Rayburn warned the President.

Nevertheless, Kennedy decided the advantages outweighed the attacks, which he felt would abate. Aboard the plane taking Jackie, three-year-old Caroline, the infant John, and close aides to Palm Beach, he told Dave Powers, "What if he does happen to be my brother? I want the best men I can get, and they don't come any better than Bobby." Continuing in that vein, Jack waved the cigar he was smoking in the air, the smoke curling around the baby's crib. Jackie promptly told the President of the United States to leave. He did, still talking about how much he needed his brother.

Bobby had lengthy discussions about the job with Jack, his father, Teddy, Ethel, "and a couple of my sisters." Finally, on Tuesday, December 8, he called Jack Kennedy.

He told him he had decided. The answer was no. ("I considered it all, and my mind was definitely made up that I wasn't going to do it," he said later.)

Jack asked him to come to breakfast the next morning.

Accompanied by John Seigenthaler, he drove the six miles from Hickory Hill to Kennedy's narrow little Georgetown house on N Street in twenty minutes. There, Jack Kennedy delivered one of his most persuasive, eloquent speeches to an audience of two.

For forty minutes, he argued that all of the people selected for the cabinet were virtual strangers, who might be "yes" men and hence the most risky types for any President to surround himself with; that it was crucial for him to have somebody close with whom he could discuss problems in detail and know he would get a no-holds-barred, honest appraisal of whether he was right or wrong, and that, finally and very simply, "I need you."

Bobby capitulated.

His first appearance in public as Attorney General may have provided confirmation in some people's minds that he was too young for the job.

He was sworn into office in the family's private quarters on the second floor of the White House. A large group of New Frontiersmen and their guests, invited for a post-ceremony reception in the East Room in his honor,

124

were standing in the main foyer waiting to be summoned into the East Room.

While they milled about, the new Attorney General made his appearance by sliding down the bannister of the great curved staircase that led from the second floor. He was followed by a squealing Kathleen, who was ten years old, and Michael, almost four.

11

The AG—At Work

*H*E DIDN'T look the part.

In his enormous two-story office, seated in a deep leather armchair at a six-foot-square mahogany desk, he looked small, very young, somewhat fragile, and entirely out of place, like a boy who had been chosen Attorney General for a day and would soon leave for his more familiar surroundings of a high school classroom.

Usually he tossed his jacket on a table and worked in rolled-up shirtsleeves, top button undone and tie pulled askew, running his hand frequently through his hair. The room on the fifth floor, forty-two by twenty-six feet, was not cluttered by Kennedy memorabilia but kept reasonably formal. On one of the walnut-paneled walls hung a portrait of Bobby's late brother Joe junior, in naval uniform; on the other, in a stately row, were framed pictures of former Attorneys General.

There were some personal touches: a sailfish he had caught in Acapulco in 1960, which he hung over the fireplace behind his desk; a three-foot Chinese junk Jack had given him and Ethel as a wedding present; a Civil War Springfield rifle; a bust of Abraham Lincoln. Almost daily, he would bring in new artistic accomplishments of his children—watercolors they had painted, poems they had written, cutouts of animals they had made—and place them on the wall nearest his desk with Scotch tape. Once he put up a copy of the Mona Lisa that Bobby junior, then nine years old, had painted and kept asking aides if they thought the boy had talent.

On the office wall was an autographed photo of Floyd Patterson, who had defeated Ingemar Johansson to regain the world's boxing heavyweight championship. When Sonny Liston defeated Patterson in 1962, Bobby had the picture removed. Kennedys don't like losers.

Desk-top decorations included a wood carving of the Nativity, a football given "The Kennedy Tigers" by the Baltimore Colts, and a handcarved God of Fertility he got in Indonesia, at the presentation of which he had muttered, "Ethel doesn't need it."

Also on the boxlike desk, which Ethel had found for him, were seals, photographs, and books, two special ones among them. One was a volume of *The Enemy Within* in a red leather binding, presented to him after the election by his sister-in-law, who had written on the flyleaf, "To Bobby, who made the impossible possible and changed all our lives, Jackie." Next to it was another bound copy, in which was inscribed, "To Bobby, the brother within, who made the easy difficult, Jack, Christmas 1960." Near these, he had placed a carved ivory monkey, at the base of which were the words: "See no evil."

Back of this formal chamber was a smaller room, which Bobby also used from time to time as an office or for consultations. It was here that he brought and scattered around the photographs he kept lugging in—dozens of pictures of Ethel and the children at all ages, of his brothers and their families, of Joe and Rose, his nephews, nieces, and sailing scenes on Nantucket Bay.

He was now two months past his thirty-fifth birthday, still five feet ten and 150 pounds, but he had slumped so much he developed a stoop that made him appear smaller and deceptively fragile. There were streaks of gray in his light-brown hair and deeper lines in his forehead and face, particularly the diagonal creases from his nose to his mouth. He was told that he should use glasses for close work, got them, but often forgot to put them on.

He no longer had the boyish good looks of Harvard years, the loss of fat pads on his cheeks making his slightly curved nose seem prominent. His eyes were still a pale blue, and his smile, wide and toothy, was contagious. Less handsome than Jack or Teddy, he nonetheless was ruggedly attractive, like a Steve McQueen or a Spencer Tracy.

Bobby came to work at odd hours. Some days he would be at his desk before 8 A.M.; other times, when the President called, he would not arrive until mid or even late afternoon. He was chauffeured around Washington in a black Cadillac limousine, where he seemed almost lost in the roomy back seat. The limo embarrassed him. He would take care to explain: "The government provides them for all Cabinet officers. It rents them for about $500 a year, which isn't a bad deal."[1]

His first stop would often be the White House, where he would confer with his brother and be present at high-level meetings. When the ill-fated invasion of Cuba was being considered, a special office was set aside for him at the headquarters of the Central Intelligence Agency. It would be late afternoon before he could begin his full day at Justice.[2]

The first months, Bobby prowled the corridors of Justice, wanting to know what people did even at the clerical level, where improvements could be made, how much red tape existed, and where it could be cut. Anybody on any floor could expect him to pop into an office and introduce himself: "I'm Bob Kennedy. What's your name? What are you working on?"

"Little Brother is watching" was revived as a whispered warning, but this time there was a subtle difference: there was a note of affection in the remark.

Offices of the department around the country were not exempted from his personal surveillance. Once, in a Midwest city, he came across a secretary reading a novel at her desk. He said nothing to her but on leaving he snapped to the attorney general for the district, who was accompanying him, "Sack her." Afterward he learned her bosses were to blame. The woman had brought a book to the office as a protest against the *lack* of work given her. The firing order was rescinded, and her superiors got blistering rebukes.[3]

Another time he saw an aide waiting to make a call on a phone being used by another. Bobby tossed a book at him, catching him in the stomach. "Get to work and start doing something useful," Kennedy said. "Why don't you try reading my book?" The volume he threw was *The Enemy Within.*[4]

A boss like this could soon arouse hatred, but a strange alchemy, something that would become more pronounced in the years just ahead, affected those who worked for him. "He inspired us," said one former aide. "He was a zealot, and we loved his zeal." Walter Sheridan, who had come over from the rackets committee to head up a new section on organized crime, declared, "He turned a huge, slumbering, bureaucratic government department into a vibrant, exciting, effective organization."

Lights were on at all hours throughout the building soon after he took over, including Saturdays. John Seigenthaler, who was called in as administrative assistant to Bobby, the job he had during the Presidential race, exclaimed, "This is no longer an eight to five agency. We're working long hours, and the idea is catching fire all over the building." Most other offices in other departments in Washington were deserted by all but cleaning personnel before 6 P.M. from late Friday afternoon until Monday morning.

He was the young King Henry V at Agincourt, rallying around him "we few, we happy few, we band of brothers." That exhortation, the Saint Crispin's Day speech from Shakespeare's play, was Robert Kennedy's favorite Shakespearean quotation:

And gentlemen in England now a-bed
Shall think themselves accurs'd they were not here,
And hold their manhoods cheap whiles any speaks
That fought with us upon Saint Crispin's day.

One day, while dining with Richard Burton in Rome, he asked the actor, who had played the role numerous times, to recite the speech. Robert knew it so well that, after applauding the rendition, he told Burton he had spoken a few words in one line incorrectly. The actor was amused; he was sure he was right. Later, Bobby looked it up, found *he* was right, and called Burton, who yielded.

Day and night, the Attorney General's office, once a restful haven, took on the look of a political campaign headquarters, something Ed Guthman noticed the first day he arrived on the job as public information head. Mail has heaped on the floor and tables, telephones rang incessantly, people "strode purposefully in and out of the inner offices." He remembered thinking, "My God, it's just like the Biltmore Hotel!"

Young, talented professionals, catching the fever from those already recruited, flocked to enlist. The staff was unique.

Bobby named Whizzer White, who had known JFK since the war and had performed superbly in the campaign, as his first deputy and persuaded Nicholas de B. Katzenbach to leave his law professorship at the University of Chicago to take charge of the Office of Legal Counsel. Both were former Rhodes scholars. He lured Archibald Cox away from Harvard Law School to become Solicitor General and Burke Marshall from a leading Washington law firm to be chief of the Civil Rights Division. Herbert J. Miller, a Republican, was named head of the Criminal Division because Bobby felt he was the best man for the job. Ramsey Clark, the son of Supreme Court Justice Tom C. Clark, who was a former Attorney General, ran the Lands Division.

They were bright, energetic, idealistic—and, like Bobby, mostly in their thirties. Clark, the youngest, was only thirty-three. Once, at a staff meeting, Ed Guthman looked around and became aware—"reluctantly"—that he was the dean of the group in terms of age. Guthman was forty-two.

One day, while tossing a football across his office with Whizzer White, Bobby wondered if the building had any exercise facilities for the staff. There weren't any, he was told. So he had a fully equipped gymnasium built on the roof.

Ethel, too, helped make the working environment more pleasant. She came by one day and noticed that employees who brown-bagged their lunches had to sit in the sun-baked courtyard of the huge Department of Justice building on Constitution Avenue. She got an idea, which she passed along to one of Bobby's aides, who told it to Bobby.

In a short while, chairs and tables shaded by large striped umbrellas were scattered around the sparkling fountain in the courtyard. Employees were delighted; the only problem was that envious workers from Internal Revenue across the street tried to crash the oasis and had to be shooed away.

His staff applauded him for the gym and the outdoor café atmosphere but was unenthusiastic about an order he issued on air travel.

Bobby always flew economy class and told his lawyers and investigators he expected them to do the same. The staff grumbled that they found it difficult to work in the more cramped confines of the tourist cabin, often surrounded by crying babies.

Nobody complained to Bobby, but one former department attorney recalled, "Every time we made a reservation, we were hoping that the cheaper seats would be sold out, so that we'd have a good excuse to go first class."

He planned his schedule to utilize every minute of his long day. Walter Sheridan learned one of his time-saving techniques back in the rackets committee days. Scheduled to leave for Chicago, Sheridan had made a reservation on a noon flight. In midmorning, Bobby saw him in the file room.

"I thought you were going to Chicago?" he said. When Sheridan replied that he had a twelve o'clock reservation, Bobby told him, "I never go anywhere at noon. It wastes the whole day."[5]

Bobby cut through not only red tape but a few departmental rules with which he didn't agree. One day he invited 125 children of Cabinet members, representatives, and heads of federal agencies to a picnic and barbecue. It was a cold day in late January, and the grounds at Hickory Hill were not suitable for the event. So he asked them all to come to his office. Ethel and the wives of his staff pitched in, brought hot dogs, hamburger meat, and everything else needed for the cook-in, which Bobby was planning to do himself in the large fireplace.

An assistant attorney general, William A. Geoghan, in charge of the arrangements, came to Bobby with a worried look and warned that an indoor barbecue in the office of the Attorney General might be in violation of some rule or other. Why not just bring in some chicken—already fried? Bobby, seeing his point, at first agreed, then stiffened his resolve to have the barbecue.

"You're getting old and crotchety," he told Geoghan, who was thirty-seven. "We will not get to the moon with this attitude."[6]

Bobby cooked, the kids ate, and nobody cared.

Bobby cracked the rules wide open when he took his dog to work. In the

Hickory Hill menagerie, which had a changeable population of domestic animals, never fewer in number than two dozen, a dog named Brumus and Bobby Kennedy took to each other at once. Brumus soon became almost as famous as FDR's Fala and Richard Nixon's Checkers.

Brumus was a black, sad-faced Newfoundland who loomed as large as his bulk—the size of a pony—in RFK's family life. He was given the run of the house and usually parked in back of Bobby's chair at mealtime, when he was fed from the table. Often Brumus didn't wait to be offered food: at dinner parties, he would help himself to whatever was nearest and available, to the consternation of uninitiated guests. Brumus also nipped at times, was known on at least one occasion to lift his leg and relieve himself on the stockings and shoes of a dignified matron at a Kennedy garden party, and was always in the way.

His single redeeming feature was fidelity: he loved Bobby. When Bobby left in the morning, Brumus would sit on his haunches and whine until he returned. Kennedy, whose compassion for animals was boundless, couldn't stand the thought of Brumus's daily heartbreak, so he put him in his limo and took him to the office.

Bobby protected Brumus as closely as any of his children. Once, the family went to a local horse show in which some of the children were entered. Brumus leaped into the car with them. On the grounds, friends and parents were told to remain behind a railing while the judging was going on. Everybody obeyed, but Brumus, wanting to be closer to the action, went into the enclosure, annoying the ringmaster. Trying to get him back behind the fence, he nudged Brumus with a foot.

Instantly, Bobby, white-faced with anger, leaped over the fence and shouted, "Don't kick my dog!" Flustered, the ringmaster protested he had just pushed him slightly, but Bobby was not appeased. "Don't tell me you didn't!" he snapped. "I saw you."

Standing with the family behind the fence, Jackie Kennedy sighed and muttered loud enough for LaDonna Harris, who had gone along, to hear, "There goes the chance any of the kids had to win."[7]

At the office, Brumus did not have as much opportunity for getting into trouble as he did at home, but he was no angel either. Ramsey Clark recalled, "One day, Justice John Marshall Harlan came in to swear somebody into office. Brumus, who had a head as large as a goldfish bowl, dashed around and scared a lot of people, including Justice Harlan."[8] Aides quickly restrained the exuberant Brumus.

He quickly became the center of a controversy. Dog lovers were on his side when FBI Director J. Edgar Hoover complained that Kennedy was demeaning the dignity of the Department of Justice. Then someone discovered that the Attorney General was facing a thirty-day jail term and a fine of fifty dollars for violating Section 201, Chapter 8, Title II of the Rules and Regulations for Public Buildings, which states, "Dogs and other animals, except for Seeing Eye dogs, shall not be brought upon property for other than official purposes."

After Arthur Krock, one of the country's most influential political journalists, devoted an entire column to the Brumus case in *The New York Times*,[9] Bobby capitulated. Brumus stayed home.

It was not surprising that a lasting feud developed between J. Edgar Hoover, then sixty-one and accustomed to having presidents pay him every courtesy, and his brash young boss, a quarter of a century his junior. Bobby knew this and tried, he said, "to make a fuss over him," massaging the Director's ego by arranging private lunches with him and John Kennedy, but he wasn't always successful.

Bobby was disgusted at the way Hoover was coddled by important people and the extent to which they would go to please him. Each winter, the Director was invited to spend some time in Florida as a guest in their palatial homes. One of his hosts, who had grape arbors on his grounds, knew that Hoover was especially partial to them. Unfortunately, they were out of season when the Director arrived. "So every morning early they would come and tie grapes to the trees so that when he'd come out he'd be able to pluck the grapes," Bobby said in amazement.[10]

Trouble began on Bobby's first day at work. He upset Hoover by flouting the carefully-built-up protocol of the Director's office; he dropped in without calling first.

Luthur Huston, public relations man for the outgoing Attorney General, William P. Rogers, came to Hoover's office. "I had arranged to see him at a particular time, but I had to wait because the new Attorney General was there."

"He hadn't called or made an appointment," Huston says. "He just barged in. You don't do that with Mr. Hoover. Then my turn came, and I'll tell you the maddest man I ever talked to was J. Edgar Hoover."[11]

Although Bobby described his relationship with Hoover as "reasonably cordial,"[12] this seems a somewhat rosy picture of a strained situation. Ramsey Clark says flatly, "They did not get along."[13] Courtney Evans, a section chief from the criminal division, acted as a liaison between the Attorney General and the Director of the FBI.

"Evans would go in to talk to Hoover about something Kennedy wanted, and he would abuse the Attorney General. Then Evans would go in to carry the message back to the Attorney General, and Bob would say things about Hoover."

Evans and Bobby became very friendly, a fact that did not escape Hoover's attention. He said nothing. However, the day after the assassination of John Kennedy, Hoover began to carp at Evans. When it continued, Evans queried Sullivan and Al Belmont, another top FBI man, about his future with the bureau.

"Court," Belmont said bluntly, "you don't have a future."[14]

The hapless Evans soon resigned.

Beneath the surface, a game of one-upmanship developed. Kennedy ruled that all speeches and press releases had to be cleared through his office. In addition, all announcements were to be made in the name of the Department of Justice.

Hoover was infuriated. This had never been done before. Again he bided his time. After the JFK assassination, when newspapers carried a story of an arrest made public by the FBI, Ed Guthman checked with reporters. He discovered that Cartha D. DeLoach had issued the releases in the name of the bureau, without the title of the Justice Department, and then collected them so there would be no physical evidence that Justice's name had been left off.

Hoover blamed Bobby for stories leaked from the Attorney General's office that Bobby had dropped in on Hoover and found him napping on a couch; that the FBI Director had eavesdropped on Kennedy's tapped phone only to hear him say that Hoover "is just too damned old"; and, most important, that Hoover was on his way out.

Even Ethel got into the act. At a Justice Department Christmas party, she had a short conversation with Hoover. As she was leaving, Ethel slipped a note into the FBI suggestion box. It read, "Chief Parker of Los Angeles for director of the FBI." Hoover hated Parker, an outspoken critic of the FBI.

At Bobby's request, a hot line had been installed between their offices. The first time Bobby picked it up, Helen Gandy, Hoover's secretary, answered.

"When I pick up this phone," Bobby told her coldly, "there's only one man I want to talk to—get the phone on the Director's desk."

Miss Gandy did as she was told. After Jack's death, when Bobby again picked up the hot line, Hoover let it ring. "Get that phone back on Miss Gandy's desk," he told an aide.

Bobby's habit of bypassing Hoover and going directly to agents in the field was a continuing source of irritation to the Director. One day he got even in a way that earned the Attorney General demerits with the press.

During the steel crisis, after United States Steel announced a six-dollar-a-ton rise in prices, news reports hinted that the company was pressuring Bethlehem Steel stockholders to increase its prices to conform with the new rates. After reading the accounts, Bobby told Hoover he wanted the writers of the stories who covered the stockholders' meeting questioned "immediately."

Hoover obeyed—literally—and issued orders to his agents. FBI men in Philadelphia and Wilmington, Delaware, woke reporters in the small hours for questioning. To the howls of protest that followed, Hoover explained that he was only following orders from his chief.

Kennedy supporters were surprised that the President did not fire Hoover. Ben Bradlee recalls a post-dinner conversation shortly after the election in the President-elect's Hyannis Port home with Jack and Bill Walton. Playfully, JFK posed a question.

"Okay, I'll give each one of you guys one appointment, one job to fill. What will it be?"

Quickly, Walton replied. "Replace Hoover." Bradlee suggested that Kennedy drop Allen Dulles and appoint a new head of the CIA. Jack made no comment.[15]

However, the next day, while he was waiting to interview Robert Kennedy for a *Newsweek* cover story, Bradlee overheard JFK place two telephone calls to Washington, one to Hoover and another to Dulles. He invited each man to remain in his Cabinet.

Kennedy sought to dispel the opposition of his campaign staff to Hoover's appointment by citing his narrow margin of victory, which made it "unwise" to offend the FBI chief's conservative supporters. Sophisticated Washington observers felt a more probable reason was to keep Hoover from releasing his file on JFK's sexual activities. William C. Sullivan, who rose to become the number-three man in the bureau, says Hoover "kept this kind of explosive material in his personal files, which filled four rooms on the fifth floor of headquarters."[16]

On May 10, 1962, the thirty-eighth anniversary of his appointment as Director of the FBI, Hoover received a graceful congratulatory message from John Kennedy. Bobby had planned a cake-cutting ceremony in his office. But Hoover was in a snit. He let it be known he wanted no party, and certainly not one hosted by Bobby. He spent the day at his desk, following his usual routine, and Bobby's children ate the cake.

After John Kennedy's assassination, Bobby and Hoover no longer spoke to one another. For a time, a bizarre situation existed: the FBI Director, who was under the jurisdiction of the United States Attorney General, reported directly to the White House and received his orders from President Johnson. "In every possible way he can think of," Bobby said, "he caused difficulty for me."

In 1964, Bobby was asked by Anthony Lewis, "Do you now think that Mr. Hoover is a dangerous person, or just nasty?"

"No," he replied, "I think he's dangerous."

Interviewed by John Bartlow Martin another time, he had a stronger opinion: "He's rather a psycho," he said.[17]

12

The AG—At Home

HICKORY HILL, Bobby and Ethel's estate in McLean, pointed up a striking contrast in the lifestyles of the three Kennedy brothers and their wives.

Jackie brought grace, elegance, and exquisite taste to her Georgetown home before Jack was elected President and transferred these attributes to the White House, adding a measure of glitter not seen in the mansion since Dolley Madison's day 150 years before.

The household was haute cuisine, haute culture, and, to a great extent, haute monde in her three years as First Lady. Upstairs in the family quarters, as well as on the main floor, the house had a special aura of good breeding and understated luxury. A French chef presided over the dinners of state, as well as the First Family's private meals, which Jack and Jackie would have by candlelight.[1] Jackie insisted on this; it was romantic and very, very genteel.

With the President's approval, Jackie swept away the dullness of the Eisenhowers, who would watch television while dining on trays, and made her home a focus for all the arts. Only four days after she moved in, she asked George Balanchine, the eminent choreographer, to tea and spent the afternoon discussing dance and dancers. When she heard that a young black mezzosoprano named Grace Bumbry was creating a sensation, she arranged to meet her. Isaac Stern, the violin virtuoso, and the famed cellist Leonard Rose played at a dinner honoring André Malraux, the renowned French novelist who was France's Minister of Culture. She entertained the Grand

Duchess of Luxembourg with a program of Elizabethan poetry and music and the President of the Sudan with an evening of Shakespeare. Her guests were served lobster en Bellevue, stuffed bar Polignac, supreme of capon demidoff, pheasant aspic salad, and bombe glacé mandarin, with Dom Perignon and the finest of other wines. John Kennedy once remarked with a grin, "This is becoming a sort of eating place for artists, but they never ask us out." Jackie's idea of a sporting good time was to ride at Middleburg, Virginia, in the Orange County Hunt.

Ted and Joan's five-bedroom brick house at 1607 Twenty-eighth Street in Georgetown was sedate, inside and out. Vines climbed the walls of the big square building, which squatted on a quiet street, and the children played almost noiselessly in their rooms or the hedge-enclosed garden. Mozart and Bach, turned low, was background music most of the day. Rusty, a small poodle, was the only animal around. Ted and Joan gave few parties and went to even fewer. Many evenings Ted, as the new young senator from Massachusetts, worked in his study, while Joan watched television with the children and put them to bed, afterward reading quietly or playing the piano before retiring herself. Later, they moved to a large gray-shingled house perched on a bluff at 636 Chain Bridge Road, a mile from Hickory Hill. Costing almost $750,000, an enormous sum in those days, it had 200-year-old paneling gathered from all across the country, white damask walls in the dining room, a cork tennis court, a forty-four-foot swimming pool, and a staff of four to take care of it all. Still, while the luxury level had been raised significantly, the low-key atmosphere had not: the children still played quietly, the parties were few, and the only animals were inanimate ones from a toy farm.[2]

Hickory Hill—official address: 4700 Chain Bridge Road—which became the best-known residence in the nation, next to the White House, was nothing like either of these.

It was Hyannis Port in the growing-up years crossed with the Skakel household, a day camp for hyperactive children, and an undisciplined frat house. Ethel herself correctly labeled it a "madhouse" and, even before the 1960 elections, admitted to being depressed when she returned from a visit to Jackie's orderly, tight-ship Georgetown house. Her own establishment was messy, mussy, slightly daffy, and entirely unpredictable. Even Bobby junior felt overwhelmed. Having lived there eight of his ten years, he pleaded to be sent to boarding school, "to get away from this confusing family." Bobby senior, seeing his point, sent him to Georgetown Prep.

Little Bobby himself contributed to the confusion by maintaining a zoo in the basement consisting of a reptile house, home for a varying population of snakes and iguanas; caged birds; members of the rodent family; and, for a brief period, a coati. Often tamed as pets, coatis are gregarious animals with long bodies and tails and upturned snouts.

Bobby's coati was allowed the run of the basement until the day he attacked Ethel. Apparently frightened, he leaped on her as she was showing Bobby's zoo to some journalists and dug his sharp teeth into her stockingless legs. The coati was banished.

The estate also lost its resident seal, one of the dozens of livestock on the premises. Kept behind a chain-link fence not far from the pool, the sixty-pound baby seal named Sandy performed for guests, who were charmed but went away wondering why anybody would want one. Sandy ate ten pounds of fish each day and soon learned to flip out of confinement and waddle down to the parking lot. One day, Sandy appeared in the doorway of a store a mile away, terrifying the owner and his customers. That did it— next day he was shipped off to the Washington Zoo.

"The house and grounds were anarchic," one Kennedy friend of long standing recalled. "Orderliness was unheard of. Children and animals were everywhere, inside and outside. You'd see them charging around the lawn, riding horses, splashing in the pool, and blowing up balloons, which they would burst behind you.

"There was a jukebox at the largest of the two pools—one was for beginning swimmers—which was always turned up to high volume. Once I saw John Kennedy hold a conference with high-level advisers at the poolside with the damned jukebox going full blast and kids racing and diving into the water. I got to wondering what important matter of state was decided, and if the participants got it right."

His bemused recollections are echoed by visitors, most of whom remember the place fondly, although there were some notable exceptions. One of the latter was a young member of European royalty who walked up to a smiling Ethel on arriving and shook her outstretched right hand. Ethel whipped out a tube of shaving cream she had been hiding behind her back in her other hand and sprayed him full in the face.

By 1961, Ethel and Bobby had seven children, with four more to come. Gradually the twelve-room house was expanded to nineteen rooms, with a barn added for horses and a huge bathhouse constructed near the swimming pool, which also served as a private movie theater. All the rooms were connected by a communications system that, as one observer stated, "would do credit to the Pentagon." All the rooms, too, were filled Kennedy style, with photographs—pictures of baptisms, swimming and boat races, campaigns, and—in places of honor—the inauguration and the parade that followed.

Five swings and a rope ladder hung from towering trees; a pony and cart provided transportation for the children; a tree house was a refuge if they needed one; the paddock contained hurdles for practice jumping; and all were in use most of the time.

The number of help employed to keep the household running ranged between ten and fifteen. There were always two cooks, a governess, laundress, nurse, several maids, a groom for the larger livestock, and often two secretaries. Ethel bought expensive furnishings—an Aubusson carpet for the living room, Etruscan pottery, French period furniture, a sofa from one of the palaces of Emperor Francis Joseph of Austria. But since none of the rooms was ever off limits to the children, the expensive antiques bore scars, and the carpets were stained.

Bobby and Ethel's room, done in pink and white, was the size of a classroom, with an emperor bed, a thick rug, a small desk for Ethel, and, slipped beneath the glass of the night table, a list of people to call if needed: the doctor, the dentist, the police, the fire department.

In a small study on the main floor was a picture of President Kennedy with two of Bobby's children peering from behind the desk. On it, JFK had written, "Dear Bobby, they TOLD me you had your people placed throughout the government!"

Bobby and Ethel's parties were as unbridled as Jack and Jackie's and Ted and Joan's were decorous. Nobody ever broke a bone at the other brothers' homes, but chipped fingers, wrist fractures, loosened teeth, torn muscles and ligaments, and even broken legs were not uncommon at Hickory Hill. Pat Newcomb broke several ribs when she was persuaded to ride a horse for her first time and fell. Off the premises, Ed Guthman attended a physical fitness party at the Chevy Chase ice skating rink, and before it was half over he was significantly less fit than when he arrived. An ambulance took him away when he fell and broke his arm.

In sharp contrast to White House fare, nobody ever had anything French-sounding at Ethel's table. She served lamb chops, chicken, steak, roast beef, clam chowder, baked potatoes, green salads, milk, and ice cream with chocolate sauce.

Ethel's energy astounded everyone, and dismayed more than a few. "It would finish off anyone else," said Lord Harlech, the former British ambassador to Washington. "I remember playing a hard game of tennis with her only six weeks before one of her children was born, and going out on a family boating picnic with her a week after the birth."[3] She won high marks for her broken-field running from Whizzer White, who couldn't tag her in a touch football game, but low ones from one guest when she called for a footrace just after they had finished a large dinner. All but this visitor dashed after Ethel. "I've already had one coronary," he said as he found his way to an easy chair, "and I'm not looking for another."

Bobby, too, was apt to challenge his guests to physical encounters. One day he called for a push-up contest. First, he easily dusted off Kenny O'Donnell, then took on author Theodore White. Bobby, to his chagrin, pooped out at thirty-two, while Teddy kept on. Then Bobby proposed a round of arm wrestling, pitting White against Georgi N. Bolshakov, a Communist editor and interpreter with whom Bobby had become very friendly and who served as a conduit to Moscow. (We will soon hear more about Bolshakov, who became known as "Bobby's Russian.")

White, short but muscular, soon had Georgi's arm pressed back close to the table. For Ethel, peering from inches away, it was the United States versus the U.S.S.R. "We're winning," she shouted. "Our side is winning!" When Georgi, violating arm wrestling rules, raised his elbow, she shrieked: "You're cheating! He's cheating! He's *cheating*!"

All her guests fascinated Ethel and the children. One day LaDonna Harris, who is part Indian and was then married to Senator Fred Harris of Oklahoma, took her Comanche grandmother for a visit. The children were fascinated by the little old lady, who wore a long dress and had her hair in braids. Kerry told them she wanted to draw a picture and ran into the den.

She returned with a drawing of a large Indian tepee. "Mrs. Harris," she asked, "do you live in a tepee?"

"No, Kerry," LaDonna answered. "We all have houses now. Grandmother lives in the country but she has a very nice house."

Ethel spoke up. "You know," she told LaDonna, "I have always envisioned you growing up in a tepee." Relating the story, Mrs. Harris observed, "She would often say things like that."[4]

Much has been written about Hickory Hill pool-dunkings and, on the other end of the intellectual scale, the monthly seminars. The first were childish nonsense, ended by Presidential order when the wide publicity threatened to make the Administration seem like freshman hell week; the second were a more significant milestone in Bobby's growth than has been generally noted.

What the family called "the Boat Treatment" was given to unsuspecting visitors who would wander too close to poolside. Some Kennedy, usually Ethel, would push him/her in, clothes and all. Ethel herself was not exempt. "She and Bobby showed their affection for each other," LaDonna Harris recalled. "They might be walking by the side of the pool, arms around each other—and then Bobby would push her in."

Parties were the times when the "treatment" was given most frequently. At their twelfth wedding anniversary party, June 17, 1962, attended by 300 dignitaries, the historian Arthur Schlesinger, Jr., Peter Lawford, and Ethel herself (wearing a new red evening gown) found themselves in the water. Others dunked at various times included Pierre Salinger, Senator Kenneth Keating of New York, and any number of lesser lights. Once Ted Kennedy, who had surprised everyone by shedding his brash jock image and behaving as a model young freshman senator, got into the spirit and jumped into the pool fully clothed. His father took him aside and gave him hell. When the "treatment" threatened to make the Administration look ridiculous, President Kennedy told Ethel and Bobby to stop.

The seminars, impiously dubbed "Bobby's Night School" and "Hickory Hill U" by New Frontiersmen, were monthly gatherings to which selected members of the Administration were invited. They heard lectures by sociologists, philosophers, historians, and scientists on abstruse philosophical sciences, the broad sweep of American history, and the relationship between economic development and democratic institutions.

Bobby would let nothing interfere with the seminars, not even an invitation to a private dinner at the White House. "Bobby can't come to see us tonight," Jackie told the President one day, "because some professor is lecturing about space or something."

The President, amused by the seminars, told his close aides that his brother was more at home, and more useful to him, by finding realistic solutions to practical problems rather than pondering the life and destiny of man.

If Jackie and the President did not take Bobby's night school seriously, he did. The seminars were the outward signs that the reeducation of Bobby Kennedy had begun. He had started to examine himself and had discovered that he had absorbed all too little at Harvard and only law at law school.

"The guy realized how little he really knew about literature, philosophy, history," Kenny O'Donnell asserted. "He told me he hadn't read enough books at school and wished he had. Well, he was right. At school, I hadn't read enough either. We spent a lot of time talking about politics and, of course, athletics, but not enough in reading."[5]

Bobby was a major power in the Administration, and he knew it. But he also was keenly aware of his limitations. These two facts of life at age thirty-five drove him to want to read, question, and learn more than he had ever done before.

He asked questions constantly of brilliant younger men and brilliant older ones. His intellectual insecurity made him tense and nervous as he bulled ahead, much as he had done on the football field, asking, prodding, eliciting as much information as he could.

From time to time, Cabinet members and senators would come to lunch with the law clerks of the Supreme Court justices. One day, Bobby attended and sat near young Peter Edelman, then clerking for Justice Arthur Goldberg, and later an aide on Kennedy's Senate staff.

"All the time this tough guy was asking questions," Edelman remembered, "his hands were shaking under the table and were knotted up with one another and moving back and forth, and his knees were going up and down a mile a minute. . . . It did mean that he was not all that cool a cookie. In addition to that, his mastery of the kinds of questions that were asked him, and you can imagine the Supreme Court law clerks were a very snotty crew, was quite impressive."[6]

"He came to understand," declared Harris Wofford, "that his wisdom consisted in knowing what he did not know, and taking it as a mandate to learn."[7]

He began to read more widely in history, biography, and philosophy, to listen to serious music, watch great drama, and learn about ballet. He listened to recordings of Shakespearean plays while shaving. Soon, like his brother, he would take a speed-reading course. Books by Goethe, Churchill, and Robert Frost were stacked on the night table.

Moreover, he was beginning to see the country and the world around him, and he was not liking what he saw. He was starting to tune in to the new generation's feelings of emptiness, which matched his own, and its yearning for a common purpose in which it could believe. He was beginning to glimpse, though just barely, that something was not quite right, that national achievement could not be measured by the size of the gross national product. Penalties in the form of increased air pollution, the death of lakes and streams, and health-wrecking work in mines and many types of farms and factories must be paid for the endless amassing of goods by which we judged economic progress.

"In a few short years," Harris Wofford said, "this man would switch from being a terribly authoritarian, terribly rigid, terribly illiberal person to being exactly the opposite."[8]

The process was beginning.

As Bobby emerged from the shelter of his privileged world, his father's influence diminished. And then, as sometimes happens in life, an unexpected cataclysmic event occurred that instantaneously reversed their roles, and Joe Kennedy became the dependent.

In December 1961, while playing golf at the Palm Beach course, Joe felt dizzy and faint after playing the sixth hole, and his niece, Ann Gargan, took him home. Hours later, he was rushed by ambulance to St. Mary's Hospital, unconscious. Tests revealed he had suffered a massive stroke caused by a blood clot in an artery of the brain.

The news was telephoned to Bobby in Washington, and he called Jack at the White House. The President had just returned from a trip to Latin America, climaxed by a stopover to visit his parents. The brothers boarded Air Force One for the flight back to Palm Beach.

The Kennedys maintained a vigil at the hospital for two days. On the third morning, Joe's eyelids flickered, and he regained consciousness. However, the stroke had left him sadly handicapped. The muscles on the right side of his face were slack, distorting his face. From time to time, he drooled, and, often, tears filled his eyes and ran down his cheeks as he was unable to make himself understood.

After his discharge from St. Mary's, Joe recuperated at home and then entered Horizon House at the Rusk Institute for Rehabilitation in New York for physical and speech therapy. Bobby, who accompanied his father, sought to lighten the tenseness of the occasion. Poking around the private tiled bathroom, he flushed the toilet. "Everything works, Dad," he reported.

Over the next years, his father's illness brought great sadness into Bobby's life. Rita Dallas, Joe's nurse, reveals that Bobby's eyes would "fill with tears, and a look of deep sorrow would cloud his face," as he watched his father struggle through his therapy regimen.[9]

Once when he and President Kennedy were in New York City at the same time, they decided to call on Joe together. Informed of the impending visit, Joe excitedly selected his clothes with care, refusing to put on his leg braces.

Mrs. Dallas wheeled Joe to the patio where Bobby and Jack, accompanied by a doctor, soon joined him. As the doctor explained Joe's progress, Joe became increasingly agitated and suddenly tried to rise out of his chair, staggering without his brace.

Bobby grabbed for his father, and Joe, struggling to get free, began to hit him with his cane. Ducking to avoid the flailing cane, Bobby and the doctor got Joe back in his chair. Bobby whispered to his father, "Dad, if you want to get up, give me your arm, and I'll hold you till you get your balance."

He kneeled beside the wheelchair. "That's what I'm here for, Dad," Bobby said. "Just to give you a hand when you need it. You've done that for me all my life, so why don't I do the same for you now?"

For a few moments, a tense situation involving a painful dilemma had existed. Had the patriarch, in his uncontrollable excitement, attacked the President of the United States with his cane, the Secret Service agents standing nearby would have had to restrain him forcibly. But if they had done so, according to Dallas, both sons would most likely have stopped the agents from performing their duty of protecting the President. "None of us believed that either son would have allowed their father to be manhandled regardless of his behavior," she said.[10]

When Bobby was at Hyannis Port, he insisted that attendants notify him when his father was taken to the pool for water therapy. He would come loping across the lawn and dive into the water with Joe. Sitting on the edge of the pool, he dangled his legs and applauded encouragingly as Joe performed his exercises. Senator Harris says that Bobby would excuse himself from his guests about an hour before dinner and go to the big house for a one-sided conversation with his father.

Later, when he campaigned for the United States Senate, Bobby would discuss campaign strategy with Joe. Patiently, he would explain his plans and ask his father's advice. Joe, of course, while he may have understood, could not give intelligible answers.

It was full circle. But now the strength and determination and driving passion to win had shifted from father to son.*

* Joe Kennedy outlived both his sons. He died in November 1969, a few days before the sixth anniversary of Jack's assassination and a year and five months after Bobby's death.

13

The Man to See

*I*N THE EARLY MONTHS of the new Administration, writer Budd Schulberg, at work in his home in Mexico City, got a phone call from Jerry Wald, the movie producer, in Los Angeles.

Bobby Kennedy, Wald said, wanted him to write the screenplay for his book about the rackets investigations, *The Enemy Within*. Wald, expecting a shout of exultation from Schulberg, heard instead, "Jerry, wait a minute . . . I need time to think." Wald explained that Kennedy had been impressed with Budd's treatment of labor racketeering in his film *On the Waterfront,* winner of an Academy Award in 1954, and felt he could do a similarly excellent job with his book about the work of the McClellan committee.*

Schulberg still hesitated. Recalling the conversation, he declared, "I said something like, 'If he turns out to be difficult . . . or if it turns out I just plain don't like him . . .' "

Wald exploded. "Don't *like* him! You're talking about the number-two man in the United States!"

Word had gotten around. Even the President had heard. A few days after Bobby took over as Attorney General, a direct line was installed on his desk to the Oval Office. One day it rang when the President was in the midst of

---

* Joe Kennedy checked the contract Bobby had signed with Twentieth Century-Fox, which was to release the film, and told the studio that some clauses had to be rewritten. When an executive explained that the Attorney General of the United States himself had given his approval, Joe, who had spent four years in Hollywood, wasn't impressed. "What the hell does he know about it?" he said. Wald died in July 1963, and the project was eventually abandoned.

an important conference with his chief aides. Kennedy picked it up, smilingly telling the group around the office, "Will you excuse me a moment? This is the second most powerful man calling."[1]

John Kennedy may have smiled when he said it, but others did not. Bobby was indeed the most influential person in his Administration, his brother's most trusted, most intimate agent and adviser.

He was the President's number-one dispenser of patronage. He was John Kennedy's chief—and often his only—confidant. He was the foreman who carried out what the boss wanted in every department of government, in every area, foreign and domestic. He was also John Kennedy's conscience, trying (but not succeeding too well) to damp down his brother's sexual fires, so that they would not scorch his reputation.

The brothers spoke to each other on the telephone five to ten times daily. Bobby, who had free access to the Oval Office, was there at least twice, sometimes more, each day.

He was problem solver, troubleshooter, and the man to see about jobs, as J. Edward Day, the Postmaster General, began to discover even before he was officially appointed. On December 16, the day before John Kennedy named him to the post, Day flew to Palm Beach aboard the *Caroline* for meetings about the shape of the new Administration.

"Both Kennedys briefed me about my new job," Day said. "Significantly, Bobby did most of the talking."

Day declared, "He passed on applicants for the top, appointive positions in the [Post Office] department. He telephoned in person or sent word through his staff about certain appointments of postmasters and rural letter carriers."

No job was too small to concern him. Once, he talked by telephone three times in a single day with the PMG on the appointment of a single rural letter carrier in a small Mississippi town.[2]

Away from the White House, the brothers communicated constantly— "almost telepathically," Ted Sorensen said, one seeming to know exactly what the other was thinking before a word was spoken. Later at the Cape, Nurse Rita Dallas, in charge of Joe Kennedy's care after he suffered his stroke, noticed the same phenomenon. "They constantly communicated by sight, even when they were not talking together," she observed. When they did confer in words, they were a riveting sight, sitting hunched over, face to face, Bobby doing most of the talking, and the President listening intently.[3]

Another time, the head of the Democratic Committee of a large, heavily populated state emerged from an interview with President Kennedy under the impression that the decision on job appointments would be his and his alone. When he reported this to a Presidential aide, he was told he had got it all wrong. "All recommendations are to clear through the Attorney General," the aide said.

One day Bobby slid down in his big chair in his office at the Department of Justice, ran his hand through his hair, and said with a puzzled look on his face, "Let's see. What am I doing? I've got so many jobs, I can't remember."

He may have been joking, but his wide-ranging positions in the Administration, official and unofficial, would have confused anybody. He even had a hand in Presidential public relations.

When writer Gene Schoor wanted to write a biography of John Kennedy for young people, he called Lem Billings, who advised him, "Get Bobby's okay." Schoor made an appointment with the Attorney General.

"He looked at me with the coldest, steeliest blue eyes I had ever seen," Schoor recalled. "He said, 'Lemoyne told me you were a boxer in college. Were you a street fighter?' "

Schoor bristled. "I never had a street fight in my life," he said.

"What kind of a record did you have?"

Schoor, irritated by the line of questioning, which he felt was far removed from his qualifications to write a book, replied with some asperity, "I won the national welterweight championship, and I was on the Olympic boxing team, and I coached boxing, too." Then, his voice rising, he leaned forward and said, "And I can beat the shit out of anybody in the Administration!"

Bobby stared, then burst out laughing. "Damn it," he said, "you're on our ball club." Schoor had met Bobby's standards of combativeness and athleticism, and got his interviews with the President.[4]

He was called a "major power in U.S. government," and with reason: whenever a crisis arose, and there were many, the President would call the department head involved, then invariably follow with the order: "Get Bobby." Bobby advised, and often took over, in problems of all stages of severity. Some examples:

Small: The Post Office Department has jurisdiction over some 25,000 leases of property throughout the country. When a controversy erupted over a continuation of one of them, Bobby sent a personal aide to investigate the situation.

Medium: Rafael Trujillo, the corrupt dictator of the Dominican Republic, was assassinated on May 30, 1961, after ruling the nation since 1930. John Kennedy was on his triumphant state visit to France with Jackie, who dazzled the French people. As soon as Bobby learned about the murder, he established a command post on the seventh floor of the State Department and took personal charge of the situation.

He approved sending U.S. warships to the area as a show of force, to back Dominicans who were opposed to Trujillo yet were also anti-Communists. When the President returned from abroad, he was unperturbed by his brother's assumption of the powers of Commander-in-Chief. Bobby acted, he explained, "because I was out of the country." He did not mention that Lyndon Baines Johnson, constitutionally empowered to act in the President's absence, was in his vice presidential offices and available.

Large: In the Bay of Pigs, Berlin, missile, and other major crises of the Kennedy Administration, Bobby was at his brother's side, helping to get things done.

He was as blunt as he had been during the campaign. Rank, age, and a distinguished career did not spare anyone who, Bobby felt, was not working fast enough or giving the President his fullest measure of support.

Averell Harriman, who had served as governor of New York and was then Assistant Secretary of State, had already become a close family friend, dining often at Hickory Hill. Later, Bobby would name his ninth child Douglas Harriman. Yet, when Harriman acted too slowly on an order Bobby had issued curbing the travel of U.S. diplomats in Eastern Europe, he became furious.

Harriman was a dinner guest when the subject came up. When Bobby heard the order had not yet been implemented, he struck the table, rattling the dishes, and said angrily to the seventy-year-old diplomat, "You get on that first thing in the morning!"

But Harriman understood. "His [Bobby's] value was in his most extraordinary loyalty, his understanding of his brother's objectives, and his fierce instinct to protect him in every way he knew."[5]

Bobby called Chester Bowles, the Under Secretary of State, a "gutless bastard" because he opposed sending American troops to the Dominican Republic during the turmoil that followed the slaying of Trujillo.

When he thought the CIA wasn't working hard enough on the Cuba problem after the Bay of Pigs, he was less than gentle with Deputy Director Richard Bissell, whom he told to "get off your ass about Cuba."

Jack Kennedy was well aware that Bobby was trigger-tempered, overly abrasive at times, and more ready to knock heads together than to use them wisely. "He can be a pain in the ass sometimes," he acknowledged to an aide.[6] The President had recruited brilliant people who could, and did, light up the sky with their ideas, but, he said, "the problem is to make them work." Bobby did that better than anybody. "He's the best organizer I've ever seen," Jack said. Even in touch football, it was Bobby's team that won, though the sides were evenly balanced. "He created the best plays," said Jack.[7]

The President trusted Bobby, the pragmatist, to tell him if an idea was woven of moonbeams and good intentions, or if it could actually work; to crack through the outer shell of a problem quickly and get to the core; to warn him of self-serving individuals and groups; and to do all this and more with no regard for personal gain.

Nevertheless, Jack Kennedy did not heed his brother's advice all the time, often learning the hard way that he should have listened.

In August 1961, Bobby and Ethel visited the Ivory Coast in West Africa as his brother's emissary to help commemorate its first birthday. He returned home with deep suspicions of the left-leaning Kwame Nkrumah, president of Ghana, the Ivory Coast's neighbor to the east. Ghana, he told the President, should be denied the $135 million loan it was seeking for construction of a power project on the Volta River.

But John Kennedy had liked Nkrumah when he had visited the White House four months earlier. He had been touched by a hand-written note on legal paper vowing friendship to America, which Nkrumah had scribbled aboard his plane before he left Washington. Besides, a dam on the Volta would open the way to a bright economic future for Ghana.

That summer, however, Nkrumah was traveling around to Iron Curtain nations, expressing undying affection. Bobby grew angrier as Nkrumah's embrace of communism became warmer. In the fall, the issue of the loan came up at a meeting of the National Security Council.

Usually, Bobby attended every session, refusing to sit at the table; instead, he stood, leaning against the wall, a little to the right of the President, his eyes darting from one member to another, listening, watching, absorbing. Jack Kennedy polled the members, who agreed to the loan.

"The Attorney General has not spoken," Kennedy said, not looking at his brother. "But I can feel the hot breath of his disapproval on the back of my neck." Everyone smiled except Bobby as the money was okayed.

Bobby had lost, but John Kennedy's faith in his brother's judgment was strengthened immeasurably when Nkrumah began turning his country into a dictatorship, cruelly stamping out his enemies and establishing himself as the country's sole ruler. "In 1963," wrote Arthur Schlesinger, "Kennedy evidently wished he had been tougher in the first place."[8]

There were other times when Bobby didn't get his way.

In 1962, he wanted his friend Arthur Goldberg, then Secretary of Labor, to serve on a review committee overseeing counterintelligence activities against guerrilla forces in Laos and Southeast Asia. General Maxwell D. Taylor, chairman of the Joint Chiefs of Staff, who headed the special group (CI), did not want Goldberg on the committee. Bobby insisted, but Taylor would not yield, even when the other members, polled by Bobby, approved.

Bobby blew up. "Well, shit!" he exclaimed as he left the room. "The second most important man in the world just lost another one."

He had another tantrum a short time later when he was questioning a representative of the Agency for International Development, which worked closely with the CIA in intelligence operations. U. Alexis Johnson, a member of the special group, who later became chairman, recalled, ''Bobby got up and slammed his chair on the floor and stalked out of the room, slamming the door.'' Experiences such as this led Johnson, a Deputy Under Secretary of State, to give up the chairmanship of the group.

Jim McShane, Bobby's portly aide in the rackets investigation, who was a great friend and admirer, thought a little lesson in humility would do no harm. He contrived a beauty.

One day, McShane, who became chief United States Marshal for the District of Columbia, invited Bobby to come with him to a well-known Manhattan restaurant and bar. ''To meet some New York friends I haven't seen in some time,'' he explained. Bobby went along, expecting to be the center of attention, as usual. Jim had other plans.

He had instructed his pals on how to act. When he and Bobby walked in, everyone surrounded Jim, greeted him effusively, and hoisted him atop the bar to make a speech. Bobby, elbowed aside, was completely ignored.

After Jim's little talk, his friends swept out the door with him, leaving Bobby alone, nursing a glass of beer and wondering why nobody recognized him.[9]

The Ivory Coast trip was followed soon after by a global journey as the President's ambassador without portfolio. He and Ethel were accorded honors approaching those of a head of state. Bobby had high-level discussions with kings, princes, prime ministers, and dictators.

He set out with Ethel in January 1962, for Japan, to damp down anti-American feelings, which had run so high that President Eisenhower had been forced to cancel his trip there just before he left office. They spent several days in Japan, mostly trying to shout down hecklers at universities, which Bobby did superbly well.

In Indonesia, he was instructed to placate President Achmed Sukarno and try to keep him from grabbing West New Guinea, thus averting a war between Indonesia and The Netherlands. Bobby didn't get along with Sukarno, partly because of his politics, which he felt were immoral, and partly because of his sexual tastes, which offended his puritanical soul. Sukarno's luxurious palace was decorated with photographs and sculptures of nude women in the most explicit poses. ''I think he's got very few redeeming features,'' Bobby concluded.

Bobby made no startling diplomatic coups, though he earned high praise from veteran American diplomats. On their return, one newsman observed, ''Bobby made the speeches, but this was Ethel's trip.''

Her vivacity, adventurousness, and occasional gaffes and naive remarks enlivened the journey, captivating (and sometimes baffling) her hosts. In

149

Djakarta, Indonesia, she blacked out Sukarno's entire Presidential palace when she inserted her hair dryer into an electrical outlet and blew every fuse. Earlier in Tokyo, Bobby had wisely declined an invitation to test his skill with a judo expert at an exhibition, but Ethel cheerfully agreed to go to the mat with a woman specialist. She was sorry even before she left her chair. As soon as she reached out her hand, the woman applied pressure that made Ethel yelp with pain, and the bout never began. In Rome, Ethel got aboard a motor scooter presented to her in a restaurant by foreign journalists. Starting it up, she raced out the door and into the Piazza Fontanella Borghese, where she sideswiped a car and bruised her leg.

On the return leg in West Germany, Bobby's Irish wit got him in trouble in West Berlin with literal-minded Mayor Willy Brandt. Ethel and Bobby had been joined by Teddy. Brandt was host that evening at the dinner honoring the Kennedys. Rising, he proposed a toast to the President, government, and people of the United States.

Bobby stood and, with a straight face, raised his glass and said, "That's the three of us—the President, that's my brother; the government, that's me." Then, turning to Teddy, he added, "And you're the people." Brandt, jotting his reactions into his journal, took Bobby's remark seriously, saying the Kennedys' "political expansion" caused him concern. If Bobby and the Kennedys were contemplating a dynasty, as many believed, he would hardly have announced the ambition in West Germany.

Bobby's trips as his brother's ambassador drew criticism from Republicans, who wondered why a young lawyer, almost totally inexperienced in diplomacy, was being entrusted with missions of such sensitivity and gravity. Representative John V. Lindsay of New York, a strong liberal despite his Republican affiliation, wrote to Secretary of State Dean Rusk: "We question whether it is necessary for you and your office to be either burdened or embarrassed by freewheeling foreign missions on the part of highly placed amateurs."

At the same time, Richard Nixon, who had retired to private life, surprised everyone by saying on national television, "Except for lack of experience, he [Bobby] has many of the qualifications that could make him a very effective leader in the field of foreign policy. He's tough-minded, he's quick, he's intelligent. He is one who has a tremendous will to win."

Bobby Kennedy's role in White House decision making was galling to Lyndon Johnson. A proud man, he expected to be called upon for advice and counsel after the election.

This didn't happen. Invariably, Jack turned to Bobby instead of his Vice President.

"Every time they have a conference, don't kid anybody about who is the

150

top adviser,'' Johnson remarked bitterly. "It's not McNamara, the Joint Chiefs of Staff, or anyone else like that. Bobby is first in, last out. Bobby is the boy he listens to.''

Not only wasn't LBJ the number-two man, his brother Sam said, "He was the lowest man on the totem pole.''

Nor was that all. Lyndon was openly snubbed even by second-echelon White House staffers who mimicked "Uncle Cornpone's'' southwestern twang.

"Some of their smart-aleck jokes extended to my sister-in-law,'' Sam asserted. Jackie Kennedy had observed during the campaign, "Lady Bird would crawl down Pennsylvania Avenue on broken glass for Lyndon.'' The wisecrack, widely repeated, had reached Johnson. Sam Johnson said that the "supposedly civilized New Frontiersmen had a great time repeating that remark.'' He added that Lady Bird would do precisely that, as would Eleanor Roosevelt, Bess Truman, and Mamie Eisenhower for their husbands.

Sam was not one to turn the other cheek. "Still,'' he said, the venom dripping, "I'm not too surprised that Mrs. Onassis would look down her elegant nose at that kind of wifely loyalty.''

The new crowd's scornful attitude toward Johnson's nowhere status in the capital was a burr under the saddle, hurting and infuriating him, because he knew he could neither remove it nor fight back. He suffered through the three "most miserable years of his life,'' according to Sam Johnson. Lyndon had to endure a constant stream of "in'' digs, the most popular of which on the cocktail circuit was, "Say, whatever happened to LBJ,'' followed by raucous laughter.[10]

Knowing this, he would be present at conferences in the White House on matters of high importance to which the President courteously invited him, but he would sit silently, his head resting on his hand, rarely offering any comment. He was grim-faced, as though he opposed the actions being discussed but wasn't about to say so. Often, he was simply sulking.

The feud between Bobby and Lyndon, one of the most bitter in recent political history, had some strange touches.

On the surface, both men frequently exhibited civility and at times even graciousness toward the other. Bobby, for example, was always correct in speeches he made that referred to Johnson and in personal meetings he had with him. Numerous times profane remarks about LBJ were attributed to him in the press, but Fred Dutton, who worked closely with him in the 1968 campaign and was a special JFK assistant, said, "I never heard Bobby call him a son of a bitch, although I read it in the paper.''[11]

When Adam Walinsky, one of Kennedy's bright, though outspoken, young aides voiced uncomplimentary sentiments about Johnson, Bobby rebuked him sharply: "Okay, Adam, that'll be enough of that.''

Johnson was personally upset when one of Bobby's sons, using an umbrella as a parachute, jumped from a roof at the Cape and fell through a greenhouse. He telephoned, offering to send a Presidential helicopter to move the boy to a hospital if the family wished. When Kathleen fell off a horse, Johnson sent her a bowl of tight yellow roses in the shape of her mount with a personal letter.

Loyal to the President, Johnson did not oppose the appointment of Robert as Attorney General, spicing his approval by comparing the two Kennedys thus to Bobby Baker, then Secretary of the Senate: "Jack is thoughtful, but that snot-nosed brother . . ."

It was just one of many choice terms Lyndon applied to Robert, for if Bobby would not tolerate harsh words about the Vice President in his presence, LBJ had no such inhibition. A man with a wide-ranging profane vocabulary, he used some of his ripest expressions when discussing Bobby, to whom he would refer as "that little shit-ass," "little runt," "punk kid," "little bastard," and terms even more colorful. Bobby was rarely just plain "Bobby" to him, but "that son of a bitch Bobby."

The animosity between Bobby and LBJ had its roots in the 1960 primaries, when Johnson and Jack Kennedy were both seeking the Democratic Party nomination for President in a hard campaign fraught with public charges and leaked information.

Lyndon Johnson had infuriated all the Kennedys, but especially Bobby, at the Washington state caucus when he made a caustic reference to the patriarch. "I wasn't any Chamberlain-umbrella policy man. I never thought Hitler was right," Johnson had said, clearly alluding to Joe Kennedy's support of the British Prime Minister, Neville Chamberlain, who had tried to appease Hitler in 1939.

Said Kenny O'Donnell, "I've seen Bobby mad, but never as mad as the day he heard what Johnson had said about his father."[12]

Johnson flared up when rumors were spread in Dallas, Houston, and Austin, just before the Texas state convention, that he had died of a heart attack. LBJ told everyone whom he suspected: "It was that little bastard Bobby."

Bobby smoldered, then exploded a short while afterward in a coffee shop filled with convention delegates. In Los Angeles, standing in line at the Biltmore for a breakfast table, he was spied by Bobby Baker, who was already seated with his wife Dorothy. Baker invited him to join them. After they had ordered, Baker said he felt Teddy had been "a little rough" when he said in Texas that Johnson had not recovered fully from his heart attack, which he had suffered five years before.

Bobby became enraged. "You've got a nerve," he said, his voice rising. "Lyndon Johnson has compared my father to the Nazis, and John Connally and India Edwards* lied in saying my brother was dying of Addison's disease.

"You Johnson people are running a stinking damned campaign, and you're going to get yours when the time comes." Baker reported that Bobby's face had become flushed with rage and his fists were clenched.

An incident that fanned the flames of hostility to a roaring intensity was revealed in an oral history by Correspondent Peter Lisagor, the Chicago newsman.

During the primaries, Lyndon Johnson appeared on a "Face the Nation" program in Oklahoma City. Lisagor, accompanying Johnson, was aboard the plane after the program, seated next to Mike Marlow, its producer. Johnson, prowling through the plane, sat down next to them.

Lisagor began to question Johnson about the Kennedys, and all of his pent-up hostility poured out.

"Jack Kennedy is a scrawny little fellow with rickets and God-knows-what other kinds of diseases," Johnson said. "Have you ever seen his ankles? They're about so round [making a small circlet with his fingers]. If he ever got elected President of the United States, his father, Old Joe Kennedy, would run the country."

He continued in that vein for a long time.

Word filtered back to Bobby, who remembered but said nothing. One day, after the convention, he was flying in a campaign plane with Lisagor as one of the correspondents. As Pete was walking down the aisle, he felt a tug on his sleeve. It was Bob Kennedy, who looked up at him and said, "I hear you have an interesting story to tell about how Lyndon Johnson feels about Jack."

Lisagor hesitated. A kindly man, he did not want to hurt feelings or fan the flames of a feud he knew existed. "Well, I do, Bob," he replied, "but I don't see why I should tell that story now. You're all in bed together now."

Bob insisted. "Please tell it to me, will you?" he asked. Lisagor still saw no point in opening wounds, but Bob "beseeched" him to talk, and finally he did. "I'll use all the language he used in telling me," he said.

And he did. Bob sat silently throughout the recital. "I don't think I left out a single word," Lisagor said, "four-letter or otherwise." Bobby finally said, "I knew he hated Jack, but I didn't think he hated him that much."[13]

---

* Connally, who would later become governor of Texas, and Edwards, a powerful figure in the Democratic Party, were leading backers of LBJ. In Los Angeles, they had called a press conference at which they questioned Kennedy's life expectancy because of reports that he had Addison's disease. Edwards said Jack's illness made him look "like a spavined hunchback."

14

Three Worst Foreign Crises

"**W**HAT TIMES stand out in your mind, when it came right down to the crunch, when you were deeply and closely involved?" asked journalist John Bartlow Martin, who later became ambassador to the Dominican Republic.

Robert Kennedy replied, "The major, most difficult foreign times were the Cuba Bay of Pigs, the Berlin crisis of 1961, and Cuba '62."

CUBA ONE

The ill-fated landings at the Bay of Pigs were the first major defeat in John Kennedy's life, and from then on he wanted Bobby, with his pragmatic, clearheaded approach to problems, at all critical meetings. He told Kenny O'Donnell, "I should have had Bobby in on that from the start."[1]

The "start" actually took place before his presidency began. In March 1960, during Eisenhower's second term, the CIA and the Joint Chiefs of Staff began a plan of covert action designed to overthrow the Castro government. By April 1961, some 1,200 Cuban exiles had been armed and trained at bases in Central America and Florida. A fleet of World War II B-26s, some obsolete transport planes, and amphibious landing craft had been assembled to assist in the landings in the Bay of Pigs in a remote area on the southern coast of Cuba about 120 miles southeast of Havana.

Kennedy learned of the plan only after he was elected. He was briefed in Palm Beach by the pipe-smoking, fatherly looking Allen Dulles, CIA head, and Richard Bissell, his six-foot-three, debonair deputy in charge of covert actions. In the Oval Office, the day before he was sworn in, President Eisenhower fleetingly referred to the plan and urged his successor to give it full-scale support.

Robert Kennedy became aware of the training program about the time his brother became President in January 1961. "I just don't know when I learned of it, but I suppose I must have known of it," he declared much later. About a week before the date set for the landings, he got a telephone call from Jack. "I want to have somebody from the CIA brief you on a matter," the President said. Soon Dick Bissell arrived at the Justice Department and outlined the projected operation.

"He was enthusiastic about it," Bobby recalled. "He said it really can't be a failure, because once they land on the beaches, even [if] as a military force they don't win, they can always stay in Cuba and be guerrillas, and they'll cause Castro so much difficulty. It'll be a very important factor in bringing about his downfall."[2]

As D-day approached, Robert Kennedy was drawn into the inner circle, participating in the discussions in the Cabinet Room of the White House with Rusk, McNamara, Dulles, Bissell, and other key Administration figures. Details of the operation, including opposition on the part of some members of the White House staff, were reported in the press.

This did not sit well with Bobby. When Arthur Schlesinger sent Jack a critical memorandum, Bobby took him into a corner at a party and told him, "Everybody had made up their [sic] mind," and that he was "performing a disservice to bring it back to the President."[3]

"I remember telling him that, once the President had made up his mind, once it seemed to have gone this far, that we should all make efforts to support him and he should remain quiet," Robert Kennedy said.

Bobby also was infuriated by a report that Under Secretary of State Chester Bowles had opposed the landings and had leaked this to the press in order to embarrass John Kennedy. One published account declared that Bobby, meeting Bowles in a corridor, had verbally assaulted him and punctuated his stinging remarks with jabs to the chest. Another said Bobby grabbed the sixty-year-old Bowles by his shirt front, Humphrey Bogart style.

The myth that a physical confrontation took place has endured. Both participants denied it but told conflicting stories.

Said Bobby, "We walked out of the room [Cabinet Room at the White House] into the other office. Chester Bowles came up to me and said, 'Well I hope everybody knows that I was always against the Bay of Pigs.'

"And I just said I thought it was a hell of a thing to say that now that the decision has been made, and as far as this Administration was concerned, he should keep his mouth shut and remember that he was for the Bay of Pigs."[4]

Calling the story of a physical encounter "ridiculous," Bowles declared, "It was no secret, then or now, that not only I but also Bill Fulbright [Senator William Fulbright, chairman of the Senate Foreign Relations Committee], Ed Murrow [head of the Voice of America], and Jerome B. Weisner, science adviser to the President, and several others had opposed the plan. How could such a secret possibly be kept in our government?

"As for Bob Kennedy," he added, "it was true that his initial reaction to the Bay of Pigs fiasco was emotional and militant, but he and I never discussed the question."[5]

On April 15, two days before the planned landings, Cuban airfields were hit by the B-26 bombers, camouflaged with the insignia of Castro's air force. Two of the planes, severely damaged by antiaircraft fire, landed in Florida, where the pilots told Immigration Service officials they were Cuban defectors. In the United Nations, Adlai Stevenson, who had not been told of the plans, denied United States involvement and, amid outraged cries, displayed pictures sent by the State Department that showed the Cuban markings.

Ed Guthman, who had not been briefed either, was queried about the Cuban pilots by reporter David Kraslow, who said, "We think this whole thing is a cover story. Is it?"

When Guthman called Bobby about the newsman's questions, the Attorney General admitted, "Something is up down there, but I don't think a final decision has been made."

He told Guthman to avoid answering the query. "Go fishing. Get lost," he advised.

Monday, April 17, was a beautiful sunny day in Washington, with a temperature in the high fifties. Jack Kennedy, just back from a weekend at Glen Ora with Jackie, Lem Billings, and Jean and Steve Smith, hosted a state luncheon at the White House for Prime Minister and Mrs. Constantino Caramanlis of Greece. In the afternoon, he strolled slowly across the south lawn, deep in thought. Often he glanced up at the bright, clear sky.

At Hickory Hill, Bobby and Dave Hackett stood on the grassy lawn in front of the house. Bobby was strangely quiet. Suddenly he turned to Dave.

"Well, we'll know in twenty-four hours," he told him.

"I had no idea what he was talking about," said Hackett.[6]

The following night, the Cabinet Room in the White House had become battle headquarters, receiving dispatches from the Cuban beaches. At the same time, three formal parties had been scheduled in the capital requiring the presence of both the President and his brother. Both Kennedys left the Cabinet Room at 7 P.M. dismayed at the reports that were coming in: the invasion was not going well. Still, they mingled graciously with guests at a white-tie dinner given by Prime Minister Caramanlis at the Greek Embassy in honor of the President.

After the dinner, John Kennedy whispered to his brother that he was returning to the Cabinet Room. Bobby nodded, and he and Ethel went on to the another ball. In the middle of a dance, Bobby, who was finding it increasingly difficult to hide his impatience, stopped and said to Ethel: "I've got to be with him. I know that he needs me."[7]

He returned to the White House, where disastrous news had come in. The operation was turning into a nightmare. Once again, the brothers hid their feelings as, still in white tie, they went to the East Room for the annual congressional reception. A marine band welcomed the President and Jackie by striking up "Mr. Wonderful"; he hardly felt that way, knowing he was facing the darkest hour of his Presidency. Bobby saw Jackie dancing with Senator Smathers and went up to them.

"The shit has hit the fan," he told Smathers. "The thing has turned sour in a way you wouldn't believe."[8] As soon as they could, Bobby and the President joined the Vice President, Secretaries of State and Defense, and the Joint Chiefs of Staff in the Cabinet Room.

The 1,200-man Cuban brigade had landed in the Zapata Swamp, miles from the mountains where they could start guerrilla activity. They were surrounded by Castro's troops, being strafed on the beaches and pushed into the sea where there was not sufficient naval power to rescue them. And there had been no simultaneous uprising among the Cuban natives, as the CIA had assured the President.

"It was so difficult to find out exactly what was going on," Bobby recalled. "The reports that came in were twelve or eighteen hours or twenty-four hours late so that you'd receive the information that the situation was becoming more critical and that might have been twelve hours before. The President was very upset that it was going badly. . . . It was a most frustrating period."[9]

Hours later, when the others had gone, Bobby, his voice betraying how close he was to tears, put his hands on his brother's shoulders. "They can't do this to you," he said. "Those black-bearded Communists can't do this to you."[10]

Much of his time in the next day or two was spent at the White House; he would go to the Justice Department office late in the afternoon. "It's not going well," he told Guthman. "I think we've made a hell of a mistake." When Guthman asked if there was anything to be done, Kennedy replied, "You can start praying for those poor fellows on the beach."[11]

Three days after the landing, the Cuban Brigade was forced to surrender.

157

John Kennedy wanted to know why it had happened this way; he moved swiftly to get some answers. On April 24, one week after the ill-fated expedition, the Cuba Study Group began to work in a hastily assigned office at the Pentagon. The four-man committee consisted of retired General Maxwell D. Taylor, plucked from his new post as president of Lincoln Center, Allen Dulles, Admiral Arleigh Burke, chief of naval operations, and Robert Kennedy.

Deputy Attorney General "Whizzer" White took over some of Kennedy's duties. He planned, Bobby said, to come to Justice daily, but not until late afternoon. "It will be terrible if the department improves while I'm gone," he quipped.[12]

The committee met twenty-one times over a six-week period, interrogating fifty witnesses, including all personnel that had participated in the planning and implementation of the mission. Its report concluded that the CIA venture had not been challenged because a new Administration was loath to oppose plans approved by President Eisenhower, "the greatest military man in America."

"It was Eisenhower's plan," said Bobby Kennedy. "Eisenhower's people all said it would succeed. . . . If he [JFK] hadn't gone ahead with it, it would have showed that he had no courage."

Almost two years later, in February 1963, Bobby denied reports that Jack Kennedy was responsible for the Bay of Pigs failure because he called off promised air cover.

"I can say unequivocally that President Kennedy never withdrew U.S. air cover. There never were any plans made for U.S. air cover so that there was nothing to withdraw," he explained.[13]

BERLIN

In the spring of 1961, Bobby Kennedy met a party-loving, ebullient, hard-drinking Russian named Georgi N. Bolshakov, who became his pipeline to the Kremlin. Georgi was editor of the slick magazine *USSR,* which sang the praises of the Soviet Union, press officer of the Russian embassy in Washington, and also a KGB agent.

But Georgi had Khrushchev's ear, and Bobby, aware of this, made good use of the conduit. Georgi not only opened a window into the thinking of the blustering but wily Soviet premier but, that summer, helped in no small measure to defuse the Berlin crisis, the frightening event that shook the world.

At the Vienna summit* in April, Khrushchev warned John Kennedy that

---

* Khrushchev was not as smitten with Jackie Kennedy as French President Charles De Gaulle had been a few days before. At a state dinner in the Hall of Mirrors at Versailles, De Gaulle talked with her all

a bone—Berlin—must be removed from Russia's throat. In the weeks that followed, he proclaimed that the only way to get rid of it was to sign a separate treaty with East Germany, effectively ending all Allied occupation rights in the quartered city by placing access routes under East German control.

Pressure mounted as the United States, Great Britain, and France announced they would never recognize East Germany's right to Berlin. On July 25, President Kennedy told the American people, "West Berlin has now become, as never before, the great testing ground of Western courage and will."

Meanwhile, in Moscow, Khrushchev asked the Soviet ambassador in East Germany, M. G. Pervukhin, for a map of West Berlin, which he and aides studied for the best place to install border controls. "We deliberated our tactics and set a certain date and hour when the border control would go into effect," he declared. "We decided to erect antitank barriers and barricades."[15]

The Wall was being planned. Construction was to begin on August 13. "We kidded among ourselves that in the West the thirteenth is supposed to be an unlucky day," Khrushchev said. "I joked that for us and for the whole socialist camp it would be a very lucky day indeed."[16]

At 1:00 A.M. on the thirteenth, the silence of Berlin's streets was suddenly split by the shrilling of sirens and the rumbling of trucks and tanks. Convoys, stretching for blocks, headed for border points and unloaded rolls of barbed wire, concrete posts, picks, shovels, stone blocks, bricks, and mortar. By dawn, a wall cutting Berlin in two was rising.

Four weeks later, it stretched through the city's heart in a jagged diagonal, separating friends and families and an estimated 50,000 people from their jobs, with only a few strongly fortified crossing points.

At this point, JFK estimated the chance that a shooting war could erupt as one in five.[17]

Kennedy asked Lyndon Johnson to fly to West Berlin to calm the growing agitation of the free Germans, an assignment the Vice President did not relish.

"There'll be a lot of shooting, and I'll be in the middle of it," he told Kenny O'Donnell. "Why me?"[18] Kenny buttered him up: he was the best man in the Administration to communicate America's resolve to preserve West Berlin's freedom and independence, a role Johnson performed superbly well, though only after a good deal of coaxing.

---

evening, barely touching his food. Khrushchev, however, said, "She didn't impress me as having that special brilliant beauty which can haunt men." He added, though, that she was youthful, energetic, and pleasant, and "I like her very much." He also found that "she had no trouble finding the right word to cut you short if you weren't careful with her."[14]

The tension grew. Under orders from the Commander-in-Chief, the First Battle Group of the eighth Infantry went streaking down the Autobahn with full battle gear, 1,500 strong. British and French army units were rushed to reinforce them, but all remained away from the Wall.

On September 8, American seismographs detected the explosion of a nuclear device in the atmosphere, and a few days later, Tass announced Russia had resumed atomic testing, breaking the pledge Khrushchev had made to Kennedy at Vienna and ending a three-year moratorium. More than thirty blasts were recorded that month. Kennedy responded to this brutal power play with underground testing, where there was no radioactive fallout.

Police of the East and West exchanged shots, tear gas, and oaths as refugees sought to escape into free territory. Then two divisions of fully equipped Russian troops moved into position, and a column of Red tanks drew up directly in front of the Wall.

Recognizing the risk of an incident, Bobby Kennedy called in Georgi Bolshakov.

"The President would like them to remove their tanks, to get them out of there in twenty-four hours," he told him.

Bolshakov said he would speak to Khrushchev.

In less than twenty-four hours, the big Russian tanks drew back.

"Georgi delivered effectively when it was a matter of importance," Bobby said.

By the end of September, Khrushchev began backing off. Having tested Kennedy's resolve, he told Paul-Henri Spaak, the Belgian diplomat in Moscow, "I'm not trying to put you in an impossible situation; I know very well you can't let yourself be stepped on." With the Wall built and the refugee flood all but dammed up, Berlin was not such a major problem to him after all. On October 17, addressing the Twenty-second Congress of the Soviet Communist Party, Khrushchev conceded that the western powers "were showing some understanding of the situation," and that being so, he would not insist on signing a peace treaty with East Germany "absolutely before December 31, 1961."

The Berlin crisis ended abruptly. Georgi was to surface again before long.

CUBA TWO

Eighteen months later, the Cuban volcano erupted again.

Since August 1962, U.S. intelligence had been watching developments there, using agents planted inside the island and the remarkable U-2 spy planes. They had discovered that surface-to-air missiles (SAMs), capable of shooting down the high-flying U-2s, were being installed by the Russians.

That was bad enough, but now came reports that construction of a submarine base, in the guise of a fishing village, might be underway only sixty miles northwest of the U.S. naval installation at Guantanamo.

On Sunday, October 14, 1962, the Strategic Air Command ordered thirty-five-year-old Major Rudolf Anderson, Jr., of Greenville, South Carolina, aloft to check.* Anderson, oval-faced, strong-jawed, with close-cropped dark hair, climbed in the cockpit of a Lockheed U-2 and almost literally leaped into the air. U-2s need only about four blocks of runway to become airborne.

Only thirty-five of these planes, perfected just seven years before at a secret factory in Burbank, California, were in service. Because of its slimmed-down design, it could climb to the unheard-of altitude of 70,000 feet—more than thirteen miles—above the earth.

Major Anderson flashed across the cloudless Caribbean, approaching Cuba from the south. As he neared the western tip of the island, he activated the U-2's sophisticated camera system. Lenses the diameter of a large mortar opened and shut automatically, taking photographs of the terrain. Each overlapped a small portion of the one preceding so that, when put together, a complete picture could be obtained of what was below. Complete and amazingly accurate, the cameras were so farsighted they could read house numbers and license plates from thirteen miles up.

The entire flight over Cuba took less than ten minutes. By Monday, the pictures had been flown to Washington, where they were processed and "read" at the National Photographic Interpretation Center. Experts examined the photos all that day and far into the night. By dawn there was no doubt. At least a half-dozen bases for missiles with a range of 2,500 miles were in the early stages of construction on the western end of the island. Launch and bunker sites, roads cut through the mountainous terrains, tents for workers—all were clearly visible.

At 4 A.M. West Coast time, on the sixteenth, CIA director John McCone was awakened in Seattle, where he had gone for the funeral of his stepson, and told the news. He ordered the photos to be rushed to the President. McGeorge Bundy, the national security adviser, saw them moments later and, holding them in his hand, rushed to the elevator to the living quarters on the second floor.

Kennedy, in his bedroom, was just pushing away his breakfast tray as Bundy walked in. He listened expressionless as he heard the startling story. Then, at 9 A.M., he telephoned Bobby and told him to come at once. "Bobby," he said, "we're facing great trouble."[19]

---

* Robert Kennedy said later that a second U-2 pilot was sent to Cuba that day, but Robert McNamara, the Secretary of Defense, asserted only one was dispatched. The other pilot, Major Richard (Steve) Heyser, may have gone the following day.

* * *

"The role Bobby Kennedy played in the Cuban missile crisis was vital to the United States, and John Kennedy knew it," said Pierre Salinger.

"Bobby's voice was the calm voice, arguing for a reasoned course of action against the military men and the CIA chiefs, who wanted to attack Cuba aggressively, to bomb it, to invade it.

"He told them that was not the way this country must react, that an intermediary approach was called for. He's the guy who, in the end, brought EXCOM [Executive Committee of the National Security Council] around to the idea of a blockade."

Salinger, who was present at most of the EXCOM sessions, disclosed that Bobby argued for a temperate course of action because he had inside knowledge of the mindset of Nikita Khrushchev that was not known to the others.

"Both brothers were fairly certain—not absolutely, but reasonably so—that Khrushchev would go to the brink, then draw back," Salinger asserted.[20]

This crucial knowledge had come to them through an unprecedented exchange of personal letters between the two heads of state that began more than a year before the missile crisis and continued for two years, almost to the time of JFK's assassination.

There were forty letters in all.[21] Khrushchev's were lengthy, most of them more than thirty pages. They were simple and direct, different in tone and substance from the formal statements emanating from the Kremlin.

Some reiterated the arguments being made in public between the East and West over Laos, atomic testing, Vietnam, and the prickly subject of Berlin. Others were loquacious, spinning long anecdotes about himself, historical figures he had known, and his travels. They were sprinkled with the kind of Russian similes Khrushchev delighted in using. He expressed his views on U.S. journalists and leaders in the American Congress and even made references to local problems in U.S. cities.

The letters were unique in that they bypassed the customary channels of diplomatic contact between national leaders. When Dean Rusk heard of them, he was dumbfounded. It is doubtful that Andrei Gromyko, the Soviet foreign minister, ever knew they were being exchanged.

Most significant was this: The statements issued by the Kremlin and published in *Pravda* were bellicose, warning of dire consequences if . . . But the private letters of the Soviet leader rarely were couched in the rhetoric of the Cold War. Khrushchev never accused John Kennedy, as the Kremlin did almost daily, of inflaming passions and increasing tensions between the two world powers. He put the blame on "hotheads" in "certain circles" and on far-right ideologues who had an abiding hatred and distrust of Russia and were "constantly stirring up the pot."

John and Robert Kennedy read and reread the letters, often spending hours on them. The President replied to each one, couching his replies in friendly fashion but rarely writing more than a few pages. In his answers, he was at his most persuasive best, as he argued for the defusing of tensions between the superpowers.

Salinger puts it bluntly: "We cannot underestimate the importance of these letters. They helped bring about a solution to the Cuban missile crisis."

The first letter arrived September 30, 1961, delivered personally by Georgi Bolshakov.

On September 29, Bolshakov telephoned Salinger in Newport, Rhode Island, where President Kennedy had gone to visit Jackie's mother and her husband, Hugh D. Auchincloss. Georgi told Pierre he had something of the highest importance to give him.

"I told him I'd meet him next day at the Hotel Carlyle in New York. He was disappointed that I couldn't see him earlier, again stressing the overriding importance of his mission, but said he'd fly to the city from Washington. He arrived with a bulky newspaper under his arm.

"As I watched, he unfolded the paper and took out a large manila envelope, which he handed me with a big smile.

"It was a thirty-page letter from the Soviet premier."

Thereafter, Georgi would call Salinger when a new letter arrived by courier from Moscow. Pierre, making some excuse, would slip out of the White House and meet Bolshakov on the other side of the city, away from the eyes of journalists, in a nondescript bar and grill or a dimly lit intersection. There, as in a John le Carré spy novel, Georgi would slip him an envelope and disappear into the crowds. Once, it was Ted Sorensen, one of few who knew about the correspondence, who met Bolshakov on a crowded street in downtown Washington and was handed the envelope. Both Kennedys obtained extraordinarily useful insights into the Russian leader's character from the letters.

Bobby also learned much about Nikita Khrushchev through a personal relationship that developed between him and the gregarious, party-loving Bolshakov.

"Most of the matters dealing with the Soviet Union in the United States were discussed—arrangements were made really between Georgi Bolshakov and myself," Robert Kennedy declared.[22]

They met about once every two weeks, Bolshakov imparting information of highest-level importance, verbally or written. "I don't know why they [the Russians] wanted to proceed in that fashion," Bobby said, "but they didn't want to go through their ambassador evidently. The ambassador handled the regular routine matters, and he, Bolshakov, handled other things. . . . The relationship continued until after the Second Cuba.

⅄"I met with him about all kinds of things," Bobby said.

⅄"I met with him about whether the [Vienna] meeting should take place, whether the President wanted to meet Khrushchev. I met with him about what they would discuss at the meeting."

Khrushchev, through Georgi, made the first overture about the two-day conference on June 3 and 4 about a month after the Bay of Pigs. Kennedy and Bolshakov discussed the advantages and disadvantages of the meeting, the importance of reaching an understanding on the subjects discussed, and the agenda itself—which would include the brewing crisis over Berlin, the need to arrive at a determination over the control of nuclear weapons, the Cuban problem, which was still festering, and the ideological struggle being fought in Laos between the Communist-backed Pathet Lao rebels and the pro-Western government forces.

On October 16, 1962, the sun filtered through the tall windows of the Cabinet Room in the West Wing of the White House. Sixteen of the country's highest ranking officials were seated in the black leather-covered armchairs around the dark mahogany oval table, each with a notepad placed neatly before him.

Less than three hours after the call came from his brother, Bobby and the President entered the room. They had spent two hours in private talk in the Oval Office a few doors away. John Kennedy, in a blue suit, white shirt, and narrow dark necktie, took his seat in the middle of the table, across from Vice President Johnson. Secretary of State Rusk was at his left, Defense Secretary Robert S. McNamara at his right. Bobby took a chair near the foot of the table.

The countdown of days began.*

CIA representatives, using pointers on blowups of the U-2's photographs, showed where the erector launching pads, tent areas, construction equipment, and eight missile trailers were located. To Bobby, carefully examining the pictures taken in the San Cristobal region, the area seemed innocent enough—"like the clearing of a field for a farm or the basement of a house." To the President's equally untrained eye, the place looked like a football field.[23]

---

* Besides the President, Bob Kennedy, Rusk, McNamara, and Johnson, others at that initial session were Deputy CIA Director Marshall Carter, filling in for McCone, who was flying in from Seattle; McGeorge Bundy; Ted Sorensen; Under Secretary of State George Ball; Deputy Under Secretary U. Alexis Johnson; General Maxwell Taylor, chairman of the Joint Chiefs; Deputy Defense Secretary Roswell Gilpatric; Assistant Defense Secretary Paul Nitze; Assistant Secretary of State for Latin Affairs Edward Martin; and Charles E. (Chip) Bohlen, Soviet expert for the State Department. Later, this group was joined by former Secretary of State Dean Acheson, Adlai Stevenson, Marine Corps Commandant David M. Shoup, Air Force Chief of Staff Curtis LeMay, Kenny O'Donnell, U.S. Information Agency director Donald Wilson, former Secretary of Defense Robert Lovett, and former High Commissioner of Germany John McCloy, though all did not attend every session.

Still, it was true enough. The Soviets were in the act of placing missiles in Cuba, pointed at the United States and capable of altering totally the power balance of the Cold War.

The first meeting of EXCOM on Day One of the crisis began at 11:50 A.M., and for sixty-seven minutes the members tackled the overarching problem: What should the U.S. do to counter the sudden threat at its doorstep? The following are excerpts from newly released transcripts of the two sessions held that day.[24]

At the morning meeting, McNamara, convinced that the missiles were "all over the lot," called for immediate bombing attacks by air to get rid of them. Lyndon Johnson agreed with him, saying, "I would like to hear what the responsible commanders have to say this afternoon. I think the question with the base is whether we take it out or whether we talk about it, and either alternative is a very distressing one."*

Of the two choices, Johnson said, "I would take it out . . . assuming the commanders felt that way."

Johnson expressed doubt that the United States could expect any measure of support from the Latin nations.

"I spent the weekend with the Organization of American States," he said. "I think this organization is fine, but I don't rely on 'em for any strength in anything like this."

Johnson did not want to confer with any of America's allies in the hemisphere, "even though I realize it's a breach of faith." He said, "We're not going to get much help out of them."

Bundy interjected, "There is an intermediate position. There are perhaps two or three of our principal allies or heads of government we could communicate with."

President Kennedy summed up the options that had been offered.

"What you're really talking about are two or three different operations. One is the strike on this, these three bases. The second is the broader one that Secretary McNamara was talking about, which is on the airfields and on the SAM sites and on anything else connecting with missiles. Third is doing both of those things and also at the same time launching a blockade, which . . . is a larger step.

"The fourth question is the degree of consultation . . ." At this point, the next sentence was removed from the transcript, presumably for security reasons, although one can assume Kennedy was referring to certain Latin countries.

Bobby Kennedy entered the discussion.

"We have the fifth one, really, which is the invasion. I would say that

---

* In military parlance, to "take out" means to eliminate by force.

you're dropping bombs all over Cuba if you do the second, . . . knocking out their planes, dropping it on all their missiles. You're covering most of Cuba. You're going to kill an awful lot of people and we're going to take an awful lot of heat on it. . . .

"And, and then, you know, the heat, you're going to announce the reason you're doing it is because they're sending in these kinds of missiles. Well, I think it's almost incumbent upon the Russians, then, to say, 'Well, we're going to send them in again, and if you do it again, we're going to do the same thing to Turkey, or we're going to do the same thing in Iran.' "

Thereafter, Bobby said nothing more that morning. He listened to more talk of aerial bombardments, which General Taylor proposed as a series of strikes to make sure that it would be impossible to place additional offensive weapons at the sites. As the session ended, he scribbled a note on his pad and passed it to his brother. It read, "I now know how Tojo felt when he was planning Pearl Harbor."[25]

Thereafter, EXCOM met daily at odd hours, the sessions often lasting all day, mostly in the Cabinet Room, sometimes in a seventh-floor conference room at the State Department. The full committee was rarely present; members would rush in after seeing to other duties.

President Kennedy attended only a few meetings after the first of the thirteen days, but received thorough briefings by telephone or in person from Robert and some of the others. Nobody presided at the sessions, and rank meant nothing. The deliberations were freewheeling; everyone encouraged to say what he wanted.

"The best performer," Ted Sorensen recalled, "was the Attorney General—not because of any particular idea he advanced . . . but because of his constant prodding, questioning, eliciting arguments and alternatives, and keeping the discussions concrete and moving ahead . . ."[26] Bobby also surprised George Ball who, until then, had considered him "immature, emotional, and inclined to see everything in absolute terms with too little sensitivity to nuance and qualification." Bobby was none of these, Ball found. Rather, he was "a force for caution and good sense."[27]

Before the end of the first day, Bobby was indicating that he was opposed to an air strike. Martin of State said at the evening session that his department officials had conferred with defense officials. "We felt an air strike, even of several days, against a military target primarily, would not result in any substantial unrest. People would just stay home and try to keep out of trouble."

Bobby had recoiled. But all he said then was, "Assume that we go in and knock these sites out, uh, I don't know what's gonna stop them from saying, 'We're gonna build the sites six months from now . . .' "[28]

On Day Two, at an afternoon meeting, he refused to support a bombing attack. Competition and victory may have been his lifelong mottoes, but his brother's honor and morality, as well as his own sensitivity and growing compassion, were more decisive influences.

The night before he had thought of the Japanese Prime Minister Hideki Tojo, executed as a war criminal after World War II, and could not bear the thought of John Kennedy being compared to the warlord.[29]

Too restless to remain in his seat, he had been pacing the floor. He stopped and, resting one hand on the table, said in a sharp tone, "My brother is not going to be the Tojo of the 1960s!"

To George Ball it was a powerful remark. "It altered the thinking of several of my colleagues," Ball declared.[30]

The crisis intensified as more U-2s returned with additional photographs, providing final proof that atomic-warhead missiles, pointed at major American cities, could be in operation within a week.

There was little levity in the White House, though Brumus did provide at least a small measure of humor. One day Bobby arrived for an EXCOM session at the White House, preceded by the huge dog. Before entering the Cabinet Room, he stopped in at the office of Evelyn Lincoln, his brother's secretary, and told her he was leaving Brumus there. He warned her to shut her door; otherwise, Brumus might go wandering down the hall.

Staff members, peering in, made choice comments, ranging from "Who's your friend?" to "Come out from behind that wig, Pierre." Miss Lincoln had almost become accustomed to the wisecracks when a young Senate messenger from the Labor Department entered, stared at the huge black animal, uttered a piercing scream, and fled down the hall.[31]

On Day Seven, President Kennedy, in a somber television address to the nation, announced his decision to impose a naval blockade (he called it a "quarantine"), which had received solid support from EXCOM despite vociferous objections from Air Force officials. Immediately, congressional leaders of both parties issued a strong statement of support. Despite Johnson's fears, the Latin American republics were unanimous in their backing, adopting a resolution calling for immediate removal of all missiles from Cuba by a vote of 20 to 0.

On Day Nine, at ten in the morning, the blockade went into effect, setting up a 500-mile barrier beyond which no vessel bound for Cuba could go without interception or seizure. Adamantly refusing to honor it, the Soviet Union sent a flotilla of twenty-five ships, accompanied by several submarines, toward Cuba. Low-level reconnaissance flights reported that work on the missiles was being speeded up. The Navy began deploying 180 ships into the Caribbean. The Strategic Air Command ordered its B-52 bombers aloft, ready for action with fully loaded atomic warheads. Bobby's gloomy assessment: "Direct military confrontation between the two great nuclear powers was inevitable."

By then, there were four launching pads at each of nine missile bases, able to fire thirty-six nuclear bombs. Though there was as yet no proof that atomic warheads were actually in Cuba, Bobby Kennedy had calculated that, if there were, and if they were used, 80 million Americans—45 percent of the population at the time—would be killed.[32]

In the Cabinet Room, he looked across the table at his brother. John Kennedy was betraying his inner tensions: a hand went to his face and covered his mouth; he tightened a fist, opened it, tightened it again. Color had drained from his cheeks. He seemed haggard and ill. Bobby's mind flipped back through the years to when he had sat at Jack's bedside in Japan where his brother had almost died and to the look on his face when word had reached Hyannis Port that Joe junior had been shot down.[33]

A messenger arrived at 10:25 and handed a note to John McCone. He read it swiftly, then spoke: "Mr. President, we have a preliminary report, which seems to indicate that some of the Russian ships have stopped dead in the water."

Later photographs arrived, and they were spread on the table and studied. Some Soviet vessels had indeed halted a few miles from the blockade line. Some were lying at anchor, others had turned and were steaming back.

There was an air of quiet satisfaction in the room. Jack Kennedy leaned back in his chair, unsmiling but more relaxed. However, the crisis was not over.

The missile bases were still in Cuba, were being beefed up, and still posed a threat to virtually every city in the United States.

On Day Eleven, an order was flashed to the State Department from the Oval Office to set up teams of civil affairs personnel who would govern Cuba after an invasion. To EXCOM, McNamara warned that a U.S. landing will result in "heavy casualties." John Kennedy said, "After a bloody fight, they [the missiles] will be pointed at us. And we must further face the possibility that, when military hostilities first begin, those missiles will be fired."

The day wore on. Members of EXCOM, most of them haggard-looking for lack of sleep, drifted in and out of the Cabinet Room. "Doom was in the air," Salinger remembers.

Much has been written about the two messages from Khrushchev to Kennedy, the first arriving in late afternoon of Day Eleven, the second on the following morning. Because they bear heavily on the new light Salinger sheds on Bobby's reaction, they are recalled in brief.

The first letter, sent privately to the President, was filled with the cus-

Bobby, age ten, with pet on the lawn of his father's house at Hyannis Port (1935).

Lemoyne K. Billings, (left) JFK's roommate at Choate, and a lifelong family friend, and John hoist young Bobby between them at poolside of the Kennedy winter home at Palm Beach (1934).

Bobby and Ethel on their wedding day, June 17, 1950, arrive at the bride's home for one of the most lavish receptions Greenwich, CT, had ever seen. First to greet them are three of the many dogs at the Skakel family residence on Simmons Lane. Bill Stettner Photo.

Bobby Kennedy, as chief counsel of the Senate Labor Rackets Committee, questions Teamster boss James R. Hoffa (1957).

The Kennedy brothers at the White House in March 1963. Bobby, as "Number-two man," consulted with the President on all major problems confronting the Administration.

Scene in the Cabinet Room on October 29, 1962, the day after Khrushchev announced he would withdraw missiles from Cuba. EXCOM (Executive Committee of the National Security Council) members had been meeting for thirteen days as the crisis worsened. RFK is standing at left. Far right, the President leans over the table as Secretary of State Dean Rusk watches. Secretary of Defense Robert McNamara is at JFK's left. Opposite, making notes, is Vice President Johnson.

Attorney General Kennedy addresses demonstrators protesting discrimination against blacks outside the Department of Justice building in March 1961.

The Attorney General meets with civil rights leaders outside the White House on June 22, 1963. RFK is flanked by Martin Luther King, Jr., on his right and Roy Wilkins of the NAACP. LBJ is at Wilkins's left.

Bobby, Jacqueline, and Ted leaving the White House on November 25, 1963, to follow the body of John Kennedy to St. Matthew's Cathedral.

Senator and Mrs. Robert Kennedy on the lawn of their Hickory Hill home with eight of their nine children. From left are Kathleen, 15; Joseph, 14; Robert, Jr., 13; David, 11; Mary Courtney, 10; Michael, 8; Kerry, 7; and Christopher, 3. Wide World.

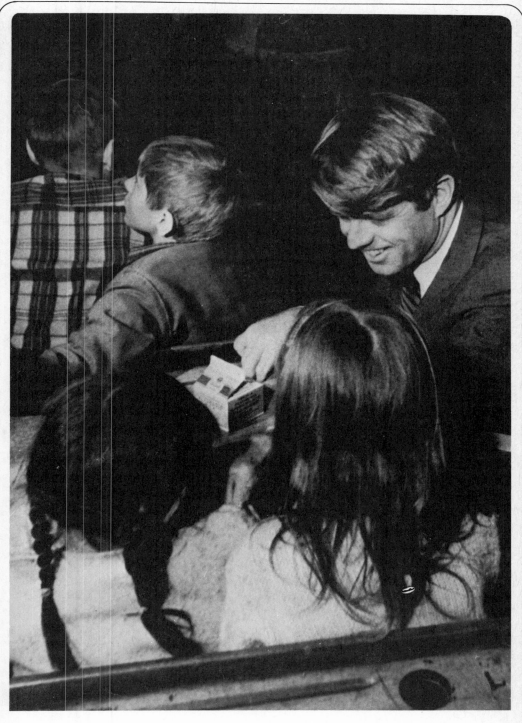

RFK, Senator from New York, chats with children in a one-room school-house in Kentucky during a tour of the poverty-stricken Appalachia area in 1968. Wide World.

Senator Kennedy, as chairman of the Senate Committee on Indian Education, visits a Head Start program on the Kashiah Indian Reservation north of San Francisco in 1968. Wide World.

tomary threats and denunciations but offered a trade: the missiles would be removed in return for a pledge not to invade Cuba.

The second, received on the morning of Day Twelve, was entirely different. This one was not private but made public by the Kremlin's Foreign Office. The tone was harsh, and the demands were escalated. Now Khrushchev insisted the United States also remove Jupiter missiles it had based in Turkey before he took the missiles out of Cuba.

EXCOM met late that morning in the White House. "It was unmistakably Black Saturday," George Ball remembered. Many were utterly confused. The "more blood-thirsty members," in Ball's words, called for an air strike as early as Sunday morning. The parallel to Pearl Harbor was not unnoticed by Bobby.

The President was calm, refusing to be swept into irrevocable action, but he was seething with anger. The Jupiters were obsolete, and Polaris subs in the area could protect Turkey from Russian invasion far better anyway. But, as Bobby said later, he wasn't about to withdraw missiles from Turkey under threat of the Soviet Union.

"That meeting continued all day long—ten hours, maybe twelve hours," recalled Donald Wilson. Once again, it was Bobby who was the strong man in the room. It should have been Dean Rusk, but he wasn't the man to take hold.

"Bobby didn't sit in his chair much. Most of the time he was pacing the room. President Kennedy deliberately did not attend for long periods because he didn't want the others to agree with what they thought he wanted."[34]

In the midst of the deliberations came more alarming news. Major Anderson, flying a photo mission, was shot down by a SAM missile, presumably fired by Russian soldiers. His U-2 crashed near Nipe Bay. Anderson was killed on impact. To Bobby, the act meant the Soviets were preparing to wage war. "The noose was tightening on all of us," he said, "on Americans, on mankind."[35]

"Toward five in the afternoon," Don Wilson said, "Bobby stopped his pacing and, in a quiet voice, told EXCOM, 'Let's ignore the second letter. Let's answer the first.' "

Pierre Salinger, in his customary seat against the wall, explained: "He just didn't believe the second message came from the same person who wrote the first. 'The first one *sounds* like Khrushchev,' he said. 'It's got his words, his flavor, his mind, his stories. But the second sounds like some other group deep inside the Kremlin.' "[36]

That proposal, which led to the solution of one of history's most dangerous crises, did not pop newborn into Bobby's head. Rather, Salinger said, "It was based on a shrewd reading over the past year of Khrushchev's mind and emotional makeup."

By that time, Georgi Bolshakov had delivered about a dozen letters from Khrushchev to Kennedy. In one, the Russian premier told a story of two goats who approached each other from opposite sides of a narrow bridge suspended across a deep precipice. The animals, he wrote, met at midpoint, but each was too stubborn and too stupid to move. Heads down, they butted one another on the span until, finally and inevitably, both tumbled into the chasm and were destroyed.

In another, he spun a yarn about a peasant in a Russian woodland area who came upon a bear. Barehanded, he grappled with the animal, trying to bring it back to his cottage. But the bear, grasping the peasant, would not allow himself to be taken. The result, the Premier indicated, had to be disaster for both man and animal. Khrushchev applied the metaphor to the efforts of French President De Gaulle to exert influence over Konrad Adenauer, the German chancellor. De Gaulle sought the dismemberment of Germany into a larger number of independent Germanies while Adenauer's aim was to unite East and West into a single German state. The moral was clear: deadlock over any issue gets nobody anywhere.

A similar metaphor was contained in Khrushchev's first letter on the missiles in which the Soviet Premier likened the crisis to a rope, in the middle of which was a knot. The more each side tugged on the rope, the tighter it would become, he said, adding the following, which Bobby read and reread many times:

> . . . and then it will be necessary to cut the knot, and what that would mean is not for me to explain to you, because you yourself understand perfectly of what terrible forces our countries dispose. Consequently, if there is no intention to tighten the knot, and thereby to doom the world to the catastrophe of thermonuclear war, then let us not only relax the forces pulling on the ends of the rope, let us take measures to untie that knot. We are ready for this.

Bobby had also studied with great care Pierre Salinger's long report, dictated to relays of secretaries, of fourteen hours he had spent with Khrushchev between May 11 and 16 that year. Sent to Russia by JFK to discuss a freer policy on the exchange of information, Salinger met the Soviet Premier at a dacha twenty-two miles from Moscow.

Khrushchev, in a good mood, was a magnificent host. At a massive lunch, he confided, "I've escaped from my doctors today, and I'm going to have a good time." Salinger lost count of the number of glasses of vodka he drank, and of the number of courses at lunch. At the end of three hours of dining, a huge platter of shish kabob—lamb and rice—was placed on the table. Already thoroughly full, Salinger went at it gamely, and between

170

them, they polished it off. The Premier was still not finished. He ate dessert and drank five glasses of cognac.

Bobby was less interested in Khrushchev's good living than in the remarks and incidents, which Salinger, who had received permission to make a full transcript of their conversations, was able to provide.

Once Khrushchev told Salinger, "We already have fought more than once and well know what war is and therefore do not want it. Although both we and you possess completely adequate means of destruction, at present it is indispensable to measure our forces not by the quantity of weapons but by the quantity and quality of reason on both sides."

On another occasion, the Premier showed Salinger a collective farm near the grounds of the dacha, proudly saying that he had helped plant many of its trees himself. "You see," he said, "trees are life, but weapons are death."

Another time Khrushchev said he liked Averell Harriman very much and tried to hire him, but he refused. When Salinger protested that Harriman couldn't possibly accept because he already had a job as adviser to President Kennedy, Khrushchev was undaunted.

"Why can't he advise us both?" he asked quite seriously. "He could bring about world peace. You tell him I still want him."

Bobby was not naive. He knew that Khrushchev, wily as well as earthy, could have been playing a game by publicly planting statements he knew would be transmitted to the United States. "But the more he looked at the broad range of his private messages and conversations, the more he was convinced that the Russian Premier would not step beyond the brink," Salinger said. Bobby believed he had the answer to Khrushchev's bold challenge, which puzzled them all and had General Taylor asking, "Was there something in the situation which escaped us? Surely such an astute fellow must have some trick up his sleeve, which we did not perceive."[37]

Privately, Bobby talked over his belief with his brother, who agreed that the diagnosis of Khrushchev's mind, though made up of fine threads, was nonetheless accurate.

The first letter was thereupon answered: Russia, the President wrote, would remove the weapons, and the United States would, in turn, end the "quarantine" and give assurance that Cuba would not be invaded.

Few slept that night as the reply was awaited. On Sunday morning, EXCOM members received envelopes containing their evacuation orders. The U.S. capital was well within range of the missiles. Each man was told where to go outside the city, accompanied only by a bare complement of personnel. Families could not come with them; so heartbreaking calls were made to wives, urging them to leave. John Kennedy, too, in the upstairs quarters, asked Jackie to take the children and go. Jackie refused. She would stay in the White House as long as he was there.

On that Sunday, Day Thirteen, one of the goats on the narrow bridge above the chasm drew back. One of the antagonists pulling the rope with the knot in the center released his hold. Khrushchev stepped back from the edge, as he had done in Berlin, sending a note to JFK that he had accepted his offer. The missile bases would be dismantled if the United States promised not to invade. The crisis was over. Bobby Kennedy's shrewd assessment of Khrushchev had been correct.

Two months later, the Donald Wilsons held one of the series of Hickory Hill seminars at their home. Bobby called Susan Wilson and asked if he could bring Georgi Bolshakov and Maya Plitsetskaya, the prima ballerina of the Bolshoi Theatre. Mrs. Wilson agreed.

After the discussion, Bolshakov said at the buffet supper, "I want to make a toast." The group fell silent. He raised his glass of rum and Coke and shouted, "To Cuba libre!"[38]

The strain ended, even Bobby was able to laugh with the others at Georgi's sly thrust.

15

Of Sex and Marilyn

ONLY ONCE was Robert Kennedy linked to a woman other than his wife.

The stories, it must be underscored, are not new, though the furor created in late 1985 made it seem so. The first allegation of a reported involvement with Marilyn Monroe was published in 1964 and was promptly picked up and spread by Bobby's arch-foe in the Administration, the FBI Director himself.

"It spread like wildfire, of course," said William C. Sullivan, head of the bureau's Domestic Relations Division, "and J. Edgar Hoover was right there, gleefully fanning the flames."[1]

Tales of a Jack-Bobby-Marilyn link surfaced intermittently after this for two decades, with accounts published in countless magazine articles, gossip columns, and a number of books. In 1985, there were two television documentaries on the subject: one was produced in the United States but not shown; the other, made by the BBC, was broadcast in Britain and later in the United States.

The stories assert that John Kennedy met Marilyn Monroe through his brother-in-law, the late actor Peter Lawford, in the 1950s and had a now-and-then relationship with her for several years. Bobby reportedly met her shortly after his brother's election, beginning a relationship that continued until the actress's death in August 1962. He, too, was introduced to Marilyn by Lawford at a party in his lavish Santa Monica beach house. Bobby was flattered to have the world's reigning sex symbol attracted to him; she, in turn, was impressed by his brains and prestige; and, according to rumor, they slipped from the house and made love in the rear seat of a parked automobile.

Marilyn was seen publicly for the first time with the Kennedy brothers on May 19, 1962, at the forty-fifth birthday party for the President in Madison Square Garden in New York City. The President had invited Gene Schoor, the writer, who was now preparing a boys' book on Bobby, to attend the celebration.

Schoor was standing between John and Robert just below the podium as a radiantly smiling Marilyn, swathed in three-quarter-length white fur, mounted the steps to the lectern.

Schoor noted that John Kennedy was watching every undulation. Not taking his eyes off Marilyn, he murmured appreciatively to Schoor, "What an ass, Gene—*what* an ass." Bobby said nothing.[2]

There were gasps from the audience of 15,000 as Peter Lawford, who introduced Marilyn, helped her remove the fur coat. She stood spotlighted in a flesh-colored, skin-tight beaded gown that revealed every line and curve of her body. Her husky, sexy rendition of "Happy Birthday, Dear Mister President" drew from Jack the wry comment, "I can now retire from politics after having had Happy Birthday sung to me in such a sweet, wholesome way."[3]

At a party afterward, Marilyn was the center of attention, attracting, among others, Arthur Schlesinger, Adlai Stevenson, and Robert Kennedy. Stevenson noted, somewhat ruefully, in a letter to Mary Lasker that he had to break "through the strong defenses established by Robert Kennedy who was dodging around her like a moth around the flame."[4] Schlesinger, in his diary, wrote, "Bobby and I engaged in mock competition for her—she was most agreeable to him and pleasant to me."[5]

Robert made several trips to the West Coast that summer for discussions with Jerry Wald on the film version of *The Enemy Within*. While there, he and Marilyn met a few times, usually at dinners or parties at Peter and Pat's beach home.

Marilyn's neighbors were reported to have seen Kennedy visit her Brentwood home on a number of times during June and July. Marilyn reportedly placed many telephone calls to Bobby's office at the Justice Department, considered significant because the phone company records were impounded by Los Angeles police after Marilyn died and have never been released. A more sinister theory has it that Bobby Kennedy was actually at Marilyn's home the night she died, to make sure nothing could be found there that could link his brother to her and damage his reputation. The theory of love unrequited has it that Marilyn swallowed too many pills in despair because Bobby would not divorce Ethel and marry her.

The evidence that Bobby had a sexual relationship with the star is at best circumstantial, but cumulative enough to be a possibility. In the BBC documentary, witnesses were produced who saw Miss Monroe alone in her apartment with him.

One was Eunice Murray, her companion-housekeeper, who had testified after Monroe's death that she had seen a light shining under the bedroom door. When she awakened in the morning on that August 5 and saw the light still on, she summoned Marilyn's psychiatrist, Dr. Ralph R. Greenson of Beverly Hills. They broke into the room and found Marilyn's body sprawled on her bed nude, a telephone clutched in her hand. Twenty-three years later Miss Murray, by then eighty-two years old, added to her earlier testimony that she had seen Robert Kennedy inside the house the day before.[6]

Another witness, a blond actress named Jeanne Carmen who was a neighbor, was visiting Marilyn in her apartment when she answered the doorbell. "I went to the door," Miss Carmen said, "and I opened it up and there stands Bobby Kennedy. I went bo-ing! Marilyn came rushing out of the bathroom all of a sudden. She jumped into his arms, and they started kissing madly." Miss Carmen added that "they settled down," and the three had a glass of wine together, after which Marilyn made a sign to her which she said meant, " 'Jeannie, go back to your apartment,' which I did."[7]

In October 1985, prior to the BBC broadcast, a thirteen-minute segment in ABC's "20/20" was killed by Roone Arledge, president of ABC News and Sports, because it lacked authentication. Calling the report "gossip column stuff," Mr. Arledge declared, "It set out to be a piece which would demonstrate that because of alleged relations between Bobby Kennedy and John Kennedy and Marilyn Monroe the presidency was compromised because organized crime was involved. Based on what has been uncovered so far, there has been no evidence."[8]

Claims over the years that Robert Kennedy had anything to do with Marilyn's death or arranged in some way to dispose, or have someone dispose, of all proof of her relationship with him and/or his brother John rest on shaky foundations. Among the bizarre stories circulated is that Bobby was present when an unknown doctor injected a lethal drug into the star's heart. A number of the tales involve a missing diary, reportedly kept by Marilyn, which would have been ruinous to Bobby's career.

Fact, conjecture, and hearsay are interwoven in attempts to reconstruct the events surrounding the death of Marilyn Monroe.

Fact: About 7 P.M., August 4, the night she died, Peter Lawford telephoned to invite her to dinner and poker "with me and some friends." Marilyn declined, pleading she was too tired.[9] That night she was found dead.

A few days later, Lawford confirmed he had made the call. Alarmed at what he heard, Lawford telephoned his agent, who in turn called Milton Rudin, Marilyn's attorney. Years later, Earl Wilson, the *New York Post* columnist, disclosed that on that night Marilyn, talking in a "slurred voice," had told Lawford: "Say good-bye to Pat. Say good-bye to the President. Say good-bye to you because you've been a good guy."[10]

That explains why Lawford made the hurried call to his agent who found Rudin and asked him to check. Rudin called Eunice Murray, Marilyn's housekeeper, and was reassured that all was well because her bedroom light was still on and the phone had not been transferred to another room, which she always did before going to sleep. It may also explain to whom Marilyn was talking when her body was discovered, her white phone off the hook and in her hand.

Speculation and hearsay: Among the "friends" who would be present at Lawford's home that night would be Bobby Kennedy, and Lawford was setting up a tryst. Marilyn was trying to reach Bobby on that last night of her life. Lawford destroyed a suicide note she left and the "friends" rushed Bobby out of Los Angeles before police were called.

Nobody actually knows for certain if Bobby Kennedy was even in Los Angeles on that Saturday, August 4, though numerous efforts have been made to prove his presence. Ed Guthman, Kennedy's press secretary, who was with him that weekend, says flatly: "He was never in Los Angeles at the time."

Guthman continues: "He was staying in the Bay area at the ranch of friends near Atherton, having flown in from Washington. He was there with his wife and his four oldest children. He was scheduled to address an American Bar Association meeting in San Francisco that Monday and then take his family to the World's Fair in Seattle, then fishing on the Washington coast and camping on the Olympic Peninsula with Justice Douglas. It was a combination of business and vacation."

Guthman met Bobby in San Francisco on Sunday. "We talked about the terrible tragedy. He said, 'How sad it is.' Next day, he spoke before the ABA, then we all went to the Fair and, after that, on a fishing trip off the Washington coast. I went off to Seattle, my hometown, while the Kennedys went camping with Justice Douglas.

"All this time, he was about 350 miles from Los Angeles."[11]

It is true that Guthman did not see Bobby Kennedy on that crucial Saturday. But he asks, "Is it likely that he would leave his wife and children to go down to Los Angeles to see Marilyn? Does it make any sense?"

John R. Bates, a highly respected San Francisco attorney who owns a ranch near Gilroy, California, about an hour's drive southeast of the city, was host to Bobby, Ethel, and the children on the weekend of August 3 to

5. On Saturday, the Kennedys had a full active day, including a touch football game. Mr. Bates declared that Bobby was never out of his sight, except from after 10 P.M., when he retired, until early the following morning at breakfast.

On the BBC broadcast, Mr. Bates was asked why a number of persons had said they had seen Bobby in Los Angeles the night of August 4. He replied, "I just can't speculate on their misinformation or their lack of information or what they think they saw, but there was no way he could have been in Los Angeles unless he had a twin." He also told *The New York Times,* "There's no way in the world he could have left, no way."[12]

Pressed again on the persistent reports by individuals that Bobby had been seen in Los Angeles, Mr. Bates stated, "I would like to cross-examine them."[13]

Ethel heard the rumors about Bobby and Marilyn but never believed any of them. One friend said, "She was as certain of him as a woman could be of a man." Once, after they both had attended a dinner at Peter Lawford's home, she kidded Bobby because he had danced with Marilyn several times. He, in turn, had remarked on her fondness for Whizzer White, now a Supreme Court Justice.

Said John Seigenthaler, "He teased her excessively about it, and she teased him about Marilyn, that night and a couple of other times."[14] It is not likely that Ethel Kennedy, a prim woman who is uneasy with liaisons between unmarried persons and takes a dim view of divorce, would have publicly joked about Bobby and Marilyn if she placed any credence in the stories.

Legally, the Marilyn Monroe case remains closed. On November 8, 1985, the Chief Prosecutor of Los Angeles County found no reason to reopen the investigation into Miss Monroe's death, which in 1962 had been ruled a "probable suicide" caused by acute barbiturate poisoning, following an autopsy and a police inquiry. District Attorney Ira Reiner, responding to a claim that new evidence existed about the star's death, found there wasn't even a "bare suspicion" that she was murdered.[15] Two weeks later, the Los Angeles County Grand Jury rejected a request from the county's Board of Supervisors to reopen the case, announcing that it "will not pursue the Marilyn Monroe case any further."[16] In December 1982, the Los Angeles District Attorney's office had concluded after a new probe that "our inquiry and document examination uncovered no credible investigation supporting a murder theory."[17]

The accurate facts about the Bobby-Marilyn relationship will probably never be known. Both are gone, and authenticated evidence of a continuing affair is sparse. In all likelihood, it will remain as much of an historical mystery as Thomas Jefferson's reputed thirty-eight-year liaison with a slave

woman named Sally Hennings, who allegedly bore him several children. Some claim the story is true; others say it is unproven.
In both cases, nobody knows for sure.

The Marilyn Monroe affair, whatever its extent, stemmed from the fascination all the Kennedys, from the patriarch to the present generation, find in show business and its celebrities.

Stars of screen, stage, sports, and journalism have always been an integral part of Kennedy social life, whether in Washington, Cape Cod, New York, or Hollywood. They are the people to know, to watch, to surround yourself with, and to gossip about. Through Peter Lawford, who was a "ticket to the stars," the Kennedys met, among others, Frank Sinatra, who became a favorite of Jack.

Said Ken O'Donnell, "His [JFK's] fondness for Sinatra, which perplexed a lot of people, was simply based on the fact that Sinatra told him a lot of inside gossip about celebrities and their romances in Hollywood." Sinatra was the "President's private Rona Barrett," reported Gary Wills.

John Kennedy's behavior in Marilyn's company was something short of Presidential. At parties in Lawford's home, he would take her for a stroll around the large swimming pool and tell her raunchy stories while his hands roamed around her body. At dinner one evening, he sat beside the blond star and, dropping one hand below the table, moved it over to her thigh. Encountering no resistance, he moved the hand further, until he found that Marilyn wore no underclothing beneath her dress. Quickly he drew his hand away. "He hadn't counted on going that far," Marilyn said with a grin.[18]

Bobby, too, was drawn to the glamorous blond personality. He was a man, and he was flattered by her attention, he told Kenny. Discussing the stories, he said, "I didn't think I was that good, especially in light of my reputation at Harvard." At Cambridge, he had been considered a "square."

"I guess I must have come a long way," Bobby declared.

His intimate friends—who may, of course, have a bias in protecting his reputation but at the same time know more about the man than anyone else—are convinced that a heavy relationship with any woman other than Ethel would have been wildly out of character.

"Bobby had a Calvinistic moral sense," said Andrew Glass, a Washington newsman who knew him well. "He really believed in absolute right and wrong, and this strict code guided his moral life."

Knowing this, brother Jack would not invite Bobby to the White House on evenings when he wanted to relax from state business. JFK knew that Robert could not, and would not, sit around, tell dirty jokes, and gossip about who was sleeping with whom.

Dave Hackett, the friend and confidant since Milton days, points to Bobby's "strong basic values."

"Fidelity was one of these," he emphasizes.[19]

Robert was committed to his wife and family, says John Seigenthaler. "Part of it was religious," he says. "He was a devout Catholic, a mass-attending, confession-going, communion-receiving Catholic. He set for himself standards, and he lived by them."

George Terrien traveled with Bobby and Jack through southern France in 1948 and recalls that "Jack and I went girl-hunting quite openly, but while Bobby had dates, he wasn't lustful." In later years, despite the large number of pretty girls in the Attorney General's office, he "never in any way indicated any interest," says Ramsey Clark.

Journalists who covered Kennedy's movements—many of whom became close friends of Bobby and Ethel—reported the same thing. "In the middle of huge crowds and motorcades he would always look around and ask, 'Where's Ethel?' " says Andrew Glass. "If he was ever separated from her in a crowd or a social setting, he would always inquire where she was and he would move over to her."

Both Glass and Dick Schaap also stress Bobby's religious convictions as guiding his behavior. "He seems to have an utter faith in himself," Schaap has said, "complete trust in his own morality. He kids his own Puritanism. 'It isn't that I'm a saint,' he has said, 'it's just that I've never found it necessary to be a sinner.' "

O'Donnell summed up the Monroe-Kennedy stories somewhat inelegantly, calling them "absolute bullshit."

Not that Bobby was unaffected by attractive women. "He was something like Jimmy Carter when it came to pretty girls," José Torres asserted. He noticed the beautiful, shapely ones and, like Carter, might have had lust in his heart for some of them, but he never went beyond that.

Torres recalled a press conference during the 1968 Presidential primaries. "There was a young woman there named Ponchitta Pierce," he said, "a beautiful black journalist for *Ebony* magazine. She was stunning. Every male writer there was paying close attention to her, and Bobby, answering questions, was not impervious to her beauty either.

"Standing close to Bobby, I whispered to him, 'I never went to journalism school, but if I had, and she was there, I'd have stayed forever.' Bobby, still looking at Ponchitta, and only half-listening to me, said, 'She is one beautiful woman.' "

During a whistle-stopping campaign trip through Oregon, Kennedy and an aide were hunched over a speech he was to deliver. As they talked, a pretty girl reporter walked down the aisle, stopping several rows in front of them. Leaning over to chat with a colleague, her miniskirt hiked up, exposing a great deal.

The voice of Bobby's aide trailed off. Head down, still studying the typescript, Bobby asked a question, got no answer, and looked up, puzzled.

179

The aide was staring at the young woman. Following his gaze, Bobby, too, stopped work and looked. Not until the girl straightened up several minutes later did Bobby and the aide return to the speech.

He liked having pretty girls in the Senate office. When students applied for internships, personal attractiveness counted more heavily than grade-point averages for selection. Most of the female clerical help at Justice ranged from good-looking to gorgeous.

On the Sunday after JFK's inauguration, Bobby invited a group of friends, including Dave Hackett and Sam Adams, to Hickory Hill. Among the guests was the actress Kim Novak. Four inches of snow remained on the ground, excellent for tobogganning on the hills.

Kathleen Kennedy, then ten years old, organized the teams and the order of slides but wasn't too successful when it came to seating people. "The guys were scrambling to sit in front and behind Kim," Adams recalled, "and no wonder. With her blond hair and long legs, she made a beautiful picture."

Bobby managed to get the seat behind the movie star and wrapped his arms around her. Ethel, watching, called out to him, "Bobby, do you want to play football now?" Usually Bobby would play football whenever he was asked, but this time he wasn't interested. "Can't a father toboggan with his daughter?" he grinned at Ethel, as—still holding Kim—he slid down the hill.

Ethel's prudishness matched Bobby's. Once Torres, who had recently been married, began talking to her, innocently enough, about other women he had known. Ethel cut him short. "Come on now, José," she told him sharply. "You're finished with that. You're a married man now."

The sexual revolution, then getting underway, shocked her beyond words. "On a trip abroad," Andy Glass said, "she learned somehow that a male and a female journalist, each married to someone else, were having an affair. She wouldn't even look at the couple, much less talk to them, so acute was her embarrassment."

Bobby was aware of the reputation for sexual adventurings of all Kennedy males, from his three brothers to his father, who had a lengthy affair with Gloria Swanson. And he didn't like any of them. In the Administration, he took on an additional portfolio, one he considered of the highest importance: protector of the President's moral image.

By that time, Bobby knew Jack was unstoppable. His brother's affairs no longer surprised or shocked him. He accepted them as being a part of Jack's makeup.

He hardly needed reminding that Jack liked girls, but J. Edgar Hoover made certain that, at least once a month, the Attorney General received information that something might be going on. Memos cascaded from the

Director that members of the Kennedy family or their friends, from the President on down, were involved in some kind of hanky-panky or other.

Bobby read them with increasing annoyance. He believed Hoover was testing him to see if he would actually investigate reports of sexual liaisons that involved the President or even himself.

One memo quoted an informant who said that, once a week, Bobby and Jack would sequester a group of girls on the twelfth floor of the LaSalle Hotel. The Secret Service, the memo continued, would surround the place, while the Kennedy brothers went upstairs for, presumably, an afternoon frolic.

Bobby gave Hoover no reason to claim that he was protecting his brother or himself. He routinely looked into the charges, as well as similar ones made about goings-on at the Georgetown Inn.

"A lot of it was so farfetched that, even on the face of it, it didn't make any sense," Bobby said. "I mean, if you were going to do that kind of thing, you wouldn't go on over to the LaSalle Hotel with the Secret Service surrounding the place." The media would almost certainly find out, wonder why the agents were there, and the country would be treated to one of its juiciest scandals in decades.[20]

If there were no sex scandals at Washington hotels, two surfaced during the Kennedy years that caused Bobby deep concern. These were real. Both could have made the country an international laughingstock; worse, one of them could have damaged irreparably the reputation of his brother.

The first came to light in the summer of 1963. Some of the most prestigious senators and representatives, as well as high government officials and lobbyists, were finding their way to a private retreat conveniently located on Capitol Hill, where they were entertained by attractive party girls.

A sometime hostess and guest at this watering spot, called the Quorum Club, was a twenty-seven-year-old model named Ellen Rometsch, a five-feet, five-inch beauty with long dark hair, sensuous lips, and a slender figure. According to J. Edgar Hoover, Elly charged $200 a night for her services. Another young woman, a twenty-four-year-old friend of Elly, said later, "I know a lot I wish I didn't know."

The story was dug up by Clark Mollenhoff, the ace reporter for the *Des Moines Register and Tribune*. Before publishing it, he went to Kennedy and asked what he knew. Bobby checked the FBI files and learned that Elly was involved with a number of people in the capital. He told Mollenhoff, however, that nobody in the White House had ever been "entertained" by her at the club or anywhere else.

Kennedy was angry when the story came out and did mention the White House. "That," he said, "was the most damaging part."

Investigating further, Bobby found that the club membership of some

200 persons cut across all party lines. The suite of rooms the club occupied had a bar, dining room, lounges, and card tables, and was surely not a brothel.

But hostesses on occasion showed up for the entertainment of members, and it was this that sent Bobby racing to the Oval Office. He told the President that what was happening "was very damaging to the reputation of the United States," and that, although nobody at the White House was involved, "it would just destroy the confidence that people in the United States had in their government."

Was Bobby Kennedy airbrushing the truth when he said nobody in the White House was "involved"?

Bobby Baker had this to say in 1978: "What the newspapers did not say, possibly because I've never admitted it before—*but which Robert F. Kennedy definitely knew*—was that Ellen Rometsch had been one of the women Jack Kennedy had asked me to introduce him to. I accommodated his request" (author's italics).

By August, Elly Rometsch and her husband, Sergeant Rolf Rometsch of the West German Air Force, had been whisked out of the country. In Bonn, shortly thereafter, Sergeant Rometsch was granted a divorce on grounds of "conduct contrary to matrimonial rules." The activities of the club came to an end.[21]

By the beginning of 1962, Bobby had virtually written off Hoover in his mind as a nasty, hate-filled man who never should have been reappointed. The memos convinced him, he told a close associate, that "the man collects dirt better than a carpet sweeper." He was no longer paying much attention to the monthly sex-related notes, all raw, unchecked charges, until February 27, 1962.[22]

The memo delivered that day was charged with trouble. FBI agents, Hoover told Bobby, had discovered that the President had been having a relationship for the past two years with Judith Campbell, a woman who was at the same time friendly with a Mafia don.

Bobby knew one man well: he was the dapper, jewel-flashing Salvatore (Sam) Giancana who had giggled his way through his testimony before the McClellan rackets committee. "I thought only little girls giggled," Bobby had told the Chicago mobster contemptuously.

He had hated the oily, boastful man, who was for him the quintessence of corruption. He had hated him even more when he discovered only a few months before that Giancana had been recruited by the Central Intelligence Agency to head up an undercover operation to overthrow Castro's Communist regime.

If Bobby's Puritanical soul was revolted at the idea that his brother and a Mafia chieftain might be sharing the same mistress, his pragmatic mind was even more appalled. This was truly dangerous stuff, raising the spectre of blackmail by organized crime, the "enemy within" that Robert Kennedy had sworn to crush.

It was not until years later that the whole sorry tale came into the open. In 1975, a bipartisan Senate Select Committee investigating intelligence abuses, headed by Senator Frank Church, reported that in an eighteen-month period between late 1960 and mid-1962 a "close friend" of John Kennedy made seventy telephone calls to the White House. The "friend," not named by the committee, was soon found by the press: she was now Judith Campbell Exner. (Two years later she published a book detailing her simultaneous affair with the President and Giancana.)

What Bobby told the President in the White House or on their walks together in the Rose Garden will never be known. The questions are tantalizing: Did he plead with his brother to stop seeing the woman, warn the philandering Jack that his careless sexual habits left him vulnerable to disgrace? "It wasn't something he would tell a lot of people," Ed Guthman says dryly. What cannot be doubted is that Bobby was anguished. Suppose this beautiful woman, with the kind of refined features and carriage that appealed most to Jack, had been planted by the Mafia to incriminate the President? Would organized crime, with such a stranglehold on the Oval Office, then have the nation by the throat?

The pain finally ended for Bobby on March 22, 1962. On that day, there were no more telephone calls to the White House from Judith Campbell. J. Edgar Hoover had a one-on-one luncheon meeting with the President, and, while neither ever divulged what transpired, there is little doubt that the FBI Director produced enough proof of the woman's Mafia connection to cool the President's ardor for her.[23]

After that, Bobby lived with Jack's continuing affairs, but never again did the President skate on such thin ice.

16

Passage to Commitment

FROM THE time of his exposure to the real world at the start of the 1960s, his social conscience developed rapidly. The moralism that had made Bobby Kennedy embrace the McCarthy crusade and the war on labor racketeering found a new cause in racial injustice.

It was during the primary campaigns that he began to learn that there was another, and more sinister, enemy within, this one striking at the heart of America's principles of equal justice. In May he had come to Harris Wofford with a confession: "We don't know much about this whole [civil rights] thing. We've been dealing outside the field of the main Negro leadership, and we have to start from scratch." He asked Wofford to head up a civil rights section.

In May, Chester Bowles, who was chairman of the Democratic Platform Committee, drew up a strong civil rights plank. Bowles's strategy was to begin at the top with a "maximum plank." Then, he said, "we'll negotiate." He submitted it to Bobby, who stood on a chair in his suite at the Biltmore Hotel in Los Angeles and, addressing key campaign workers, accepted the "maximum" and told everyone to go "all the way" with it.

Was this the beginning of commitment, or a political strategy to deliver as many black delegates as possible at the July convention?

"It was part of both," asserts Wofford. "Bobby knew that his brother had to be elected to achieve reforms in civil rights, but he was beginning to understand that the reforms needed to be made."[1]

"Bobby best understood things by feeling and touching them," declared Richard Boone, one of his aides. As he saw the legal, social, and economic inequities faced by blacks, his sense of moral justice was offended. He had an almost uncanny ability to burrow into other people's feelings and, almost literally, experience what they did. Once he was lowered into a coal mine in northern Chile, emerging with a blackened face and a look of horror at the conditions under which the men were forced to work. When he was told the majority of the miners were members of a Communist union, he responded, "If I worked in this mine, I'd be a Communist, too."[2]

The first actual manifestation of a concern that was to grow rapidly had come less than two weeks before Election Day.

On Wednesday, October 19, Martin Luther King, Jr., entered Rich's department store in downtown Atlanta, walked into the Magnolia Room, and asked to have lunch. When he and about a dozen followers were refused service and would not leave, they were arrested for trespassing on private premises. More than fifty other blacks sitting in at other lunchrooms in the city were also jailed.

Within days, all were released pending trial, but King had been rearrested for violating probation. The previous year, he had been fined $25 and put on probation for a year by a judge in DeKalb County, Georgia, for driving with an Alabama license, illegal in Georgia. Now he was sentenced to six months at hard labor.

King was awakened at 4:30 A.M. in the county jail and, hands cuffed and ankles chained, driven 300 miles to a state prison in Reidsville. Exhausted, his wrists and ankles rubbed raw, he was given a prison uniform and thrust into a small cell reserved for hardened criminals.

Robert Kennedy was finishing breakfast at Hickory Hill when John Seigenthaler, his administrative aide, arrived for a brief conference before Bobby took the shuttle flight for New York. The two men left for National Airport in Bobby's blue convertible. Several days had passed, and King was still in jail.

As they drove down Chain Bridge Road, Bobby spoke: "I want to call that judge," he said. "I want to tell him that everybody in this country—everybody—has a right to bail under the Constitution. He had no right to sentence him without granting bond."

"The more he talked," Seigenthaler recalled, "the angrier he became. I tried to calm him. I questioned the propriety of a lawyer to raise hell with a judge over bail in a case with which he wasn't connected. The news would be splashed over the front pages and be on national television for sure, and very likely would detract from the thrust of the campaign, which was geared to other issues." There would be a tight race in Georgia, and a bold act such as this might well lose the state.

As he left him at the airport, Seigenthaler urged Bobby to think it over.

Meanwhile, he planned to ask Sargent Shriver and Harris Wofford to plead with Bobby not to call.

In midmorning, a news service sent out a story from Georgia that Bobby had telephoned and excoriated the judge. Seigenthaler couldn't believe it. Incensed, he told Roger Tubby of the campaign staff to issue a denial.

As Tubby left, Bob Kennedy called from New York. He had indeed spoken to the judge. "Cancel the denial if you denied it," Seigenthaler yelled to Tubby.

Recalling the conversation, Seigenthaler quoted Bobby as saying, "I couldn't get it out of my mind. The more I thought about it, the more outraged I got. On the plane I got angrier and angrier. It's the man's right to make bond! If he leaves the jurisdiction, he'll be back. Johnny isn't a lawyer, so he couldn't call. I am, and I can, and I did."[3]

Within hours, the judge allowed King to post bond pending appeal.

Candidate Nixon, a lawyer, too, had said nothing. Candidate Kennedy had only called Coretta King to offer his support. But Bobby had gone far out on a limb. Swept away by his passion, he had breached the Canons of Professional Ethics of the American Bar Association, which specifically bar attorneys from communicating privately with judges on pending cases.

To Nixon, it was a "grandstand" play. At Democratic campaign headquarters, many thought the act had been dumb and dangerous, certain to cost heavily in southern white votes. Bobby, too, realized afterward it had been wrong. Next day, looking contrite, he asked aides, "Couldn't you just say [to the press] I was inquiring about Dr. King's constitutional right to bail?"[4]

He had responded emotionally to moral outrage. His act of courage paid off on Election Day in astonishing fashion. Kennedy defeated Nixon in Georgia by 458,638 to 274,472 and won two-thirds of the state's black vote.

"You are now an honorary brother," Louis Martin, a black journalist who worked at national headquarters, told him. But Bobby was not yet thinking as a brother. "At this stage," declared John Seigenthaler, "he was like many liberal northerners who have never been exposed to the racism of the South. They had a sense that what went on was wrong, but not the rage nor the frustration and the bitterness. The trauma of the black experience was still beyond his grasp."

After he was sworn in as Attorney General, a world never visible to him as a young man came into direct view, and with his built-in capacity to *feel*, education came fast. His boyhood friend Dave Hackett, who had been named to head a government agency on youth delinquency, took him on a walking tour of New York's Harlem only a few weeks after he took office. Bobby couldn't stop talking about what he had seen.

A week later, he discovered the pitiable condition of Washington's schools, during a drive through the ghetto areas with Ed Guthman. "These were all private visits," Guthman said, "no notices to the press or anyone else." The enrollment of the schools was overwhelmingly black.

At Dunbar High at First and N Streets in the northwest section, only a mile from the Capitol, he learned that the swimming pool had not been used for eight years because of needed repairs.

"So he wrote to the school board and asked how much it would cost to fix it," Guthman said. "They told him $50,000, but he got a contractor who said he'd do it for $35,000. Then he got in touch with Catholic, Protestant, and Jewish philanthropic organizations and raised the cash.

"That summer, the pool was opened, and used, not only by the students but the community."

Even worse than the physical condition of the schools was the staggering dropout rate. At Cardozo High, within sight of the White House, he was told that nearly 500 quit every year.

"How many can you help?" he asked the superintendent.

"About fifteen."

At Justice, Bobby called an afterhours meeting of his top aides and came up with the idea for a benefit show. Hosted by Ella Fitzgerald, the noted black singer who had entertained at his brother's inauguration show, $50,000 was raised, enough to keep 400 students in school by providing counseling, and cash when needed.[5]

That February of 1961 Bobby told John Seigenthaler, "I don't know anybody in this department. Let's take one day a week and go on some walks."

Seigenthaler recalled: "The walks went on for weeks. We worked our way through every division housed in that big block-square building and then into all the offices located elsewhere in the city. One day, after we had gone through the lands division behind the Federal Courthouse, he asked on the way back, 'Does anything strike you strange about the personnel?'

"I said, 'No, not especially.'

" 'In the weeks we have been doing this, how many Negroes have we seen?'

"Except for some secretaries, cleaning women, and maintenance people, I realized there had been none at all."

In March, Bobby asked his three chief southern aides, Ramsey Clark of Texas, Louis Oberdorfer of Alabama, and Seigenthaler of Tennessee to find out exactly how many blacks were employed in the department. Without waiting for the result, he began a recruitment program, ordering letters to be written to all the deans of law schools and the heads of bar associations in major cities, asking them to recommend qualified black attorneys.

All division heads cooperated in the count except J. Edgar Hoover, who ducked every memo Seigenthaler sent him. He pleaded he didn't know, because federal law barred him from listing personnel by race. When Seigenthaler pressed him to assign someone to make a head count, Hoover said it would be impossible to get an accurate result because some agents had "mixed blood."

Finally Seigenthaler asked Sal Androtta, Assistant Attorney General for Personnel, to try to get some answers from the Director. Androtta visited Hoover and told him that, since none of the other divisions had thus far come up with any blacks, he wouldn't look all that bad if the FBI didn't have any either.

Thus reassured, Hoover sent in his report: the bureau had two black agents.

"So I had to tell the Attorney General he had two black G-men working for him," Seigenthaler said. "He was outraged at the Justice Department's record and astounded by Hoover's—until Androtta checked and learned that the two agents were assigned to Hoover as his personal chauffeurs."

Bobby's recruiting campaign bore fruit. From just ten black lawyers who eventually were found working at Justice, the number rose to more than one hundred in two years. About a dozen were prominent black attorneys who were telephoned personally by Bobby and persuaded to accept appointments.

Getting blacks into the FBI was much tougher. Hoover claimed none could be found who could pass the tests and was convinced he knew why. One day, an aide to Bobby who had talked to the Director on a business matter reported that Hoover had told him, "Everybody knows that Negroes' brains are twenty percent smaller than white people's."[6]

Word that the 6,600 agent corps was entirely white spread rapidly. One day in March, a large crowd of angry blacks gathered outside the building, protesting the discrimination. "Bobby got a bullhorn and went out to talk to them, telling them something will be done," said Ramsey Clark. "It was a milestone in the department. His predecessors would have closed their doors, and their ears."

Next day Bobby summoned Hoover. "There was a stormy scene," Clark recalled. Hoover took his familiar position that hiring was done strictly on merit. "You show me a black man who is as well-qualified as a white man, and we'll take your man," he said. Observed Clark, "We weren't even talking about women in those days!"

"Bobby would have gotten better results with diplomacy," Clark asserted, "but he slammed ahead, bluntly demanding the Director to change policy. Hoover, who resented any criticism from anywhere, bucked. Slowly, though, a number of blacks were appointed."[7]

Troubled as he was by what he viewed as a scar on America's face,

Bobby was still talking in terms not unlike those of other moderates: "We must move strongly and vigorously . . . I do not think this is a matter that can be solved overnight. . . . We're not interested in pushing things down people's throats. . . . We're trying to work these matters out."[8]

Early in February, he talked face to face with Martin Luther King for the first time.

It was an historic meeting of the activist and the government official charged with enforcing the laws. During their three-hour talk, they discovered that they were in total disagreement on how the problem should be remedied. "King, the idealist, and Kennedy, the pragmatist, saw and heard one another and realized they were poles apart," Seigenthaler, who was present, declared. Kennedy stood for slow but steady progress within the framework of laws; King stood for freedom now.

They met in Bobby's office on a wintry morning. Tie askew and hair rumpled, as always, one foot resting on an open desk drawer, Bobby faced a dark-suited, immaculately groomed King. The visitor, speaking softly, made it clear that he and his followers would attack civil rights violations on a broad social front, peacefully targeting segregation practices in public facilities.

Kennedy listened respectfully but told King that protests, even though nonviolent, would almost certainly result in bloody violence when the inevitable clashes occurred. Voter registration, he told King, would be the way to proceed. It was the conservative, cautious approach, avoiding direct confrontations, and King, of course, knew it. He shook his head.

"Look," Bobby said, leaning toward him. "You know that Negroes are permitted to register and vote in many parts of the South, but simply do not. If you can get enough of them on the voting rolls in Mississippi, Jim Eastland wouldn't be so fresh." James O. Eastland, the rich planter who venomously decried "mongrelization of the races," was chairman of the Senate Judiciary Committee.

"It was a terrific line," commented Seigenthaler. Eastland had been trying to bottle up civil rights legislation in the Judiciary Committee for years, and succeeding much of the time.

Dr. King, impressed by Kennedy's remark, softened. "I'm not saying we won't be interested in voter registration," he said, "but right now the full thrust of my movement has to be directed at the abuses every Negro experiences every moment of every day."

Kennedy walked to the door with Dr. King, and the two men shook hands warmly, each knowing the road the other would take.[9]

It was not until more than two years later, after the Freedom Riders had been clubbed, stoned, and fire-bombed as they moved through the South in busloads, that Bobby began to comprehend the depth of black fury, grief, and despair.

The start of this climactic stage of his education can be pinpointed to a single day: May 24, 1963.

On that afternoon, he met with a small group of black artists and intellectuals and a few white supporters in the apartment his family owned on Central Park South, near the Plaza Hotel.

At that session, Bobby was subjected to a three-hour verbal assault that left him angry and resentful but, in the end, opened his eyes.

For some time, Kennedy had wanted to ask leading northern blacks for whatever advice they could offer on further steps the Administration could take to end racial discrimination. He had also felt that successful blacks up north could increase their efforts on behalf of their less fortunate brothers and sisters fighting the civil rights revolution in the South.

Early in May, he called James Baldwin, the writer and essayist whom he knew and liked, and suggested the meeting to discuss the situation, then at another boiling point in Birmingham. Baldwin gathered together the singers Lena Horne and Harry Belafonte, the playwright Lorraine Hansberry, the actor Rip Torn, the psychologist Dr. Kenneth Clark, and a few others, including a young leader of the Congress for Racial Equality.

When Kennedy, accompanied by Burke Marshall, arrived, they were all gathered in the small lobby, waiting for him. He led them upstairs, and the session began, the whites seated on one side of the living room, the blacks on the other. To Lena Horne, who had flown in from Palm Springs, California, the seating arrangements symbolized the character of the meeting.[10]

It began on a note of sharp criticism of the Administration and never let up.

"Those of us, like you and me, who are blessed . . . " Bobby told the group. Baldwin interrupted sharply: "Blessed!" he said. "You don't know what the hell you're talking about. My life is not blessed. I live in hell!"

Kennedy stared at him in astonishment. Jerome Smith, the young CORE official who was still ill from beatings in the South, demanded to know why the government hadn't sent more marshals to protect civil rights demonstrators. Stammering in his urgency to express his pain and the disgust he felt at the Kennedy brothers' inaction, he told Bobby, "Being at this meeting makes me want to throw up."

It got worse. Bobby tried to explain that Congress had before it a civil rights bill, and another, stronger one was being drafted. Neither Smith nor the others listened. Smith's rage had ignited theirs; the hostility poured out unchecked.

Baldwin turned to Smith and asked if he would go to war for the United States. "Never, never, never!" Smith replied. Kennedy was profoundly shocked. "How can you say that?" he demanded. Smith said he could indeed say it, and said it again. When Bobby tried to explain that his own grandparents, newly arrived from Ireland, had been the victims of discrimination, Baldwin told him, "Your family has been here for three generations. My family has been here longer than that. Why is your brother at the top, while we are still far away? That's the heart of the problem."

The blacks were not hearing his arguments that the government was doing more than any other previous Administration. "There is no logic in the way the Negro has been treated," Lena Horne said later, "and so, to suddenly start asking the Negro to be logical and reasonable and patient in his demands, which is what Mr. Kennedy was trying to do, seemed ridiculous to me."[11]

The blacks, Miss Horne declared, were past listening to "reasonable" explanations. With police dogs being loosed on black children in Birmingham and black women swept down the streets by jets from fire hoses, they felt agony, impotence, and burning rage, no longer willing to grasp the hand held out in goodwill. Jerome Smith, they felt, "just put it like it was. He communicated the plain, basic suffering of being a Negro," Miss Horne asserted.[12]

The meeting ended with both sides exhausted by the emotional outbursts. Bobby, seething inwardly, was convinced they knew nothing about what was being done and didn't want to learn. The blacks were just as certain they hadn't gotten through to him at all.

"He was deeply depressed when he returned to the office that evening," Seigenthaler declared. "He had truly believed that the seeds of ending discrimination had been sown and the plant was beginning to grow, but that the black intellectuals had pissed on the plant. He had hoped to challenge them, and they had wound up challenging him."

In the weeks that followed, Bobby thought a great deal about the events of that day; the more he dwelled on the emotions that had spilled out, the clearer the magnitude and depth of the problem came into focus.

The black people he admired, artists, singers, people of significant accomplishment who were earning large sums of money, felt themselves discriminated against just as much as the southern blacks who were far lower on the economic scale. Despite their fame and wealth, blacks who had "arrived" felt excluded in the white world.

"If there ever was a maturing time in Kennedy's life," Seigenthaler declared, "this was it. It took a while, but Bobby Kennedy came to realize that integration could not be accomplished by laws alone; that segregation and discrimination were not confined to the southern states; that the young man who had said he wouldn't fight for his country was not as wrongheaded as he had believed.

"The problem was not to change the young man, but to change America," he said.[13]

17

Quarterback for Civil Rights—1
Rides for Freedom

*T*HE REAL thrust of the Kennedy Administration policies regarding the black race were principally the work and ideas of his brother Robert Kennedy rather than the President himself."[1]

Many years after the civil rights struggles of the 1960s, Bobby won this tribute from James Meredith, the first black admitted to the University of Mississippi.

Since his graduation from Ole Miss in 1963, Meredith has worked for the full participation of blacks in the American system. The authors spoke with him after he completed a year as a visiting professor at the University of Cincinnati.

Recalling the early years, he said, "Jack Kennedy, who had been in the House and Senate, was a typical rich Irishman who did whatever he did from political necessity. Bobby was different. When he was in the Kennedy government, he was much less of a politician than his brother.

"It was he who made the core decisions on civil rights."[2]

He was the gadfly in the Administration. When Jack Kennedy was moving so slowly that he was tagged the "reluctant emancipator," Bobby told him in private conversation that action must be taken, because it was right to do so and wrong not to. Kenny O'Donnell, his liberal friend and football teammate, said, "On civil rights, Bobby was the quarterback."[3]

John Kennedy, worried lest the Freedom Riders racing into the heart of

Dixie might embarrass him at the Vienna summit, angrily told his special assistant for civil rights, "Get your friends off those buses!" Bobby, identifying with the embattled blacks, wished they would stop because he was fearful for their safety and, when they would not, gave them all the protection he could under the law.

John Kennedy dragged his feet almost two years before he signed an executive order banning segregation in public housing funded by the government. In October 1960, he had pledged its elimination by "one stroke of a pen," a promise he regretted when, soon after he took office, thousands of pens and gallons of ink were mailed to the White House by civil rights advocates.

Looking at the cartons, Kennedy joked, "Who the hell got me to make the promise?" Told it was Harris Wofford, he said, "Then send the pens over to him." They were stacked in Wofford's office until the President finally signed the executive order.

On May 6, 1961, Bobby Kennedy flew in the *Caroline* to the Deep South, where he bluntly told his almost all-white audience that the Kennedy Administration intended to enforce civil rights laws vigorously.

The occasion was the Law Day address at the University of Georgia at Athens; in the audience of almost 1,800 whites—students, faculty, and parents—was Charlayne Hunter, one of two young black women whose entrance, suspension, and subsequent reinstatement had precipitated riots on the campus several months earlier.

It was his first major speech as Attorney General, and he used it to give a complete picture of how the Kennedy Administration would tackle civil rights.

"You may ask, will we enforce the civil rights statutes?" he declared. "The answer is: Yes, we will.

"We also will enforce the antitrust laws, the antiracketeering laws, the laws against kidnapping and robbing federal banks and transporting stolen automobiles across state lines, the illicit traffic in narcotics, and all the rest.

"We can do no less."

As he spoke, a group of seven black and six white members of the Congress of Racial Equality (CORE) was embarking on a journey that would test these vows. They had left Washington by bus on May 4 on a ride that would take them through Virginia, North and South Carolina, Georgia, Alabama, and Mississippi, all the way to New Orleans. They planned to use—and integrate—waiting rooms, eating facilities, washrooms, and barber shops in the terminals, which were barred to blacks.

There had been some minor troubles. In Charlotte, North Carolina, one young man had been arrested for refusing to leave a barbershop. Three young people had been assaulted in Rock Hill, South Carolina, and another two arrested in Winnsboro. But the worst was yet to come.

On Sunday, May 14, in Atlanta, Georgia, the Freedom Riders divided into two groups; one boarded a Greyhound bus and the other, a Trailways for the ride to Birmingham. Six miles outside of Anniston, Alabama, a mob of Ku Klux Klansmen attacked the Greyhound bus. A fire bomb was thrown, burning the vehicle and injuring twelve persons. That evening the Trailways bus was met at the Birmingham bus terminal by other Ku Klux Klansmen carrying chains, clubs, and blackjacks; the Freedom Riders were subjected to an unmerciful ten-minute beating.

Where were the police? An FBI informant had tipped off the agency to the impending violence, and authorities in Anniston and Birmingham had been notified, but no police were in the area. Eugene (Bull) Connor, Birmingham Police Commissioner, said it was Mother's Day, and he had given his men the day off.

"I knew about it from reading the paper next morning," Bobby told Anthony Lewis.[4] He conferred with John Seigenthaler and Burke Marshall and took a telephone call from Simeon Booker, a reporter for *Jet* who was in the Birmingham bus terminal. Booker confessed he was frightened. "I don't think we are ever going to get out of here," he declared.

"John, you'd better go down there," Bobby told Seigenthaler.

Twenty-four years later, Seigenthaler, now executive editor of *USA Today,* recounted the story in his office on Wilson Boulevard in Arlington, Virginia. Just back from an early morning tennis game, he spoke quietly, recalling the details easily, the horror apparently etched deeply in his memory.[5]

"I was his friend, and he sent me down there so he would have somebody close on the scene. He called the President and told him I was going. I was on the first plane out. They [the Freedom Riders] had been taken to the hospital and the Birmingham airport. I went there.

"A mob surrounded the airport. The police were hostile. They [the Freedom Riders] would go to the bathroom in twos and threes so that nobody would accost them. They had been badly beaten. They were in bad shape. A guy named Peck had his head bloodied, swathed in bandages, his ribs broken."

That afternoon, Bobby spoke to some of the injured people in the hospital; they had decided to abandon the ride. Seigenthaler accompanied them to New Orleans and had just about settled in at his hotel when the telephone rang at 2 A.M. It was Robert Kennedy calling from Washington. Another group of students was coming from Nashville to Birmingham to continue the Freedom Ride.

"Can you go back up, John?" Kennedy asked.

In Birmingham, the new Freedom Riders waited to board a bus, but none was leaving the terminal. Bobby spoke to Bull Connor, who said the police would protect the bus station but could do nothing once the bus had left the terminal. He called Alabama Governor John Patterson, who agreed to guarantee the safety of the Riders on the road; several hours later he had changed his mind. For the next few days, with the Riders waiting in the terminal, Patterson was unreachable by phone, even to the President. Bobby ordered Burke Marshall to assemble a force of federal marshals who would go to Alabama to maintain order.

Patterson finally returned JFK's calls, interrupting a Cabinet session one afternoon. He agreed to meet with a personal representative of the President, and Seigenthaler flew to Montgomery, where, in a two-hour meeting, he received assurances that the state could and would protect the new Freedom Riders.

Greyhound representatives protested there was no driver available, so Bobby again reached for the telephone. In an angry exchange with George E. Cruit, the company's Birmingham representative, he warned, "Somebody better get in the damn bus and get it going and get these people on their way."

The next morning, twenty-one students boarded a bus for Montgomery—ultimate destination, New Orleans. The FBI notified the Montgomery police its agents were on the way, but none was visible when the bus pulled into that city's terminal. As the Freedom Riders debarked, a crowd of more than 1,000 was waiting.

John Doar, chief assistant to Burke Marshall in the Civil Rights Division, called Bobby from the United States Attorney's office, overlooking the terminal, and described what was taking place.

"The bus is in," he said. "The people are just standing there watching. Now the passengers are coming off. They're standing in a corner of the platform.

"Oh, there are fists punching. A bunch of men are beating them. There are no cops. It's terrible. There's not a cop in sight. People are yelling, 'Get 'em, get 'em.' It's awful."[6]

Seigenthaler remembers: "I was in a car with John Doar. I was driving. He had a hearing in court, and I let him out at the Federal building, which adjoins the bus station. There was a mob waiting at the station. There were no police anywhere.

"The bus pulled in, and the passengers started coming off. The Freedom Riders were standing at one corner of the platform. Somebody yelled, 'Get 'em, get 'em,' and the mob moved in and started punching. I drove around the terminal. Two white girls, Susan Hermann and Susan Wilbur, were trying to get away. A large woman hit one of them on the head with her purse. As she backed off, somebody was hitting her from behind.

"Instinctively, I bounced the car over the curb, leaning on the horn. I leaped out of the car and yelled at one of the girls to get in the back. I grabbed the girl who was being beaten and tried to push her in. She was a young student and said to me, 'Mr., I'm nonviolent; this is not your fight. You're going to get hurt.'

"I said, 'Get your ass in the car.' I almost got away. But somebody grabbed me from behind and said, 'Who the hell are you?'

"I said, 'You get back, I'm a federal man.' I turned back to her, and the lights went out, I mean literally. I was hit with a pipe over the ear. When I went down, they kicked me and bounced on me. The two young women escaped from the other side of the car and ran to a church halfway down the block and escaped inside. I was left lying on the ground for a half-hour.

"When I came around, the first thing I did was I looked down. I was blood-soaked, and I was wearing John Doar's shirt. It was wet and sticky. I had left my coat with my billfold in the motel and the only thing I had was a notebook. It had telephone numbers for the White House, the Attorney General, for Hickory Hill, Fred Shuttleworth, a black minister, Governor Patterson, Bull Connor, the FBI, and Floyd Mann, head of the Alabama State Police. A police lieutenant was standing over me, and he had my notebook in his hand.

" 'You had some trouble, Buddy,' he told me. He had pulled me from under the car and put me into the passenger seat, where I was sitting when I came around.

"He said, 'Can I call anybody?' I had the presence to say, 'Yes, call Mr. Kennedy.'

"He said, 'What Mr. Kennedy?'

"I said, 'Either the President or the Attorney General.'

"Then he asked, 'Who the hell are you?'

"I said, 'I work for the Justice Department. My name is John Seigenthaler, and I'm the Presidential representative here to get these people through.

"Then he said, 'We've got to get you to a hospital.' He started to lift me, and I immediately passed out. The next thing I remember I came to on an X-ray table in Dr. Bartlett's clinic. Dr. Bartlett was talking to Whizzer White on the telephone.

" 'I think he's going to be all right,' he told Whizzer. 'He had a bad head wound, and he's badly bruised, maybe a broken rib. We're going to keep him here.'

"Whizzer got on the phone with me and said federal marshals were on the way. That night Bob called me. 'How's my popularity down there?' he wanted to know.

"I said, 'Bob, if you ever run for public office, don't do it in Alabama.' "

Bob Kennedy had just returned from horseback riding when Burke Marshall called to report on the events in Montgomery. He rushed to the Department of Justice, stopping on the way to throw out the first ball of the season at an FBI game. All that day and throughout the night, he was on the telephone, with the President, with Martin Luther King, Jr., with Governor Patterson, and with Whizzer White.

King decided to fly to Montgomery to speak at the First Baptist Church. That night, with some 1,500 blacks, including the Freedom Riders, inside the building, another crowd began to gather in the park across the street. Rocks were thrown; a car burned. When the mob advanced on the church, White's marshals, brandishing nightsticks and flinging tear gas, forced them back. State troopers and the National Guard arrived and formed a wall between the church and its attackers.

Dr. King called Bobby from the church and berated him for not providing enough protection.

"Now, Reverend," Kennedy replied. "Don't tell me that. You know just as well as I do that if it hadn't been for the United States marshals you'd be as dead as Kelsey's nuts right now." The reference to an old Irish slang expression may have been unknown to King, who ended the conversation abruptly.[7]

A few minutes later, Kennedy was at the receiving end of another angry outburst, this time from Governor Patterson, who called to protest that Alabama was being invaded.

"John, John," Kennedy replied. "What do you mean, you're being invaded? Who's invading you, John? You know better than that."

When Patterson charged that Kennedy had sent the Freedom Riders into the state and was responsible for the violence that resulted, Kennedy said, "Now, John, you can say that on television. You can tell that to the people of Alabama, but don't tell me that. Don't tell me that, John."

Patterson repeated the accusations and told Kennedy, "You're destroying us politically."

"John," Kennedy told him quietly, "it's more important that these people in the church survive physically than for us to survive politically."

The blacks remained in the church until 4 A.M., when they were escorted home by the members of the Guard. Kennedy left his office at six o'clock to go to his home.

He felt the right of the Freedom Riders to travel through the South had to be established. After "more than thirty" telephone conversations with Senator Eastland, the Freedom Riders traveled by bus from Montgomery to Jackson, Mississippi, under the protection of the state authorities. They were arrested for trying to integrate facilities at the Jackson terminal.

There were more rides and more arrests in the next months. The Interstate Commerce Commission, upon the request of the Attorney General, issued regulations forbidding segregated facilities, and the Justice Department began, city by city, to enforce them. By the end of 1962, the "white" and "colored" signs had disappeared from stations and terminals in the South.

18

Quarterback for Civil Rights—2
Blood on the Green at Ole Miss

O N SATURDAY morning, January 21, 1961, a slender young black man typed out the following letter on a Smith Corona portable: "Please send me an application for admission to your school. I would like to have a copy of your catalog and any other information that might be helpful to me."

It was addressed to the registrar of the University of Mississippi and signed J. H. Meredith. James Howard Meredith drove three-quarters of a mile down a hilly dirt road to a cluster of mailboxes, where he deposited the letter into the one bearing his father's name: "Moses Meredith, Route 2, Box 10."

He was now twenty-nine years old, married, and the father of a two-year-old son, John Howard. The seventh of thirteen children of "Cap" Meredith, who had worked a small farm in Attala County all his life, James had returned to his hometown the year before, after nine years in the Air Force and a brief period at Jackson State College, a black school. A political science major, he needed another year and a half of credits for his degree, and the University of Mississippi offered the best courses in his field.

But "Ole Miss" had not enrolled a black student since it was founded 113 years before. The letter Meredith mailed that day started a chain of events that epitomized the full immensity of the legal, social, political, and, finally, the violent aspects of the civil rights revolution.

199

The day before, former Staff Sergeant Meredith had listened by radio to the inauguration address of John Kennedy. In the living room of his father's house, four miles from the Mississippi hill-country town of Kosciusco, he had heard the forty-four-year-old President proclaim that "the torch had been passed to a new generation." Excited by the promise of the New Frontier, he became convinced that the new Administration would work hard to obtain the rights of citizenship for black Americans.

Trouble began almost at once. Meredith received an application on January 26, which he filed five days later, affixing a photograph in the space calling for it, unmistakably a black face, and explaining in a covering letter that he was "an American—Mississippi-Negro citizen." On February 4, he received a telegram from the registrar informing him that all applications arriving after January 25 could not be considered and advising him not to appear for registration.

Meredith appealed to Thurgood Marshall, then chief of the NAACP's legal defense staff. The lawyers hesitated: Mississippi was the toughest nut there was. Already civil rights advocates had fought and died there. The NAACP wanted to know if Jim Meredith was tough enough to stand up against the ordeal that would surely come. Over the telephone, the ex-Air Force man bellowed, "Just try me."

Convinced, the NAACP took the case in his behalf. All that winter, spring, and summer, suits were fought in the courts, Meredith losing at first, then winning but being blocked by a series of stays. Finally, on September 10, 1961, Supreme Court Justice Hugo L. Black nullified the final stay of an injunction and ordered James Meredith admitted to the university.

Mississippi would not yield. Bearing the standard in the fight was the fundamentalist sixty-four-year-old Governor Ross Barnett, an ardent believer in the supremacy of the white race, who had no use for Kennedy or Johnson. In 1960, he had bolted the Democratic ticket to back Virginia's Senator Harry Flood Byrd for the Presidency.

Three days after the Supreme Court ruling, Barnett issued a proclamation that all public schools and institutions of higher learning in Mississippi would be run under state supervision, answerable only to state laws. Challenging "the evil and illegal forces of tyranny," he called upon the state's leaders to follow him into a prison cell if that were needed to keep Ole Miss white.

In Washington Bobby Kennedy heard Barnett's defiant call and immediately said, "The man's a looney." When United States marshals armed with a court order escorted Meredith to the Oxford campus, they were met by 2,000 jeering students singing, "Glory, glory, segregation," and by Barnett himself acting as a "special registrar." Meredith was turned away then and on two other occasions. The fourth attempt, on September 27, was canceled when Justice Department officials heard that 2,500 students and 200 police armed with clubs had been deployed around the campus to stop him.

Bobby Kennedy arrived at the Oval Office at 7 A.M. on Sunday morning, entering through the Rose Garden door to avoid the media. All day and night, without sleep, he shuttled between the Cabinet Room, which was designated command headquarters, and the President's office.

His greatest fear was that emotions, rising to the flashpoint, would explode in a bloody shootout between American troops and Mississippi sheriffs, police, and civilians. Sitting at the President's desk, the brothers discussed that grave possibility.

"We could just visualize another great disaster like the Bay of Pigs," he said later, "with a lot of marshals being killed."[1] He did not exclude from the worst-case scenario yet another horror: the body of James Meredith hanging from one of the tall trees on the Ole Miss campus.

The thought chilled him. "Oh God," he said to Budd Schulberg, who had dropped in at Justice, "I hope nothing happens to Meredith. I feel responsible for him. I promised we'd back him up all the way—and I'm worried for McShane [the D.C. chief marshal] and the others, too. It seems so simple, so simple to us, and down there it's bloody hell."[2]

At 7:30 on Friday evening, John Kennedy had called Barnett at the domed state capitol in Jackson. Once and for all, Kennedy demanded, would the governor cooperate in enforcing the court order to admit Meredith? Barnett hedged again, but he had an idea.

Why not register Meredith secretly in Jackson and announce on Monday that it had been done? That way, a confrontation might be averted. Kennedy said he couldn't care less how and where the admission took place as long as it did.

But two and one-half hours later, Barnett called Bobby and said he had changed his mind about the secret admission plan. What he did not tell Kennedy—and has been unknown until now—was that James Meredith refused to be signed into the university under any cloak of secrecy, but insisted on being registered in exactly the same way as any other student.

Neither Kennedy was aware of this at the time. Bobby hung up and, bitter and angry, called the President. A few minutes past midnight, Jack Kennedy went to the newly restored Treaty Room and, on the massive walnut table around which Cabinet members of ten Administrations had sat, signed Executive Order 3497, which brought confrontation immeasurably closer.* The order authorized the Secretary of Defense to "take all appro-

* Kennedy went to the Treaty Room to sign the order to symbolize its importance. It was here that, on October 7, 1963, he signed the partial nuclear test ban on behalf of the United States.

priate steps'' to enforce all orders of the court, to use any armed forces he deemed necessary, and to call into active service the Mississippi Army and Air National Guards.

On Sunday morning, Barnett called again, once more begging Bobby, ''Can't you postpone this matter?''

''That's not possible,'' Bobby replied.

The governor thereupon proposed a ludicrous scenario: Bring Meredith to campus, escorted by a large, armed Army force. He would pass through a phalanx of unarmed Mississippi highway patrolmen and deputy sheriffs, who would be standing in front of a mass of students and other civilians. The governor would read a proclamation barring Meredith, the Army men would draw their weapons, and the defenders would yield.

Bobby instantly saw the possibility, if not probability, of calamity if the defenders did not surrender and told Barnett it would not do.

Throughout the week, Bobby had kept his temper. Now he lashed out. ''The President is going on television tonight,'' he shouted over the phone, ''and he's going to tell the entire nation you made an agreement with him to register Meredith and then broke your word.''

Barnett sputtered, ''That won't do at all.''

''You broke your word to him,'' Bobby repeated.

''You don't mean the President is going to say that tonight?''

''He is.''

Bobby called in Nick Katzenbach and, in a tone as casual as though he were inviting him to Hickory Hill for a cookout, asked if he was ''doing anything'' that afternoon. When Nick said he was free, Bobby asked him to fly down to Oxford and ''take charge of things.'' Nick said he'd go down with Ed Guthman, Norbert Schlei, and Dean Markham, one of Bobby's close friends from Harvard days. As Nick left, Bobby called after him with characteristic mordant humor, ''If things get rough, don't worry about yourself. The President needs a moral issue.''

As Katzenbach was about to leave, Harold Reis of the Office of Legal Counsel wandered into Bobby's office. ''Are you ready to go, Harold?'' asked Burke Marshall, who was with Kennedy.

Reis, who thought he was going into downtown Washington, said he was. ''He didn't know until he was in the car that he was going to Mississippi,'' Bobby said. ''Next time,'' Reis declared later, ''I'll ask, 'Go where?' ''

When they reached Andrews Air Force Base, they discovered they were assigned to a Jet Star, and that the runway at the small Oxford airport was short by at least 200 yards to land it.

Nick called Bobby, who, as always, expected his people to get things done. Laconically, he told Nick, ''Well, I'm not going to be on that plane, so just go ahead and land it.''

Katzenbach sighed, then wondered how they would take off if they did succeed in landing safely. Bobby, straight-faced, replied, "You can take the plane apart and put it on a truck and take it to a new airport and then reassemble it."

Nick figured out a way: they would jettison enough fuel to enable the aircraft to land and take off.[3]

Earlier, Ed Guthman, accompanied by John Doar, who was in charge of voting rights cases, and big Jim McShane, the D.C. marshal, had taken off for the huge Millington Naval Air Station north of Memphis, Tennessee. Seventy-eight miles from Oxford, Millington had been designated as a staging area for the corps of marshals and federal troops. Jim Meredith had been taken there for security.

By late afternoon, 300 marshals had ringed the Lyceum, a large red-brick building in the center of the campus that housed the Administration offices where Meredith insisted on being registered. Surrounding them, about a hundred students and townsfolk had gathered. As the afternoon waned, more and more came. Shouts began: "Where's the nigger?" "Kill the nigger-loving bastards!" By early evening, the mob, rapidly growing uglier, numbered more than 1,500.

Unknown to them, Meredith was a mile away in Baxter Hall at the western edge of the campus, having landed at Oxford airport at 3:45 P.M. in a green twin-engine Cessna. Surrounded by a swarm of marshals, he had been whisked in a caravan to Dormitory Row, where he was assigned two bedrooms, a living room, and a bathroom. True to his Air Force training, the first thing he did was make his bed.

In the White House, JFK had postponed his television address from 7:30 to 10 P.M. Washington time, hoping Barnett would permit the registration. But the governor saw that an avalanche was gathering speed.

From neighboring southern states, cars were pouring into Oxford and onto the campus, driven by furious segregationists who had filled their trunks with stones, metal pipes, and, in more than a few, there were shotguns. Some 200 police, armed with clubs, had been deployed around the campus. Barnett's aides were reporting to him that the mood on the campus was ugly and getting worse, with cries of resistance, "regardless of the cost in human life." On Friday Barnett had begged Bobby, "Can't you get him out? I can't protect him."

Bobby's answer was a masterpiece of humorous understatement under the circumstances: "But he likes Ole Miss."

Massive forces were also being assembled by the government. In addition to 541 marshals and deputies, among them tough men trained in riot control from federal prisons in Leavenworth, Atlanta, Terre Haute, and the federalized Mississippi National Guard, MP battalions, and United States combat troops had been put on alert in Fort Bragg, North Carolina, and Fort

Benning, Georgia. Cyrus Vance, then Secretary of the Army, set up a war room at the Pentagon, with large maps of Mississippi and red pins ready to mark strategic locations. As far away as Fort Dix, New Jersey, the 716th MP Battalion was ordered to be ready to move out in hours.

Close to 8 P.M., a sixty-man unit of the National Guard, commanded by Captain Murray C. Faulkner, nephew of the late novelist William Faulkner, arrived. Faulkner had lived in Oxford, and this added indignity infuriated the southerners who had ringed the building. They threw rocks, eggs, and metal pipes at the convoy, injuring one of the guardsmen.

It was now 7:58. President Kennedy was due to go on national television in two minutes (Washington time). He had already left the Cabinet Room for the Oval Office and was unaware that violence was beginning. In the Cabinet Room, Bobby picked up the phone. Katzenbach, from a pay station inside the Lyceum, told him, ''Bob, we're very sorry that we had to fire tear gas. We had no choice.''

Bobby yelled the information to Burke Marshall, who sprinted toward the Oval Office a few doors away. By the time he reached it, John Kennedy, at his desk, was saying to the nation, ''Good evening, my fellow citizens . . .''

Unaware of developments, Kennedy proceeded to deliver an impassioned, eloquent address telling the country that Meredith was safely on the campus of Ole Miss. Even as he continued to appeal to reason, hidden snipers were firing rifles and shotguns, soda bottles filled with gasoline and acid were being hurled at marshals, and stones, clubs, concrete blocks, and pipes were thudding against the Lyceum walls.

Bobby was chagrined as the President concluded, ''The honor of your University and State are in the balance. I am certain that the great majority of the students will uphold that honor.'' Shortly after the President returned to the Cabinet Room, Katzenbach called to say that a group of students had commandeered a bulldozer from a construction site and tried to ram the Lyceum. It had veered against a tree and stalled. They got it going again, but in a counterattack led by marshals, a canister of tear gas hit the driver's seat and drove off the attackers.

A new wave soon menaced the marshals. Katzenbach, alarmed, asked Ramsey Clark, who had been assigned to man a command post in Bobby's office at Justice, ''Can the marshals draw their guns?'' Clark relayed the question to Bob in the Cabinet Room with his own recommendation that authority not be given. Kennedy agreed: he said no.

Minutes later, as the mob, now numbering more than 300, pressed closer, came a second request. Once again Bob's reply was, ''No guns.''

Those two ''no's'' by Bob Kennedy in all likelihood prevented a massacre. Kennedy himself said they were the most crucial decisions made that evening, and Ramsey Clark concurred. "If guns had been drawn," he said, "the situation could have escalated pretty badly."[4]

Another fear assailed Clark. They knew at the command posts that Meredith wasn't at the Lyceum, but the mob did not. "Over at Baxter Hall," Clark said, "he was being guarded by only three or four marshals." If the crowds found out and rushed the dormitory, Clark had visions of "a great tragedy."

"Very fortunately," he said, "they never found out."[5]

The President went to his office and once again tried to reach Barnett to demand that he give in before bloodshed forced him to yield. While awaiting the return call, he paced the floor. When the phone rang, Evelyn Lincoln, who was at his desk, picked it up and, as the President looked on in amazement, began a pleasant conversation. After a few moments, she handed him the phone with a broad smile. "It's Red Fay," she said brightly. "He just wants to say hello." Paul B. Fay, Jr., an old friend from PT-109 days, was Under Secretary of the Navy. Said Kenny O'Donnell, who was watching, "I thought the President was going to grab the telephone and throw it out the window."[6]

The violence continued. Television mobile units were firebombed, and other automobiles on campus were burned and overturned. Deadly barrages of jagged concrete, stones, and whatever else could fly and hurt were thrown.

Southern officers were little help. Outside the Lyceum, one U.S. marshal asked a Mississippi state trooper to move the mob back from the building and was told, "To hell with you, you son of a bitch. I didn't invite you down here." When a young boy hacked away at the tire of an Army truck, a local patrolman advised him, "Don't fool around letting the air out that way. Just cut the valve stems right off." A coed, terrified by what was happening, asked a cop to do something. He turned away, saying, "Go talk to your federal buddies about it."

"How's it going down there?" Bobby asked Ed Guthman as rocks thudded against the Lyceum walls.

"Pretty rough," Ed replied. "It's getting like the Alamo."

"Well," Bobby said, "you know what happened to those guys, don't you?"

"The light remark," Guthman said later, "raised our morale and helped us through the night."[7]

Gallows humor such as this also eased the intense pressure building up in the Cabinet Room.

At the height of the battling, John Kennedy observed, "We have riots like this at Harvard just because some guy yells. . . . Remember the riot at Harvard? These guys go around and start asking for your identity card?"

"The university police," someone interjected.

"Yeah," Kennedy said. "That's the only thing that scared the shit out of me."

Burke Marshall, the telephone at his ear, told the meeting that the defending marshals had just driven the attackers a few dozen feet back from the Lyceum.

"We just got three points in the match!" came the dry observation from the end of the Cabinet table.

The reports grew increasingly ominous. Just before midnight in Washington, Barnett called again.

"Make sure and take that boy [Meredith] out of there and everything will be all right," he told someone who had picked up the phone in the Cabinet Room, probably Larry O'Brien.

"The son of a bitch," Bobby said when he was told, "he's always just . . ."

The President interrupted. "He wants to be able to say that he asked me to get him off. And I refused. [The problem is that] you've got to get law and order, and then you can discuss what to do about Meredith. But he can't do anything. He doesn't even get ahold of the head of the state police."

Bobby spoke to Nick, "How's it look?" It looked very bad. Two men had already been killed, and hundreds had been injured, some seriously. Paul Guihard, a thirty-year-old newsman for Agence France-Press, had been shot in the back, and a few minutes before, word had come that a local jukebox repairman named Ray Gunter had been taken by a fatal bullet in his head as he watched the action.

Katzenbach said the time had come to use the combat troops. JFK, who had hoped it would not reach that point, phoned Cyrus Vance at the Pentagon, who called Brigadier General Charles Billingslea at Memphis, which had been designated as a staging area for troops from a half-dozen bases. Billingslea, assistant commander of the Second Infantry Division at Fort Benning, Georgia, would be field commander on the campus.

But hours passed, and no troops arrived on the Ole Miss battlefield.

President Kennedy continued to ask about them and was assured they were on the way. "They're five minutes from landing," Bobby said they were told. "They're in the helicopters." But when he called the Memphis staging area, the troops still had not left. "Over and over," Bobby said, "we'd be told the same thing. And they hadn't been called out of their barracks to get into the helicopters yet."

Finally, JFK boiled over. "He had the worst and harshest conversation with Cy Vance and with the General that I think I've ever heard him have," Bobby reported later.

Finally, at 4 A.M. Mississippi time, MPs were bussed onto the campus, where they disembarked and fixed bayonets. Amid shrieks of derision from coeds along Sorority Row and a hail of stones and bricks, they marched to the Lyceum and stood around the building, facing the rioters.

The main body of troops was yet to come. The attackers multiplied and threatened to overwhelm the small MP force. A half-hour later, not a minute too soon, convoys rumbled onto the campus from every direction, surrounding the mob. After one final desperate lunge at the Lyceum by 100 students, peace finally was restored to the campus.

Even then, there was an aftershock to be dealt with. New rioting broke out at 9 A.M. in the town of Oxford, just one mile west down University Avenue, and continued for three more hours. By noon, after the troops had fired over the heads of the mob, the battling ended.

The lovely campus was a mess. Burned and wrecked vehicles, acres of broken glass, jagged pieces of masonry, torn clothing, and empty tear gas canisters littered the once-beautiful grounds. In addition to the two killed during the fifteen-hour riot, 166 marshals, 40 soldiers and guardsmen, and hundreds of students and civilians had been injured; two hundred rioters were arrested.

The man who was at the center of the storm slept through it all. James Meredith read a newspaper that Saturday evening and went to bed at 10 P.M. At intervals during the night, the distant gunfire roused him, and there was some commotion—door-banging and shouting—in the corridor outside his rooms.

"In the Air Force," he said, "you get used to noise, so I slept fairly well. In the morning, sometime between six and seven, I looked out my window and saw soldiers in combat gear. There was a slight odor of tear gas in the room, not too pungent, but unmistakable. With no radio in the room, I had no notion of what had happened or who or how many had been hurt. About eight, some marshals arrived and told me."

Outside was the same car used in his attempt to enroll eleven days before. It had been shiny and spotless then; now bullets had shot out the windows and scarred the sides and fenders. The marshals drove him to the Lyceum, where the university registrar, sitting behind a desk, handed him the forms. Meredith filled them out and was registered at last.

"Are you happy?" he was asked outside.

His eyes scanning the debris-strewn campus, he replied, "This is no time for a happy occasion."

For almost eleven months, James Meredith attended classes under constant guard by United States marshals. They lived with him, went where he went, and drove him on visits off campus. No day passed without shouts of "Hey, nigger . . . there's that nigger." He recalled one student, an especially foul-mouthed antagonist, who would typically barrage him with the

207

nastiest curse words ever uttered. "He called me every manner of sons of a bitch, mother f-s, coconut-headed baboons, and bastards," Meredith said.

One morning he saw that someone had created a new symbol for Ole Miss. Instead of a southern colonel, a man's face, painted coal black with large thick lips, had been drawn. Underneath were printed the words "Kennedy's new colonel." When he went to classes for the last time, he dressed in the same dark suit, white shirt, and red necktie he had worn when he registered. There was one difference: he had picked up a large button inscribed "NEVER, NEVER" from the grass. This had been Ross Barnett's slogan. He pinned it on his lapel, upside down.

On August 18, 1963, his degree in his luggage, Meredith left the campus and, still under escort, was driven up Route 55 to Memphis, where his cousin Katherine lived and his parents were waiting. Here he shook hands with the marshals and bade them good-bye. A close friend, Robert L. Smith, had accompanied him out of Oxford. As they left Ole Miss behind for the last time, Smith said to him, "I don't see how you stood it. I just don't see how you could take it."

In April 1963, when the University of Alabama was preparing to enroll three black students, Bobby Kennedy was determined to forestall any repetition of the turmoil in Oxford. He wanted to know what Governor George Wallace, an outspoken segregationist who had vowed to stand in the doorway himself to bar this registration, was going to do. Wallace refused to take his phone calls, so Kennedy had intermediaries arrange a meeting. On April 25, accompanied by Ed Guthman and Burke Marshall, he flew to Montgomery.

More than 600 state troopers ringed the capitol as Kennedy approached the building. Guarding the spot where Jefferson Davis was sworn in as President of the Confederacy was a white-clad, middle-aged woman, a member of the United Daughters of the Confederacy, whose chief duty was to prevent anyone from stepping there.

"They had the biggest state troopers you ever saw all guarding the way in, and they all had big sticks," Kennedy related later. "One of them took his stick and put it in my stomach . . . belted me with the stick.

"They were unfriendly . . . the point was to try to show that my life was in danger in coming to Alabama because people hated me so much."[8]

During the conference, Wallace was not very friendly either. "I will never myself submit voluntarily to any integration of any school system in Alabama," he declared.

Replied Kennedy, "I have a responsibility that goes beyond integration, to enforce the law of the land and to ensure court orders are obeyed."

"I understand your position," Wallace told him, "and I'm sure you understand mine, and it looks like we may wind up in court."

Bobby told Wallace, "As long as we wind up in court, I'll be happy, Governor. I just don't want it to get into the streets. I don't want to have another Oxford, Mississippi; that's all I ask."

When the meeting was over, Kennedy was convinced that Wallace was determined to defy the court order so that the Administration would have to use force. He "was dumbfounded by Wallace's attitude."

On May 21, a federal court ruled that blacks must be admitted to the summer session of the university. Three applicants were qualified—Vivian J. Malone, twenty, of Mobile; Jimmy A. Hood, twenty, of East Gladsden; and David M. McGlathery, twenty-seven, of Huntsville. Federal Judge Seybourn Lynne warned Governor Wallace not to obstruct their registration, hinting that failure to obey his order might get him a jail term.

As the June 10 date for the summer session drew near, Kennedy and his Justice Department aides planned carefully. Army reconnaisance planes photographed the Tuscaloosa campus, and aerial maps were drawn. Deputy Attorney General Katzenbach was again dispatched south, with a team of Justice Department aides and United States marshals. At nearby Fort Benning, Georgia, 400 army troops, trained for riot duty, were waiting, ready to go by helicopter to the campus.

In Washington, Bobby had set up another command post in his office. An open telephone line and a radio-telephone hookup linked him with Katzenbach's group; television and radios also would enable him to follow the events as they occurred.

Wallace, too, had made some preparations. Two air conditioners had been installed in an office just inside the entrance to the building where registration takes place. Al Lingo, the state highway patrol chief, had painted a white line in front of the building. A few minutes before ten, the time Katzenbach had told reporters the students would appear, Wallace arrived on the campus, accompanied by state policemen in full combat gear.

Minutes later, Katzenbach drove up in a border patrol car. Students Malone and Hood were parked nearby in vehicles driven by the federal marshals. After much deliberation, Kennedy and Justice Department aides had decided it would be best for Katzenbach to confront Wallace alone, thus giving him no chance to obstruct the students' registration and force the Administration to arrest the governor of Alabama.

A broiling sun shone overhead, and the temperature was near the 100-degree mark as Katzenbach strode to the entrance. Wallace, a microphone hanging around his neck, came from the building and stood before a lectern which had just been placed there.

"Stop," he called out as Katzenbach approached the line. The tall, balding Katzenbach, his forehead glistening with perspiration, stopped barely four feet from the short, pugnacious Alabama governor. He asked Wallace to give "unequivocal assurance that you will not bar entry to these students."

Wallace interrupted. "We don't want to hear any speeches," he declared, then proceeded to read a five-page proclamation, which concluded with a denunciation of "this illegal and unwarranted action by the central government."

When Wallace finished speaking, Katzenbach suggested that "he didn't know what the purpose of this show is."

"From the outset, Governor, all of us have known that the final chapter of this story will be the admission of these students," he asserted.

"Two students who seek an education on this campus are presently on this campus . . . it is a simple problem scarcely worth this kind of attention."

Wallace did not reply.

"Very well," said Katzenbach and he left.

From his office, Bobby spoke to Katzenbach and then called the President, who gave the order to call up the Alabama National Guard. That afternoon, Brigadier General Henry V. Graham, assistant commander of the Thirty-first Infantry, Alabama Guard, appeared before Wallace.

"It is my sad duty to inform you that the National Guard has been federalized. Please stand aside, so that the order of the court may be accomplished," he said. After Wallace left the campus, Malone and Hood went into the building.

"Hi, there," said the registrar to Malone, "we've been waiting for you."

Two days later McGlathery registered at the Huntsville extension center for night classes. There was no one there to protest.

In mid-1963, Martin Luther King, Jr., was driving to a speaking engagement in Connecticut with John Maguire, the university professor and civil rights fighter. Maguire asked Dr. King how he evaluated Bobby Kennedy's actions in the struggle.

"Umm, I believe he's comin' around," Dr. King replied with a small smile. "I believe he's comin' around."[9]

A few days later, Bobby and James Meredith met face to face for the first and only time. In the big Justice Department office, they shook hands and appraised each other.

"I met a man I could respect, a man who believed that blacks should control their own destiny, not accept what the white man thinks his destiny should be,'' Meredith asserted.

Bobby understood that. Said Meredith, ''The Kennedy Administration, mostly because of Robert Kennedy, was the first in American history to add moral authority to the black struggle.''

Bobby Kennedy was indeed comin' around.

19

"Someone Turned Off His Switch"

A T SIX in the afternoon of November 20, 1963, forty of Bobby Kennedy's staff at Justice, led by Ethel, trooped into his office for a surprise birthday party. Bobby, thirty-eight years old that day, was at work at his littered desk, reading glasses halfway down his nose. He looked up bewildered. He had completely forgotten his birthday.

Ethel, who had organized the party, had also thought up the gag gifts that he accepted with a shy, embarrassed grin. He got an old putter from his golf bag, tied with a pretty ribbon; only later did he recognize it as his own. He received a game of Monopoly with different signs pasted over the squares rimming the board. One read, "Land on White House Lawn"; another, "Get Camp David Free." He was handed a plastic "hot line" telephone in recollection of the days at the Democratic convention when it was in constant use.

He was toasted with beer, bottles of which were stacked on the table in the office, fed chocolate-covered cupcakes, and had "Happy Birthday" bellowed at him. After a half-hour, the staff left, and eight of his closest associates remained.

Despite the outward show of fun, an undercurrent of disquiet was being felt by the staff. Ramsey Clark remembered it as "a very gloomy evening." The Attorney General's office, and Kennedy himself, were under bitter attack for civil rights activities and some of its criminal prosecutions, particularly the continuing, unrelenting pursuit of Jimmy Hoffa and the Teamsters. The words "unfair" and "vendetta" recurred continually in the media.

From all across the nation, letters of protest were pouring into the AG's office, from private citizens as well as organized groups. "We had never received mail in the volume that we were getting it then," Clark said.

All this was uppermost in Bobby's mind that evening when he suddenly mounted the bottle-and-pastry-strewn table and delivered a mock political oration in which he cited all the voting blocs he had succeeded in alienating for his brother.

"My fellow Americans," he said, sawing the air with his right hand, "I want you to appreciate what a wonderful asset I am to the President. As Attorney General, I was responsible for convincing many segments of our population to support him. Now, take, for example, the Teamsters. John Kennedy has their undying backing, thanks to his little brother. And who do you think clinched the South for President Kennedy? Robert Kennedy, that's who. When he runs for a second term in 1964, the entire South will flock to his banner because of what I have done for civil rights.

"And I don't want to forget the civil libertarians. Now that's a large voting segment, and we managed to sew up their votes by wiretapping."

Ethel led the claque, calling out, "Let's hear it for the Teamsters! . . . Yeah for the civil rights!" But the applause from the eight was unenthusiastic.

Later Bobby, Ethel, and several aides went to the White House for the annual judicial reception, a highlight of the year for lawyers and other staff members of the Justice Department.

Upstairs, the President and Mrs. Kennedy were hosts at a small dinner party for the nine sitting and two retired Supreme Court justices and their wives. Jackie was masking a mood of petulance. She had arrived only hours before from their newly built summer home, Atoka, in the Virginia hunt country near Middleburg, where she had wanted to stay and rest for the trip to Texas on the twenty-first. But the President had telephoned the evening before and insisted she return. The justices and high judicial officials would be offended if the First Lady did not consider the event important enough to attend.

Jackie sighed and said she would be there. A helicopter picked her up, and she reached the White House shortly before 2 P.M.

Dinner in the yellow-walled, beige-carpeted dining room was low key. Jackie, beautiful in a dark purple velvet gown, was at her most charming. Afterward, the Kennedys and the justices descended to the densely packed East Room for the reception. In the crowd of some 600, which spilled over into the other rooms on the floor, Archibald Cox, then Solicitor General, and Clark talked about Bobby's funny-strange speech, wondering if he had been trying to tell them all something.

Cox thought he had. There had been reports that Bobby was feeling he might be a burden to his brother because of the antagonism he was creating. "I believe Bobby was saying to us that he won't remain in the department much longer," Cox asserted. "I bet he'll be gone before the end of the year."

Clark was inclined to agree. "He's always been a lightning rod for Jack," he said, "trying to take the heat away from the Presidency. It's not important what happens to him. What is important is what happens to Jack.

"I would say few men have ever loved a brother more."[1]

The reception was over by 9 P.M. Bobby left for Hickory Hill where about sixty friends had gathered for a more formal birthday party. He didn't get to bed until past 2 A.M. In the middle of the night, Ethel woke up, remembering suddenly that she had completely forgotten to give her husband his birthday present, a sauna that had been delivered a few days before and that was still in a huge crate in the basement. It had slipped her mind because there was so much to do and enjoy. "It's all going so perfectly," Ethel had told Whizzer White earlier that evening.[2]

Next morning John Kennedy played with his children for ten minutes while he was breakfasting in bed, worked for a while in the Oval Office and, at eleven, took off in a helicopter from the South Grounds for Andrews Air Force Base and the flight to Fort Worth and, afterward, Dallas.

That last evening at the White House, Bobby had for the first time talked to Clark about the trip his brother would make the following day.

The journey, intended to calm down the factional feud raging in the state Democratic Party between Governor John Connally and Senator Ralph Yarborough, would be "useless and unnecessary, a strain on busy people."

"I don't want him to go," Bobby had said.[3]

After the assassination of his brother, Robert Kennedy "seriously considered" bypassing the Constitution and preventing Lyndon Johnson from functioning as President of the United States.

Johnson, who had been sworn into office in Dallas hours after John Kennedy died, made that accusation.

On Saturday, November 23, the morning after the murder of the President, he prepared to go to the Oval Office. He had been advised by Dean Rusk and Robert McNamara to take over the duties of the Presidency swiftly, to minimize any danger of dislocations of the massive governmental structure. Johnson agreed and had asked Evelyn Lincoln, Kennedy's personal secretary, to have all of the late President's personal belongings removed by 9:30 A.M.

Mrs. Lincoln hurriedly summoned workmen, who arrived and began to crate the books, ship models, pictures, and objects on his desk. Jackie came in, followed by J. B. West, the White House chief usher, and watched the dismantling of her husband's office. Seeing her, the workmen left in embarrassment.

Jackie remained only a moment. She had just gone when Bobby, who had spent the night in fitful sleep in the Lincoln bedroom, arrived. He had not gone into the East Room, where his brother's body was lying on the catafalque. That day, it would be moved into the rotunda of the Capitol.

Bobby stepped inside the Oval Office and was looking at the half-crated belongings when he saw the new Chief Executive approach.

He walked to the doorway, spread his arms out, and, facing Johnson, said, "You can't come in here. You don't have any business in here. Don't come in here!"

Johnson stared at him in astonishment.

"Bobby," he said. "You're making a big mistake. I'm the President of the United States, and you have no business in any way to interfere with my constitutional duties."

Bobby would not stand aside. The words sputtered out repetitiously, and his voice almost rose to a shriek: "You should not be here! You don't deserve to be here."

A week later, Johnson related the story to Senator George Smathers. "Bobby was so overcome that his grief drove him to that extreme," Smathers declared.

On August 12, 1969, seven months after he left office, President Johnson again recalled the bizarre incident and added details he had not set down before.

He was interviewed for an oral history by William J. Jorden, a former Deputy Assistant Secretary of State and reporter for *The New York Times*. The interview, which Johnson knew was intended for historians and researchers, was conducted at the LBJ ranch on the banks of the Pedernales River in Texas and is now at the Lyndon Baines Johnson Library in Austin.

"I think he seriously considered whether he would let me be President," Johnson asserted, "whether he should really take the position that the Vice President didn't automatically move in. I thought that was on his mind every time I saw him the first fews days, after I had already taken the oath. I think he was seriously calculating what steps to take. For several days, he really kept me out of the President's office. I operated from the Executive Office Building because it was not made available to me. It was quite a problem."[4]

Bobby never talked about his attempt to keep Johnson out of the Oval Office. All he said of the incident was that he wanted his brother's belongings removed before the new occupant took over. In May 1964, he said, "I wanted to make sure the desk was gotten out of there and all the papers were out."[5]

If Johnson's suspicions that Bobby sought to keep him from performing as President were correct, the probability is that the intense shock of the assassination had temporarily twisted the younger Kennedy's mind to the point of irrationality.

After the funeral, Bobby and Ethel had gone back to Hickory Hill, accompanied by John Jay Hooker, the Tennessee lawyer who had served on the Presidential campaign staff.

At seven, the younger children's bedtime, they all knelt on the floor of the den. Bobby said prayers, and the children kissed their parents and went upstairs. The three then sat silently for a half-hour, watching the tapes of the funeral on television. Hooker said he will never forget the pain on Bobby's face as he saw the state funeral reenacted: the caisson draped in black carrying his brother's body; the riderless, skittish sixteen-year-old Black Jack with a sword in scabbard hanging from the black saddle; the largest gathering of heads of state in modern times; the twenty-one-gun salute in three volleys at Arlington National Cemetery; the jets of the Air Force roaring by and dipping their wings in final salute; the sight of Jackie, Teddy, and himself, one after the other, touching a lit torch to the Eternal Flame over the grave of John Kennedy.

Except for that night he never discussed the details of the assassination in public or in private. More than a year later, the journalist Oriana Fallaci asked him, "His memory persecutes you, doesn't it?" He would not reply. "For a long time now, I have refused to speak of it. . . . Please do not ask me. Let us forget the question."[6] Luella Hennessey Donovan, the nurse who has seen the family through all its illnesses and tragedies, notes that the tragic events are never brought up within the family. "They put the past behind them," she said. "They do not ever sit and talk about the terrible events that have happened. It is one of their secrets of survival."[7]

But that evening the killing of the President was too new and fresh in his mind.

"We talked about the unbelievability of the whole thing," Hooker said. Bobby declared that there were parts of the burial ceremony that he was unable to recall. For example, he told Hooker, he had no memory whatever of Air Force One flying over the grave at Arlington.

"And then he reached over and picked up the telephone* and said to the White House operator, 'You know, my brother always told me that one of the worst things about leaving the White House would be leaving the White House telephone operator. But I guess where he has gone now, he doesn't need telephones. . . .' In this moment of absolute deprivation and despair—

---

* A direct line had been installed at Hickory Hill to the White House.

it is hard for me to even partially convey what Bobby Kennedy felt and showed on his face, or how he felt. He alluded to afterlife in the same sort of certain casual manner that he did the first time I ever saw him, when he said that his brother Joe had gone to heaven."[8]

Fearing for the safety of his family, Bobby asked Jim McShane, the chief United States marshal, to assign some men to protect them. The marshals were at Hickory Hill until late May. One of them recalled that "he [Bobby] was so undone by the assassination he could barely talk to his wife."[9]

That winter, unable to sleep, he would leave the house in the middle of the night and, with the mercury hovering around zero, would roar down the driveway and onto Chain Bridge Road in his convertible. Often he would not return until dawn. The marshals, who were not permitted to accompany him, never knew where he had been.

In the months that followed, his bereavement was so profound, his behavior so frighteningly different, that his friends and family feared for his sanity. Watching him, Dave Hackett felt he was a lifeless man going through the motions. The vibrancy, the spirit, were gone.

"It was as though someone had turned off his switch," Hackett said.[10]

"It was a shattering thing," Smathers said. "You couldn't talk to him. He would look at you, listen to you, but would not respond. You got the feeling he was there in body but he wasn't there at all."[11] Said John Seigenthaler, "The pain never left him. He hurt when he went to bed at night, he hurt when he got up in the morning, and he carried the pain with him all day."[12] To Jack Newfield, his journalist friend, Bobby was "in the deepest kind of mourning" he had ever seen in a human being.

Jackie, too, was affected deeply, more than everyone believed. In public, she was magnificent during the grueling days of the lying-in-state, the memorial service, and the funeral procession. Privately, she would break into unpredictable and uncontrollable sobbing over a period of a year or longer.

During the four terrible days before the funeral, she seemed unable to stop reliving the tragedy, repeating every detail to friends. Benjamin Bradlee, then with *Newsweek* magazine, describing her first night back in the White House, said, "She moved in a trance to talk to each of us there and to new friends as they arrived, ignoring the advice of doctors to get some sleep and to change out of her bloody clothes." Mary Barelli Gallagher, her personal secretary, recalled that, tears streaming down her face, she cried out, "Why did Jack have to die so young?"

That first morning, she appeared confused and disoriented. After she left the half-dismantled Oval Office, she walked down the hall and opened the door of the Cabinet Room where Kennedy had helped shape momentous events. She had motioned to West, the White House usher, to come with her.

Sitting at the great mahogany table, she ran her fingers over the polished wood and turned to West. She stared into his face, "As if," he said later, "she might find the truth there." Unaccountably, she talked, not of the murder, but Caroline and John.

"My children," she said, "they're good children, aren't they?" she asked.

"They certainly are," West replied.

Jackie was silent as she looked out the window at the sandpile and trampoline where they played in the afternoon.

"They're not spoiled?" she asked.

"No, indeed," West assured her.

Again she stared into the face of the gray-haired, bespectacled chief usher, on whom she had leaned heavily for three years.

"Will you be my friend for life?" she whispered.

West, who had been at the White House since FDR's day and had known at first hand how the death of a President can affect a First Lady, was so overcome by emotion at Jackie's obvious helplessness that he was unable to speak. He nodded. Jackie fell silent, then after a minute rose and went upstairs.

Away from the spectators and the television cameras, she had revealed for just an instant that she was a thirty-four-year-old young mother who had suddenly lost a husband, was left with two small children, and was frightened of the future.

After she left the White House to live in Georgetown, she broke down when she opened boxes containing a collection of small figurines that Kennedy had started. She was unable to stop crying for minutes, recalled Billy Baldwin, the decorator she had asked to help her with the refurbishing. James Reed, a close family friend, said that in Hyannis Port, four months after the tragedy, she sobbed on his shoulder "and couldn't stop for a long time."[13]

In Shakespeare's dramas, tragic events are relieved, at moments when more might be unendurable, by the grotesqueries of the clowns. The drunken porter in *Macbeth,* who rambles on about the knocking at the gate, eases the tensions between murders. As the terrible week ended at the White House, an incident occurred that snapped the unrelieved gloom for the White House staff.

Mr. West had given orders to decorate the East Room for the mourning period, which was to last a month. After dinner one evening, he and his wife Zelda went over to see if it was being done properly. As they stepped inside, they stared in horror. The catafalque upon which the coffin of John Kennedy

218

had rested was still in the center of the room. Stretched out upon it, eyes shut and holding a lily in his hands, was one of the White House carpenters.

The Wests' shock gave way to helpless laughter. "The week of tension collapsed," he said. "The White House would survive."[14]

Early in December, Bobby asked a group of associates from Justice and some other close friends to the Palm Beach house. The first morning there, he organized a football game. Pierre Salinger, who was in the party, will never forget that match.

"It was the roughest, wildest game I have ever seen. Everybody was trying to get the hate and the anger out of their systems. There had never been anything like it at Hyannis Port, Hickory Hill, or anywhere else.

"Bobby was absolutely relentless. He attacked the man with the ball like a tiger, slamming, bruising, and crushing, and so did everyone else. One guy broke a leg, and you couldn't count the bloodied noses and contusions. It was murder. I was never so battered in a game before. For a week I could hardly walk. Every bone in my body hurt."[15]

After his return, Bobby created a miniature shrine in his brother's memory in a corner of his large office. It was in an obscure place, and only a few of his closest friends were even aware it existed. Bobby placed photographs, books, and small reminders there. He would go there many times during the day and stand in front of it, lost in thought.

He would try to work, but within minutes of his arrival, associates would find him staring out a window. He would get up suddenly, go downstairs, and stride in the great courtyard of the block-square building. His eyes were always red and swollen from weeping. Most of the time he cried alone, at night, in Hickory Hill; sometimes he was unable to contain his tears before others.

A week after his return from Palm Beach, the black journalist Simeon Booker was summoned to Bobby's office. Bobby wanted to discuss a story, but he was unable to focus his attention on what he had wanted to tell Booker.

"At his huge desk," Booker remembered, "the Attorney General covered his head in his hands and when he lifted his head, I saw he had been crying. His eyes were red and wet."

Booker, a large, kindly man, told him, "Come on, now. You've got to forget the past. Hell, you're Irish and supposed to be tough. I'm Negro, and you think you can push me around."

The joshing words, recalling as they did the bitter criticisms of the black intellectuals, jolted Bobby. He managed a smile. "Booker," he said, "you always know how to knock somebody off balance."[16]

During this long bleak period, he canceled all social engagements but one, a Christmas party at the Justice Department offices for 800 children from Washington public schools and the St. Joseph's Home. Toys had been ordered weeks before, and the invitations had gone out. On December 21, all the guests showed up.

So did Bobby. In a huge room filled with food and piled with presents, he shook hands with each child, smiled at them, and wished them Merry Christmas. A clown band performed, the actress Carol Channing sang, and James Symington, son of Senator Stuart Symington, led the children through "Jingle Bells" and "Silent Night." When it was time to go home, Robert Kennedy thanked them all for coming, said he hoped they had a nice time and that he had, too.[17]

"It was one of Bobby's greatest performances," an aide said, "and one of his toughest."

Bobby did not undergo psychotherapy during his period of grief, so no clinical diagnosis of his mental state was ever made. "I don't believe in any of that couch stuff," John Kennedy once said, and neither did Bobby. Still, he was exhibiting many of the major symptoms of clinical depression listed by the American Psychiatric Association.

He was unable to sleep. He couldn't concentrate on work, or anything else. He became preoccupied with the idea of death. He brooded incessantly. He lost interest in his usual activities. He was engulfed by feelings of sadness, hopelessness, and discouragement.

In January, Johnson sent him on a diplomatic mission to the Far East, to try to persuade Sukarno and Malaysia to settle their squabbling. Averell Harriman, concerned by Bobby's continuing despondency, had suggested to LBJ that the trip might help lift his spirits. Bobby returned two weeks later, still in shock, the journey having provided only a brief distraction.

In February, Seigenthaler, who had returned to Tennessee, came back to Washington for a brief period. He saw Bobby having his hair cut in his office. It was the first time they had seen each other in three months.

They sat and looked silently at each other for a long while. Finally, Bobby said, "How do I look?"

"You look like hell," Seigenthaler replied bluntly.

Bobby said, "I know. I can't sleep. I'm having a hard time sleeping three, four hours a night." He looked away. Tears were welling in his eyes.[18]

It was survivor guilt in classic form: by what right am I granted life while he was not? It was mourning for a much-loved brother, a frightening disequilibrium everyone experiences at a severe loss. But it was more and worse.

Craggy-faced, long-limbed Lem Billings, who saw Bobby constantly during this period, offered the closest and clearest insight into Kennedy's mind. Billings, who died in 1981, spoke to the authors six years after the assassination of JFK in his ground-floor apartment at Eighty-eighth Street in New York. Aping the Kennedys, whom he genuinely loved and admired, Billings had dozens of photographs of the family, many with himself in them, in every room. He was proud of his association with the family, of the open invitations he had had to Hyannis Port, Palm Beach, and the White House. Caroline and John, who lived nearby, visited him frequently, he said, listening raptly to stories he spun about their father's adventures at prep school.

"When Jack died," Billings asserted, "a large part of Bobby died, too. I saw that life extinguished. He had tied up so much of his own self, his own career, to that of his brother. He had been totally involved, totally dedicated to helping and furthering the work of John Kennedy. Hitching himself so completely to Jack, he established no identity of his own and never wanted one. So when they buried Jack Kennedy in that grave at Arlington, they buried much of Bobby, too."[19]

In this period, Bobby discovered Albert Camus, the French author who rose from poverty to become a Nobel Laureate in literature in 1957, and who wrote of people helpless in life's grip. Isolation and loneliness run through much of Camus as he explores the dilemmas of the twentieth century.

Kennedy bought every Camus novel, play, and essay, and read them all carefully, marking passages and making marginal notes on every page. He read *Resistance, Rebellion and Death, The Rebel,* and *The Notebooks* until they were dog-eared, searching their pages for the meaning of life, wrestling with the most fundamental philosophical questions of human existence. Why are we on earth? Why were we born? What, after all, is the purpose of our being?

Unable to sleep, he would read Camus in his den until the early hours, seeing much of himself in the man, who, like him, was a moralist and, like him, a humanist with compassion for human suffering, an abhorrence of violence, and a challenger of tyranny and oppression. And more: Camus died violently, killed in an automobile accident in 1960 at the age of forty-seven, only a year older than Jack.

Camus turned Bobby Kennedy into a fatalist. "He became convinced that senseless tragedy can befall us, that even the murder of his brother was senseless, and that [Lee Harvey] Oswald may not even have had a reason for killing him," said Jack Newfield.

The dark view that he was powerless to alter events emerged in his speeches. When he contemplated running for the Senate in New York in 1964, he told a roomful of advisers, "I don't know that it makes any difference what I do. Maybe we're all doomed anyway." On another occasion in 1964, he said in despair, "Man is not made for safe havens. If it's going to happen, it's going to happen." A political adviser cautioned him against taking a stand, as a senator, on a thorny issue that might come back to haunt him. "I can't be sitting around here calculating whether something I do is going to hurt my political situation in 1972," he replied. "Who knows whether I'm going to be alive in 1972."[20]

Bobby quoted Camus so much and so often that, on arriving at an Indiana airport during the 1968 campaign for the Presidency, he was greeted by signs reading: "KENNEDY AND CAMUS IN 1968."

Ted Kennedy, whose tastes in reading run from light novels to biography and recent history, also developed a strong fatalistic outlook after Bobby was killed. Once he told David Burke, then his administrative aide, "Whatever is going to occur in life, will occur." In a conversation with Gerard Doherty, who helped run his political campaigns in Massachusetts, he said, "What God will ordain will happen."

Silent proof that he is ready for a personal tragedy, should such a crime ever occur, is found in a copy of Shakespeare's *Julius Caesar* that the author saw on his desk in Room 431 of the Old Senate Office Building. He had underlined in red ink these lines spoken by Caesar in the second scene of Act Two:

> Cowards die many times before their deaths;
> The valiant never taste of death but once.

The passage ends on the note that some power or force has already predetermined man's fate:

> It seems to me most strange that men should fear;
> Seeing that death, a necessary end,
> Will come when it will come.

"Bobby wasn't quite dead inside. Ethel pulled him out of it," Lem Billings said.

"Ethel was as wrapped up in Bobby as he was wrapped up in his brother's career. Her entire purpose from the day she married him was to make his life more comfortable, more happy. Now he was in the deepest trouble she had ever seen. And she was there for him. If it weren't for her, Bobby's melancholia might have lasted for years, or he may never have come out of it all."[21]

An early biographer wrote, "It is deeply resilient Ethel, with her vitality, her gift for living in the present, her demonstrativeness and her determination, who has been Robert Kennedy's personal bulwark since his brother died. . . . She is a pioneeer wife in a modern sense and her husband's friend."[22]

"Her personality ultimately had the effect she intended," says Ed

Guthman. "It was contagious, and she brought him out of his gloom and disorientation." And a close friend declares, "It wasn't so much what she did as what she was. She wouldn't allow anybody to dwell on the sadness, or to be sad around him. She didn't like silences or morbidness. She saw to it that there would always be people in there and things to do on weekends, that there would always be jolly company. She herself never allowed him to see her sad."

So there were always parties at Hickory Hill, not as rambunctious as before, but the football games and the tennis matches resumed, the dinner table conversation was always upbeat, and there was much laughter. "Bobby, feeling himself in the midst of normalcy, surrounded by people he loved, was thereby reinforced," explains Dave Hackett.[23]

Surely not least was Ethel's strong religious faith. She reminded him daily of her own belief that nothing happens in life that God does not permit, or permit indirectly, and that whatever does happen is for eternal interest, even though, with finite vision, those on earth cannot see the connection.

Bobby had gone through a period of questioning his faith after Jack was killed. That first night, when he slept in the Lincoln Bedroom, he sobbed and cried out, "Why, God, why?"[24] "But he never broke faith," said his friend Sam Adams. "He went through the same experiences as Job in the Old Testament, who was tested by God and learned that God's judgment is beyond the understanding of man."[25]

After the initial wounded cry, "Why, God, why?", his faith deepened and strengthened. He prayed daily at home and never missed mass on Sunday at St. Luke's Catholic Church in McLean. At 6 P.M., he would pile his entire family into a station wagon and drive back to the church for a folk mass. On the ride home, he would discuss the service with the children, asking questions and explaining.

When he found that the children were not getting the point of the sermons, he became concerned and argued with the pastor, the Reverend Albert F. Pereira, about it. "My kids are pretty bright," Bobby told him, "and if they don't get it, other people won't either." Bobby told the clergyman his sermons should be like his own political speeches, "simple and clear, going directly to the point." When the pastor facetiously suggested Bobby send over one of his speechwriters to help with future sermons, Bobby apologized.

"I didn't mean to be so intent," he said, "but religion is so important in life. I want my kids to like it. You all should not be talking about God up there so much. I want to know what God is like down here, how He is concerned with what we do here. I want to know how my life should be lived here now."

Though he did not voice it, he also wanted to know what he was to do with the rest of his life.

20

For Love of a Brother—A Coverup

THE ASSASSINATION of John Kennedy did not change Bobby's character one bit. He remained after Dallas what he was before: a moralist who challenged evil with anger and impatience, using all the levers of power available to him.

What changed were his goals. He stepped up the crusades he was on and acquired new ones. Civil rights became a high priority; he warred on poverty in cities and rural areas, on violence in the world, and on war itself. Donald Wilson may have found the key when he said, "Through the pain of his own suffering, he learned volumes about others who suffered."[1]

If he raged against communism and labor racketeers before Dallas, he raged against indifference to human needs afterward. If he was uncompromising with what he looked upon as evil before, he bit his lips in anger when he talked in private about the impenetrability and immovability of institutions and people who could do something about poverty, ignorance, and hurt, and did nothing.

Once, Stanley Tretick, the photographer who covered him for years, said to him in a hotel suite, "What you really are is a revolutionary. You should be in the hills with Castro and Che Guevara."

Bobby was silent for several minutes, then said quietly, "I know it."[2] He was as passionate in the pursuit of his goals as they.

One of the very few times in his life when he did not apply his moralistic yardstick of right and wrong occurred after the murder of JFK, but it was for his brother's sake.

After the Warren Commission had finished taking its testimony, it sent a letter to all persons who had testified, asking if they had recalled any material information they had not given and wanted to add. Although Robert Kennedy had not appeared, he received one of the letters.

On the face of the letter, Bobby scrawled, "What do I say?" and sent it back to Joseph Dolan, an assistant attorney general who had forwarded it to him.

There was a great deal that Robert Kennedy could have told the commission at the time, and did not.

The reason was understandable. He wanted to put the entire painful episode behind him. He never read the Warren Commission report when it was made public and discouraged all efforts at further investigation. Indeed, Nick Katzenbach believed Bobby had not wanted any probe at all.[3]

Without telling Bobby, Katzenbach sent a memo to Bill Moyers, then President Johnson's special assistant, saying, "The public must be satisfied that Oswald was the assassin" and that "speculation about Oswald's motivation must be cut off."

Big questions arise. Why didn't Bobby want an investigation? Why didn't he accept the commission's invitation to pass along relevant information?

Was it to spare himself further grief? Or was it because he was in possession of significant facts that would have opened a whole new avenue of exploration into the murder of the President?

This is what Bobby knew and kept to himself.

Beginning in the Eisenhower years and continuing into the Kennedy Administration, covert operations had been underway to overthrow Fidel Castro. In 1975, Senator Church's committee issued a report on murderous diplomacy, "Alleged Assassination Plots Against Foreign Leaders," which disclosed attempts to kill leaders of the Dominican Republic, the Congo, South Vietnam, Chile—and Cuba.

Schemes to eliminate Castro, some of them of mind-boggling zaniness, were hatched by the CIA in 1960, the Church committee revealed.

The Technical Services Division, for example, sought to create a chemical that when secretly given to him, would cause his hair and beard to fall out, thus undercutting the soldierly image he needed to maintain power. Chemists also worked on drugs that could be sprayed into a radio and TV studio to disorient the Cuban leader, making him babble like an idiot during his lengthy speeches.

Early in 1963, a task force was assigned to determine if an exotic seashell, rigged to explode, could be placed in a part of the ocean where Castro liked to go skin diving. Another idea was to contaminate a skin-diving suit with a dangerous fungus and the bacterium that causes tuberculosis and present it to him as a gift. One plan was to offer him a box of cigars treated with deadly botulinium toxin. In a grisly coincidence, on the day Kennedy was shot, a CIA official met with a Cuban agent in Paris and gave him a ballpoint pen in which a hypodermic needle had been inserted. When he wrote with it, Castro would get an injection of Blackleaf-40, a deadly poison.[4]

If these notions were ludicrous (some were ultimately discarded as impractical), an effort to enlist Mafia leaders to put out a contract on Castro was not. From the summer of 1960 until mid-1962, the CIA set up a working relationship with Sam Giancana and John Roselli, the same underworld crime figures Bobby had prosecuted in the rackets committee, to hire Cuban hit men to do the job.[5]

Eliminating Castro was being given much attention. On at least two occasions, President Kennedy himself brought up the subject of the assassination of the Cuban leader.

In March 1961, he asked his friend George Smathers how South America would react to the slaying of Fidel Castro. Smathers replied that, much as he disliked Fidel, he did not think the idea should even be considered. Kennedy, he said, agreed with him.[6]

Eight months later, in early November, Tad Szulc, then a reporter in the Washington bureau of *The New York Times,* met with JFK after being invited to an off-the-record conference with Bobby Kennedy. During their private one-hour talk in the Oval Office, the President asked Szulc, "What would you think if I ordered Castro to be assassinated?" When the newsman replied that the United States should not be a party to murders, he reported the President as saying, "I agree with you completely."[7]

In notes he made of the meeting several days later, Szulc wrote, "JFK said he raised the question because he was under terrific pressure from advisers (I think he said intelligence people but not positive) to okay a Castro murder, sed [sic] he was resisting pressure."

But John Kennedy, deeply distrusting the CIA, wanted a separate covert action program to be set up independent of the agency. So the same month that the conversation with Szulc took place, Operation Mongoose was created, with the same objective—to get rid of Castro.

The broad outlines were put together by General Edward Lansdale, who had considerable experience in counterinsurgency techniques; Richard Goodwin, a Presidential special assistant; and Bobby. At the end of November, JFK sent a memo to Dean Rusk to permit Mongoose to get underway. "Let us use our available assets . . . to help Cuba overthrow the Communist regime," the President wrote.

Action came swiftly. A Special Group (CI, for counterinsurgency) was formed, consisting of a half-dozen of the most important figures in the diplomatic and defense establishments: CIA Director John McCone, National Security Adviser McGeorge Bundy, Deputy Defense Secretary Roswell Gilpatric, Deputy Secretary of State U. Alexis Johnson, and General Lyman L. Lemnitzer, then chairman of the Joint Chiefs. Within days, this was expanded to Special Group (SGA), to which were added nine other high-ranking officials, including Robert Kennedy and General Maxwell D. Taylor, soon to become chairman of the Joint Chiefs.

Bobby Kennedy was the spark plug of the operation. With the passionate pursuit of an objective typical of his character, he kept after the SGA, demanding action. He telephoned, sent memos, held meetings at which he pounded his desk and told them to get off their asses. He was clearly dissatisfied with the progress of Operation Mongoose.[8]

Spurred on by Bobby, the Army adopted measures that were even more absurd than the plots of the CIA. Robert Amory, deputy CIA director, disclosed that every Army school on every post in the country received a directive from the Chief of Staff to devote one-fifth of its teaching time to counterinsurgency techniques.

Responding, the finance school began instructing students on how to rig typewriters so that pressing the keys would make them explode in the faces of the typists. The cooks and bakers school offered a course that included a different recipe for pies: add one live hand grenade that would detonate on carving.[9]

When a year passed with insignificant results, Bobby told the SGA he would himself be chairman of the meetings. But he was no more effective in making things happen than the others. Some thirty-three plans were discussed (use chemical warfare to ruin the sugar harvest, offer bounties for killing or capturing known Communists), but none was adopted.[10] Mongoose languished.

Was there knowledge of, and authorization for, the assassination of Fidel Castro on the part of any senior official of the Kennedy Administration? Nothing was ever put in writing, no memos, directives, or orders issued. But Richard Helms, the CIA's deputy director, in charge of clandestine services, felt that no direct command was needed.

"I believe it was the policy at the time to get rid of Castro, and if killing him was one of the things that was to be done in this connection, that was within what was expected," he said. One does not discuss assassination with the President of the United States, Helms asserted. "We're hired to keep those things out of the Oval Office." At the same time, nobody told him assassination was ruled out, and he had the distinct perception that, if Castro went, "they would not have been unhappy."[11]

Ultimately, though, the Church committee concluded there was insuf-

227

ficient evidence that any President, Eisenhower, Kennedy, or Johnson, or any of their close advisers, or the Special Group of Operation Mongoose, had authorized the murder of Castro.[12]

What about Bobby? His role is murky.

On May 22, 1961, he had been informed of the Mafia link. On that day, Hoover sent a memorandum to the Justice Department summarizing a CIA report on the employment of Giancana and other crime leaders. "None of Giancana's efforts have materialized to date," the statement of the CIA said. "But plans were still working and might eventually pay off."[13]

The statement never mentioned assassination, but did it have to commit the word to writing? Did Bobby know that a murder plot was in the works, but at the same time didn't want to know? The Church committee admitted to being baffled: "We will never know for certain whether in May of 1961 . . . anyone realized that there were ongoing assassination plans and yet did nothing about them."[14]

One year later, in May 1962, Bobby was informed by CIA officials Lawrence Houston and Sheffield Edwards of the plan to recruit the crime leaders to murder Fidel. Bobby had reacted angrily, Houston told the Church committee. His eyes became steely, his jaw set, and his voice became low and precise. "I trust that if you ever try to do business with organized crime again—with gangsters—you will let the Attorney General know," he said.

Murkiness again. Was Bobby Kennedy angry because the CIA was trying to murder Castro, or because it was using the "enemies within," whom he regarded as the incarnation of evil, to do the job?

In 1966, when the journalist Jack Anderson wrote that Bobby had "played a key role" in the assassination plot, Kennedy angrily denied any culpability. "I didn't start it. I stopped it," he said. "I found out that some people were going to try an attempt on Castro's life, and I turned it off."[15]

The Church committee did not absolve Robert completely. Its report stated, "Despite the fact that the Attorney General, the Director of the FBI, and General Counsel and the Director of Security of the CIA, all discussed assassination plots against Castro, *no written order was levied upon all CIA employees banning such actions*"[16] (author's italics).

Even though no documentary evidence exists to implicate the Kennedy brothers directly in the murder plots, it is hard to believe that they did not know and approve. Vice President Nelson Rockefeller, under whose direction the Church select committee was set up, asserted, "I think it's fair to say that no major undertaking by the CIA was done without the knowledge and/or approval of the White House." Senator Barry Goldwater, a member of the Church committee, noted that the CIA would not have attempted to murder any foreign leader without the approval of the President.[17] "I am convinced as I am sitting here," he said, "that the action would never have been taken without the President knowing about it."[18]

Syndicated columnist Mary McGrory, always a staunch friend of Robert Kennedy, wrote, "John Kennedy, the graceful master of Camelot, slyly steered several conversations to the subject of killing Cuba's Fidel Castro and, upon getting negative answers, unconvincingly denounced assassination and complained to one caller of 'terrific pressures' to consider it."

About Robert, she wrote sarcastically: "Robert Kennedy, turned an icy blue glare at shamefaced officials of the Central Intelligence Agency who reported recruitment of two hoods to help murder Castro. He tells them not to do it again—not to hire mobsters without consulting him, that is."

The complete story of that unsavory episode may never be known, but this fact is indisputable: the Warren Commission, created to learn all it could about the murder of President Kennedy, was never made aware of a crucial set of events that could have provided a motive—the attempts on Castro's life. John McCone, who was told about the plots in 1963, said nothing. Allan Dulles said nothing. Both men had been directors of the CIA and—incredibly—Dulles was one of the seven members of the commission!

And Bobby Kennedy, too, said nothing. Can one doubt that his suffering because of the assassination of John Kennedy was intensified by the struggle with his conscience? Right was right, wrong was wrong: it was right to tell what he knew, wrong not to tell. But his brother's Administration had been involved, at least to some degree, with murderous plots. Bobby, too, had played a key role in an all-out secret project to undermine and overthrow Castro. Actually, his efforts were not counterinsurgency at all. Castro was not an "insurgent," as the Viet Cong were, but a legitimate head of a foreign government. It was the people of Mongoose who were the insurgents. And more: vicious mobsters were part of the scheme.

Had all this come out, the honor of his brother's Administration would have been sullied. Declares Ramsey Clark, "For Bob, the important thing was now the memory of the President, and he wanted it to be pure and golden."

While Bobby was not legally required to tell what he knew, he had a moral obligation to history to bring all the facts of his brother's assassination into open view. Moreover, as the chief law officer of the United States, he should not have hesitated to come forward.

Lacking the information Bobby and several other high Administration officials could have given it, the Warren Commission found "no credible evidence" that Lee Harvey Oswald was part of a conspiracy to assassinate the President, and "no evidence that the Soviet Union or Cuba were involved." It is entirely possible, of course, that even with the new knowledge, the commission would have discovered no link. In 1978, Castro told a House Select Committee on Assassinations that murdering Kennedy would have been "tremendous insanity," inviting an American invasion of Cuba.

On the other hand, Castro was well aware of the attempts to kill him. On September 7, 1963, he told an Associated Press correspondent, "Kennedy is the Batista of our time, and the most opportunistic President of all times . . . United States leaders should think that if they assist in terrorist plans to eliminate Cuban leaders, they themselves will not be safe."

In July 1973, four years after he left office, Lyndon Johnson told Leon Janis, a former aide, "We had been operating a damned Murder, Inc. in the Caribbean." (The reference was to a notorious murder-for-money ring operated in Brooklyn, New York, in the 1930s.) "A year or so before Kennedy's death," Janis wrote, "a CIA-backed assassination team had been picked up in Havana. Johnson speculated that Dallas had been a retaliation for this thwarted attempt, although he couldn't prove it."[19]

Finally, Bobby Kennedy must have thought a Cuban connection existed. Why else did he tearfully ask the agency's chief, John McCone, soon after Dallas, "Did the CIA kill my brother?"[20] McCone replied that it had not, but Robert Kennedy knew what had gone on since 1961.

At the very least, the Warren Commission should have had opportunity to pursue the Cuban link. It did not, because Bobby, deciding he wanted the entire horrible, painful story wrapped up and forgotten, participated in a coverup of essential evidence.

21

Indecision

*I*NEVITABLY BOBBY began to consider his future. He thought he might teach, he told a friend, or perhaps write another book. Maybe he would take his family and live abroad for a year. Most intriguing of his options, he thought, was the possibility that Lyndon Johnson would offer him the vice presidential spot on the Democratic ticket.

In January, New York political leaders came up with another solution to Bobby's dilemma: Senator Kenneth B. Keating's term would be up the following year. Why didn't Bobby run for his seat?

John English, Nassau County's young, energetic Democratic Party leader, broached the subject to Steve Smith for the first time on January 19, 1964. "I remember the date because it was my daughter's birthday," he said.[1] Smith, who masterminded the Kennedy family's financial and political affairs from his office in the Pan Am Building, nodded.

"Maybe we ought to look into it," he told English noncommittally, but within the next few weeks other important Democratic figures were voicing similar sentiments. In Washington, Buffalo Democratic leader Peter Crotty called Bobby and said, "Do it." Former Supreme Court Justice Arthur Goldberg told Kennedy he ought to be in public life, and New York was the right place. Franklin D. Roosevelt, Jr., publicly supported the Kennedy candidacy.

The idea began to take hold in Democratic political circles. "We had lost President Kennedy," explains John Burns, former mayor of Binghamton and chairman of the New York State Democratic Committee. "We transferred our allegiance to Robert Kennedy."[2]

Kennedy had several talks with English, admitting he was tempted. "Do you really think it's feasible?" he wondered. "Yes," English said, but Kennedy shook his head. He pointed out that Hickory Hill happened to be in the gently rolling hills of Virginia, not New York, the issue that could torpedo any campaign he launched. For the first time, he used the term that would be repeated over and over in the coming months: "Carpetbagger," he said. "Can't you just hear it?"

English could, but argued that Kennedy's candidacy would not violate the election statutes, which only stipulated that a senator live in the state at the time of the election. Moreover, he reminded Bobby that he had lived in Bronxville and Riverdale—New York communities—until the 1940s, when his father had become Ambassador to the Court of St. James, and his family still had an apartment in New York City.

Kennedy wished he could be as certain as English, countering with, "Look, I'm a registered voter in Hyannis Port, I live mostly in McLean, and I'm going to the [Democratic] convention as a delegate from the state of Massachusetts!"[3]

Kennedy was aware, too, that a move toward the Senate required a delicate balance: a bull's rush for Keating's seat could destroy his vice presidential ambitions, which still remained his prime priority. "He did not want to give Johnson an excuse for avoiding the fact of his availability as a running mate," said William vanden Heuvel, who had been a special assistant to Kennedy at Justice.

Still, the Senate notion tempted him enough to ask Steve Smith to travel around the state, taking informal soundings on the support he would have among the leading Democratic bosses. Smith began a long tour to amass information.

Carpetbagging charges were only one of the high hurdles Kennedy faced. Looming large, too, was the fact that the state's Democrats had not been able to unite and elect a senator since 1950. Representative Samuel Stratton of upstate Amsterdam, a tough campaigner, wanted the Keating seat and was claiming the support of twenty-two county organizations, but many Democrats were dubious about his ability to topple Keating. For English, Bobby was the only one in sight. "We wanted someone who could win," he said.

New York's Mayor Robert F. Wagner, the state's most powerful Democrat, was another problem: he wasn't thrilled at the prospect of having a Kennedy enter state politics and probably usurp his place as party head.

Finally, many among New York City's reform Democrats bitterly opposed Kennedy's nomination on the party ticket. "Bobby Kennedy is a ruthless, unprincipled, frighteningly ambitious young man who intends to use the New York State Democratic Party to launch his Presidential ambitions," reformers told Wagner.[4]

"The New York liberals who opposed him didn't like his history," says Burns. "Somewhere along the line, he had become a reformer but he wasn't one to start with. They looked on him as an interloper who hadn't worked his way through the system. They wanted one of their own."

The assaults continued, but Steve Smith kept coming back from his journeys around the state with good news about pledges of support and local poll results. "You could win," he told Bobby, but Bobby was still backing off. On May 20, reporters cornered him in New York, where he had gone to speak on behalf of Charles A. Buckley, the Bronx Democratic leader who was in a tough battle for his seat in Congress—and got an answer.

Asked about his plans for the Senate race, Bobby said he had none, that he would remain in his job as Attorney General, and that "all things being equal it would be better for a citizen of New York to run for the position."

It was not a Shermanesque "no," and Bobby never intended it as such: he was closing the door but had not triple-locked it. At least one month later, he was still changing his mind almost daily. "Yesterday I thought I'd like to do it," he said in mid-June, "today I don't."[5]

Reform groups, however, threw their hats in the air—and other names in the ring: United Nations Ambassador Adlai Stevenson; Dr. Ralph J. Bunche, Under Secretary General of the United Nations; New York County District Attorney Frank Hogan; Ambassador Averell Harriman; and Wagner himself were suggested. None was interested. No one but Stratton wanted the job.

In mid-June, Kennedy's chances for the vice presidential nomination suffered a sharp blow. Voters went to the polls in California and gave the conservative Barry Goldwater a thumping victory over Nelson Rockefeller in the Republican presidential primary. For Bobby, the meaning was only too clear: if LBJ would be facing the conservative Goldwater in the November election, he would have little need for the liberal Kennedy in the northern states where Bobby's support was strongest. It would be down below, in the southern tier, that Johnson would need help, and it was there that Bobby was weakest.

In Washington Johnson, an inveterate reader of public-opinion polls, was beaming that spring. "He liked the polls of the Oliver Quayle organization," said his brother Sam Houston Johnson. "They . . . went right to the heart of an issue, with detailed analyses of voter profiles, depth perception, potential shifts in sentiment, and all kinds of testing. . . .

"The figures that gave him the greatest satisfaction were those that demonstrated he could win quite easily without having Bobby Kennedy as the vice presidential candidate. . . . According to any Quayle poll, none of his potential running mates (Kennedy, Humphrey, Stevenson, McCarthy, Dodd, Pastore, Wagner) could add or subtract more than two percent from the probable vote for LBJ.''

Sam came to dinner in the upstairs living quarters at the White House one June evening. The President fished a newspaper clipping from an inside pocket, where he stuffed the poll results for a later look, and waved it at Sam.

"Look't here," he said, "I don't need that little runt to win. I can take anybody I damn well please."

Said Sam, "He wouldn't have made that kind of statement in public, for he was pretty closemouthed about his resentment against any of the Kennedys or their clique. If nothing else, his pride wouldn't let him reveal how much they had humiliated him."[6]

Bobby didn't need to know what was being said about him at the White House dinner table. In his own dining room at Hickory Hill, he told Ethel glumly that the Vice Presidency was slipping away. As for the Senate, he still couldn't make up his mind.

On a sunny day late in the month, he drove home for lunch along the usual route, which took him across the Memorial Bridge over which the funeral cortege of his brother had passed. Directly ahead, up the grassy slope, was the Custis-Lee mansion in Arlington Cemetery below which John Kennedy was buried. His companion noted that Bobby did not show pain as he passed the point, only a few hundred feet from where the Eternal Light burned over the grave, and appeared more relaxed than he had seen him in months.

Never garrulous, he was now talking freely, almost animatedly. World and national issues, which had roused little interest in him since late November, now concerned him again. He was upset about the growing problem in Southeast Asia. He worried about the still-burning racial issue. New violence had erupted in Mississippi and Alabama. Action, fast action, was essential. Why was Congress still dragging its feet on JFK's civil rights bill?

"The monosyllabic curtness of recent months was gone," his companion said. "Now again he was involved." It was a good sign that the depression was lifting.

New signs of recovery were apparent at home. Ethel, watching him closely, saw that he took obvious delight in playing and roughhousing with his children again. He gave David diving lessons, played hide-and-seek with the younger ones, and lectured Bobby junior on a bad report card, threatening to take his reptile house away if he didn't do better. Once he led his entire brood around the grounds in a hunt for a four-foot iguana that had somehow escaped from young Bobby's zoo.

That summer, Caroline and John Kennedy, Jr., were such frequent visitors at Hickory Hill that some of the younger children thought they were their brothers and sisters, Lem Billings said. After Jack died, Bobby had taken on the role of surrogate father to his children, bringing them into his own family circle. When Jackie moved out of the White House, he visited her often at the three-story brick home she purchased at 3017 N Street in Georgetown. He would have dinner with her and spend hours playing with Caroline and John.

"I've got ten now," he once told Lem sadly. (Four years later, Ted Kennedy, in a chilling reprise, would voice the same thought: "I'm the father of sixteen now." Three were his, two were Jack's, eleven, Bobby's.)

That day as he watched John and Caroline playing with his own brood, Bobby said, "That John, he's a little rogue." Caroline, going through her own period of grief, was different. "She doesn't let people get close to her," he remarked.

Caroline's feelings of utter sadness would last considerably longer than her Uncle Bob's. Like most children her age, she had little knowledge about death except to know that her father would never return to her. Feelings of guilt and self-blame are almost universal among children when a loved one dies, and Caroline doubtless was experiencing this, coupled with a devastating sense of being abandoned by a father she adored.

It was hardly surprising, then, that her personality altered almost completely. The verve and vivacity of the White House years were gone. John could be playful and teasing with Bobby, but Caroline remained solemn, grave, bewildered, and withdrawn.

Bobby did not tease her or joke with her. Once he put an arm around her shoulder, in a protective gesture. She looked quickly at him, then away. He asked about her new home. She told him quietly that soon she was to move to New York with her brother and mother. Jacqueline Kennedy had purchased a $200,000 fourteen-room apartment that occupied the entire fifteenth floor of a gray limestone building at 1050 Fifth Avenue.*

On Friday afternoon, June 19, Bobby flew to Hyannis Port just as the Senate neared its final vote on the historic Civil Rights Act of 1964.

He had remained in Washington long enough to know the outcome of the bill he and his brother had sent to Congress almost exactly a year before. The House had passed the measure decisively in February, 290–130, and

---

* Caroline had kept her sorrow within her. After the assassination, she told a classmate at the White House school she was attending, "I only cried twice." In New York, where she was enrolled in the Junior School of the Convent of the Sacred Heart, six blocks north on Fifth Avenue, none of her classmates or teachers heard her talk of the tragedy, or saw her weep.

that day the Senate had finally accepted the compromise hammered out by legislators of the two houses, 73–27.

When he got the news by telephone, Bobby appeared diffident, as though it no longer mattered. An aide recalled, "He was not especially elated. He had lived with it so long, had so many ups and downs with it, that the victory was an anticlimax." Mike Mansfield responded more emotionally. "I have never known such a feeling of relief as I did when that vote came," he said. Nine days before, cloture had shut off a seventy-three-day filibuster by the southern bloc, only the sixth time in history; never before on a civil rights issue had the Senate yielded up its jealously guarded privilege of limitless debate. That had effectually put the bill over. All that remained was the Senate's final stamp of approval.

Ted Kennedy was on the Senate floor, impatiently waiting for the balloting to begin. It was a crucial day for him, too, not just because his brothers' fight for a civil rights law was being won but because he was on the verge of a unanimous nomination for a full six-year Senate term. The day before, Massachusetts Democrats had opened their state primary convention at the Eastern States Exposition Grounds in West Springfield and were ready to name him by acclamation.

Late in the afternoon, a pilot named Edwin T. Zimny had telephoned to tell him the plane he had chartered, a two-engine Aero-Commander, would be waiting at the National Airport whenever he showed up.

The voting started at 7:40 and went quickly. At 7:59, it was finished. By 73 to 27, the act became a law, to be signed by President Johnson on July 2 following. Ted didn't wait to join in the jubilation. He walked quickly to his office, No. 431 in the Old Senate Office Building across the park, where Indiana's Senator Birch Bayh, who had walked even faster, was already waiting with his wife, Marvella. Bayh was to deliver the keynote address at the convention.

The Bayhs, Ted Kennedy, and Edward Moss, his administrative assistant, were driven to the Butler Aviation operations office near the airport, where their pilot was waiting. At 8:25, Zimny got clearance and took off for the eighty-minute flight to Barnes Airport in Westfield, a few minutes from West Springfield. The night skies were clear as the six-passenger aircraft headed north, but murky weather was closing in on central Massachusetts.

Bobby had gone to bed before 11 P.M., after he got word that the Civil Rights legislation had been passed. A few hours later, there was a knock on his door, and someone—he never could remember who—came into his bedroom and woke him up.

The Aero-Commander had crashed in dense fog into an apple orchard four miles from Barnes Airport. The pilot had been killed instantly when the plane's nose had crumpled on impact. Ed Moss, who had been sitting in front with Zimny, had suffered severe head injuries and was not expected to live. The Bayhs had been thrown clear and were not seriously hurt. But Ted's back had been broken.

With his sister, Jean Smith, Bobby raced in a state police car to Cooley Dickinson Hospital in Northampton, where Ted had been taken, arriving at 3:40 A.M. Climbing the steps three at a time, he raced to Isolation Room No. 1 on the first floor where Ted lay in an oxygen tent, tubes in his nostrils and blood being transfused into his veins. Though semiconscious, he recognized his brother. Bobby sat at his bedside for twenty minutes, alongside Joan, who had arrived an hour before.

On the main floor, Bobby joined Jean and another sister, Pat Lawford, who had caught a plane from Pittsburgh. In the morning, Dr. Thomas F. Corriden, the senior surgeon at the hospital and a family friend, told them that three vertebrae in Ted's lower back, along with their supporting transverse processes, were fractured; two ribs on the left side were cracked, his left lung had been punctured, and he was in shock from internal bleeding.

While Joan telephoned Richard Cardinal Cushing in Boston, Bobby, as he had done so often after the murder of his older brother, walked off by himself. Ed Moss had died just before 6 A.M. At the door of the hospital, Bobby took off his slate-gray jacket, held it under his arm, and, hands sunk deep in his pockets, went across the street to a park. He put on dark glasses against the rising hot sun, and, for a half-hour, he walked alone, head sunk to his chest. Inside the park, he sat on the grass, absently yanking up tufts, working over in his mind the new turn of events. Another thirty minutes later, he rose and returned to the hospital.

By then, the Kennedys and key members of the brothers' staffs had converged from all over, a dozen and a half of them sitting at tables in the small wood-paneled coffee shop.

After nine, Bobby went to the same phone Joan had used and called his mother. Rose handed the phone to his paralyzed father, and he repeated the story, trying to keep his voice calm and saying no more than absolutely necessary.

Bobby hung up and went to the counter, where he ordered a soft drink. There he told a friend in a grim voice, "I guess the only reason we've survived is that there are so many of us. There are more of us than there is trouble."

Staring into his glass, he said aloud what he had been thinking during his lone walk through the park earlier.

"If my mother did not have any more children after her first four, she would have nothing now. My brothers Joe and Jack are dead and Kathleen is dead and Rosemary is in the nursing home. She would be left with nothing if she only had four."

A newsman asked Bob, "In view of all your tragedies, will the Kennedys now retire from politics?"

Kennedy's chin jerked up, as though lifted by a puppet string. His tone was hard and sharp: "The Kennedys intend to stay in public life. Good luck is something you make, and bad luck is something you endure."

Privately, he wasn't too certain this philosophy was entirely accurate. To Walter Sheridan, he said, "Somebody up there doesn't like us," adding, "It's been a great year for giggles, hasn't it?"

By Monday, Bob learned that, although Ted faced a lengthy period of convalesence, his life was no longer in danger. Before returning to Washington, Bobby went to say good-bye. Ted had a final question for him: "Tell me," he asked. "Is it true that you're ruthless?"[7]

His crisply worded avowal to stay in politics notwithstanding, Bob Kennedy was more uncertain than ever about his future. The new personal crisis of Ted's accident had been a setback. The feelings of sadness and isolation that had dominated his life the previous winter and spring returned. He renewed his solitary walks, and again he would sit for hours staring into space.

Rose noticed his dark mood on his next trip to the Cape. She wrote in her diary, "Bobby is here, but seems to be distracted by the confusion and uncertainty surrounding his own plans. He feels he should do nothing to prevent his being chosen by President Johnson to run as Vice President, although he thinks it unlikely that will happen. Sometimes he talks about going abroad for a year to write a book, or just to get away from it all."[8]

In late June, he received an invitation from West Berlin Mayor Willy Brandt to unveil a plaque of John Kennedy in the great square facing the City Hall where the late President had proclaimed that free men everywhere stood with Berlin against the Russians. His *"Ich bin ein Berliner"* had roused a million Germans to a joyous frenzy.

It was yet another opportunity to pay tribute again to his slain brother, and he accepted. With Ethel and their three oldest children, Kathleen, Joe, and Bobby junior, he flew to Berlin and received a tumultuous ovation from a quarter-million Germans lining the streets.

Addressing a huge audience at the Free University of Berlin, Bob spoke the thoughts that had been in his mind those bleak months, and which he had written himself on the flight across the Atlantic.

"The hope that President Kennedy kindled is not dead but alive; it is not a memory but a living force. . . . For me, that is the challenge that makes life worthwhile; and I hope it will be the same for you."

Afterward, the Kennedys and their entourage flew to Poland to be met at their Warsaw hotel by hundreds of Poles who had learned of the visit from broadcasts of the BBC, Radio Free Europe, and the Voice of America.* The next day was Sunday, and the Kennedys went to mass in a centuries-old cathedral. Both the church and the square outside were filled with Poles, men, women, and children carrying flowers, all waiting to glimpse and perhaps touch a Kennedy.

When the family emerged, the crush was so great it was impossible for them to reach the car where Ambassador John M. Cabot was waiting. Bobby had to elbow his way through; the rest followed his path. But the great crowds hemmed in the car; it could not move. Kennedy forced the door open and leaped out.

"Come on, Ethel," he cried. He grabbed her arm, helped her to the roof of the car, and climbed after her. The children followed. Then with Polish secret police and Kennedy aides opening a path, the car slowly moved along, Bob, Ethel, and the children waving. In the midst of all this, John Nolan, a Kennedy administrative aide, felt a tentative tap on his shoulder. Leaning out the car window, the ambassador made a request: "I say there, would you tell the Attorney General the roof is caving in?"

Next stop was Cracow, where jubilant students at the Jagellonian University hoisted him on their shoulders and carried him to the campus. Later, Bob, Ethel, and the children rode on the roof of a government car to the town square, where 15,000 persons were waiting. A woman began to sing *"Sto Lat,"* a Polish folk song that translates to "May you live a hundred years," and the crowd took it up, climaxing by pelting the Kennedys with flowers.

Grinning, Bob said, "Now we'll sing something for you." He conferred with Ethel and the children and soon the delighted audience was treated to a carefree—and off-key—rendition of "When Polish Eyes Are Smiling."

That afternoon, Kennedy was stunned by an unexpected question when he met with twenty students and civic leaders in the office of Cracow's mayor, Zbigniew Skolicki. Politely and apologetically, the head of the Polish Student Union in Cracow, twenty-five-year-old Hieronym Kubiak, asked Bob for his version of his brother's death.

"We always greatly respected President Kennedy," the young man declared. "We hope you will forgive us for asking such a direct question, but we really would like your view."

Kennedy aides looked at each other and waited. They knew he had never publicly discussed Lee Harvey Oswald. Then, quietly and soberly, Kennedy said, "It is a proper question which deserves an answer.

"I believe it was done by a man with the name of Oswald who was a

---

* The Polish government did not announce the visit until the Kennedys had been in the country for two days.

239

misfit in society, who lived in the United States and was dissatisfied with our government and our way of life, who took up communism and went to the Soviet Union.

"He was dissatisfied there. He came back to the United States and was antisocial and felt that the only way to take out his strong feelings against life and society was by killing the President of the United States.

"There is no question that he did it on his own and by himself."[9]

Three months later, a few days after the Warren Commission issued its report, Bobby was asked by an American student—this time at Columbia University—if he agreed with the finding that Lee Harvey Oswald acted alone. Again, he appeared stunned by the question. Tears came to his eyes, and he half-turned from the audience to hide them. Many in the crowd stirred with embarrassment at the obvious reaction the question had caused. After a few minutes Bobby regained control and replied, "As I said when I was asked this question in Poland, I agree with the conclusions of the report that the man they identified was the man, that he acted on his own, and that he was not motivated by Communist ideology."[10]

These were the only two times that Kennedy ever said publicly that he believed the murder of his brother was committed by one individual.

On Monday morning, July 27, Lyndon Johnson telephoned Kennedy and asked him to come to the White House after lunch.

When he hung up, Kennedy turned to Ed Guthman and said, "He's going to tell me I'm not going to be Vice President. I wondered when he'd get around to it."[11]

At 1 P.M. on July 29, "oil and water," as Averell Harriman described Johnson and Kennedy, met in the Oval Office. The President, seated at his desk, motioned Bobby to a straight-backed chair to his right. Usually, he conducted personal discussions informally on a sofa at the other end of the room, but the unsmiling Johnson wanted this session to be strictly businesslike. He was going to dispose of his Bobby problem once and for all.

Johnson, of course, knew of Kennedy's wish to be his running mate, but he had no intention of accepting him and thus bring the Kennedy aura into his administration. All that spring and summer, he waited for a chance to shoot down Bobby's hopes. Toward the end of July, he was told that a twenty-minute eulogy to the late President would be shown at the first evening session of the forthcoming Democratic National Convention, which would open August 22. At the same time, he heard rumors that Jackie might show up at the convention hall to help Bobby.

There was, he felt, a significant risk that an emotional tide might sweep Bobby into the Vice Presidency, or even to the top of the ticket. He confided to his brother, Sam, that it was time to take "direct action." Bobby would have to be told he wasn't going to be Vice President.[12]

Three days in advance of the meeting, Johnson wrote down what he would say and had his notes ready when Bobby sat down. Referring to them as he spoke, he said stiffly, "You have a bright future, a great name and courage, but you have not been in government very long. I have given you serious consideration but find it inadvisable to pick you."

Then he turned folksy: "You would be unhappy as hell as Vice President," he said. "You would be crazy all the time and driving me crazy." Kennedy listened quietly and, fairly certain the interview was being taped, said only that he would accept LBJ's wishes and would support him in the campaign.

Johnson, aware that dumping Bobby completely would bring on his head the wrath of the Kennedy supporters within the Democratic Party, offered him virtually any high office he wanted—except the position where he would be a constant threat to his Presidency. Kennedy could direct Johnson's campaign and, if he was elected, have his choice of Cabinet jobs or the ambassadorship to the Soviet Union, Great Britain, France, Italy, or anywhere else.

Kennedy said he needed time to consider the offers and, on leaving, told him, "I could have helped you, Mr. President."

Back at his office, Bobby telephoned Ethel. "Now I have to decide what to do," he told her, "either run for the Senate in New York or work for Lyndon." Certain that Johnson would not wait long before leaking the interview to the press, Bobby buzzed for his key aides to tell them before they read about it or heard the news on television. Ramsey Clark, Burke Marshall, John Douglas, Harold Reis, and John Nolan trooped in and sat in a semicircle around the huge desk. Bobby briefed them on what had happened in the Oval Office.

"It was an emotional moment for all of us," Ramsey Clark recalled. "Next to the murder of the President himself, this was the heaviest blow to fall since the start of the Kennedy Administration. We all knew that Bobby would now leave the department and that it marked the end of the most exhilarating experience we had ever known, or perhaps would ever again know.

"We sat there stricken, and it showed on our faces. The only guy in the room who took Johnson's decision with good humor was the victim himself. While we were being swept by powerful emotions, Bobby was wisecracking."[13]

Bobby's suspicion that LBJ would not hold the secret long was correct, but he did not anticipate the lengths to which the President would go to get rid of him. The next evening, Johnson asked for television time and announced that he had eliminated not only Bobby and the entire Cabinet but any of those who met regularly with the Cabinet for consideration as the vice presidential candidate. Nothing like it had occurred in American politics before.

"All of Washington guffawed at the clumsiness and transparency of the ploy," said Rowland Evans and Robert Novak.[14] Hubert Humphrey, who had not heard the President's announcement, was told by a reporter and flatly disbelieved him. "He must be having hallucinations," Humphrey said.

Kennedy, still wryly cracking wise, said, "I'm sorry I took so many good men over the side with me."

On August 21, Bobby drove to Atlantic City to introduce the JFK film at the convention. Pat Lawford, Jean Smith, and Eunice Shriver were already there. Next day, Joan Kennedy flew in from Massachusetts. With Ted still strapped prone in his Stryker orthopedic frame at the New England Baptist Hospital, Joan had taken on the entire burden of the campaign, driving to Boston each day from the Cape to confer with Ted, then hitting the trail for ten or more hours at a stretch. Ted won by 1,129,245 votes, 76.5 percent of the total cast. Kennedy's campaigning was limited to a single speech, taped from his bed. For years afterward, James King, who headed up the Boston campaign, would remind the senator, "You didn't win in 1964. Joan won in 1964."

At the evening session, Bobby was introduced to the delegates.

He emerged from an enclosure behind the platform and walked to the rostrum. When the delegates caught sight of the small figure in a dark suit, they rose to their feet and roared in a spontaneous ovation that lasted for twenty-two minutes. Each time he tried to make himself heard, the waves of sound drowned out his voice. Bobby stood quietly, biting his lower lip, as the Democrats, many in tears, cheered him in the most highly charged emotional moment of the convention.

When a hush finally came over the great hall, Bobby thanked the delegates for the "encouragement and the strength you gave John Kennedy after he was elected President of the United States." Then he read a quotation from Shakespeare's *Romeo and Juliet,* which Jackie had suggested:

> When he shall die,
> Take him and cut him out in little stars,
> And he will make the face of Heaven so fine
> That all the world will be in love with night,
> And pay no worship to the garish sun.

When he had finished there were few dry eyes in the hall.

The lights went out, the film began, and Bobby returned to the room behind the platform. He had kept his composure during his talk, but now his control broke and he began to weep. Tears streaked down his face, and for minutes he was unable to speak.

At that moment, George McGovern entered the room and saw him. "It was never again possible for me to accept a description of him as a ruthless, hardhearted human being," McGovern said. "Indeed, he was the most sentimental, the most thoughtful, and the most idealistic member of the remarkable family that gave him to the nation."[15]

Steve Smith, still taking soundings around New York, called Kennedy. "To hell with them," Smith said bluntly. "Come up here and run."[16] He already had 450 delegates lined up of the 700 needed for nomination.

Kennedy's Hamlet-like indecision continued most of that sweltering August. He invited old friends to Hyannis Port and talked endlessly about his future. Arthur Schlesinger, Dave Hackett, Kenny O'Donnell, Larry O'Brien came up together and singly.

Out of these discussions, during solitary walks on the beach of Nantucket Sound, after long nights lying awake and pondering, Bobby finally made up his mind. He would run. And yet, it seemed to Ramsey Clark, he was not motivated by a burning desire to attain the Senate so much as he was "being pushed forward by a momentum outside him, carrying on less because he really wanted to than because people told him he had to."

Having cast the die, Kennedy began boning up on New York. Invited for a cruise on IBM Chairman Thomas J. Watson's yacht, he arrived lugging a heavy book on the history of the state. For hours each day, he sat on the deck as the fifty-four-foot *Palawan* sailed up the Maine coast, studying and expressing dismay at how little he knew.

Back in New York, his supporters pressed on to secure more delegates. Smith, English, and Harriman contacted Democratic Party regulars; Schlesinger and Alex Rose concentrated on the "liberal" vote; R. Peter Straus, president of radio station WMCA, and William Haddad of the Peace Corps worked on getting Jewish support; and Ronnie Eldridge and Albert Blumenthal urged reform Democrats to come out for Bobby.

By August 21, Mayor Wagner knew Kennedy had won; he told City Hall reporters he would support Kennedy's nomination. "There can be no question of his personal eminence—of the appealing nature of his great public achievements, nor of the dazzling magic of his name," Wagner conceded. Wagner could do little else: no other Democrat on the horizon stood a chance to topple Keating.

Four days later, at 11:07 A.M., the front door of Gracie Mansion, the historic residence of New York City's mayors, opened, and Wagner, followed by Bobby and Ethel Kennedy, emerged.

The Attorney General, clad in a black pin-striped suit and black tie, descended a short flight of steps leading from the porch and then climbed to a small, wooden platform that had been erected on the broad lawn. Standing between Ethel, in a lavender maternity dress, and the Mayor, his hands trembling ever so slightly, Kennedy addressed the more than seventy newspaper, radio, and television reporters gathered on the lawn.

He said he was running because "all that President Kennedy stood for . . . is threatened by a new and dangerous Republican assault," but admitted his recent out-of-state residence would probably cause "misgiving" among some voters.

A few hours later, Ken Keating welcomed Bobby to New York: "As his senator," he said, "I would be glad to furnish him a guidebook, road maps, and other useful literature about the Empire State which any sojourner would find helpful."

Much of the media was not kind. "Mr. Kennedy apparently needs New York," said *The New York Times,* which had supported his brother in 1960, "But does New York need Bobby Kennedy?" The *Los Angeles Times* published a cartoon of Bobby carrying a huge carpetbag, waving a finger in the air and saying, "Ask not what I can do for the State of New York; rather ask what the State of New York can do for me . . . !" *The New York Herald-Tribune* assailed the candidacy of an out-of-stater as "abhorrent to tradition."

The torrents of criticism prompted author Richard Condon to suggest that Kennedy declaim to his audiences, *"Ich bin ein New Yorker."*[17]

Ethel topped it with an idea for a campaign slogan: "There is only so much you can do for Massachusetts."

22

"Ich Bin Ein New Yorker"

KENNEDY SETTLED Ethel and their seven oldest children in an elegant three-bedroom suite on the eleventh floor of the Hotel Carlyle. Jackie and her children were temporarily housed on the twenty-fourth floor while her Park Avenue apartment was being decorated.

Steve Smith, confident of the outcome of the race, had also taken a two-year lease for the Kennedys on a twenty-five-room mansion in an exclusive area of Glen Cove on Long Island's North Shore. Owned by fashion designer Philip Hulitar, the house had been built in 1830 and renovated several times. The three-story farmhouse with its Olympic-size swimming pool and private beach and playhouse charmed Ethel Kennedy, who, with political adroitness, announced that "the best thing is that it is in New York."

For the next few weeks, the Carlyle apartment teemed with activity, as political advisers, speechwriters, and secretaries devised blueprints to nail down the nomination and plan the senatorial campaign.

The night before the Democratic state convention at the Seventy-first National Guard Armory, Kennedy attended a party to meet reform delegates. Entering a spacious apartment on Central Park West, he was greeted by a portrait, almost life-size, of his late brother. It was one of the few friendly faces in the room that night. Ronnie Eldridge, coleader of the West Side Reform group, who supported Bobby, said: "Everybody was sitting there waiting for this ruthless, aggressive man to come in. They were filled with resentment. . . .

"The doorbell rang, and this scared little guy came in. Very shy, his eyes down on the floor all the time, and it just took everybody by such surprise because they were really there to eat him up, and there wasn't anything to eat up."

Bobby's relationship with McCarthy, his relentless prosecution of Hoffa, and what they regarded as a disinterest in civil liberties had created a distrust. "There is a whole group of liberal people that he never did get to in the time he was here," Eldridge said.

The next day, September 1, Bobby emerged from the shower and stood before the television set in bare feet, a white towel wrapped around his middle, watching himself swept into the nomination, 968 to 153. Just as the voting ended, the seven Kennedy children came home from a visit to the zoo.

All the Kennedys, father and children, dressed—he in a dark blue suit, his three daughters in white cotton dresses, his four sons in identical navy-blue blazers. He lined them up—Joe, eleven; Bobby junior, ten; David, nine; Michael, six; Kathleen, thirteen; Courtney, seven; and Kerry, four. All were neat and newly washed, and all nodded in understanding when he explained they were going to a convention and they must behave. He cautioned young Bobby: "I know you're my namesake, and if someone at the convention yells out 'Robert Kennedy,' now don't you go up and make a speech."

To the strains of "When Irish Eyes Are Smiling," all the Kennedys entered the red-brick armory on Park Avenue. The children climbed to the balcony and joined Pat Lawford and Eunice Shriver and their children, Christopher Lawford and Robert Shriver. Aides cleared a path to the rostrum for Bobby and Ethel.

The delegates roared as Bobby, speaking too rapidly as usual, began his acceptance speech by addressing them as "my fellow New Yorkers." Obliquely replying to the "carpetbagger" charge, he told the delegates, "For every citizen who is a New Yorker by birth, there is one who is a New Yorker by choice, or whose parents were."

The campaign began inauspiciously. Ethel and Bobby drove to the Sheraton Atlantic Hotel, where an elaborate buffet had been set up for the delegates. Bartenders and waiters were standing by; pretty "Kennedy girls" were waiting in the lobby. After a while, it became obvious something was wrong. Only a few delegates had shown up; a hurried investigation revealed that someone had goofed and no invitations had gone out. Campaign aides scurried about and began to dragoon people in from the streets to "shake hands with Bobby Kennedy." The candidate, who learned later of the boner, said, "I knew there was something wrong. Not enough people were wearing delegate badges, and too many were carrying boxes marked Macy's."[1]

Bobby now had to resign his post as Attorney General. He and Ethel flew to Washington, where President Johnson received them privately in the Oval Office. When they left, reporters asked Bobby if he had any plans for himself for the White House.

"I think there's someone there," he commented. "I keep reading that, and I never see any statement that he's willing to move out. I think he'll be there for some time."[2]

Back in New York City, the advertising firm of Papert, Koenig & Lois, the agency that had handled Senator Jacob Javits's 1962 campaign, began to prepare Bobby's. The sum of a million dollars was budgeted for a full-scale media onslaught for the eight-week period. Posters appeared showing Kennedy, his shirt-sleeves rolled up, bearing the message. "Let's put Bobby Kennedy to work for New York." Bobby was heavily involved in the planning.

When agency head Fred Papert told Bobby, "We're going to present you as a warm, sincere individual," the candidate deadpanned, "You going to use a double?"

Aides brought out a layout for a campaign brochure, which Kennedy read hurriedly and then pointed to a picture that showed him shaking hands with another man.

"Can't you dig up a better picture than this?" he complained.

"Why, what's wrong with this one?" he was asked.

"He's in jail," snapped Kennedy.[3]

From the start of the campaign, the size of the crowds was astonishing. That first week more than 500,000 persons came out to see Bobby; middle-aged and older men and women, teenagers, and younger children jostled, pushed, and shoved to shake his hand, touch his clothing, even grab a handful of hair.

In Syracuse, where he was to dedicate the new John Fitzgerald Kennedy Park, more than 800 persons waited for the *Caroline* to land at Hancock Airport. He deplaned and walked quickly to the iron fence where the crowd had lined up and began to shake the outstretched hands. After a while an aide, noticing that the line appeared to be endless, checked.

"Bobby," he whispered, "as soon as they shake your hand, they run back to the end of the line."[4]

Later at the Syracuse State Fair, Bobby addressed an audience of 50,000. He told them he had read in the newspapers one morning that California had replaced New York as the most populous state. Feeling himself challenged to do something about it, he said, "I moved to New York and in just one day

I increased the population by ten." And, he added, "another half." Ethel was five months pregnant.

If women had jumped up and down at the sight of John Kennedy, they went totally mad about his younger brother.

What one reporter almost enviously called "his damned sex appeal—a combination of his tousled hair and bashful demeanor" charmed females of all ages. Homer Bigart, a *New York Times* reporter, commented, he "can evoke shrieks of pleasure from women and girls, who predominate in the crowds, simply by running his hand through his tousled hair."[5]

When he tried to walk along the beaches on Long Island on a hot Labor Day weekend, he was almost knocked down by hundreds of semihysterical teenagers. "It's Bobby," one girl screamed. "The one with the dirty blond hair." In upstate Johnson City, a middle-aged woman, her hair in curlers, an apron shielding her clothes, darted out of a beauty parlor and ran up to his car to shake his hand.

Bobby attracted larger crowds upstate than any candidate in the region's history. On September 9, John Burns met Kennedy at the airport for a tour of upstate communities. "I never saw it before or since," he recalled. "It was like watching the eye of the storm to see him go from the plane to a car. The crowds were clawing at him and pulling off his clothes. His people would have to hold him by his belt or he'd be pulled out of the car."

That day, said Burns, his clothes were ruined, the buttons ripped off his coat, and his PT-109 tie clasp was lost.

The Kennedy entourage arrived in Buffalo two hours late. Crowds lined both sides of the ten-mile route from the airport to downtown Buffalo, growing to six deep as they approached the city. Police struggled to hold back the mob, many of whom carried signs saying, "RFK all the way" and "We love Bobby." Every now and then an enterprising fan would break through the barricades to try and reach Bobby. In the black district, the excitement really erupted, and Kennedy had difficulty keeping upright as the crowds surged past the police barriers.

That night at the Hotel Statler, Ed Guthman commented on the size of the crowds. "Don't you know," replied Kennedy, "they're for him. They're for him." It wasn't until years later, said Guthman, that Bobby finally believed the crowds were for him, not Jack.

As the *Caroline* approached Glens Falls, five hours behind schedule, Bobby sipped a cup of tomato soup and wearily asked Guthman, "Do you think anybody will be there?"

Moments later, he got his answer, when he emerged from the plane and cheers came from the field where 500 Glens Falls residents, many with children in pajamas, were waiting to greet him. Kennedy climbed to the roof of a waiting car and, obviously touched, said, "Thank you for waiting."

The motorcade again drove through streets lined with people, and in the town center Kennedy made a promise to the 5,000 persons waiting there.

"I'd like to make my very first commitment of the campaign," he said. "Win or lose, the day after the election, I'm coming back to Glens Falls."[6]

Both Kennedy and Keating courted New York City's big ethnic vote. About 90 percent of the city's 2,500,000 Jews had voted for Jack Kennedy in 1960. But Bobby was viewed as being much like his father who, as American ambassador to Britain, had warned against war with Nazi Germany. Many Jews disliked him because of this perception.

Keating was well-liked in Jewish circles. He had a fifty-acre forest in Israel named after him; he attended many Jewish-oriented events, appearing at bar mitzvahs, weddings, and fund-raisers in a yarmulke. He ate kosher hot dogs, pickles, and cheese blintzes in Lower East Side delicatessens, where one restaurateur prominently displayed a sign, "Keating and Israel go together like bagels and lox."

Very much aware of this, Bobby courted the same constituency. He, too, turned up at Jewish functions, a yarmulke on his head, but was less knowledgeable than Keating. Lunching in a Lower East Side restaurant, however, he eschewed the unfamiliar foods and asked for melon, split pea soup, and chocolate milk. At a kosher Jewish delicatessen, he asked for a glass of milk.

When he was advised by a local politician who was accompanying him to wish Jewish voters a "Happy New Year," Bobby asked, "How will I know who to say it to?"

"When I say 'Now,' " was the reply.

It worked fine until a TV cameraman stepped on the politician's toe and he loudly yelled, "Ow." Bobby, mishearing, promptly wished "Happy New Year" to the black man whose hand he was shaking.

In Coney Island on a warm October afternoon, Kennedy, his shirt-sleeves rolled up, his tie loosened, climbed to the roof of his automobile and addressed a small crowd that had gathered in front of Nathan's Famous, at Surf and Stillwell Avenues, which had been founded by Nathan Handwerker in 1916 as a nine-foot hot dog stand and had grown to a vast business. It was a traditional stop in political campaigns. Bobby made another boner.

"How many of you," he asked, "know that this establishment is owned by a man named Hamburger?"

Kennedy walked into the kitchen where Handwerker, although in his seventies, was personally supervising the operation. Handwerker shooed away Bobby's entourage, the police, politicians, everybody but thirty-one-year-old Jay Cohen, then manager of the stand, and led Bobby up the stairs into his office. He seated Bobby on the couch, pulled up his own chair, and leaned back. Puffing on a cigar, he smiled benevolently and asked, "So, how's the family?"

"Ethel's fine," Bobby replied. "She's home with the children. We've got eight, you know." They swapped child-rearing stories, and then Nathan asked hospitably, "How about a cold drink and something to eat?"

A little more cued in to local dietary habits now, Kennedy asked for an orange drink and a "couple of hot dogs." He devoured them, called them "great." When he left, Handwerker asked for his address. "I'll send you a pack of these," he promised. Later ten pounds of hot dogs were delivered to Hickory Hill.[7]

As the campaign heated up, Keating accused Kennedy of settling the government case against the General Aniline and Film Corporation in a way that would turn a large part of its assets, more than $60 million, over to Interhandel, a Swiss firm the United States government had charged was a Nazi front.

Bobby was infuriated. Next morning he told a crowded press conference at the Hotel Carlyle, "I never have heard of a charge as low as this one. . . . I lost my brother and my brother-in-law to the Nazis. I'm not about to make any deals with the Nazis."

At a state convention of the NAACP, Keating released to reporters the text of a speech charging Kennedy had "abandoned" the civil rights movement by resigning his Justice Department post. Charles Evers, who had followed his late brother, Medgar, as head of the NAACP in Mississippi, was attending the convention to which Bobby had not been invited. He heard Keating attack Kennedy.

"God, I was so mad I just bit my tongue," he said.

Discarding his prepared speech on civil rights, Evers defended Bobby's record. He told the convention, "You're fortunate to have a man of Kennedy's caliber even visit New York, much less run for senator.

"If he ran for dogcatcher in Mississippi, every Negro in Mississippi would vote for him."

Keating also played on the resentment that had grown among Italian-American groups of Justice Department release of testimony by Joseph Valachi, which featured tales of hoodlums with Italian names. Kennedy took advantage of a Columbus Day rally to accuse Keating of "hit and run tactics in his campaign by accusing me of making deals with the Nazis, of selling out the Negroes, and of being anti-Italian."

He began to attack Keating's record. A well-circulated pamphlet, the "Myth of Keating's Liberalism," resulted in a three-page letter from Keating to Bruce L. Felknor, executive director of the Committee for Fair Campaign Practices, charging the Kennedy campaign with "incredible falsehoods."

After studying Keating's charges, Felknor wrote privately to Kennedy that "your description of his position on the Nuclear Test Ban Treaty is not only fake and distorted but also appears to be either a deliberate and cynical misrepresentation or the result of incredible carelessness."[8]

Although Felknor says the letter was not meant to be public, a copy fell into the hands of a *Herald-Tribune* reporter and was printed. In the ensuing uproar, during which two committee members resigned, Felknor was forced to withdraw the letter and apologize for its publication. Kennedy aides held this was proof that Keating's charges were unfounded and Kennedy's were not.

In the final week of the campaign, the candidates had the leading roles in a slapstick comedy that could have come straight out of a Marx Brothers movie.

Since September, negotiations had been taking place for a face-to-face meeting to debate the issues. At first Kennedy, the front-runner, was unwilling to risk his lead in a debate, but as the polls showed Keating gaining ground and even ahead, he and his advisers thought it might not be a bad idea after all. But by then, Keating stalled for the same reason Kennedy did. Then, when the polls seesawed once again, Keating's camp renewed its challenge. And so it went, each side accusing the other of dragging its feet, and each side being absolutely right, because a candidate's fire to debate flares up in inverse ratio to how far he is lagging behind his opponent.

A week before the election, the Columbia Broadcasting System offered them an hour of prime time for the debate. Both sides promptly accepted, and just as promptly fell into a disagreement on a format. The CBS effort collapsed.

Finally Keating, in disgust, purchased a half-hour of TV time on October 28 at 7:30 P.M. and announced that since Kennedy did not want to appear, he would place an empty chair on the stage and direct his arguments to the Kennedyless seat. The trick had been tried many times before in political campaigns and had a certain dramatic effect, which Keating well knew.

When Kennedy heard, he promptly bought the 8 to 8:30 time period for his own appearance.

Still, the idea of a ghostly TV presence that could not talk back bothered Kennedy, so he went to the CBS studios on the evening of the debate to sit in the chair Keating would provide. At 7:29 P.M., he appeared at the door of Studio 45, where a CBS aide stood guard.

"Your studio is that way." The man pointed down the corridor.

"I said I wanted Mr. Keating's studio. Where is it?" Bobby demanded.

"I'm sorry, sir. I can't let you in."

"I'm here to debate," Kennedy declared. "Senator Keating has invited

251

me to debate. Senator Keating said he would have an empty chair for me. I'm here, and I want to go in.''

''I'm sorry, sir,'' the CBS man said. ''Mr. Keating has purchased this time, and I can't permit you to enter.''

Newsmen crowded around to hear and flashbulbs went off, as Kennedy demanded to be allowed to enter. Inside the studio, it had just been announced that, ''Senator Keating has invited his opponent to debate him tonight, but Mr. Kennedy has not appeared.'' Then, with his fellow Republican senator, Jacob Javits, Keating proceeded with the ''debate.''

Outside, Kennedy, in a loud voice, denounced Keating's tactics as ''unfair,'' then went to his own studio to attack his opponent's ''political trickery.''

While Bobby was on the air, Keating emerged from Studio 45, and waiting reporters began to close in. Not wanting to answer any questions about the ''barring'' of Kennedy, he tried to dash from the building. Aides overturned chairs, tables, and potted plants in his wake, to prevent reporters from getting near him. Shins were barked, and knees skinned, as the newsmen tripped and fell in their chase after the candidate.

At that moment, Ethel Kennedy appeared on the scene. She had watched the undignified exit of the silver-haired senator from a staircase, but she was all dewy-eyed innocence as she raised her arms halfway to the ceiling and, affecting a movie ingenue chirp, asked, ''Is anything wrong?''

Next day, one journalist recounted his experiences of the evening under the headline: ''I Ran the Keating Obstacle Course.''

The evening was a flat-out disaster for Keating, and Kennedy took fullest advantage. After his own speech, Bobby put on another comic show, as he described to reporters (with considerable exaggeration) the Keating program. ''There were Javits and Keating,'' he said, ''on television really giving it to this empty chair. I've never seen any of them better. They kicked that chair all over the room. And there I was trying to get in. But Senator Keating had a guard (or three guards) bar me from the studio.''

As Kennedy moved about the state, the Republicans whaled away at the carpetbagger issue. Said Keating, citing a well-known Brooklyn waterway, ''Bobby thinks the Gowanus Canal is part of the lower intestinal tract.'' Another time he told an audience, ''There are people who have been standing in line at the World's Fair longer than he has been living in New York.''

Robert dealt jocularly with the charge. In Jamestown, which is in the western part of the state, he explained to a cheering crowd that his accent was ''pure Glen Cove.'' And on Long Island, where Glen Cove is located, he said that, try as he could, he was unable to eliminate his western New York accent. One time he was almost accurate: in the Bronx, he was greeted with signs saying, ''Why don't you go back where you came from?'' He replied that he did come from there. Riverdale was indeed in the Bronx, an exclusive section of fine homes and schools, but the Bronx nonetheless.

To reinforce his New York roots, Kennedy took three-year-old John Kennedy, Jr., to see the large two-story stucco house in Riverdale where Bobby had lived as a boy. On the way they stopped at St. Margaret's Roman Catholic Church on Riverdale Avenue. "Your father went to communion here," he told the little boy.

Kennedy was roundly criticized for "exploiting" the child. Even staunch supporter Averell Harriman called it "stupid, pretty damn stupid." More vitriolic was TV producer David Susskind, who said, "Bobby Kennedy's running for the Senate is not an immoral grab for power, but his using his late brother's son in this campaign is a terrible violation of good taste."

Opponents of Kennedy's race included his arch-enemy Gore Vidal, who, with the late television personality, Lisa Howard, organized the "Democrats for Keating." The group included Susskind, Archibald MacLeish, the poet, writers Barbara Tuchman and Joseph Heller, actor Paul Newman and historian Arthur Schlesinger senior, whose son, Arthur junior, had been an aide in the Kennedy White House.

The junior Schlesinger was also heavily involved in lining up celebrity support for Bobby's campaign. At a party hosted by William vanden Heuvel in his Dakota apartment on Central Park West in New York City, guests included John Gunther, Paddy Chayefsky, Leonard Bernstein, Gloria Vanderbilt, Lauren Bacall, Lillian Hellman, and Jackie Kennedy. The guests heard Schlesinger and economist John Kenneth Galbraith extol Robert Kennedy.

Later, reminiscent of Hickory Hill days, playwright Arthur Kopit, author of *Oh Dad, Poor Dad,* declared that he still favored Keating. Writer and editor George Plimpton toppled him over a sofa. "You see, the swimming-pool syndrome is still with us," Kopit charged.

Despite her pregnancy, Ethel accompanied Bobby on walking tours, gave two-minute telephone speeches from Hickory Hill to women delegates, where she spent most of her time, and was hostess at teas at Glen Cove.

At one campaign stop, Bobby and Ethel were surrounded by autograph seekers. Already behind schedule, Bobby made his way to the car. Ethel, however, continued to sign the bits of paper shoved before her. "Ethel," Bobby finally called, "remember I'm the candidate."[9]

Near the end of the campaign, without knowing it, Bobby rode and joked in the same blue Lincoln convertible in which his brother was riding when he was murdered in Dallas.

The unreported incident occurred on the Sunday before Election Day, when President Johnson came to New York. Air Force One landed at the Republic Aviation Corporation airfield in Suffolk County, where it was met by Bobby and Ethel, Averell Harriman, and Nassau County Executive Eugene Nickerson. The President was accompanied by Lady Bird Johnson and Rufus Youngblood, the Secret Service agent who had flung Johnson onto the floor and covered him with his own body when John Fitzgerald Kennedy was shot.

The group moved to the shining Lincoln, which was parked nearby. It had been rebuilt, the upholstery changed, and a bubble top installed; the appearance had been so changed that it was unrecognizable.

Bobby and Ethel entered and sat with the President, Mrs. Johnson, and Eugene Nickerson. During the ninety-minute drive, Johnson talked of nothing but the poll results, which he pulled from an inside pocket. He stuck his right hand out of the car window and waved to the crowds but did not look out; his attention was focused on the slips of paper in his other hand. Flipping them, he smiled at good news and furrowed his brow when he came across one that reported a dip of below 58 percent.

In between, the Kennedys began a comedy routine, pretending to remember towns and places as though they had been natives of Nassau County. "There's Franklin Square," Bobby said, pointing to a village off the parkway. "You remember Franklin Square, don't you, Ethel?" "Why certainly, Bob," she replied, "remembering" shopping centers, restaurants, and other towns that neither had ever seen or heard about. They grinned widely as the game went on.

Bob never knew he and his wife were riding in the death car. Nobody in the President's party told him; perhaps no one had noticed.[10]

Election Day, Bobby and Ethel, who could not vote in New York, took their children to the Bronx Zoo to feed peanuts to the elephants. That night he watched the election returns at Steve Smith's duplex apartment at 950 Fifth Avenue, along with Jackie Kennedy, Rose Kennedy, British Ambassador David Ormsby-Gore, and other Kennedy relatives and supporters. Shortly after the polls closed at 9 P.M., Bobby became impatient.

"I can't find out anything here," he said, and grabbing Ethel's hand, he hurried to a tenth-floor suite at the Statler Hilton, crowded with Democratic politicians, aides, and celebrities, including Marlene Dietrich, Maria Cooper (Gary's daughter), and actress Shelley Winters.

After midnight, Keating conceded the election to Kennedy. Bobby had won by a total of 3,823,749 votes to Keating's 3,104,056, a win many political observers said was made possible by Johnson's "massive victory" in New York State, which he carried by more than 2.5 million votes.

The telephone rang, and someone called out, "Bobby, it's for you. It's the President." Kennedy took the call in the bedroom and then descended to the grand ballroom to thank his campaign workers. Later, he celebrated with a victory party at the Hotel Delmonico and went to the Fulton Fish

Market, the first stop on his campaign some weeks earlier. "It smells a lot better now," the grinning senator-elect said.

Several hours later, he boarded a plane to fulfill the promise to return to Glens Falls. A reporter asked if he was glad the campaign was over. "Yes," he laughed, "now I can go back to being ruthless again."

23

The Freshman Senator

ROBERT KENNEDY came to the Senate with a recognition factor unmatched by any other freshman in the upper house. "He was an instant national figure," said Ted Sorensen. Within a few weeks he was also a tourist attraction.

Everywhere he went, he drew crowds. He would stand at a street corner on his way to the Capitol and, before the light changed to "Walk," would be surrounded by pedestrians. Teenagers and senior citizens followed him in long strung-out queues.

On January 4, 1965, he was sworn into the Senate alongside Teddy, who was making his first appearance in the chamber since his plane crash. A large contingent of Kennedys, including Ethel, her four oldest children, Joan, Eunice Shriver, and Jean Smith, watched from the gallery as the brothers were escorted by the senior senators from their states—Robert by Jacob Javits and Ted by Leverett Saltonstall, both Republicans.

Bobby walked to the last row of the chamber, where two new desks had been added for him and Senator Joseph D. Tydings of Maryland. The Johnson landslide victory had brought the number of Democratic senators to sixty-eight, and they could not fit into the traditional four semicircular rows of seats. Walter Mondale of Minnesota and Fred R. Harris of Oklahoma also sat there. "At least I got into the building," Bobby said.

Kennedy's small rooms in the Old Senate Office Building were a sharp contrast to the lavish suite he had occupied at Justice, and it was impossible to squeeze in all his possessions. "This will have to go!" Kennedy said to

Angie Novello, his secretary. "This" was a stuffed, ferocious-looking Bengal tiger, gift of the Indonesian government.

On a cold January day, Bobby had wood brought in and a fire lit. Unfortunately the fireplace had been blocked up and the ducts incorporated into the air conditioning system. "Soon," recalls Senator Harris, "aromas of oakwood filled the corridors and spread through the building."[1]

Bobby was later assigned three rooms in the new Senate Office Building, much too small for his staff of thirty-seven, one of the largest in the Capitol. Jeff Greenfield, then a legislative intern fresh out of Yale Law School, says the office reminded him of a college newspaper—"total chaos, totally cramped, six people working in a space that was designed for two."

Bobby's own office, carpeted in blue, again displayed familiar Kennedy memorabilia, portraits of Jack and Joe and the framed doodlings of the late President's last Cabinet meeting. On the wall behind his desk were the ubiquitous watercolors painted by his children.

The outer rooms teemed with activity. The staff handled close to 60 phone calls and 1,000 pieces of mail daily, and a constant stream of constituents and tourists who wanted to see Kennedy. Wes Barthelmes described the atmosphere as "very free form, free flow," but "everybody worked a six-day week and secretaries were expected to be on call."[2]

This dedication to duty of Kennedy employees was noted by biographer Laing, who writes, "It is plain that most of them work for love or loyalty rather than money." She quotes one unidentified man as saying, "None of us would be here if it were an ordinary job. It's working for him that makes the difference. I would rather be doing this than anything else in the world."[3]

Many of the Kennedy people, like Ed Guthman, Joseph Dolan, Peter Edelman, and Adam Walinsky, had worked for him at the Justice Department and when he ran for senator. Guthman left after a few months to return to newspaper work in Los Angeles, after telling Barthelmes, his replacement, "You've got to learn to read the pauses, those long silences."[4]

Walinsky, a graduate of Yale Law School, and Edelman, from Harvard Law, were Kennedy's legislative assistants, writing most of the speeches, bills, and amendments; Dolan was the administrative assistant.

Edelman's job interview took place in an alley between the White House and the executive offices, where Kennedy had gone for treatment of a knee injured playing touch football. Kennedy emerged from the doctor's office, hoisted himself onto the hood of a car, and asked, tentatively, "Well, are you going to come aboard?"

"I thought he was going to ask how many A's did you get in school or what do you think about the nuclear test ban or write something for me, but nothing like that," Edelman said.

"I told him I have this problem. I'm going to be out of law school three and one-half years, and I still haven't worked in a law office or practiced law." Bobby nodded and replied, "I had that problem myself, but I managed to work it out."[5]

Requests for interviews poured in. "Kennedy could literally have spent all his waking hours just being talked to by the press," said Barthelmes. Reporters wanting to see him might hitch a ride to the National Airport with Jim Boyd, the chauffeur, wait until Kennedy deplaned, and interview the senator between the airport and the new Senate Office Building.[6]

When David Kraslow of the *Los Angeles Times* made such a request, RFK said, "Sure, come on out, if you want to do it while I'm putting my cufflinks on." Kraslow went to Hickory Hill and followed Bobby around while he dressed for an evening affair.

Reporter Warren Weaver, assigned to write a rush piece for *The New York Times Magazine*, found that the only time he could see Kennedy was to take the Eastern shuttle back to New York City with him. Weaver waited at the airport for three hours on a Friday afternoon as Kennedy missed one flight after another. Finally Kennedy appeared, and the two boarded the plane and found seats in the rear of the aircraft.

A few minutes later, Senator Javits came aboard, saw the two in the back, and joined them. Weaver was loath to conduct the interview with Javits listening, so the three just chatted. He planned to continue his questioning of Kennedy when they landed at LaGuardia.

Once down, however, Kennedy, motioning to a waiting car, politely asked Javits, "Jake, do you want a ride in?" Javits accepted, and Weaver's story was shot.

While some of the press (like Andrew Glass, Peter Lisagor, and Joseph Kraft) had immediate access ("They simply had to come through the door and into the office"), others were not so fortunate. Visiting newspapermen who dropped in seeking a Robert Kennedy interview "as a trophy" to take back home often could not be accommodated into the busy schedule. And Bobby was often cold to foreign newspaper people, whom he accused of making stories up.

He was outraged when a correspondent for a "reputable Sunday newspaper" obtained a copy of one of the speeches on Vietnam, took some quotes from it, and sent a dispatch beginning with "Senator Kennedy, relaxing in his office over a long cigar, told me," implying that he had been granted a personal insight into the Senator's feelings.

He wanted nothing made up and would not cooperate in interviews that stretched accuracy even a harmless bit. He said "no" when a crew from the United States Information Service, filming "A Day in the Life of a Senator," suggested he ride the Senate subway to the Capitol.

"I don't do that," he said, "that isn't how I go to the Capitol. I walk across the campus."

Some months later, a Columbia Broadcasting Company crew doing a half-hour program with a similar theme and title suggested to Angie Novello, "You look over his shoulder as if you're reading the mail."

"Angie doesn't look over my shoulder at the mail," Kennedy objected. "Adam comes in and talks to me about legislation or something, but Angie doesn't do that, so it wouldn't be true."

Not everyone in Washington displayed the same interest in Kennedy as the press and public. Many of his peers virtually ignored him.

"If I'm here fifteen more years," one senator remarked, "I'll never develop rapport with Bobby."

"It's painful when Bobby comes in the dining room," another senator declared. "We try not to look. Nobody likes him yet."

Harris explains. "Some senators did feel that way. I did until I met him. I was sure he was one person I would not like." Harris enumerated the reasons for his initial dislike.

"There was a big difference in our backgrounds. He was a rich man, and I came from a poor family. He had worked for Joseph McCarthy and I had been very active when I was a student against McCarthy. I felt he had won his election primarily because he was a celebrity. And I had just had a hard campaign against another celebrity [Charles "Bud" Burnham Wilkinson, coach of the Oklahoma Sooners]. I resented him."

Harris met Kennedy on November 1, 1964, the day he took office to fill the unexpired term of Oklahoma Senator Robert S. Kerr, who had suffered a fatal heart attack. He and Kennedy and Joseph Montoya of New Mexico, also filling an unexpired term, had been invited to tea in the office of the Senate majority leader, Mike Mansfield.

"I was very impressed with how shy he was. I had expected him to be more aggressive, brusque, like his public image. Instead I found him to be a shy, appealing, wistful, and funny man."[7]

He could be blunt, making no effort to mince words so as to avoid offending. Sometimes his questioning was "almost too mean." At hearings on automobile safety, Kennedy, who was attending his first meeting, felt that Frederic G. Dunner, president of General Motors, was not responsive enough to questioning by Subcommittee Chairman Abraham D. Ribicoff, the senator from Connecticut. He leaped in and demanded to know what proportion of the annual expenditure of the company was being spent on automobile safety.

"You mean to tell me that you're the president of General Motors, and you don't know how much is being spent by your corporation on automobile safety?" Kennedy asked incredulously.

Similarly, when Ralph Nader, testifying before the same committee, was repeatedly interrupted by Senator Carl Curtis, Bobby complained. "What I don't understand is why you don't let Mr. Nader read his statement to find out if in fact . . . ' '

Although Curtis interrupted again to say, "I have no objection to his reading his statement," Kennedy continued: "Then maybe we would understand his position.

"I don't know how you can reach a conclusion about his position. First, you admit you haven't read his book; and secondly, you haven't heard his testimony. Why don't you listen to his testimony and then criticize?"

When Curtis floundered, "I have no objection to hearing his testimony, but when he loses me with . . . ''

"With big words?" Kennedy queried in an acid tone.

Kennedy made his first major speech a scant month after he took office,* antagonizing Javits with an amendment to the Aid-to-Appalachia Bill calling for the inclusion of thirty-three counties in New York State among those to receive federal funds. Javits was outraged.

"It was an internal management amendment for a state in which both senators generally join," explained Javits. "It would have embarrassed me politically if it were mostly his and not mine also."

"I thought it was very rude, and I told him so in no uncertain terms." Javits, a master at parliamentary protocol, also proceeded to point out to the neophyte senator that the measure had to be amended to include the names of the counties, as well as the approval of Governor Rockefeller. Kennedy accepted the amendments and invited Javits to join him in sponsoring the measure, which subsequently was passed.

"With him and his staff, you had to be alert," Javits said.[8]

That both men were keenly aware of their rival status was humorously indicated by their reaction to a joint television appearance on a Channel 2 show.

Driving back to the office from the CBS studio at 2020 M Street, N.W., Kennedy told Walinsky and Barthelmes, "I never want to do that again."

"Why?"

"Javits is so facile. He's computerized. He's very garrulous. He dresses himself up on camera; he has the motions; and he's not phlegmatic. I imagine it's going to be a terrible show. I wish I hadn't gone on with him. I don't ever want to do that again."

Ten minutes after arriving at the Senate Office Building, Barthelmes got a call from Javits's press secretary. His boss wasn't too happy either. "Javits bitched and bitched at me all the way back."

---

* Jack made his first speech after five months in the Senate; Teddy, after fourteen.

"Don't ever put me on with Kennedy again," he ordered. "He's glamorous. He's got the name. People will just turn it on to see him. They won't remember what I said."[9]

While both Kennedys were assigned to the Labor and Public Welfare committees, as was Javits, they forged separate areas of interest; Robert concentrated on education, and Teddy on health and medical research. Also, each was perceived differently by his fellow senators. Bobby was a loner. He was aggressive, intense, energetic, and probing. Often he was moody. Dun Gifford, who worked in Teddy's office and later was a campaign aide in Bobby's 1968 campaign, said, "You always had the feeling that Bobby was going to explode." "He was bold," said Javits, "with something of a taint of arrogance because of his boldness."

Teddy operated differently. He was more cautious and would painstakingly explain his positions and how he came to them. More open and friendly than Bobby, he had forged good relationships with senators of both parties, as well as the White House, where an aide recalled, "We've felt freer being frank with him [Ted], telling him what the problem was on something without worrying what he would do with it."[10]

In committee, where they sat together, and on the Senate floor, they both joked and needled each other.

At one Labor Committee hearing, Robert had bogged down explaining the intricacies of a measure he had proposed. Behind him, Adam Walinsky and Edelman winced as it became clear that he didn't know much about it. The committee chairman pressed Robert. "What are you trying to do?"

"I haven't the slightest idea," Robert replied undaunted, "so let's do it anyway."

Persistent questioning to "explain it in more detail" brought forth a note from Ted. "I don't care about the other fellows. I understand it, Bobby."

On another occasion, when Bobby rambled on in an attempt to explain a complicated amendment drawn up by one of his legislative aides, Teddy sent another note: "Well, you just lost Lister [Lister Hill, chairman]. Stop talking, and let's vote or you'll lose all the others, too."

The Kennedy brothers often took their jibes at each other public. Teddy had "Bobby jokes." He told one audience, "Bobby is house-hunting. There's a house he's interested in on Pennsylvania Avenue, but it is already occupied, and the present owners give no intention that they want to move out."

Bob returned the sally at the Massachusetts Democratic state convention, assuring all candidates that "my brother Ted favors an open convention," defining it as one "where the delegates fully consider all the possibilities, debate all their merits, and then pick whomever Ted selects."

Notes were also passed back and forth in the Senate chamber between

Bobby, Fred Harris, and Walter Mondale. "We laughed a great deal," said Harris. "I remember a time or two when very serious matters were being discussed in the Senate, we worried about how we looked down there on the floor, giggling and trying to hide it." Harris says Kennedy's humor was unlike that of a southern senator, who might lean back and spin a long anecdote. "He was full of quips, topical humor, spur of the moment."

The Kennedy humor could also be directed at himself. When Senator Joseph Clark congratulated him on a speech, Kennedy replied with a note of thanks. "Why do you have to be so polite?" asked Clark. Kennedy shot back, "I'm trying to conceal the ruthless side of my nature."[11]

Or at an aide. Passing Peter Edelman's cluttered desk, which was covered by a foot-high pile of papers, Kennedy queried sarcastically, "Is your mind like that?"

Kennedy commuted several times weekly between Washington and New York City, where he had offices on the fourth floor of the post office building on East Forty-fifth Street in Manhattan. The offices of Senator Jacob Javits were one flight up. "His schedule was fantastic," said John English. "He'd see one guy in the bathroom and another someplace else. He'd be taking a bath and conferring with his aides. He was always doing something."

His staff was encouraged to concentrate on projects that would involve large groups of constituents, especially children. Accordingly, plans for new playgrounds, school lunch programs, and parties for ghetto kids streamed from the office.

"He would get frustrated in New York when he couldn't get things done fast enough," says Burns. "He hated the time it took to deal with bureaucracy."

Kennedy became enraged at one planning session for a Christmas party for elementary school children. An assistant superintendent of schools suggested that attendance be limited to children from the second through the sixth grade.

"How about first graders?" queried Bobby.

"They can't come."

"Why not, they'd enjoy it?" Bobby persisted.

"Well, Senator, we've decided they get too excited, and they wet their pants."

"That's absolutely ridiculous," Kennedy exploded. "You get the superintendent [of Schools] on the phone. I want to talk to him." Ronnie Eldridge, also at the meeting, recalled that eventually the younger children were invited.

He was bored by the partying aspects of political functions and would arrive five minutes before he would be called upon to speak, dismaying the politicians who looked forward to having a Kennedy grace the dais. Representative John Murphy of Staten Island, a staunch Kennedy supporter, invited him to a cocktail party and dinner at his political club. Barthelmes checked the time and told Murphy, "He'll come and he'll say a few words and he'll leave."

"You Kennedy people sure drive a hard bargain," sighed Murphy. But that's how it was.

He accompanied Abraham Beame as he campaigned for mayor against John Lindsay in New York City in the fall of 1965. At a long taping session for a thirty-minute program to be broadcast later, Kennedy, who had been coaching Beame, suddenly broke off and began to pound on the table.

"Damn it, Abe, look alive," he scolded. "Don't just sit there." Beame, a small, placid person, meekly promised, "I'll try to do better."

Kennedy added more controversy in that election when he and Ethel were waiting in line to vote for Beame at the polling station in P.S. 6 on Madison Avenue and Eighty-first Street, one of the most desirable public schools in the city. City Councilman Theodore R. Kupferman, a Republican running for reelection in that district, entered the polling place.

"What are they doing here?" he asked an election official. "I thought he lived in Glen Cove." Kupferman checked the rolls, which revealed that Bobby and Ethel had registered from the Hotel Carlyle. He approached Kennedy.

"Senator," said Kupferman, "I don't believe that you really live at the Hotel Carlyle, so if you just leave quietly we can avoid any problems."

Bobby looked at him coldly. "Who are you?"

"I'm the councilman from this district, and my name is Kupferman," was the reply.

"How do you spell that?" asked Kennedy.

Kupferman spelled his name, and Kennedy simply said, "I expect to vote," thereby precipitating a challenge from the councilman.[12] Bobby and Ethel were asked to take an oath that they lived at the Carlyle and were permitted to vote. When newsmen, who had been following the Kennedys all day and had just gone out for coffee, returned, the whole incident was reenacted for the television cameras. "It's nice publicity for that smart guy," Bobby told reporters.

The Kennedys rented a high-floor apartment in the elegant United Nations Plaza as a base of operations and began to partake in the city's social and cultural life. They attended the theater, went to the ballet, and dined in the most fashionable and costliest restaurants.

At the legendary Le Pavilion, Kennedy's favorite restaurant, proprietor Henri Soule recited a list of the special dishes for the day, painstakingly describing the ingredients and the intricate preparation, when he was interrupted by a halting, "Do you have cold chicken?" For dessert, Kennedy would eschew the crepes and tortes for a bowl of vanilla ice cream, covered with chocolate sauce.

Bobby, like Jack, seldom carried any money. His aides became accustomed to handing Bobby cash for incidentals. One day, he decided it would be useful for him to personally experience a New York City subway. He and Barthelmes went to the Seventy-second Street station of the Broadway line. Walking briskly, he tried to belly through the turnstile without depositing the fare. The turnstile, which was just about the level of his abdomen, did not budge, and he received a jolt that caused him to double up. "You can really lose your life that way," he gasped, as he waited for Barthelmes to deposit the fare. He never again forgot, though, that he needed money before he could pass painlessly to the train.

Once he was attending a luncheon at the old Willard Hotel in Washington when he was told that the buzzer had sounded in the Senate for a vote on a housing amendment. Having dismissed his car, he raced downstairs for a cab, then raced back again and cornered Barthelmes. "I got a cab all right, but I don't have any money. I need five dollars."

One day Bobby and Barthelmes were returning to Washington on the shuttle flight from New York. At the Eastern Airlines terminal at LaGuardia Airport, he drifted off to chat with some constituents. In a few moments, Barthelmes said he heard a "plaintive voice" over the hum of passengers waiting for the plane. "Wes, I want a Hershey bar, and I don't have any money." Sometimes, Barthelmes would have to buy his boss two or three chocolate bars a day.

Author Peter Maas once made an accounting of cash laid out for Bobby Kennedy. Maas watched him dig fruitlessly through his pockets for change to buy a magazine, and he told him, "Listen, Bobby. This has gone on long enough. I've been keeping count. Newspapers, magazines, candy bars, grilled cheese sandwiches. You owe me $176.30." Observed Maas, "To my delight, he appeared to be genuinely needled."

But it happened again. When Maas accompanied Bobby to Korea in January 1964, they attended church services in an Army chapel near the border between North and South Korea. As a soldier came by with the collection basket, Maas watched Bobby digging through his pockets and again coming up with nothing. When the basket was extended, Maas sighed and put in a dollar bill for himself, and another for Kennedy.

Bobby, mindful of his name and position, stage-whispered to Maas, "Don't you think *I* should give more?"[13]

Nothing melted Kennedy faster than a call from his family. He would interrupt any conference if Ethel or one of his kids was on the wire. He would listen patiently, answering questions, soothing ruffled feelings, making no attempt to hurry the call, says an aide. And he was never the one who ended the conversation.

The children visited him at work often. Esther Newberg recalls the day Matthew and Christopher came by: "They were eating crackers; Matthew was sitting on my lap trying out the typewriter, his mouth full of cracker crumbs. The senator came to his doorway. 'Show the lady how you learned to whistle,' Christopher told Matthew.

"Matthew turned around to show me. Crackers everywhere. It was just a mess." Bobby guffawed, but Esther was not amused. "I wanted to slap the kid in the face," she said later.[14]

Predictably, it was not only his own children who brought out the gentleness, the teasing, and the concern. Close friends noted that a mystique seemed to develop between Robert Kennedy and children whenever they met up. Like a Pied Piper, he drew them, singly and in crowds.

"He was magic with the kids," said Jennie Littlefield, who lives on a farm in Wayland, Massachusetts, about forty minutes from downtown Boston. She campaigned for Bobby as a twenty-year-old Barnard student and later married Allard Lowenstein, who became a close supporter of Kennedy.

"Once at a rally near the Barnard campus at 115th Street and Broadway," she recalled, "Bobby was surrounded by kids, black kids, white kids, Spanish kids. He said a few words in Spanish with his Boston accent and had them in stitches.

"He ended by asking, 'Now, who are you going to vote for?' And, of course, they all yelled back 'Kennedy!' Unfortunately nobody in the crowd was over fourteen."

John Burns, who accompanied Bobby often on visits to schools, remembers the kids all called him "Kennedy."

"It was never Bobby, always Kennedy. Just like his brother, Jack. They felt Bobby cared about them. They are very suspicious of politicians, but in the case of Kennedy they felt he cared."

Once, Burns recalled, he picked up Kennedy at the airport and drove with him into Manhattan. The car stopped at a red light, and a boy, about nine, recognized Robert.

"Hey, Kennedy," he called out. Bobby turned and saw the boy was smoking. "That's terrible for you," he remonstrated. "Promise me you'll stop." The boy threw away the cigarette, the light changed, and the car drove on.

About a month later, "Unbelievably," says Burns, "we were driving on the same street, stopped for a light, and there was this kid. He recognized the car and Kennedy and came over. He wanted Bobby to know he had not smoked since their previous encounter."[15]

Kennedy's remarkable rapport with youngsters was due in large measure to his sense of fun, his ability to forget formality and enjoy himself with them. Once, in East Harlem, Kennedy was slated to appear at ceremonies honoring young trainees who had just completed a Vista (Volunteers in Service to America) program.

"The street was roped off," recounted Wes Barthelmes. "It was crowded, mostly with kids, and there were older people leaning out of the windows of the brownstones, which lined 102nd Street. In the middle of the street there was an improvised platform with some folding chairs."

Waiting were two officials of the Office of Economic Opportunity, but it was obvious that there was no planned program. Kennedy, impatient at the lack of foresight, said, "Well, I'll give the certificate, but isn't there some oath?" There was none, so Kennedy said, "We'll make up an oath."

Kennedy told the two dozen volunteers to "line up and raise your right hand and say, 'I solemnly swear that I will be faithful and true to the Vista concept and help my own people and take care of my baby brothers and sisters and vote for Robert Kennedy in 1970.' "

The young people laughed, but the bureaucrats were "stunned and outraged; it was something that just wasn't done." The ceremonial part over, Kennedy left the platform and joined a group of young men who had a stick and a rubber ball.

"Let's play stickball," he suggested. "You be Willie Mays," he told one, "and you're Orlando Cepeda," pointing to another. "And who will I be?" he asked. "I'll just be myself." He threw the ball into the air and swung with the club. And for the next few minutes the senator from New York played ball in the street with some of his constituents.[16]

In Tulsa, Oklahoma, he was riding to the airport with Senator Harris when they passed an elementary school. Bobby stopped the car and went to the fence, where the children quickly clustered.

Using a bullhorn, he asked, "What's the name of this school?" The children shouted their response.

Then, "Do you know who I am?"

"Yes."

"What's my name?"

"Kennedy."

Pointing to Harris, their state's senator, he asked, "Do you know who this is with me?"

When he got a mixed chorus of yeses and nos, Kennedy turned to Harris and teased, "I don't see how you ever got elected in Oklahoma."[17]

Traveling through the country, he would always find the time to stop and speak with children. Peter Edelman says Kennedy told him often he preferred to be with children who provided "a special kind of release"

266

during a campaign. Anecdotes abound about his encounters with youngsters and his unusual sensitivity to their needs.

Years after it happened, seventeen-year-old Eddie Guthman remembered going to an all-star football game in Buffalo with his father, Bobby, and Joe Kennedy III. Bobby and Joe got autographed footballs, and when Kennedy saw that none was given to young Eddie he tossed his ball to the boy.

Campaigning in Oregon, Kennedy saw a little boy standing at the edge of the platform where he was speaking. The child silently held out a box of chocolate-covered cherries. Kennedy took the box and selected one and offered the box to the boy, who also selected one. Then, while the crowd watched, the two chewed chocolate companionably.

24

Catharsis

*B*OBBY HAD recovered from the acute stage of bereavement, but John Kennedy's influence on his personal behavior remained uncommonly strong.

He began by aping his brother's mannerisms. He started to smoke cigars, adopted the habit of chopping the air with his hand when he made speeches, and quoted him constantly. John Kennedy's heroes became his heroes. He wove into his talks quotations from Goethe, Churchill, Robert Frost, and John Emerich Acton, the liberal Catholic baron who left a deep imprint on historical study.

Searching through Jack's wardrobe, he selected several items, which he wore or carried constantly. One was an old blue coat he would drape on a chair and often leave behind; some distance away, he would remember and race back to retrieve it. In New York City during the Senate campaign, he left the coat at a school. The next morning, a frantic call came from Bobby's staff, but the school was closed for the weekend. That evening, at the showing of a movie, *The Guns of August*, Bobby sat behind Ronnie Eldridge. Tapping her on the shoulder, he said, "I'm very anxious to get the overcoat back. It belonged to my brother." The overcoat was later recovered, only to be lost and found many more times.

That same year, he went sailing in rough seas off the Maine coast with his longtime friend, Charles Spalding. The weather worsened, and soon fifty-mile winds were buffeting the vessel, which was listing in five-foot-high waves. Bobby had taken along Jack's windbreaker. He tied the sleeves around his shoulders as he worked the sails with the help of a small crew.

Suddenly a powerful gust tore the jacket from his shoulders and blew it overboard. Ignoring the possibility of drowning in the icy, churning water, Bobby dived over the side, swam toward the jacket, and retrieved it. With considerable difficulty the crew maneuvered the boat around to pick him up. He lay on deck, shivering and exhausted, his brother's jacket safe.[1]

In the spring of 1965, Bobby risked his life again, this time to make an assault on a 14,000-foot mountain in the Yukon that no man had ever conquered. "I climbed," he said, "for personal reasons that seemed compelling. I'm glad I went."[2]

He had never climbed a mountain before, and he was afraid of heights. Yet, he went because the Canadian government had renamed the peak Mount Kennedy after the assassination, and the National Geographic Society had invited both surviving brothers to join in the effort to scale it. Ted's injury in the Massachusetts airplane crash left Bobby to take up the challenge alone.

As a newly elected senator from New York, as the father of nine children, prudence should have told him to stay home and attend to his family and his work. But the pull to honor his dead brother was too strong.

Roped to James W. Whittaker, the mountaineer, and Barry Prather, a specialist in glacial formations, he spent three days and nights on the peak, his head throbbing every moment and his hands shaking.[3] Once he fell through a crevasse and was hauled to safety. The final leg was an almost vertical climb of 200 feet, with a 6,000-foot drop just to his left.

At one in the afternoon of the third day, Bobby waded knee deep in snow to bury on the summit a copy of JFK's inaugural address, a batch of PT-boat pins, and the Kennedy coat of arms, three gold helmets on a field of black. On a pinnacle, with breathtaking views all around them, Jim Whittaker told Bobby, "This climb and mountain have some meaning now for President Kennedy."

Bobby himself signaled that the climb up the snow-and-ice-covered mountain was the final act of catharsis that brought to a close his long period of personal mourning. He said, "It [the climb] was done with mixed emotions. It was with a feeling of pain that the events of sixteen months and two days before had made necessary. It was with a feeling of relief and exhilaration that we had accomplished what we set out to do."[4]

He never forgot, of course. There were some times afterward when remembrance struck suddenly and forcefully. He would stop work and sit with his head sunk into his chest. In planes and cars during campaign trips, he would stare in moody silence out of a window. "Those of us who were around him much knew enough not to try to start a conversation but to wait until the sadness left and he would speak,'' said John Burns, chairman of the New York State Democratic Party.[5]

Once, a volunteer came into an office late in the afternoon and unexpectedly found him standing before a photograph of his brother on the wall. Nobody else was there. He turned a tearstained face toward her. ''I loved him,'' he said softly, and brushed past her.[6]

Bobby's devotion to the memory of his brother and his distorted sense of family loyalty caused him to monitor closely media portrayal of the Kennedys. Not only did he maintain a close watch on what had already appeared in print—keeping tabs on who was for and who was against them—he also tried to exercise tight control before the fact. Once, in California in 1966, infuriated by a planned story, he berated the reporter before a dozen colleagues for ''sensationalism.'' That wasn't enough: he had an aide follow the attack with a telephone call to the man's editor.[7]

At times Bobby was skillful and tactful in his attempts to satisfy the sensitivities of the Kennedys; on other occasions he was abrasive and difficult. The most celebrated of the Kennedy media quarrels preceded publication of William Manchester's *Death of a President* and resulted in a personal and political backlash that was disastrous for his image.

During his 1964 senatorial campaign in New York, he screened every television commercial and looked at every photograph. ''He was really a very intensely critical guy about it,'' recalls Donald Wilson, ''and I don't remember him ever being completely satisfied with anything that was ever done on television or the printed page, ever. He was rarely satisfied with pictures that were taken of him and his family.''

Wilson, an executive with Time Inc., said Bobby, like Jack before him, would call ''at the most outlandish hours'' with questions about planned stories in the company's magazines. ''He'd ask what did I think of such and such a guy who was doing the interviewing and how did I think he'd get treated.''[8]

Earlier, in December 1961, William Peters, a freelance writer, sent a draft of his article for *Redbook*, ''What Makes Teddy Run,'' to the younger Kennedy brother's office for ''review and comment.'' Teddy sent it on to Bobby, detailing his objections to the piece.

He did not like, he said, what he called ''a dynasty reference,'' in which Peters quoted the seventy-five-year-old mother of a Harvard roommate who, when told that Teddy might run, asked, ''Wouldn't you think they'd be satisfied?''

He objected to a quoted comment from Joan, in which she characterized her background as ''cloistered as you can imagine'' and confided ''I actually never met a Jew as I was growing up.''

Joan's description of the Kennedy compound also made him uneasy. "Besides all that sports equipment—boats, water skis, tennis courts, riding horses, nearby golf courses and everything else, they have their own projection room for movies," she said. "If you want a steam bath, they have that, too."

The article included a description of an elaborate collegiate caper in which Ted bought a one-way ticket to Cairo on his credit card for his Harvard classmate Edward Carey, who was to make his way back on his own. With a half-dozen classmates Ted drove Carey to Logan Airport, where Kennedy had serious second thoughts and tried to call the bet off. Carey, however, adventure-minded, refused and boarded a plane to New York's Idlewild, now Kennedy International. There, he was summoned to the telephone by Ted in Cambridge who, visualizing headlines, not to mention his father's wrath, frantically urged him to come back.

Carey again refused, but took a plane to Hartford, Connecticut, spent the night at his home in Westfield, and returned to Harvard in the morning, to Ted's enormous relief.

Ted Kennedy had misgivings about the Carey story, too.

He told Bobby that his aide, Hal Clancy, felt publication of the article would be politically damaging and had suggested a "strong letter" to the editor of *Redbook* that "we consider the article to be inaccurate and distorted."

"We want to stop the article in its present form," Clancy wrote in a memo to Ted Kennedy.

Robert Kennedy's approach was more diplomatic. He read the article carefully, looking for ways to present a more positive side of Ted. The result was a four-page list of changes that eliminated the reference to the seventy-five-year-old mother, the Carey prank, and the projection room and steam bath.

"I would just say you don't think it adds anything and it might appear that it shows our bragging about being more fortunate than others," Bobby wrote in reference to the luxuries of the compound. He also suggested that Peters be asked to tone down the last third of the article, which he felt was anti-Ted.

When the article appeared in the June 1962 issue of *Redbook*, most of Robert Kennedy's suggestions had been accepted.[9]

If Bobby handled the Peters article deftly, minimizing any possible damage to Teddy's image, he was astonishingly inept five years later in the Manchester affair, the fallout from which was a public relations debacle for him.

The story is well known.[10] Briefly, the Kennedys selected Manchester, who had written an early biography of JFK described as "adoring," to do

271

the authorized account of the events in Dallas. He would have full cooperation from the family and sole access to files, documents, and oral history tapes. In return the author promised, in writing, that Jacqueline and Robert Kennedy would have final approval of the text.

The agreement forbade a movie or television adaptation but permitted magazine serialization. "I don't want anyone to make a killing out of my brother's death," Robert Kennedy told Manchester at the start of the discussions.

Manchester resigned his post on the faculty of Wesleyan University and moved to Washington, where he lived frugally, renting "cheap rooms," walking miles to save taxi fare, and typing his own notes.* For the next two months he immersed himself in the assassination, interviewing every person in Washington and Texas who might have some knowledge of the event. He worked ten, sometimes twenty, hours a day; he became so exhausted that his doctor put him into the hospital for twelve days.

In March 1966, the finished manuscript went to Evan Thomas, who would edit the book for Harper & Row. Over the next four months, Thomas conferred with Ed Guthman, John Seigenthaler, Richard Goodwin, and Arthur Schlesinger about the manuscript. On July 28, Bobby sent a telegram to Manchester saying, "Members of the Kennedy family will place no obstacle in the way of publication."

It was scheduled for publication in January 1967, and the serialization rights were sold to *Look* magazine for $665,000.

But the magazine sale infuriated Jackie, who said, "I thought that it [the book] would be bound in black and put away on dark library shelves." In spite of what he said in his telegram, Bobby now tried to persuade Harper and Manchester to abrogate the agreement with *Look*. He urged *Look* executives not to publish the serialization. Finally, he sent a telegram to Evan Thomas, declaring he felt the book should not be published or serialized and asked him to break the news to Manchester.

When conferences in Washington, Hyannis Port, and New York could not resolve the conflict, Jackie filed suit to prevent publication and magazine serialization of the book. Eventually, an out-of-court settlement resulted in the deletion of personal details Jackie considered offensive (much of which had already been leaked) and unfavorable comment about President Johnson, which Bobby and his staff felt would hurt him politically.

The damage, however, had already been done. Widespread publicity was given to the suit and to the attempts of the Kennedys to suppress the book. Manchester, in his *Look* article, declared, "It was as though the first and fourteenth amendments had been struck from the Constitution."

* In an article in *Look* magazine, April 4, 1967, Manchester said he received a small advance from his publisher, Harper & Row. The Kennedys did not underwrite any of the expenses.

"Manchester's contribution to history may prove not to be writing the book so much as being the unwitting agent who allowed the innocent millions an unexpected glimpse of a preternaturally ambitious family furiously at work manipulating history in order that they might rise," wrote Gore Vidal.

Elie Abel, discussing the episode with Bobby, says Bobby kept referring to Jackie as "the poor little thing, the poor little thing."[11]

Pete Hamill, too, feels that acceding to Jackie's wishes was uppermost in Bobby's mind. "RFK didn't really believe that Mrs. Kennedy's objections were worth the trouble," he said, "but she was his brother's widow—and the Kennedys have nothing if they do not have a ferocious sense of family loyalty."[12]

He was becoming increasingly absorbed in the struggles of minority groups, feeling an urgency to help find practical solutions to often desperate problems. One day, he went for a walk through the streets of Bedford-Stuyvesant in Brooklyn. Bed-Stuy was once home to a solid, white, middle-class population who lived in three- and four-story elegant brownstones along tree-lined streets. But on February 4, 1965, the day of Bobby's visit, it was a huge black slum, second in the United States only to Chicago's South Side. More than 450,000 persons were squeezed into the 500 square blocks. It was the most depressed black community in America.

Kennedy saw vacant, rubbish-strewn lots, burned-out houses, uncollected garbage spilling out of cans. Unemployed men and youths hung around the corners and the bars. Inadequately dressed children played in the streets, unprotected from the February cold. Later he met with community leaders, who lashed out in their frustration.

"You're another white guy that's out here for the day; you'll be gone, and you'll never be seen again. We've had enough of that," said one leader. State Supreme Court Judge Thomas R. Jones told Kennedy, "I'm weary of study, Senator . . . weary of speeches, weary of promises that aren't kept. The Negro people are angry."[13]

Kennedy told Adam Walinsky, "I want to do something about all this." For the next nine months, key members of his staff, headed by Walinsky and Thomas Johnston, worked on the project, traveling all over the country, seeking suggestions to revitalize Bedford-Stuyvesant.

Kennedy felt it was essential to enlist the aid of white affluent and influential business leaders who could give practical guidance to the Bedford-Stuyvesant community. He began to recruit among his personal friends and acquaintances. Men like Douglas Dillon, former Secretary of the Treasury, Thomas J. Watson, head of IBM, William Paley of CBS, David Lilienthal, former chairman of the Tennessee Valley Authority, Roswell

Gilpatric, former Under Secretary of Defense, and Andre Meyer of Lazard Freres agreed to participate, Meyer upon the condition that Kennedy make another anti-Vietnam speech.

Benno Schmidt, managing partner of J. G. Whitney & Company, an investment banking firm, received a phone call from Kennedy asking to see him immediately. Schmidt, a Republican who had voted for Richard Nixon in 1960 and Kenneth Keating in 1964, did not know Kennedy and was somewhat surprised at the request.[14]

"I'll be in my office all day," he responded, "if you'd like to see me."

"I have a vote at three o'clock, which I should make," said Kennedy. "I can catch the four o'clock shuttle, which should put me at your office by a quarter to six."

Late that afternoon, Kennedy appeared at Schmidt's thirty-eighth-floor Rockefeller Center office and urged him to join the others to bring "managerial know-how, banking know-how, technological know-how" to Bedford-Stuyvesant.

"I promise you this is not a political project," he said. Schmidt, after conferring with Mayor John Lindsay and Senator Javits, "who urged me to do it," agreed, later devoting as much as 25 percent of his time to the undertaking.

Ten months later, on December 6, 1966, Kennedy unveiled his plan before more than 1,000 Bedford-Stuyvesant residents meeting at P.S. 306 on Monroe Street. Flanking him on the platform were Lindsay and Javits, the latter calling it "Kennedy's finest hour."

After Bobby Kennedy's assassination, Javits asked Ethel to take her husband's place on the board saying, "It was the greatest memorial she could give him, because it was the single act of the greatest virtuosity with which he was connected."

The plan called for parallel organizations; the Bedford-Stuyvesant Restoration Corporation, composed of community leaders and residents who would determine what was needed, and the Bedford-Stuyvesant Development and Services Corporation, which would advise and counsel and help raise funds.

Kennedy took an active part in the implementation of the plans, attending almost every meeting of the D and S Board and assigning several members of his staff to work with the community residents. Dissension from young, militant blacks, who were opposed to "whites" taking over, was handled by appointing their representatives to the board.

"We had a standing in Bedford-Stuyvesant because of Bob that we could never have had without him," recalled Schmidt. Kennedy "spoke to me with more enthusiasm about this one effort than any other he had ever undertaken," says Ted Sorensen. And to another aide, Kennedy declared,

"If I could do what I really wanted to do, I would resign from the Senate and run Bedford-Stuyvesant."

Some twenty years later, were Robert Kennedy to take that same walk in Bed-Stuy, there is much that is different. More than 4,000 homes have been spruced up by neighborhood youths, who paint and fix the facades of the buildings, caulk and replace windows, redo stoops and sidewalks through a "home improvement" program that operates from July through October. Owners pay a fifty-dollar fee; the Restoration Corporation absorbs the rest.

Two "superblocks" have been closed off to traffic, and parks designed by I. M. Pei, architect for the John Fitzgerald Kennedy Library, provide attractive, tree-shaded strolling and sitting areas. More than 1,500 new and rehabilitated homes have been constructed, and millions of dollars in mortgage money have been made available for people who want to buy homes.

There are many black-owned small businesses and a huge IBM computer cable plant in the area. Much of the construction and many of the businesses provide employment for Bed-Stuy residents. There are shopping, banking, recreational, and social services available, including the Billie Holiday Theater, a skating rink, and a Center for Art and Culture.[15]

He knew little of the plight of the migratory grape workers in California, so his emotions were not engaged in their struggle, but once he saw—as he did in Bed-Stuy—Bobby Kennedy underwent an almost instant conversion to their cause.

Kennedy was a member of the Migratory Labor Subcommittee of the Senate Labor Committee, which was chaired by Senator Harrison Williams of New Jersey. One day in early 1966, Walter Reuther and Jack Conway of the United Auto Workers telephoned Peter Edelman to suggest that Kennedy go to Delano, California, to the committee's hearings on the strike of the grape workers.

Since 1962 Cesar Chavez, the short, soft-voiced Mexican-American head of the United Farm Workers Organizing Committee, had been urging the grape pickers to join La Causa, a nonviolent crusade for better working conditions. Chavez's grandfather, Cesario, had crossed the Mexican border at El Paso, Texas, in the late 1880s after a dispute with the owners of the hacienda where he lived and worked. Chavez had been born in Arizona in 1927 and, as a young boy, worked with his family picking cherries, lettuce, grapes, melons, and all the other crops of "Sunny California" after his father lost his grocery business during the Depression years.

It was those years when he experienced firsthand all the miseries of the migrant laborer that provided the impetus for his battle to unionize farm workers. However, California growers, often aided by local police, had fought back bitterly, bringing in workers from other areas, forbidding organizers on the fields, and setting dogs and spraying insecticides on the pickets.

Now, finally, the Senate was going to investigate what was happening in those fields, and Kennedy was wanted in California because his presence would attract public attention. Although he and Chavez had met when the latter was registering Mexican-American voters in 1960, Kennedy knew little about the situation in Delano. On the plane heading west, he asked Edelman, "What am I going out for?" Edelman briefed him on what was happening.

They were met at the airport by Chavez and Dolores Huerta, vice president of the United Farm Workers, who took them to the vineyards where the strikers were picketing the cold storages in the fields. Bobby went to the picket line and shook hands with each of the strikers.

"It was a turning point for us," declares Cesar Chavez, now a little heavier, gray streaks running through his hair. "He came to the strike hall and held our flag. And people said, if Bobby Kennedy says it's good, it must be good."[16]

Kennedy also went to the hearings in the high school auditorium, which was filled with farm workers who occupied every seat and crowded in the doorways and windows. Witness after witness testified to the deplorable conditions under which they worked, and Kennedy listened.

His questioning, says Chavez, was the "highlight of the whole hearing."

Just before the lunch break, Kennedy asked county sheriff Leroy Galyen why forty-four workers had been arrested three months earlier. "I hear they were peaceful; they were nonviolent, they were picketing lawfully," he said.

"Why did you arrest them?"

The sheriff replied, "Well, I got a call from a supervisor of the company who told me that these people who were out there earning a living had said if we don't get the picket line out of there they were going to come and cut their hearts out. So I came and removed the cause to counter the effect."

Kennedy asked, "The cause of what?"

"The cause of the problem," explained the sheriff.

"So you came and arrested forty-four people because somebody else was going to come and attack them?" Kennedy demanded.

"Yes," replied the sheriff.

"But they didn't violate any law," Kennedy pointed out. "How could you do that?"

"Well, we were just protecting them," was the reply.

"I would suggest to the sheriff," Kennedy said acidly, "that in his lunch break he take the time to read the Constitution of the United States."

276

Kennedy supported the grape pickers in their strike after the hearings, forging with Chavez a warm, trusting relationship upon which each could call. "Always after that, we helped Cesar Chavez in any way we could," says an aide. In return, the farm workers were the first organized group to come out for "Kennedy in '68," Chavez says.

He began to look at how other groups lived. LaDonna Harris remembers that he questioned her about Indian reservations, about Indian education and Indian problems.

"Once at Hyannis Port, I asked Eunice why Bobby was so involved with Indians," she recalls. "Eunice said both Jack and Bobby felt very bad when the federal government condemned Seneca land for a dam and whole tribes had to be relocated."[17]

Bobby was especially disturbed by the 75 percent dropout rate of Indian schoolchildren. He went to their schools to see what they were being taught about Indian history and culture. He checked the libraries for books on Indian lore, almost exploding with rage at one school, where the only book touching on Indian history began with a chapter on the scalping of whites.

In a Concho, Oklahoma, school where he was conducting a hearing, he lashed out at an elementary school principal who blamed Indian parents because their children could not read.

"It was maddening," Mrs. Harris says. "I had testified, the parents had testified. We pointed out the children had no textbooks about Indian history. There were no courses where they could learn about their ancestry. They had no role models, and this gave them a low self-image. That's why they weren't learning to read.

"And this principal. All he could say was 'In Oklahoma, we love our Indian people.'

"Bobby got very emotional. He banged on the table and shouted at this man. 'What are you saying? Is that all you have to say?' "

This kind of empathy, followed by action on Kennedy's part, struck a special chord in Indian hearts and memories. Elizabeth Lohah-Homer, who works with Mrs. Harris at Americans for Indian Opportunity, says she grew up admiring and respecting Robert Kennedy.

"I was ten when he was killed. I remember my father, who was a judge, came home and hugged my mother. Then we all just stayed in the kitchen and cried."

This feeling was emphasized by Senator George McGovern, who declares, "The Indians had a special response to him that I never detected with any other politician."

In 1967, John Burns accompanied Kennedy and Senator Javits to a migrant workers' camp about thirty miles outside Rochester, New York, where they were met by the owner carrying a gun. The migrants were living in old, burned-out buses with no toilet facilities. Everywhere there was dirt and squalor.

"Kennedy was angry and disgusted," says Burns. "I can't believe this can exist," he kept repeating. "There are laws already on the books, which are not being enforced."

The camp owner, "a big, burly guy," motioned with his gun. "This is private property," he declared. "Get out of here."

Kennedy refused. "This is an outrage," he told the man. "You should be ashamed of yourself."

The owner called over one of his workers, a black man, who looked terrified. " 'How do I treat you?' he asked. The poor guy, he just said, 'You treat me fine,' " Burns recalls.

The obvious phoniness of the scene disgusted Kennedy, who snapped at the camp owner: "You should be shut down!"[18]

25

"What Shall I Do?"

ON August 4, 1967, a hot Sunday, Bobby attended early mass in New York and raced to the airport with Pierre Salinger, barely arriving in time to catch a plane for San Francisco. Jesse Unruh, the speaker of the California state assembly and a power in national Democratic politics, had personally asked him to come to a fund-raising dinner. They stretched out in first-class seats, a luxury Bobby was no longer denying himself.

Back in the economy section, a youthful-looking man in a golfing jacket, his shirt opened halfway to his waist, was peering at a sheaf of papers through thick-lensed glasses. This was Allard K. Lowenstein, thirty-eight, who had spent all of his adult life pursuing causes. His restless social conscience had blossomed at the University of North Carolina, where he had become a passionate advocate of civil rights. By the time he was twenty, he had been elected president of the National Student Association and in the next ten years, with the help of other students, had put together something of a political movement among Mississippi blacks. By 1967, he was nationally known in radical liberal circles as an implacable enemy of racism, injustice, and the exploitation of minorities.

Lowenstein was a nonpracticing attorney who taught constitutional law at City College in New York and had a small private income from a restaurant chain his family owned. Thus he had the time, and some means, to carry on his crusades, the latest of which was begun that summer.

Furious at Johnson's conduct of the Vietnam conflict, he had formed "end the war" committees around the country, which were bombarding the White House with letters. Lowenstein, reading the mood of the nation, was certain that the rage of increasing numbers of Americans, particularly young people, against the war was fierce enough, and contagious enough, to cause a volcanic eruption from deep inside the core of the Democratic Party that would roar upward with explosive force. Lyndon Johnson would be the main casualty.

From his West Side apartment in New York City, where he and his wife Jennie lived with their just-born son Frank, Lowenstein began and led the "Dump Johnson" movement. Although the unceremonious jettisoning of a sitting President was precisely the idea he intended to convey, he let others use the strong word. Soon they did, by the many millions. Lowenstein himself, despite his zeal, felt the word was "too discourteous," asserting, " 'Stop Johnson' was as far as I ever went."[1]

Al Lowenstein could speak with remarkable persuasiveness in perfectly formed sentences, delivered urgently. From his apartment, he racked up monumental telephone bills as he mounted his crusade.

Success was seven months away on this August morning.

Lowenstein was on his way to a meeting with one Gerald Hill in San Francisco. Hill headed the California Democratic Council, consisting of upper-middle-income persons who were planning to field a slate of delegates in the forthcoming Democratic convention pledged to end the Vietnam war.

Bob Kennedy knew Al Lowenstein and about his efforts to unseat LBJ. Pierre, who had caught sight of Al while boarding, told his boss he was on the plane. "Say," Bobby said, "I'd like to talk to him."

Pierre went down the aisle to where Lowenstein was seated and squeezed himself into the economy seat, while Al went forward to sit with Kennedy.

Lowenstein almost charged up front. He had Kennedy in mind already as a Democratic candidate. "When Al started the 'Dump Johnson' movement," Jennie declared, "Robert Kennedy was his number-one choice, even though he felt Bobby was least likely to accept." Up to then, however, Al had not approached him.

Bobby himself brought up the subject. "Who's your candidate?" he asked.

Lowenstein admitted he didn't have any. "You need a movement before you can get a candidate," he said. Then, making it seem like lighthearted conversation, "But if you want to run, we'll let you."

Bobby laughed and asked Al to tell him more about the organization. "We're going to defeat Lyndon Johnson for the party nomination in '68," Lowenstein told him. "With you, we could do it much more easily—but we're going to do it with you or without you."

Outwardly, Kennedy all but scoffed at the notion that Johnson could be dumped. Later, Al said, "He took it as seriously as the idea of a priest in Bogotá deposing the Pope." At the same time, he felt that Bobby's instinct was to make the race, although he had no illusions at that time that he would ever risk it.

From the time of that serendipitous encounter, Al kept after Bob doggedly in secret meetings, arguing, pleading, even berating him. "Whenever they would meet," Jennie declared, "it was always kept off Bobby's calendar. His secretary would not put it down because, if it were known that he was seeing 'that radical Lowenstein,' everybody would know what they were talking about."[2]

The notion that Bobby Kennedy someday would succeed his brother in the White House had been in circulation for years, even while Jack was living there. Joe Kennedy's overweening ambitions for his sons fostered the idea of a dynasty unprecedented in American history, one Kennedy following the other in an unbroken torch-passing of power.

Jack himself did not look unfavorably on the scenario. "When I'm through, how about you?" he had inscribed on a cigarette case he presented to Bobby. In the 1968 campaign, Bobby drew laughs when he told rallies that Ted had been given the job of having campaign buttons manufactured. "Tens of thousands came," he said, "and when we opened the cartons, they had Teddy's name on them." While stumping for Bobby that year, Teddy said in Iowa, "Eight years ago, I was introduced as the brother of a President. Today, I'm introduced as the brother of a Presidential candidate. If about eight years from now you see me coming back to this picnic . . . . " A long pause, a wide grin, and, playing his audience like a seasoned standup comedian, a lift of the eyebrows and a drawn-out, "We—lll . . . ." The crowd roared.

These were jokes, of course, but nobody was fooled much. Jack had said, "I came into politics in my brother Joe's place. If anything happens to me, Bobby will take my place, and if Bobby goes, we have Teddy coming along." Rose, who knew her children, said of Ted just after his election to the Senate in 1962, "He is very ambitious and naturally wants to do what the other boys did."

Rose Kennedy, too, is ambitious still for her family. In the winter of 1983, the author interviewed Rose, this time by telephone, one of a number of talks over the years. She had celebrated her ninety-third birthday on July 22 and, friends reported, was noticeably weak and more frail than she had been only a year or two before. As a result of a recent stroke, her left eye was closed. She was in Palm Beach, recuperating slowly.

During the brief conversation—she had interrupted her lunch to come to the telephone—she was asked, "Would you like one of your grandchildren to become President, following in the footsteps of your son John?"

Rose had twenty-nine grandchildren, seventeen boys and twelve girls. David Kennedy has since died of a drug overdose, in April the following year.

"Oh, of course," she replied in her unmistakable Bostonian accent. "It's a great honor. The family is politically oriented, and we discuss it a lot."

"Would you like one of the dozen girls to make it to the White House as the country's first woman President?"

Without a moment's hesitation, Rose Kennedy answered, "Why certainly." She did not say which one had the best chance or which she favored. With diplomatic sidestepping, she said, "I haven't gone into it with them."

As the 1968 elections neared, Arthur Krock, an intimate friend of the family since Bobby was ten years old, was certain that Jack's younger brother claimed the Presidency "as his rightful heritage."[3] Evidence was not lacking that Bobby was gearing up for a race. As far back as 1966, his Senate office in Washington resembled a candidate's campaign headquarters a fortnight before Election Day. An unending stream of handouts poured from the offices; his major speeches were trumpeted in advance to attract the widest possible attention; his travels abroad were heavily publicized, the staff making certain there would be saturation coverage by the print and electronic media.

By the end of 1966 and all throughout the following year, talk of a Bobby Kennedy Presidency was widespread and growing. In midsummer of 1966, the Gallup organization reported that his popularity had leaped ahead of Johnson's in a poll of Democrats and independents, a finding confirmed by the Louis Harris pollsters three months later.

Ethel was elated when the results were published. "In politics, Ethel operated mainly on instincts," declared Dave Hackett, "and in this case her instincts told her he should get into the race."[4] As time passed, Ethel's conviction became so strong that she was urging him almost continually to do battle against Johnson. The odds against a successful campaign did not bother her; knowing little about political techniques, she either glossed over the formidable problem of wrestling delegates from LBJ or did not even know it existed.

But they bothered him a great deal. In a replay of the lengthy indecisiveness he displayed before the Senate race in 1964, he wavered that year and into almost a quarter of the next.

He wondered, he told a friend, "Do those good polls show support for me, or dissatisfaction with Johnson?" He wondered if he would damage his political career irreparably if he lost, if he would sunder the Democratic Party and thereby lock up the election for the Republicans, if he would stand accused of thirsting for power, if running would be viewed as the ultimate act of defiance in his too-well-known feud with Johnson.

Looming largest in RFK's mind was the Vietnam War, and his late brother's role in its escalation.

While Jack was alive, Bobby was an undeviating hawk. On his big desk at Justice was a green beret. In February 1962, on a visit to Southeast Asia, he said in Hong Kong, "The solution there [North and South Vietnam] lies in our winning it. This is what the President intends to do." When he reached Saigon, he declared, "I think the United States will do what is necessary to help a country that is trying to repel aggression with its own blood, tears, and sweat."[5]

But in mid-1964, as the U.S. military involvement steadily increased, Bobby veered toward the side of those who had begun to feel a growing disenchantment with the war. Officially, the Johnson Administration was arguing that the North Vietnamese could be defeated, but many were not so sure. By the close of the year, as the Vietcong, moving nearer to Saigon, appeared close to a victory despite huge amounts of U.S. aid to the South, Bobby's doubts were magnified.

However, he knew the figures as well as anyone: in May 1961, when the Kennedy Administration was only four months old, there had been 685 military advisers in South Vietnam aiding the regime of President Ngo Dinh Diem. By the end of the JFK years, the number had risen to 16,500.

He could disavow a war he had himself supported. That was acceptable, for a man can grow and change. But John Kennedy did not have time left to him in life to change. His record on the war was closed, and it was only too clear. Could Bobby run on a platform repudiating a policy that, however much it had been transmuted by his successor, was originally the product of a Kennedy Administration, and was still being carried out by some of the people he had appointed?

"Facing the problem was an everyday agony for him," declared Harris Wofford, and everyone who knew him saw the internal tug-of-war going on.[6]

Almost daily, Bobby and Ethel talked over his dilemma in private, often until long past midnight, picking apart the pros and the cons, Hackett revealed. Bobby looked upon Ethel as more than a cheerleading, blind supporter. He trusted her instincts. "On matters that were politically complex," Hackett said, "she did not have much knowledge. But on the broader issues, she would fall back on her basic inner feelings and was often proven right."[7]

Besides trying to convince Bobby herself, Ethel began her own private campaign that winter of 1967 to bring him around, enlisting her friends to work on him. Once, for example, Jack Newfield wrote a blistering article, in which he said, "If Kennedy does not run in 1968, the best side of his character will die. . . . It will die every time a kid asks him, if he is so much against the Vietnam War, how come he is putting party above principle? It will die every time a stranger quotes his own words back to him on the value of courage as a human quality."[8]

Ordinarily, when Ethel felt that journalists were even slightly critical of Bobby, she was unforgiving. She would scold them when they met, write sharp notes, or stop speaking to them entirely. Once when she fancied that Chet Huntley's remarks on the Huntley-Brinkley show were unfavorable, she called him from Hickory Hill after the newscast and laced into him. When he hung up, Huntley shook his head in bewilderment.

But Newfield's article was different. It was critical in a way she wanted, so she had it copied and sent to fifty friends. Later, Bobby came up to Newfield at a political meeting. "I thought he was pissed off at me and was going to pick a fight," he said. Instead, Bobby told him Ethel adored the piece.[9]

The opening gun in the Bobby-for-President drive was fired on October 8, 1967, revealing how his close advisers would be split in the coming months. Pierre Salinger's keen political sense, sharpened by his three years in the White House with JFK, was telling him that Johnson would toss in the towel the following year. "I told this to Bobby," Pierre said, "and that I wanted to call together a group of advisers to bat the ball around about running. He wasn't crazy about the idea, but he didn't say no either."

Salinger called Teddy, Steve Smith, Ted Sorensen, Arthur Schlesinger, Jeff Greenfield, and Adam Walinsky, who met at an all-day session in a suite at the Hotel Regency in New York. Teddy, Sorensen, and Schlesinger were opposed; the others, including Salinger, voted yes.

"But Bobby sat through the entire meeting, hardly saying a word, just listening and giving no clue," Pierre declared.[10]

From that time on, dozens of meetings were held in New York and Washington all through the winter and early spring. Bobby people came together at Kennedy's apartment at United Nations Plaza, in Steve Smith's apartment at 1030 Fifth Avenue, in Bobby's New York Senate office, at Hickory Hill, in his Washington Senate office. They met in airport lounges and bunched together on airplane flights while the senator was en route to a political function. Once a half-dozen of them had a heated discussion on Madison Avenue and Fifty-first Street, where Bobby's car was parked outside a Schrafft's restaurant. Bobby slipped away and had a glass of milk at the counter; when he returned, the arguments were still going on. Nobody had noticed his absence.

Teddy and Schlesinger were worried that a Bobby candidacy would be seen as opportunism and a personal vendetta against LBJ. Fred Dutton read the polls as RFK did: evidence that the public disliked Johnson rather than approving Kennedy. Burke Marshall, Robert McNamara, and Lawrence O'Brien counseled against haste. Kenny O'Donnell preferred that Bobby stay out but would follow him anywhere he went.

In early October, during a meeting at Kennedy's New York office on East Forty-fifth Street, Lowenstein for the first time asked Bobby to enter the race. He told him his organization was in full swing, with local groups fully active in a number of states. He had just gotten word that the California Democratic Council, enlarged and increasingly powerful, had committed itself to backing an anti-LBJ candidate.

"Johnson is finished," Al said. But Kennedy shook his head. Only "unforeseen circumstances" could get him to run.

"Okay," Lowenstein replied. "I'm the unforeseen circumstance."

Kennedy smiled but replied that tradition was all against the bizarre plan. Sitting Presidents had overwhelming power, and dislodging one, particularly a politician as wily as Johnson, simply couldn't be done.

Lowenstein was sad and angry at the same time. He told Kennedy, "If things were to be judged by traditional political standards, and by traditional politicians, by traditional judgments of what was possible, then of course nothing could be done. But that's the whole point. Nothing is the way it had been before, and if you don't know that, you're not nearly as smart as I thought you were.

"And if you don't try, it's hard to believe you care as much as millions of people think you do."

Bobby was stung. Reddening, he glared at Lowenstein, who glared back. "It can't be put together," Bobby insisted.

Lowenstein stood up. Furious, he raged at Bobby: "There are those of us who think the honor and direction of the country are at stake. I don't give a damn whether you think it can be put together or not! We're going to do it without you, and that's too bad because you could have been President of the United States!"

Al turned and almost ran from the office. Bobby rose and ran after him, turning him around with a hand on his shoulder. They stood looking at each other, silent in the emotion-charged moment. Bobby spoke first. "I hope you understand that I can't do it, and that I know what you're doing should be done, but I just can't do it." Lowenstein left without a word.

Rebuffed, saddened, Lowenstein scoured the country for a candidate. He asked the dovish General James M. Gavin, recently retired, who had been an airborne commander in World War II. Gavin liked the idea, but would only run as a Republican, which he had been all his adult life. Al saw no logic in that and turned to Kenneth Galbraith, the Harvard economist who had served as ambassador to India and as president of the Americans for Democratic Action. But the six-foot-six Galbraith was a Canadian by birth, disqualified by the Constitution. He tried Senator George McGovern of South Dakota but was turned down.

On October 19, Al flew to Los Angeles where Senator Eugene McCarthy of Minnesota was delivering an antiwar address. In the senator's hotel room that night, Lowenstein broached the idea. Inwardly he groaned when McCarthy's first comment was, "I think Bobby should do it."[11] Still, McCarthy was interested but wanted time to think it over. Over the next few weeks, Al kept after him, until, after an especially impassioned plea, the Minnesota senator asked, "How do you think we'd do in a Wisconsin primary?"[12]

Lowenstein was certain now that McCarthy was going in, but McCarthy still wasn't sure what Bobby would do. Back in Washington, he went to see him for a frank talk and left satisfied that Kennedy would stay out.

That brief meeting was recalled by the former senator in a talk with the author. Eugene McCarthy lives in a 200-year-old house on fifteen acres of land in the rolling Virginia countryside, an hour and a half drive from Washington. It is a peaceful, near-idyllic setting. From his terrace, he looks down on a large tranquil pond and, in the distance, the foothills of the Blue Ridge Mountains.

Dressed casually in baggy black pants and checked shirt, he had not changed much over the years: he is still handsome, white-haired, soft-spoken. He devotes his time to lecturing, writing, and serving on the board of directors of a consulting firm.

In the low-ceilinged den of his home, he recalls that brief meeting with Bobby.

"It only lasted a very few minutes," McCarthy said. "He told me then that he definitely was not going to run. He said, 'I have to think of my future.' I don't know what that meant. He didn't elaborate, and I didn't ask him.

"We shook hands on it. When a couple of politicians discuss a serious question, and one says, 'I'm not going to run,' the other assumes he *means* he is not going to run. Had he said he would run, I would have had to give very serious thought to my own candidacy, because you can't have two people running on the antiwar front."

McCarthy did not call Kennedy's ultimate decision to enter a betrayal, but he came close. He said, "If I had said what he did, under the circumstances, I would have thought that I had given my word not to run. What he thought I don't know."

At this time, McCarthy was unaware of the deep division in the Kennedy camp on running. He knew only that some of Bobby's friends and advisers had told him the "no" was irrevocable. These assurances, added to what he took as Kennedy's personal word, convinced him. On November 30, he announced that he would oppose Johnson for the Democratic nomination.

Al had his candidate, and Bobby had told McCarthy the truth: the question had been resolved in his own mind. He said to a friend after the McCarthy visit, "That's it. Now maybe I can get some other work done." But the faction that wanted him in wasn't giving up. They continued to pull and prod, urge and warn. Ethel was certain that the "no" came from the lips, not the heart, that he would regret forever *not* running because his deeper instincts propelled him to activity and combat.

On the weekend of January 20 and 21, Jesse Unruh and several associates decided to make one last attempt, because the deadline for filing in the California primaries was approaching. They flew in on the "redeye" for more arm-twisting. Bobby sighed, invited his own contingent, and the debate began once again at Hickory Hill.

The highlight of the weekend was a gag dreamed up by a couple of the Kennedy children. As the arguments became heated, they put a record on the stereo and played it full blast. It was the song "The Impossible Dream," sung by Don Quixote in *Man of La Mancha*. Everybody cracked up.[13]

A few days later, Steve Smith called Unruh on the West Coast: "He's not going to go."

On January 30, Kennedy met with a group of Washington journalists at the National Press Club for an off-the-record background session at which he intended to silence further speculation. Eugene McCarthy was already up in New Hampshire and, in Bobby's view, not likely to stir up much interest. Neither, he felt, would he. Would he support LBJ if he were nominated? Yes, albeit unenthusiastically.

At the end, Kennedy, with the help of Frank Mankiewicz, his press aide, permitted the newspeople to quote him as saying he would not enter the Presidential campaign "under any foreseeable circumstances."

That very day, the Viet Cong launched the Tet offensive—the unforeseen circumstance that ultimately would change everything.

Nobody expected it. In Paris, representatives of the warring countries were in the first stages of drawing up an agenda for peace discussions; and there had been a three-day cease-fire at the start of the New Year; not perfect, but it had held. Another three-day truce had been agreed upon for the Vietnamese holiday marking the lunar New Year at the end of January. But all month long, vast numbers of Viet Cong soldiers in civilian clothes had gone silently into twenty-seven South Vietnam cities, and others had infiltrated jungle villages.

The ferocity of the attack stunned Washington. Until then, the official pronouncements that America could win and would win had been believed by many, even half-believed by Robert Kennedy. Now, with all the major cities under assault and the U.S. Embassy itself besieged, the words of the President and his generals were exposed as utterly wrong. By the end of February, the Viet Cong had been routed from the cities, but allied casualties stood at 20,000, with 600,000 natives homeless.

Dazed by the cataclysmic turn of events, Bobby stayed home for the next few days, seeing nobody but his family, taking no phone calls.[14] As the assaults mounted in ferocity, the realization sank deeply in that the Johnson Administration's policy on Vietnam was a total failure and the war a national disaster. The size, intensity, and early successes of the Viet Cong attack showed up the falsity of the bright, confident predictions made almost daily by Johnson and his generals. The American people were being told a pack of lies. The war could not be won.

Al Lowenstein, Bobby knew now, had been right. Someone had to lead the country out of the mire into which it was sinking.

As the days went by, he began the process of second-guessing. To a columnist who had been present at the backgrounder where he took himself out of the race, he put the question, was Tet the "unforeseen circumstance" that canceled out his declaration? To Anthony Lewis, then chief of the London bureau of *The New York Times*, he wrote, "The country is in such difficulty, and I believe headed for more that it almost fills one with despair. . . . I wonder what I should be doing."

Almost pleading, he asked his Harvard classmate, "What should I do?"[15]

26

"I Am Announcing My Candidacy"

*I*T IS a long way from Vietnam to the small town of Howth on the Irish Sea northeast of Dublin. But a letter sent from there soon after Tet had a profound influence on Kennedy at this critical juncture.

In the late fall of 1967, Pete Hamill, the journalist and author, had left his newspaper job to write a novel. He saw no point in grinding through the coming campaign. "Bobby had decided not to run, and McCarthy seemed like a hopeless case," he asserted. "And Johnson seemed at the time certain to get the nomination." He took his family to Rome to research a fictional account of a plot to assassinate the Pope, later published as *A Killing for Christ*, then rented a small attached row house in Howth at the end of a quiet street.

When Tet exploded, Hamill and his family were desperate for news. Hamill's brother, John, was in Vietnam, sent over the previous year. He could get only sketchy information from the Armed Forces radio and the BBC. Not knowing whether his brother was dead or alive, overwhelmed by the realization that the Viet Cong had the ability to strike anywhere, any time, Hamill rolled a sheet of inexpensive typing paper into his battered old portable Hermes 3000 and wrote an emotion-charged letter to Bob Kennedy:

> I had wanted to write you a long letter explaining my reasons
> why I thought you should make a run for the Presidency this
> year. But that's too late. I read in the *Irish Times* this A.M. that

you made a hard announcement, and that small hope is gone, along with others that have vanished in the last four years. . . .

I wanted to say that the fight you might make would be the fight of honor . . . I wanted to say that you should run because if you won, the country might be saved. . . . If we have LBJ for another four years, there won't be much of a country left. . . .

I wanted to remind you that in Watts I didn't see pictures of Malcolm X or Ron Karenga on the walls. I saw pictures of JFK. That is your capital in the most cynical sense; it is your obligation in another, the obligation of staying true to whatever it was that put those pictures on those walls. I don't think we can afford five summers of blood. I do know this: if a 15-year-old kid is given a choice between Rap Brown and RFK, he *might* choose the way of sanity. It's only a possibility, but at least there is that chance. Give that same kid a choice between Rap Brown and LBJ, and he'll probably reach for his revolver.

Again, forgive the tone of this letter, Bob. But it's not about five-cent cigars and chickens in every pot. It's about the country. I don't want to sound like someone telling someone that he should mount the white horse; or that he should destroy his career. I also realize that if you had decided to run, you would face some filthy politics, and that there are plenty of people in the country who resent or dislike you.

With all of that, I still think the move would have been worth making, and I'm sorry you decided not to make it.

Not even sure of the address, Hamill mailed the letter in the local post office, hoping Kennedy would see it.[1] "It was one last shot," Hamill said. "There had to be another President to end the war. I didn't write the letter just to save my own brother, but to save everybody's brother. We had a half-million soldiers out there by that time."

Bobby got the letter, read and reread it, and carried it with him in his inside pocket wherever he went.

Early in March, diners at La Caravelle, a posh East Side Manhattan restaurant, were treated to a remarkable spectacle: Bobby, Ethel, and four close friends were debating the question excitedly, and loudly, so engrossed they were unaware that many in the room had stopped eating and heard almost every word.

Benno Schmidt said it would be wrong to run. Bobby replied, "I agree with you, Benno, I think if I run I will go a long way toward proving everything that everybody who doesn't like me has said about me."

Ethel interrupted. "Now, Bob, you've got to get that idea out of your head. You're always talking as though people don't like you. People *do* like you, and you've got to realize that."

Bobby said, "If I run people are going to think that I've been intending to run all the time, that Vietnam has been the issue that I've been building up, that I never accepted Lyndon Johnson as President, that I'm just a selfish, ambitious little s.o.b."

Schmidt pointed out that the key lay in delegates: "Have you got them?" Kennedy admitted he did not have the support of the majority of delegates, "and I have very serious questions whether I could get them between now and convention time even if I tried."

As they were finishing coffee, Bobby ended the discussion with, "I just think, at this stage, it would be a mistake for me to try." The diners went back to their food, having heard, they thought, Kennedy's final word.[2]

If he would not run, he could make his voice heard, and he did with increasing passion.

At Marymount College, he polled the women students on whether they favored an increase or decrease in the continuing saturation bombing. When the majority indicated they wanted the attacks stepped up, he reddened and shouted at them, "You are voting to send people, American and Vietnamese, to die! Don't you understand that what we are doing to the Vietnamese is not very different [from] what Hitler did to the Jews?"

The high percentage of black soldiers in Vietnam appalled him. Later that year, he told college students in Omaha to look about them. "How many black faces do you see here?" he demanded. "The fact is, if you look at any regiment or division of paratroopers in Vietnam, 45 percent of them are black. How can you accept this?"

On February 8, he broke cleanly for the first time with his brother's, and his own, policies. Casting aside caution, he was clear, sharp, and unequivocal in an address at a book and author luncheon in Chicago, sponsored by the *Sun-Times*. His third book, *To Seek a New World*, had just been published (the second had been *Just Friends and Brave Enemies*, a memoir of his journeys abroad).*

It was time, he said, to take a new look at the war. Tet had "shattered the mask of official illusion that was concealing the austere and painful reality." The illusion that the war could be won had been blown away by the Viet Cong, which demonstrated that "no part or person of South Vietnam is secure from their attacks." America, he asserted, had to learn that a

---

* The book was dedicated to his parents and to Ethel, after whose name he had written "Ruth I: 16–17." The passage reads, in part, "Entreat me not to leave thee, or to return from following after thee: for whither thou goest, I will go; and where thou lodgest, I will lodge; thy people shall be my people, and thy God, my God."

military victory was no longer possible, or even in the interests of ourselves or the Vietnamese, whose "tiny land has been devastated by a weight of bombs and shells greater than Nazi Germany knew." A peaceful settlement must now be sought.

Next day, more than a thousand telegrams supporting his position arrived at his office. One of the first to be opened read, "What took you so long?" In the next few days, thousands of congratulatory letters flooded in.

Bobby read them all, and they fired him up even more. On February 24, he journeyed to Philadelphia, to address a dinner of the Americans for Democratic Action, and told his audience:

> However the war may seem to us, youth see it as one in which the largest and most powerful nation on earth is killing children (they do not care if accidentally) in a remote and insignificant land. . . . They see us spend billions on armaments while poverty and ignorance continue at home; they see us willing to fight a war for freedom in Vietnam, but unwilling to fight with one-hundredth the money or force to secure freedom in Mississippi or Alabama or the ghettos of the North.

Eleven days later, on March 7, he made an even bolder and more emotional speech, this time on the floor of the Senate. His 6,000-word, forty-five-minute address was a battering-ram assault on Lyndon Johnson's war policies, the sharpest attack on a President heard in the upper house in many years.

His voice rising, one hand sawing the air, he cried out,

> Are we like the God of the Old Testament that we can decide in Washington, D.C., what cities, what towns, what hamlets in Vietnam are to be destroyed? Is it because we think it may possibly protect the people of Thailand, the people of Malaysia, the people of Hawaii, or keep certain people out of Texas or California or Massachusetts or New York? Or do we have that authority to kill tens and tens of thousands of people because we say we have a commitment to the South Vietnamese people? But have they been consulted, in Hue, in Ben Tre, or in the other towns that have been destroyed? Do we have the authority to put hundreds of thousands of people—in fact, millions of people—into refugee camps for their protection, or should these decisions be left to them?

During the cold February weeks, Bobby had been increasingly worried about his friend Cesar Chavez. Chavez had gone on a hunger strike, taking only water to drive home his message of nonviolence to members of his union who had become truculent. Weeks passed, and a nurse had been summoned to attend to him.

By March 1, his health had deteriorated alarmingly. Letters and wires came in from all over the United States, urging him to end his fast. Bobby had sent a message pointing out that, if he died or his health were impaired permanently, his movement would be dealt a devastating blow.

Word came the first week in March that Chavez, feeling his point had been made and that violence would no longer be part of union tactics, would conclude his hunger strike at an ecumenical mass of thanksgiving in a county park not far from union headquarters in Delano, north of Los Angeles.

Accompanied by John Seigenthaler, Peter Edelman, and Ed Guthman, Bobby flew to Delano on Sunday, March 10, to greet his friend and join in the mass. First, he went directly to the small room at the rear of a gasoline station on union property where Chavez was lying.

Refusing a chair, Bobby spoke gently to the pale and shrunken figure. Little was said—the customary "How are you's" and "I feel all right"— but Chavez remembered that a great deal more was communicated. He could not explain it, then or almost twenty years later, but a bond of understanding existed between the Mexican-American and the rich man's son that defied definition. "Bobby understood, and I knew he understood," Chavez says now, "and that's all I know."

The brief scene was an emotional one for both men, its tone quickly shattered when Bobby asked to use the bathroom. The union staff scurried to find the key to unlock it, but it was lost. Jim Drake, Chavez's assistant, took Bobby by the arm and led him to his home nearby. There is now a large sign in Jim Drake's home: "Robert Kennedy went to the bathroom here."

Afterward, Kennedy drove to the park, where thousands of union members were waiting in the hot sun for the mass. Chavez, weak and ill, suffering from a bad headache, sat near him as the mass began. The crowds, eager for a view of Bobby, pressed uncomfortably close. Turning to Bobby, Cesar said, "We're pretty lousy in controlling crowds." Kennedy replied, "The important thing is they're here."

After the mass, pandemonium erupted when Bobby tried to leave. Hands, reaching to touch him, scratched his, bloodying them, and tearing the sleeves of his coat. They shouted at him, "We want Kennedy!" "You've got to run!" Homemade placards, "Kennedy for President," were waved in his face.

It took Bobby fifteen minutes to push through to his car. But no sooner was he inside than he emerged, mounted on top, and began to address them—in Spanish.

Rarely were the unionists treated to a more comic moment. Said a union aide, "He was speaking Spanish with that Boston accent, and I swear I didn't understand what he was trying to say. I thought he was speaking French or some other foreign language. And all of a sudden, they started clapping. Somebody must have caught what he was trying to say—but it wasn't anything close."

At one point, Bobby stopped and turned to Chavez. "I'm murdering the language, Cesar, is that right?"

Chavez, beaming at him, said simply, "Yes."

Analyzing Bobby's appeal, Chavez makes an interesting, and revealing, comparison of the effect the Kennedy brothers had on Mexican-Americans. "They looked on John Kennedy, much as poor people during the Depression looked on Franklin Roosevelt, as the man who gives them hope. For John, there was respect and admiration. Besides, he was young, and, like them, he was Catholic.

"But with Bobby it was different. There was a kind of mystical aura about him, something that was electrifying and almost religious in intensity. We felt at once, just looking at him and listening to him, that he was ours."

Chavez had known many political figures, but none who "crossed that line" of touching the hearts of people like Bobby Kennedy. "God," he said, "I can't explain it. It was a phenomenon that cannot be explained." He reached them, and they responded with love and idolatry. It will be a long time, if ever, Chavez said, before he sees another public figure like him.

Chavez recalled that Kennedy did not respond directly to the crowd's demand that he run. However, as he was driving back toward the airport, union aide Jim Drake seated beside him, he said, half to himself, "Yeah, I think I'll run. Maybe I'll run."

"When Jim reported that to us," Chavez said, "in our minds we knew he was going to run. . . . We knew he had to run."[3]

Peter Edelman, his legislative assistant, knew even earlier. He had flown with Bobby from Washington to Los Angeles, then changed planes for the short hop to Delano. Said Edelman: "It was on that same flight from Los Angeles to Delano that I first knew for sure that he was going to run because he said explicitly; 'I am going to run. Now I have to figure out how to get McCarthy out of it.' "

Edelman asked him: "What if you can't get McCarthy out?"

"I'm going to do it anyway," Bobby answered.

Dates now become crucial.

It is popularly believed that Bobby Kennedy made up his mind to run after Eugene McCarthy's astonishing performance in the New Hampshire primaries had shown him that LBJ was vulnerable. McCarthy confounded almost everyone by winning 42.2 percent of the Democratic vote, only 7.2 percent less than the President and, in the process, picking up twenty of the party's twenty-four delegates to the forthcoming convention because of the peculiar way the delegate selection system was structured.

Primary Day in New Hampshire was Tuesday, March 12. Kennedy

learned the results late that evening. But on Saturday, March 9, Jim Drake of the grape growers' union and Edelman had each heard him make a virtual commitment to run.

While he had apparently decided, for some inexplicable reason hidden deeply in the labyrinths of his mind, he was not yet ready to make a flat-out statement. Had he done so, McCarthy supporters could not have made the harsh—and, to many, accurate—charge that his entry "was like a jackal coming to feast on the carcass after someone else had made the kill."[4]

Instead of speaking out, he made matters worse by dreadful timing. To reporters who cornered him in the corridor of the new Senate Office Building the morning after McCarthy's showing, he said, "I am reassessing the possibility of whether I will run against President Johnson." The announcement topped the television news that evening and received black headlines around the country, stealing the glory from McCarthy and arousing resentment that still festers.

Later that day, he explained why he was "reassessing," citing his concern about the war, his fear that Nixon would not offer a suitable alternative to Johnson, and his own inability to live with himself if he didn't go in.

By Thursday morning, his office suite was besieged by media people and deluged with telegrams and letters. "We want Camelot again," said a wire from Evanston, Illinois. Another, taking note of the fact that Johnson's pet dog was named Him, pleaded for a dual ouster: "Let's get *him* out of the White House."

In the evening, all the Kennedys—Bobby in a dark business suit, Ethel in a white minidress of tiered lace, all their children and pets—greeted dinner guests, thirty editors and publishers of weekly New York State newspapers and a few close friends. At the reception in the living room, where two white-coated waiters served drinks and canapes from silver trays, and at dinner over oyster soup and roast beef, the conversation never veered from the question everyone was asking: Would he get into the race?

Bobby wandered around the three tables, chatting pleasantly with his guests.[5] Along with Johannes Laursen, editor and publisher of the Merrick (Long Island) *Life*, they all knew that "candidacy was in the air," but none suspected that, when Bobby excused himself intermittently to duck into a side room, he was conferring with aides on the wording of his announcement and being briefed on how to answer reporters' questions when he made it.

Never once did he hint he had already decided, although he made a few sly jokes about succeeding to the White House. When he rose to speak for a few minutes, he pointed to the dark blue Presidential standard behind him.

"Do you think it appropriate that I am standing near my brother's flag?" he asked.*[6]

To Jeff Greenfield, then a young speechwriter on his staff, the evening was "weird and unreal." He had prepared one version of the formal announcement, Sorensen another, but Bob hadn't liked either. He and Adam Walinsky found a nearby room in which to prepare a new draft. Some women friends of the Kennedys—"who always seemed to hang around Hickory Hill"—were reading over their shoulders as they typed, offering suggestions. "They were not appreciated," Jeff said dryly.

"Art Buchwald would come drifting by and go drifting back," Jeff said. "And these ladies would come in giggling about Bobby's statement, asking to help. It was almost like a scavenger hunt."[7]

In the midst of this, Bobby was getting a lesson in international finance from William vanden Heuvel, who had been a special assistant to him at Justice. The dollar was under siege, and complex facts about the balance of payments, dollar devaluation, and the price of gold had to be digested. "What if I get a question on this godawful international currency problem?" Bobby had asked, and vanden Heuvel tried to brief him.

The guests left about midnight, still unaware that they had been in the midst of an historic event.

Kennedy delayed his announcement a full day to build up suspense. He spent all of Friday in New York, in a carefully crafted round of appearances designed to get the maximum publicity for the announcement, which he would make on Saturday—in time for the Sunday newspapers, whose circulations were half again as high as they were on weekdays.

At the Garden City Hotel on Long Island, he was "fall guy" at the Sky Island Club annual luncheon, attended by 900 businessmen and local political figures. Comedian Joey Adams ribbed him about his shaggy hair style and doubled him up with a one-liner: "The new Archbishop of New York didn't come because he didn't want to kiss Bobby's ring again." But he blushed and looked down when three scantily clad girls gyrated erotically in front of him.

By the time he got up to speak, he had recovered his aplomb. "Would you mind," he said, "if I took the girls home with me—for my sons. They're growing up, you know."

Hint after hint was dropped that day, one big one before microphones he didn't know were turned on. Reporter Daniel Meehan of radio station WMCA

---

* The Kennedy kids were not as polite to the guests as their parents were. During the dinner, Walter W. Grunfeld, president of the association and publisher of the *Independent* of Marathon, New York, left the room. On his return, two small Kennedy daughters and a son, each in nightclothes, blocked his way. The boy silently drew a gun from a holster around his waist and squirted a jet of water into the publisher's face. Sighing, he mopped off and went back to the dinner.

picked up the following conversation with Leonard W. Hall, former chairman of the Republic National Committee, which was later broadcast.

Kennedy: "Do you think I'm crazy?"
Hall: "What will McCarthy do?"
Kennedy: "He is going to stay in. So it's going to make it tough. . . . It will make it much tougher."
Hall: "Are you going the primary route?"
Kennedy: "Yeah."[8]

That afternoon of the great tease he asked clubwomen for help "in this great effort" but stopped short of spelling it out. In Westbury Manor, he came close: "These are very important days in Washington," he said. "We're very busy down there, and I'll have an announcement to make about that tomorrow morning." When someone in the crowd called out, "Do it now!" he ducked his head and, with a wave, left the podium.

Next morning he was up before sunup at Hickory Hill, pacing the floor downstairs in his pajamas, as he ran through his mind the answers to questions expected after his announcement. About eight o'clock, David Burke came over and found him in his bedroom, having his hair cut. Bobby, he noted, was intensely nervous. "Ethel was dressing him," Burke recalled, "picking out his tie."[9]

Shortly before nine, he was dressed in a dark-blue suit, a narrow red and blue figured tie, and a gold PT-109 clasp. With Ted Kennedy, vanden Heuvel, Sorensen, Burke, and other staff aides, he drove down Chain Bridge Road and into Washington. Fifteen minutes later, Ethel, in a blue coat, squeezed nine of her ten children, the boys shaggy-haired but in neat dark suits, the girls in starched dresses, into her station wagon and went off. Only eleven-month-old Douglas Harriman was left behind with his nurse.

At ten sharp, Bobby entered the Senate Caucus Room, where he had sat as counsel during the Army-McCarthy hearings, where he had clashed with Dave Beck and Jimmy Hoffa, and where, eight years earlier, his brother Jack had told the nation he was running for Chief Executive.

More than 450 persons crammed into the oblong chamber, built in 1909 to hold only 300. Opening a black notebook, Bobby began reading in a strong voice: "I am announcing my candidacy for the Presidency of the United States." By accident or design, the words were the same as those spoken by his brother from the same podium.

Pete Hamill's letter from Ireland had played a significant role in helping Bobby make up his mind. On March 16, he sent Pete a telegram: "I need your help. I'm announcing tomorrow." It reached Hamill the day after he completed his novel. Two days later, he was back in the States.

Ethel told Pete, "You did it! Your letter did it. He was carrying it around to show to everybody." Bobby, too, acknowledged the part it played. During the hectic primary campaigns that followed, he told Hamill ruefully, "Look what you got me into."[10]

Some Democratic officials were infuriated. In Georgia, Lester Maddox, the segregationist governor, fumed that he'd leave the party if Bobby were nominated. "I'd think we'd be just as well off if we had Castro on the national Democratic ticket," he raged. Chicago's Mayor Richard Daley, the Illinois delegation in his pocket, telephoned Kennedy but said later he was still a Johnson man. At the same time, he was finessing. "The place to resolve our difficulties is at the August convention," he said, signaling his readiness to switch if that's the way the political winds blew.

McCarthy, watching from the Northlands Hotel in Green Bay, Wisconsin, where he was campaigning for the April 2 primaries, showed no emotion as Bobby said, "My candidacy would not be in opposition to his [McCarthy's] but in harmony." He wasn't angry then, nor is he now, but he wondered how Bobby intended to perform that kind of magic. "We knew he would split the antiwar movement," he says, "and he did."[11]

Later, on television, McCarthy was cool to any offers of accommodation that might be forthcoming from the Kennedy camp. "I am not prepared to deal with anybody so far as my candidacy is concerned," he said, adding caustically, "It was a little lonely out there in New Hampshire."

Looking back across the years, Eugene McCarthy reflects:

"They said Bobby could have won the nomination and McCarthy couldn't, but all the polls showed me running ahead of him, against Nixon and Rockefeller. And in Wisconsin alone, the polls showed me beating Johnson two to one.

"Now if I had been running badly and he had to step in—well, that would have been a pragmatic argument. He could then say, with justification, 'I came in because the antiwar movement needed me.' But it didn't.

"If he hadn't come in, we would have beaten Johnson. We could almost have taken the primary victories for granted, and gone on to work on the States that did not have primaries. But as it was, we had to divert time, effort and money to battle in Oregon, Indiana, California, and we had none left for the other states.

"Bobby came in because he saw a chance for the Presidency and didn't want to lose it. His big tragedy was that he had to destroy his brother and his brother's position in order to establish his own."[12]

Al and Jennie Lowenstein, still up in New Hampshire, where they had campaigned for McCarthy, were packing in their hotel room to return to New York when they heard a radio broadcast that Bobby was running. Even though he was working for McCarthy, Al was thrilled by the news, Jennie said. In the city, he got a message that Bobby had telephoned.

When he returned the call, Kennedy said, "Al baby, I've decided to take your advice." Lowenstein, a broad smile on his face, said, "You bastard, why did you take so long?"

Al was now in a quandary. "I can't leave McCarthy," he told Jennie, "but I can't spend the rest of the primary campaign trying to defeat Robert Kennedy either." The arrival of a telegram several days later from Democratic leaders of the Fifth Congressional District on Long Island solved his dilemma. He was asked to run as their candidate for the House. He accepted and ducked out of the McCarthy camp.

Shortly afterward, there was an emotional encounter between Al and Bobby. As they were returning from Binghamton in upstate New York after a Democratic function, fog closed the airport and they boarded a bus for New York. Feeling wretched, Al said to Bobby, "After hammering away at you for months, I can't support you. I won't work for McCarthy, but at the same time I got him to run, and . . ."

Kennedy understood. "I know that. I can't expect you." On their arrival, Bobby handed him a note he had written on a sheet of yellow, legal-size paper. It read:

> For Al, who knew the lesson of Emerson and taught it to the
> rest of us: "They did not yet see, and thousands of young men as
> hopeful, now crowding to the barriers of their careers, did not yet
> see if a single man plant himself on his convictions and then
> abide, the huge world will come round to him."
>
> From his friend, Bob Kennedy.

Al came home before dawn and woke Jennie. Showing her the letter, he said, "I can't believe this man. I tell him I can't support him, and he writes me this." He read the words over and over until he could no longer see them because of his tears.*[13]

Before he left Hickory Hill the day of his declaration, Bobby and Ethel had a private conversation, during which they marshaled the arguments for and against entering one last time. Dallas was never far from his mind, and he mentioned it now.

"There's no knowing where this could end," Bobby told his wife.

Ethel did not flinch. Looking directly at him, she replied, "You should go ahead—no matter where it ends."[14]

---

* Lowenstein was assassinated in 1980 by Dennis Sweeney, a deranged political associate.

27

March 16 to June 4

*I*T WAS A MIRACLE that Bobby did so well, winning four out of five primaries in the eighty days that followed, considering that the much-vaunted Kennedy political machine came apart like an old jalopy, or perhaps was never even assembled.*

The organization for the greatest bid of his life was a shambles from the start and only slightly improved when it ended. As Frank Mankiewicz, RFK's press assistant from 1966 to 1968, put it, "The 'smooth-running, well oiled Kennedy machine' got to be an office joke very quickly."[1]

From the Caucus Room, where he made his announcement, Bobby raced to the airport for a commercial flight to New York to march in the St. Patrick's Day Parade. It wasn't on his schedule because there was no schedule, nor was there yet a chartered plane to take him places. He just went because he thought it was politically wise to appear there.

Seat-of-the-pants decisions like that were made frequently. Most of the time they turned out well, his receptions ranging from enthusiastic to ecstatic, although his first appearance as a candidate was not an unqualified success. That afternoon the greeting was mixed: he was cheered but also heard more boos and catcalls than ever before, including some threats to beat the hell out of him. Said one furious college student who was marching, "If he didn't have twenty cops around him, I'd punch him in the mouth."

---

* Kennedy won by substantial margins in Indiana and Nebraska on May 7 and 14, but lost in Oregon on May 28. On June 4, he won 46 percent of the votes cast in California to McCarthy's 42 percent. He also won the South Dakota primary, held the same day, 49.7 percent to McCarthy's 20.4 percent.

His appearance the next day on NBC's "Meet the Press" was scarcely more successful, because there hadn't been time to brief him adequately. When he insisted repeatedly that he was planning to "cooperate in every way possible with Senator McCarthy," he was shredded by four leading Washington journalists who wondered how he intended to do that, considering that he was going to battle the Minnesota candidate in every important primary.

Loyal Kennedy men, veterans of the 1960 campaign, dropped what they were doing, lucrative though it may have been, and formed a staff. Kenny O'Donnell, low-paid all his adult life, had finally begun to make real money as vice president of a Boston educational company. He took a leave to enlist. Salinger, also earning a good income in private enterprise, flew in from the West Coast to share press duties with Frank Mankiewicz. Sorensen, Fred Dutton, and vanden Heuvel temporarily left prosperous law practices; Donald Wilson, an executive of Time Inc., took a leave of absence. Larry O'Brien resigned as Postmaster General. Dave Hackett was everywhere. The first day he acquired an Airline Guide and went off to talk to delegates. He would be especially useful in directing the "boiler room," about which we will hear presently.

Family members, of course, were at the top of the staff pyramid: Ted Kennedy, more experienced than the days when he was "Rocky Mountain Coordinator" for John; brother-in-law Steve Smith, who looked like a grown-up Freddie Bartholomew but was tough, sharp, and a financial genius; and finally Ethel, who campaigned with Bobby much of the time and buoyed everyone's spirits at low points.

There were younger men too: liberals like Milton Gwirtzman, Adam Walinsky, Peter Edelman, and Jeff Greenfield were recruited for speech writing. Jeff had a problem that, he felt, might make Bobby reconsider using him in the campaign. He said that he was draft-prone but was so strongly opposed to the war that he would not comply with the order. Instead of dropping him, Kennedy told him soothingly that a prison term might not be the worst thing he could experience. "Don't worry about it," Bobby said. "A lot of the greatest men in history have begun their careers by spending time in jails."[2]

In Ted Kennedy's Senate office those first days, aides began drawing up plans from scratch, suddenly aware they needed a blueprint. Nothing had been done, because nobody had even thought beyond the should-he, shouldn't-he-run stage. It was, of course, too late. Begun in chaos, the drive never attained smooth forward momentum. It seemed to lurch from one stop to another and was marked by staff conflict over where the candidate should go, what he should stress, and especially who was responsible for what.

301

Friction quickly developed among the bright people who occupied three levels of a new building at Twentieth and L Streets in Washington. They held strong views on almost everything, and as a result were disgruntled and bickering much of the time. Dutton recalled, "We had so many sensitive egos," and "so many feuds."[3]

Bobby was not much help. When he managed Jack's campaigns, organization was his sole concern. Now he had no time for anything but the issues, and in his staff of dazzling intellects and intense, cause-motivated people, he didn't have a Bobby Kennedy. He made matters worse by going from one key aide to another asking, "What would you like to do?" And he muddled matters even more by asking them, "What do you think Sorensen— or vanden Heuvel or O'Donnell—should be doing?" Getting different replies, he threw up his hands.*[4]

The most efficient part of the campaign was a holdover from 1960, the information-gathering system the Kennedys invented and used with enormous success in 1960. This was the "boiler room" operation, headquartered in Washington, where a half-dozen young women spent fourteen hours a day, weekends included, on the telephone to make sure everything ran smoothly.

Each one was assigned a number of states and touched all bases. If a small city in Nebraska had run out of campaign buttons or stickers, she knew about it that day. If money problems were developing in Omaha, Indianapolis, or Sacramento, she discovered them early. She learned what functions were being scheduled, where, and if they needed speakers. She obtained the dates of local conventions, down to the precinct level.

Most importantly, each young woman kept a running count of the convention delegates from her states—who they were, where they went each day, and which ones needed convincing to swing them into the Kennedy camp. Mock counts were taken continually, so that campaign leaders knew exactly how the candidate was doing at any given time.

At the end of each day, all of them summarized their material and placed it into a "night reading" file for the Kennedy top aides, who, in turn, would order action.

The boiler room was not without its problems. Because it had to be set up literally overnight, the first days were "a complete madhouse," recalled Esther Newberg, one of the key young women. With Dave Hackett, she and the others dug through old files of names, found many no longer viable, and kept "calling, calling, calling all over" before it took shape.

---

* Fred Dutton disputes the widely accepted opinion that Bobby was ever a great campaign strategist. "It was a base canard from the beginning," he says. Bobby was very good at setting up special operations and "ramming things through, but the idea that he could lay out a blueprint for a campaign . . . never happened. That was not his cup of tea."[5]

Also a problem was the youth of the women at the phones. "They were very young girls, most of them anyway," Ms. Newberg said. She herself was only in her middle twenties. Experienced old pols who came to Washington would take one look at them and would make known their preference for dealing with top campaign aides. It took a while for the boiler room crew to convince the politicians that money, material, and other essentials could be gotten faster if they went through them.[6]

Bobby knew his campaign badly needed an overhaul, but he had to blunder along for the first few months. Things would be different in a short while, he told his staff, when they would all have a breather. He planned a total reorganization, with his brother-in-law, Steve Smith, in full charge, to streamline the operation.

But that would have to wait until after the California primary.

At 8:45 on March 31, a Sunday evening, John Burns and John English entered the American Airlines terminal at Kennedy Airport to meet Bobby, who was flying in from Denver after two weeks of hectic campaigning. His plane was due at ten, but the Democratic leaders, Burns of New York State and English of Nassau County, wanted to hear Lyndon Johnson's televised address on Vietnam. They settled down before the TV set in the VIP lounge.

LBJ's major speech had been announced several days earlier, and speculation about what he would say was intense. With two of his own party's most voter-appealing members challenging him, and the doves' wings beating stronger than ever around the country, would the President give General Earle G. Wheeler, chairman of the Joint Chiefs, the 206,000 more troops he wanted? Or would he scale down the escalation to appease the critics?

Few in Washington, where important secrets are hard to keep, knew precisely what was in his mind. That morning, Johnson had gone to the apartment of his Vice President, Hubert Humphrey, and told him. The two, who had never been friendly, had thrown their arms around each other in an unusual display of emotion. Humphrey walked away from that meeting, dazed by what the President told him and dazzled by the promise of what lay ahead. Not even Elizabeth Carpenter, the First Lady's press secretary, who had typed the manuscript of the speech, knew what he would say. The final paragraph had not been in the text she received.

In the airport lounge, Burns and English watched an unusually poised and self-confident Johnson appear on the screen. The President seemed less tired than usual, and his voice, generally more wheedling than authoritative, was strong and assertive. In this thirty-five-minute speech, he turned down Wheeler's request for more troops and announced a partial bombing halt of the North as an inducement to begin peace talks. That was startling enough. The final paragraph was staggering.

For thirty-seven years, he said, he had served the nation, but "there is division in the American house now," and he did not want the Presidency to become involved in the "partisan divisions that are developing in this political year."

A pause. "Accordingly," he concluded, "I shall not seek, and I will not accept, the nomination of my party for another term as President."

Burns recalled:

> When he came out with the bombshell, I knew Kennedy hadn't heard the word because he was up in the air; he was about to land.
>
> About ten minutes later he landed. There was a huge corps of press there and I wanted him to get the word before the press gave it to him, you know, so he'd be ready for it—that was the main thing—so that he didn't come off the plane not knowing about it and be hit with it right off the bat. So we rushed on the plane and I told him about it. He says, "Sit down, John." I was so excited, you know. So, he said, "Now tell me again what the President said." I related to him that the President said that he was not going to be a candidate for reelection as President. He was going to give all his time devoted towards peace and bringing about peace in Vietnam, and so forth. He didn't have time to campaign, and all that jazz.

Kennedy, smoking a cigar, sat quietly, absorbing the news. He said nothing during the drive to his apartment, where he began listening to a replay of Johnson's talk.

"He was transfixed," said John Burns, "but he wasn't celebrating. He thought that what Johnson had done was good, but at the same time, he seemed to have sadness in his heart for the man."[7]

The vindictiveness of the earlier years had gone, but the competitiveness remained. Later, he would say, "I'm going to chase Hubert Humphrey's ass all over the country."

In Waukesha, Wisconsin, west of Milwaukee, McCarthy was addressing a student group when a cry rose from the audience: "He's not running! He's not running!" As newsmen swarmed toward him and the students broke into cheers, McCarthy was the calmest person in the auditorium. "Come on, kids," he said, "relax." He himself did, counseling the television journalists waiting for interviews to tell their stations to play a little music until he arrived. "Or maybe they should read a little poetry," he said. "This is a night for reading poetry—maybe a little Yeats."

The final milestone in Robert Kennedy's ideological journey was passed on April 4 in Indianapolis.

He arrived on that gray Thursday morning to begin a month of hard campaigning for the May 7 primary. Two hours after checking into the Marriott Hotel, he had showered, changed, and was flying to the University of Notre Dame in the northern part of the state. In the afternoon, he was at Ball State University in Muncie.

He was greeted enthusiastically at both schools. "So far so good," he said, as he sped back to the airport for the short flight back to Indianapolis, where an outdoor rally had been scheduled for early evening in the worst part of town, a black ghetto.

A few minutes before six, he boarded his chartered plane, settled back in his seat, and closed his eyes.

At the same hour, about 500 miles to the southwest, Martin Luther King, Jr., stepped out on the second-floor balcony of the Lorraine Motel in Memphis, Tennessee, to speak to civil rights workers. Sensitive to jibes in the newspapers that he was occupying a $29-a-day room at the Holiday Inn, he had moved into the black-owned Lorraine, where the rate was only $13. In a rooming house across the street, James Earl Ray, crouching at a window, peered through a telescopic sight and squeezed off a bullet on his 30.06 Remington pump rifle, severing King's spinal column at the neck.

Within minutes the wire services were sending out flashes. Up in Muncie, reporters traveling with Kennedy heard the news from their editors before boarding the plane. One raced down the aisle and told Bobby, who stared at him. Then he turned his face to the window, saying softly: "Oh, my God!"

When the plane landed at Indianapolis, another newsman told him King was dead. Bobby covered his face with his hands and moaned: "Oh, God, when is this violence going to stop?"

At the airport, the chief of police, having heard reports of swiftly rising tensions in the black community, was not taking chances. "Cancel your speech," he told Bobby. "Nobody knows what's going to happen tonight."

"There's no way I won't give that speech," Kennedy answered. "I've got to make that speech. It's the most important thing I can do."

Ethel, who met him at the airport, also said it might be best to sit it out at the hotel. "I can't," Bobby told her, but he insisted that she go back and watch on television.[8]

With Fred Dutton, he drove to the scene of the rally, preceded by a police car and followed by the press bus. Many newspersons openly expressed fears for Kennedy's safety.

During the twenty-five-minute ride, Bobby sat silently, making no notes. Once he asked Dutton what he thought should be said. "I made a couple of inadequate responses," Dutton recalled, and Bobby lapsed into silence again.

Arriving at Broadway Christian Center, he buttoned his topcoat against the 37-degree cold and walked quickly to a flatbed truck pulled up at the side of a large paved parking lot next to the outdoor basketball court where he was to speak. There had been no attempt to keep the people from where he would talk: already the truck was loaded with spectators.[9]

The crowd of almost 1,000, most of them black, cheered and whistled when they spotted him, waving "RFK for President" banners and home-made placards with Kennedy slogans. They shouted greetings to him; some were singing. They had not yet heard.

Telling the officials who had organized the event that he wanted no introduction, Bob mounted the truck and raised both hands for silence. Slowly they quieted.

"I have bad news for you," he began, "for all our fellow citizens, and people who love justice all over the world . . ." Now there was complete stillness.

". . . and that is that Martin Luther King was shot and killed tonight."

A long gasp like the hissing of locomotives in a railroad yard came from the crowd. Shouts of "No! No, No!" pierced the dark. A woman to his left moaned loudly, and others near her echoed the long, low cry. Bobby, his eyes wet, his voice at the breaking point throughout, talked for seven minutes, without notes, delivering on that chilly April evening one of the two most moving speeches of his career, during which he made a rare public reference to his brother's assassination.

In this two-minute address, quoted here in full, he showed that his transformation was now complete.

> Martin Luther King dedicated his life to love and to justice for his fellow human beings, and he died because of that effort.
>
> In this difficult day, in this difficult time for the United States, it is perhaps well to ask what kind of nation we are and what direction we want to move in. For those of you who are black—considering the evidence there evidently is that there were white people who were responsible—you can be filled with bitterness, with hatred, and a desire for revenge. We can move in that direction as a country, in great polarization—black people amongst black, white people amongst white, filled with hatred toward one another.
>
> Or we can make an effort, as Martin Luther King did, to understand and to comprehend, and to replace that violence, that stain of bloodshed that has spread across our land, with an effort to understand with compassion and love.
>
> For those of you who are black and are tempted to be filled with hatred and distrust at the injustice of such an act, against all white people, I can only say that I feel in my own heart the same kind of feeling. I had a member of my family killed, but he was killed by a white man. But we have to make an effort in the United States, we have to make an effort to understand, to go beyond these rather difficult times.

My favorite poet was Aeschylus. He wrote: "In our sleep, pain which cannot forget falls drop by drop upon the heart until, in our own despair, against our will, comes wisdom through the awful grace of God."

What we need in the United States is not division; what we need in the United States is not hatred; what we need in the United States is not violence or lawlessness, but love and wisdom, and compassion toward one another, and a feeling of justice toward those who still suffer within our country, whether they be white or they be black.

So I shall ask you tonight to return home, to say a prayer for the family of Martin Luther King, that's true, but more importantly to say a prayer for our own country, which all of us love—a prayer for understanding and that compassion of which I spoke.

We can do well in this country. We will have difficult times. We've had difficult times in the past. We will have difficult times in the future. It is not the end of violence; it is not the end of lawlessness; it is not the end of disorder.

But the vast majority of white people and the vast majority of black people in this country want to live together, want to improve the quality of our life, and want justice for all human beings who abide in our land.

Let us dedicate ourselves to what the Greeks wrote so many years ago: to tame the savageness of man and to make gentle the life of this world.

Let us dedicate ourselves to that, and say a prayer for our country, and for our people.

The audience, most in tears, dispersed quietly.

Shortly after 11 P.M., he came back to the hotel, talked with Ethel for a few minutes, then telephoned Coretta King. She asked him to help her bring the body of her husband to Atlanta for burial; he said he would. Later his Senate office arranged for a chartered plane to return the body. At 1 A.M., in shirt-sleeves, bleary-eyed, and disheveled, he came into the room where Jeff Greenfield and Adam Walinsky were working on a speech he would deliver in Cleveland in a few days. He sat in a straight-backed chair and said nothing, staring at a curtained window.

"You know," Bobby said finally, "that fellow Harvey Lee Oswald, whatever his name is, set something loose in this country."

Jeff noted: "That was the only time I ever heard him mention his name. . . . When the news of John Kennedy's death first came out, the news reports had the name backward. And that's the way he remembered it, because he never took another look at it again."

Bobby left, but returned at 2:30 to find that Jeff, groggy with fatigue, had stretched out on the bed.

"He tucked me in," Jeff recalled. "I told him, 'You aren't so ruthless after all.' "

"Don't tell anybody," Bobby replied.[10]

307

The murder of King unloosed a wave of violence unprecedented in U.S. history. For weeks, many blacks vented their fury, despair, and sense of personal loss by rioting in 167 cities, burning stores and homes, looting, and assaulting. Entire urban districts resembled war-torn areas. Indeed, a British journalist said that parts of Washington "looked like London after the blitz."[11] In all, forty-five persons were killed, nine in the capital alone, and all except five were blacks. Before 55,000 armed troops finally restored order, 23,000 persons were arrested, 21,000 injured, and property damage was reckoned in the scores of millions.

In New York, Baltimore, Chicago, Philadelphia, and everywhere else the blacks were tearing up their neighborhoods in fury and despair. But Indianapolis, where Bobby spoke that night, was the only place where there was no major riot.

At forty-two, he had a strange young-old look. When he walked, his head down, hiding his bright-blue eyes, his hair falling over his wide forehead, his hand extended for a shy handshake, he seemed like a boy. His face, though, had become longer, bonier, harder. The teeth protruded more, the outwardly hooked nose was more prominent, the mouth with its jutting lower lip was formless. His face was now deeply lined, and his hair was streaked with gray.

His energy seemed inexhaustible. From 7 A.M., often earlier, until past midnight he traveled the country, by plane, in a motorcade, or special train, making a dozen or more speeches a day, submitting to endless interviews, walking the streets, going into workplaces, and—perhaps the most grueling test of all for any politician—standing on receiving lines to shake hands with thousands of people.

As the weeks passed, his eyes became increasingly sunken and his face grayer and gaunt. Sometimes his hands shook so that he could barely hold a pen.

In 1960, as the pragmatic politician, electing Jack was all he cared about. Now, churned inwardly by emotionalism, he ignored much of the hardheaded, practical advice he had given his brother and drilled into the campaign staff.

He had scoffed at Adlai Stevenson for wasting precious vote-getting hours by stopping to discuss world affairs at length with just a handful of workers at a rural railroad siding. Yet on his own campaign he insisted on spending considerable time with Indians. Dutton pleaded with him to cut it out, on the sensible grounds that, while Indians are citizens and thus entitled to vote, not many do. Returning from a visit to an Arizona reservation two weeks into the race, Dutton told Bob that, after he was elected, he could help the Indians but just then he needed all the ballot-box support he could get.

"So knock off the Injuns," Dutton said. Bobby, saving his voice for speech-making, wrote him a note. "Those of you who think you're running my campaign don't love Indians as much as I do. You're a bunch of bastards."[12]

He was so passionate in arguing about the plight of the American Indian that he committed mayhem on statistics. Once he quoted a horrendous number of suicides among young people frustrated by their impoverished lives on reservations. Later, on the campaign plane, the newsman Jimmy Breslin kidded him.

"Senator," he said, "you killed more Indians today than Warner Brothers. According to you, Jim Thorpe would never have become a sports legend if the rope hadn't broken."

"When it came to Indians," recalled Steve Bell, the radio and television newscaster, "there was no politicking, only genuine feeling." At Cleveland High School in Portland, Oregon, he told a white, middle-class audience about a recent visit to a reservation. On the day he arrived, a baby had died of starvation there. "When that baby died," Bobby said, "a little of me died, too."[13]

Jeff Greenfield, too, noted that he was not concerned about the political implications of his speeches. He did not ask, "Will this help me or hurt me in running for President?" He said what he believed people should know. Greenfield observed that students at some midwestern colleges were noticeably apathetic about world hunger. "You sure you want to talk about hunger?" he asked Bobby en route to another campus. "I don't think they care." Kennedy replied, "If they don't care, the hell with them."[14] He proceeded to deliver his speech, hoping to convince his audience of young people.

In southern Indiana, he castigated an audience for its apparent disinterest in the problems of the poor. He arrived late at the Ramada Inn in Vincennes, where about one hundred members of the city's service clubs had already started their lunch. After his set speech, he took questions and found the men mainly concerned with what they called "God's Time," the government-mandated Daylight Saving Time that was upsetting the farmers. Kennedy had no views on the matter, nor any knowledge of it; he quickly found an opening in a question to discuss starving children in affluent America.

"Do you know," he thundered, "that there are more rats than people in New York City?"

The club members, busily eating their Salisbury steak and worried about "God's Time," didn't know and couldn't care less. Many, in fact, had always thought of New York as something of a sewer anyway and burst into laughter.

Kennedy's face grew dark. The veins stood out in his neck as he said, slowly and grimly, "DON'T LAUGH!" The men quieted and stared at him. He completed his talk and quickly left. There was only a small scattering of applause.[15]

Except for that eloquent speech after King's death, when he was moved by powerful emotions, his usual speaking style would win him no prizes for oratory. His voice was too shrill, with no modulations. He talked too long, repeated himself continually, made numerous syntactical errors, and often chose the wrong words. He had a distracting habit of smacking his left palm with his right fist for emphasis and was always running his fingers through his hair. He became irritable and tendentious with his audience during after-speech question periods.

He wasn't very good at telling the slick one-liners his speechwriters invented for his appearances at large functions. Audiences would titter dutifully, but it was only when he became serious that they were captured. In small towns and rural areas, he abandoned stand-up comedy routines entirely and, with his informality and wry humor, developed an open, honest sense of community with people.

When he arrived in a town in the midst of a Slovak festival, he wanted to know how many Slovaks were in the crowd. There weren't any. "Well," he asked them, as a puzzled visitor might, "why are you having a Slovak festival?" There was a reason, of course, and explanations floated up to him from the throng, but they were lost in the general laughter. The give-and-take was not special, hardly brilliant, but it was homey and friendly.

In Eugene, Oregon, he told a crowd that their city was "the Eugene I like best in the country." To reporters who asked him what he would do if he lost the Oregon primary, he replied, "I might be a nice man. I'd return to being unruthless." A strikingly attractive blonde asked him in Indiana, "If you were elected President, would you appoint your brother Attorney General?" He answered, "No, we tried that once." The questioner was Joan Kennedy, wife of the senator.

He could tease the crowds, and they loved it.

At Turlock, California, in the San Joaquin Valley (population 9,116), famous for its turkeys, he asked a large throng gathered at the rail station, "Do you know what my family and I had for breakfast this morning?"

When he got a loud "No!" he said, "Turlock turkey. We have Turlock turkey every day for breakfast. Do you believe that?"

"Yes!" the throng bellowed back.

Kennedy: "Then you believe anything! Will you vote for me?"

310

Came the loudest roar yet: "YES!"

He was always asked about local issues. Sometimes he was briefed about them, most frequently there wasn't time, but knowledgeable or not, he was ready for them. At Sioux Falls, South Dakota, a middle-aged business-man called to him, "What priority are you giving to the Sioux Falls economy if you're elected President?"

Without missing a beat, Bobby assured him, "Top priority. The very *top*. Why, just this morning at breakfast I said to Ethel, 'We've got to do something about the Sioux Falls economy.' "

At an Indiana rally, there was a large sign, "BOBBY GO HOME!" in the back of a large parking lot. When he rose to speak, he pointed to the sign and said, "First I want to say that there's a little boy named Bobby whose mother wants him to come home right away." He had the crowd on his side at once, as he did in Wabash, when he grinned wickedly and said after his introduction by the mayor, "I am very happy to be in Wabash, and I want to say how grateful I am for the courtesy of your mayor—standing there with his Nixon button."

Ethel kept pace with Bobby on his sixteen-hour days, sharing the dais most of the time. Her bounce and gaiety were unflagging, and she never allowed anyone on the campaign to know that she was becoming seriously concerned about the alarming numbers of hate letters and telephone calls the family was receiving before the race was one month old. The threats were never publicized.[16]

She didn't dress down for the midwestern ladies, wearing $850 Courreges outfits, Elizabeth Arden wiglets, and patterned hose. She showed her knees in skirts two and three inches above her knees. But she went over well because she was completely natural. When a crying child interrupted a talk at a club, she giggled and said, "That makes me feel right at home." The audience loved it.

Inevitably, there were a few gaffes. Arriving in Los Angeles, she told a group how nice it was to be in Anaheim. "For Christ's sake, Ethel," Bobby whispered to her through closed lips, "if you're going to get the name of the city wrong, at least say you're glad in a low voice, so nobody can hear you!"

In Fort Wayne, Indiana, she told school children how happy she was to be in the city named for the great general who fought so gallantly in the War of 1812. "Mad Anthony" Wayne, whose name the city bears, fought in the American Revolution and died in 1796.

Quick thinking and alert ducking saved her from embarrassment when she toured a pharmaceutical company in California. Talking to employees engaged in the manufacture of birth control pills, she saw photographers approaching and ran for cover.

There were far fewer "Coffee with the Kennedys" get-togethers in neighborhoods, but Bobby had a powerful ally on his team, his mother Rose. After nearly a lifetime of campaigning, she had retired herself a few years before, saying enough was enough. As politically astute as anyone in the top echelon at headquarters, Rose saw what was happening and, although she was nearing seventy-eight, jumped in. "They need all the help they can get," she observed.

She stumped in Indiana, Nebraska, Oregon, and finally California, addressing rallies and making full use of television, which she studied carefully. "I wouldn't think of wearing a print," she said, "because they don't photograph well. I also make a point to wear light hats because they are flattering with my dark hair."

Rose also took the time to watch her candidate-son in action and offered some advice. He talked too rapidly. Rose told him to slow down; he did. "I noticed also he was letting his hair grow awfully long," she said, "perhaps because he was racing around the country with so much on his mind he didn't think about getting to a barber shop." She told him to get his hair cut, and he obeyed.

Rose made a major blunder that caused shudders in the Kennedy camp. Countless times she had been asked about the family fortune and elections, always blunting questioners by suggesting that enough had already been said about money. After the Indiana primary, when a reporter for *Women's Wear Daily* commented the campaign must have cost a great deal, she gave a different reply.

"It's our money," she said, "and we're free to spend it any way we please. It's part of this campaign business. If you had money, you spend it to win. And the more you can afford, the more you'll spend.

"The Rockefellers are like us. We both have lots of money to spend on our campaigns. It's something that's not regulated. Therefore, it's not unethical."

When she saw the headlines all across the country and heard her observation on the evening news, Rose bit her lip. She never discussed money again.

Almost daily came evidence of the remarkable rapport Bobby had with children.

In Indianapolis, he paid the politician's obligatory visit to the home of the Hoosier poet, James Whitcomb Riley, in a run-down section of town. Near the house was the Day Nursery Association of Indianapolis. About a dozen poorly dressed children from broken homes, mostly five-year-olds, were pressed against a rusting cyclone fence, which enclosed a postage-stamp-size playground in front of the house. Big-eyed, they stared at the Kennedy entourage as it passed.

Bobby saw them and stopped. After talking to the day nursery officials, he went inside the playground, knelt, and talked softly to the children, who had gathered around him. Two small girls put their heads on his lap.

"And suddenly it was hard to watch," wrote David Murray in the *Chicago Sun-Times*, "because he had become in that moment the father they did not know or the elder brother who couldn't talk to them, or more important, listen to them. . . . You can fool a lot of people in a campaign, and you can create phony issues if you want to . . . but lonely little children don't come up and put their heads on your lap unless you mean it."

All through March, April, and May, the campaign, though poor in organization, was rich in spirit. Crowds jam-packed town squares, fieldhouses, arenas, and airport terminals. More than 15,000 students, crushed together on the dirt floor of the vast Ahearn Fieldhouse at Kansas State University, literally exploded when he finished speaking, rising to their feet and screaming, pounding one another, and hitting chairs together to make more noise. Greetings were ecstatic at the University of Kansas in Lawrence and at Vanderbilt in Nashville. Some 20,000 jammed Campau Square in Grand Rapids, 12,000 turned out in Kalamazoo, and the enthusiasm was unbridled everywhere he went in West Virginia.

In places where enthusiasm was not quite so wild, the fertile brain of Richard Tuck, one of Kennedy's traveling assistants, made it appear greater than it was by his invention of the "spaghetti barricade."

Prior to the arrival of the candidate, Tuck would have fences erected in areas where Kennedy would appear, strong enough to look like fences but so fragile that a crowd pushing forward could easily knock them down and surge forward. The sight of masses of people breaking through barricades to get at Bobby made superb television and newspaper shots, not to mention news accounts, which would lead off with, "Supporters of Robert Kennedy crashed through barricades yesterday to reach the candidate for the Democratic nomination . . ."

Tuck was as politically astute as he was witty. The previous November he had been sent to Gary, Indiana, to watch out for election frauds in the contest between the Democratic machine candidate and Dick Hatcher, a black man. "[Tuck] had heard of a plot to have all the voting machines in the black wards break down at the height of the voting," said David Halberstam, "and so he sent off to nearby Chicago for ten Negro pinball machine repairmen . . . whom he tutored on a model of the voting machine. . . . On Election Day, sure enough, when the machines started breaking down, always in the black wards, Tuck's men fixed them in minutes instead of hours."

In the verdant valleys and cities of Oregon, the pep sputtered. The thin crowds didn't bother to burst through the spaghetti barricades. There were many more "McCarthy-for-President" signs than Kennedy cared to see. It was apparent he was in trouble there.

He didn't help much by going skinny-dipping in the Pacific. Walking on the beach at Astoria, he had asked photographers following not to snap pictures, and they didn't, but he neglected to ask reporters not to write anything. Next day, news accounts reported that the man who wanted to be President had flung off his clothes and swum naked in the ocean. Analysts later stated the incident cost him votes.

On May 24, McCarthy challenged him to a thirty-minute debate in Portland. Kennedy's staff, particularly the younger members, loved the idea. The primary would be held on the twenty-eighth, and this was a golden chance for their man, with his verve and emotionalism, to show up the phlegmatic McCarthy. He could do to him what his brother did to Nixon eight years before.

They didn't just tell him; they badgered him. Bobby, though, wasn't at all sure they were right. Oregonians were stolid people, and maybe McCarthy's style was what they preferred. Besides, as Donald Wilson said, "The old-fashioned political axiom is that you don't debate somebody who is less well-known than you."

Early next evening, Bobby blew his stack in the worst eruption of the campaign.[17]

He had retired to his suite at 6 P.M., after another day of thin crowds and lukewarm receptions, tired and frustrated. Ethel, too, never a good loser, began screaming at him. "She's very volatile," said one staff aide who had heard her through the closed door, "and while most of the time she was marvelous, she can be a tremendous pain sometimes."

Outside his eighth-floor suite, Walinsky, Edelman, and some of the other younger men were arguing the debate issue. Their voices rose louder than they intended, much too loud for the candidate, who had undressed and was trying to sleep before his appearance at a rally in a local high school.

When the arguing turned to shouts, laughter, and smart cracks, Bobby stormed into the corridor in his underwear. Don Wilson, who was on the floor at the time, remembered the incident vividly. "He really blew," Wilson said. "It was so rare for him to do that. I mean, he hollered."

"Why are you standing around making noise?" Bobby demanded. "If you want to do something, go ring doorbells!" To Adam, he yelled, "If you guitar-playing kids would stop making wise remarks and spend more time on writing speeches . . ." On long campaign trips, Adam and Jeff Greenfield would sometimes strum a guitar and sing old tunes.

Walinsky started toward the door, but Bobby slammed it in his face as he went back inside.

Next day, in a motorcade, Kennedy apologized to "the kids," having regretted his outburst.

Kennedy, who had lost in Oregon, finally agreed to debate McCarthy on national television but wished afterward he had trusted his instincts to skip it. The hour-long encounter in San Francisco's KGO-TV studios on June 1, three days before the primary, was a dull, dispirited fizzle. They agreed on every substantive point, prompting the moderator, Frank Reynolds, to exclaim, "Well, there don't seem to be very many differences between you on anything."

McCarthy won easily on appearance. He was handsome, self-assured, mature, and Presidential. Bobby looked too youthful, spoke too stridently, and seemed too tense. McCarthy also ran away with the crucial windup question when both candidates were asked why they wanted to be Chief Executive. His summary of his qualifications and how they met the mood of the nation was considered masterful by the daily journalists, while Kennedy's answer was rambling and repetitive.

Afterward, Newfield wondered why Bobby had done so poorly at the end. "You won't believe it," Kennedy answered, "but I was daydreaming. I thought the program was over, and I was trying to decide in my own mind where to take Ethel for dinner when they asked that last question. I was lucky I didn't answer, Joe DiMaggio's."[18]

Not long before the California primary, Kristi Witker sat next to Bobby on the campaign bus. Kennedy was half-slumped in his seat. "He looked very small-boyish, vulnerable, almost forlorn," Ms. Witker recalled.

"I told you this was going to be fun," he said, recalling their first meeting, "but there's a lot of loneliness in it, too. Do you feel it?"

"Suddenly," says Kristi, "I heard myself blurt out, 'Do you worry about it? About getting shot? Every time you make a speech I worry about it. All those crowds pushing and shoving around you, the chaos . . .' "

Kennedy replied, "There's not a minute that I'm not aware something like that could happen. But there's no point in worrying about it. It's counterproductive."

Says Kristi, "I had a feeling he wouldn't care. He looked so sad, almost fatalistic. He seemed resigned to the possibility that it might happen."

Toward the end of May, Bobby Kennedy sat cross-legged, his chest bare, on the living room floor in John Frankenheimer's Malibu Beach home, where he was staying. He had just come in from a swim in the ocean and was sipping a glass of orange juice.

The guest list for lunch that day was a glamorous one: Warren Beatty, Shirley MacLaine, Romain Gary, the French novelist, and his wife, the actress Jean Seberg, Pierre and Nicole Salinger, Angie Dickinson and Burt Bacharach, John Glenn, and the hosts, the Frankenheimers.

Two weeks earlier, Gary had said to Salinger, "You know, of course, that your guy will be killed?"

"I live with that fear," Salinger replied. "We do what can be done and that isn't much. He runs around like quicksilver."[19]

That day, Gary said to Bobby, "You know someone will try to kill you."

"The remark stopped everyone cold," says Salinger. "Bobby replied, 'Well that's the chance I have to take.' "[20]

Gary asked Bobby what precautions he was taking. Bobby shrugged.

"There's no way of protecting a country-stumping candidate. No way at all. You've just got to give yourself to the people and to trust them, and from then on it's just that good old bitch, luck.

"Anyway, you have to have luck on your side to be elected President of the United States. Either it's with you or it isn't. I am pretty sure there'll be an attempt on my life sooner or later. Not so much for political reasons. . . . Plain nuttiness, that's all. There's plenty of that around."[21]

At 11:30 P.M. on June 4, when returns showed Bobby had won the California primary, Frank Mankiewicz left the ballroom at the Ambassador Hotel, where 2,000 jubilant supporters waited for Bobby Kennedy, and took the elevator to Suite 511. Pushing through the jammed living room, he went into the bedroom and told Kennedy, "It's time to go. We've got both networks now. It's getting late. It's already nearly 3 A.M. in the East. Let's just come on down and make a speech to the crowd in the ballroom, and go over to see the writing press."

"Fine," said Bobby. Mankiewicz, Dutton, and Kennedy went into the second bedroom, which was empty, to discuss what the victorious candidate might say. Bobby scribbled some notes and stuffed them into a coat pocket.

He went out into the living room, where he drew Kenny O'Donnell aside. Alone in a corner, he said to him, "You know, Kenny, I feel now for the first time that I've shaken off the shadow of my brother. I feel I made it on my own."[22]

Watching him leave the suite, Kenny was thinking, "The guy now believes—he *really believes*—he could become President of the United States."

O'Donnell joined a dozen and a half others who trailed after Bobby and Ethel. Bobby took one elevator, she followed in another.

Postscripts

K RISTI WITKER looked down at him as he lay on the floor of the greasy
pantry. She had been only six feet behind him when the shots were
fired.

"At that moment he was conscious," Ms. Witker remembered. "We
looked right at each other, and he recognized me. From just three feet away,
I could see an alert expression on his face, an awareness, as though he were
remembering that conversation we had a short time ago, when he told me it
could happen.

"His face had a quizzical expression, which seemed to be saying, 'It
happened, it really happened.' It was as though he had known all along."

Pete Hamill was walking backward, preceding Kennedy as he left the
stage of the Ambassador Hotel ballroom through a heavy gold curtain at the
rear.

"And then we heard this sound—pow, pow! I was still watching him,
and there was this guy with his arm out who we didn't know, and there was
a rush toward him. I remember reaching over Rosie [Roosevelt] Grier and
hitting this fellow with the gun on the head and somebody saying, 'Oh, no,
it can't be Dallas!'

"And I went back to where Bobby was, and he was lying there. I
remembered looking at him, and his eyes were still open, but there was this
kind of sweet sort of smile on his face.

"I thought it was a smile of resignation that this was inevitable."

At Arlington National Cemetery, José Torres had a mystical experience
as he watched Robert Kennedy's body being lowered into the grave between

two Japanese magnolia trees. It was 10:30 P.M. Floodlights for the television cameras lit the site, a few yards down the slope from where John Kennedy lay. Torres, who had torn an Achilles tendon, rested on his crutches.

"As I looked at the casket," Torres said. "He spoke to me. I was so hurt. I had to understand what he had been trying to do. I felt it was hopeless now, that my people who had come so close to having a friend would never have one now.

"I felt we were doomed, that nobody would be able to help us. I heard, I swear I heard, the voice of Robert Kennedy. The voice said, 'I tried. Don't despair, José. Things will get better. Somebody will come. I know this. Believe it.'

"I went home and, somehow, I felt better."

When Attorney General Clark heard that Kennedy had been shot, his first act was to telephone Jim McShane, the chief United States marshal: "Get out to Hickory Hill immediately," Clark said, "and keep an eye on Ethel and the family."

Two weeks later, he received a phone call from Ethel.

"Ramsey," she said, "you know how much we love Jim, but he's got to get out of my house."

"What do you mean?" asked Clark, puzzled.

"Didn't you send him here?" Ethel asked.

"Yes, I did," Clark replied, "but he's not still there, is he?"

"He is."

Declared Clark, "It never occurred to me that Jim wouldn't go home the next day. He stayed because he was devoted to Robert and was so crushed by his death.

"Jim died later that year. People die of broken hearts, you know."

For months after the tragedy, Ethel Kennedy pushed herself beyond the limits of exhaustion to blot out the memories. Though pregnant, she raced up and down stairs, swam, and played tennis nonstop. Once she fell and injured herself painfully, but shrugged off help and continued with the game.

By day, she succeeded reasonably well in keeping away the demons, but at night, in bed, the events were replayed over and over in her mind. Then, sleepless, she would weep for hours. After seeing her distraught for many weeks, her secretary asked her, "If you think Bobby is in heaven, why don't you ask him to help you?"

Ethel sat up and replied, the tears staining her face, "I do! I go to sleep thinking about him."

Ethel believes that someday she and Bobby will be reunited in Heaven.

That is why she won't ever marry again, despite the number of men with whom she has been linked over the years. "How could I possibly do that with Bobby looking down from Heaven?" she asks. "That would be adultery."

She came close to a romance only once. After Bobby died, she and Andy Williams, the singer, who had been a family friend, were together a great deal, dancing, laughing, holding hands. "That could have developed into a deep relationship," a friend said, "but it didn't because she feels herself still 'married' to Bobby. She is so married to him that she could not make that jump, marriage to another man."

That kind of deep commitment is not rare in persons who have had a close marriage based on shared vision of life eternal.

Ethel is now "winding down," says a family friend. She still has parties, but not the tumultuous, crowded ones she once had. These days the parties are small affairs, with a few close friends. At the Cape, she spends much of the time sailing.

She has brought to a close the famous RFK Pro-Celebrity Tennis Tournament, held annually for the past ten years to raise funds for the Robert F. Kennedy Memorial. The Memorial awards fellowships to young people to work on social projects around the country that carry on Bobby's goals to help the disadvantaged.

Ethel used to devote five months of the year to the tournament, which drew together the world's leading tennis pros, who were teamed with celebrities from the worlds of entertainment, sports, government, and the arts. Said David Hackett, director of the Memorial, "They have become too much of a burden for her."

Nearing her sixtieth birthday (she was born April 11, 1928), Ethel's face is now lined and weathered by advancing years and the sun and wind. Despite much exercise, she is thicker around the middle. Outwardly, her personality has not changed a great deal: she is peppy, energetic, and fast with one-liners. She is still, on occasion, uninhibited. When Andy Williams didn't blow out the candles on his birthday cake fast enough in 1984, she pushed his face into it.

The change is inward.

The event in California has left deep emotional scars. She is unable to watch a movie that involves shooting and someone dropping dead. Films are shown once or twice weekly in the cabana near the swimming pool at her Hickory Hill estate. If a shooting scene occurs, she rushes from the room.

Once a young volunteer was blowing up balloons at a fund-raising event. Suddenly it exploded with a loud pop. Ethel, who was only a few feet away, turned white and cringed, as though ducking a bullet. "Oh, my

God!'' she cried. Everyone stared at her. In a moment, the fear passed, and she resumed work, saying nothing about the incident.

Ethel spends her summers at the compound and the rest of the year lives quietly at Hickory Hill. Pets still roam over the grounds and in and out of the house, but there is an emptiness there, the forlorn look of a place after party guests have gone. Only Rory Elizabeth, born seven months after Bobby died, lived at home in 1986, a student at the exclusive Madeira School, but she, too, will be off to college before long.

On October 9, 1984, Ethel spoke in public for the first time since her son David died from a drug overdose, the previous April 25, at the age of twenty-eight.

Sixty persons gathered in the dining room at Hickory Hill for the annual Robert F. Kennedy Book Awards luncheon. Seated next to her was Roger Rosenblatt, author of *Children of War,* who had just received one of the awards, an inscribed bust of RFK, which he had placed on the table in front of him. Ethel, who had been chatting easily with Rosenblatt, got up to speak.

"I think,'' she began, "that the thing that meant most to Bobby than anything was to make gentle . . .''

Tears suddenly filled her eyes. Her throat tightened, her lips compressed. Unable to continue, she sat down. She was trying to complete the quotation from Aeschylus her husband used so often: ". . . to tame the savageness of man and make gentle the life of the world.''

"There was silence in the room, total, complete, for a few seconds,'' Rosenblatt recalled. "I took her hand and held it. Then three of her children, Courtney, Douglas, and Rory, rose suddenly from their chairs and rushed to their mother. It was like a football huddle. They put their arms around her, and she clasped hers around them.

"All at once, amazingly, the kids started to giggle, as if to say, 'This is how we bring ourselves out of sorrow.' In a few moments, Ethel began giggling, too, with tears still running down her face, and then she began to laugh, and the spell of grief was over.''

Ethel has received a large measure of blame for what happened to David. In her grief at her own loss, she allegedly failed to give David the guidance he needed at a critical time in his life, and instead of providing understanding, she lashed out at him in rage.

Only once has Ethel responded to these charges, though indirectly.

At David's funeral, the faithful Luella Donovan was present. To her, Ethel said, "I did my best for my children, and this is the way it turned out. You can't hold their hands after they are adults. They have to live their lives themselves.''

*   *   *

When David was a teenager, he spent two summers at the home of John Seigenthaler in Nashville. "He had an insatiable desire to know everything about his father," Seigenthaler recalled. "He would stay up late each night—and sometimes all night long—listening to me tell stories of Bobby. He asked question after question, not only about his dad but all the people with whom he had ever worked.

"David worked on the newspaper with me those years [the *Nashville Tennessean*] and got seven or eight bylines. He had a real talent. Could have been a fine journalist."

After David's death, LaDonna Harris wrote a note to Ethel, saying she would always remember David as a little boy playing at Hickory Hill. She urged Ethel to remember these good times.

Ethel sent her a hand-written note in reply, saying she, too, would remember David "in the best of his times."

If Robert Kennedy had won the nomination and had been elected President in 1968, what would he have accomplished in office? Some of his close associates and friends reply:

Pierre Salinger: John Kennedy brought a new spirit to Washington. Like him, Robert Kennedy would have inspired countless numbers of young people to enter government, as a challenge to make a lasting contribution to America and for Americans.

Cesar Chavez: He would have ended the Vietnam War right away.

David Hackett: He would have provided blacks, Hispanics, and other minorities with legitimate avenues of participation in solving their problems.

John Seigenthaler: He would have been a potent reconciling force between the generations, because he understood the wide gap that had developed between young people and those twenty or more years older. He would have attacked aggressively any pervasive evil that arose in America's midst. He would have continually challenged the country to resolve their internal differences, and by this would have been a great healing force in bringing Americans together. With his vision, ingenuity, he would have created and implemented a new course to reduce the level of crime in our society.

Former Senator George A. Smathers: We would have had some form of socialized medicine in the United States, because, under President Robert Kennedy, there would have been a greater tilt toward social progress than there was in his brother's administration.

Endicott Peabody Davison, law school classmate and lifelong friend: He would have come in swinging on civil rights, and blacks would have obtained more civil liberties sooner.

Pete Hamill, journalist and author: The Administration of John Kennedy is popularly remembered as the Camelot years. But Camelot was a fairyland, a legendary place that never existed. Under President Robert Kennedy, we would have had enormous forward strides in social progress on every front, and, moreover, the CIA would never have been permitted the free rein it enjoyed under other Presidents.

That would have been the *real* Camelot.

NOTES

(Oral histories are herein abbreviated to OH)

RFK: A Prologue

1. Ghetto visit, author interview with Torres.
2. RFK, OH, JFK Library.
3. Gunther, *Inside USA,* p. 679.
4. RFK, OH, JFK Library.
5. Ibid.
6. Author interview.
7. Sullivan, *The Bureau,* p. 56. (By 1971, Sullivan was the number-three man in the FBI. He was killed the following year in a hunting accident in New Hampshire.)
8. Ibid., p. 48.
9. Statement by NAACP, October 1964, during RFK Senate campaign.
10. RFK interview with Oriana Fallaci, *Look,* 3/9/65.
11. Cohn, *McCarthy,* p. 72.
12. De Toledano, *RFK,* p. 50.
13. Ibid., p. 49.
14. Wes Barthelmes, OH, JFK Library.
15. Susan Issacs, "What It's Like to be a Kennedy," *Parents* (November 1980).

1. His Father's Son

1. Author interview.
2. Ibid.
3. Kennedy, *Times to Remember,* p. 76.
4. Gunther, *Inside USA,* p. 456.
5. Laing, *The Next Kennedy,* pp. 75–76.
6. Author interview.
7. *Fortune,* September 1937.
8. Martin, *A Hero for Our Time,* p. 33.
9. Farley, *Jim Farley's Story,* p. 115. Cited in Koskoff, *Joseph P. Kennedy,* p. 73.
10. Koskoff, *Joseph P. Kennedy,* p. 83. Koskoff found the note in the President's Personal File, No. 207, at FDR Library, Hyde Park.

2. Little Altar Boy

1. Whalen, *The Founding Father,* p. 92.
2. Kennedy, *Times to Remember,* p. 286.
3. Parmet, *JFK,* p. 14.
4. Kennedy, *Times to Remember,* p. 286.
5. Harris Wofford, author interview.
6. Luella Hennessey Donovan, author interview.
7. Schlesinger, *Robert Kennedy,* p. 18.
8. Kennedy, *Times to Remember,* p. 163.
9. Krock, *Memoirs,* pp. 353–54.
10. *The New York Herald-Tribune,* October 29, 1938.

11. Ickes, *Secret Diary,* Vol. III, entry of March 10, 1940, p. 147.
12. *The Boston Globe,* November 10, 1940.
13. Krock, *Memoirs,* p. 338. (Krock employed the euphemism *outhouse* for the word Kennedy obviously spoke. It was one of his favorite expressions.)

3. Preppie

1. Perry, Cleveland, Norris, and Adams materials in this chapter obtained by author interviews at Milton.
2. Portsmouth Priory School Catalogue, 1940–41.
3. Transcript from Gene Schoor's excellent file of early RFK materials.
4. Schoor file.
5. Author interview, 1971.
6. All St. John material: author interview, 1975.
7. Yearbook, *Orange and Blue,* Milton Academy archives.
8. Wes Barthelmes, OH, JFK Library.
9. Author interview.
10. Searls, *Lost Prince,* p. 196.

4. Turn in the Road

1. The story of how the Kennedys learned of Joe's death was related to the authors by Joe McCarthy, a Kennedy family friend and author, and by Lem Billings. Searls, *Lost Prince,* p. 290, and Kennedy, *Times to Remember,* also have accounts.
2. JFK's involvement with Arvad has been well documented. Best accounts are in Blair and Blair, *Search for JFK,* and Parmet, *Jack.*
3. Billings, Green, and Adams comments: author interviews in 1970, 1973, and 1985, respectively.
4. McTaggart, *Kathleen Kennedy,* p. 245.
5. Joe McCarthy, author interview. See also O'Donnell and Powers, *Johnny We Hardly Knew Ye.*
6. Schlesinger, *RFK,* p. 64., citing correspondence from Hyannis Port Papers and Joseph P. Kennedy Papers.
7. JFK Papers, JFK Library. Letter sent January 1, 1945.
8. Schoor file.
9. Knowles, OH, JFK Library.
10. Rodis, Adams comments: author interviews.

NOTES

11. For fuller account of EMK at Harvard, see David, *Ted Kennedy*, pp. 52–70.
12. Brady, OH, JFK Library.
13. Lawford, *That Shining Hour*, p. 18.
14. Author interview, 1971.
15. Schoor file.

5. Bobby and Ethel—The Early Years

1. *The New York Times Magazine*, November 30, 1968.
2. Burns, Clark comments: author interviews.
3. Gager, *Kennedy Wives*, p. 217, from *The Washington Post*, 1974.
4. Author interview with Harris.
5. Paar, *My Saber Is Bent*, p. 148.
6. Glass, Harris: author interviews 1970 and 1985, respectively.
7. Lin Root, author and journalist, author interview.
8. *Look*, 3/9/70.
9. Author interview, 1970.
10. Burner and West, *The Torch Is Passed*, p. 195.
11. Author interview.
12. Tremblay, Sommer, Davison statements: author interviews.
13. Bunche material based on interview with Davison.
14. See *Time*, February 9, 1976; *The New York Times*, December 10, 1975.

6. "A Royal Pain"

1. Schoor files.
2. Spalding, OH, JFK Library.
3. RFK, OH, JFK Library.
4. Schlesinger, *Robert Kennedy*, p. 98, from Hyannis Port Papers. Letter dated October 10, 1951.
5. Ibid., p. 69.
6. RFK, OH, JFK Library
7. Ibid.
8. Martin, *A Hero for Our Time*, p. 498.
9. Author interview.
10. Schoor, *Young Robert Kennedy*, p. 111.
11. RFK, OH, JFK Library
12. Whalen, *The Founding Father*, p. 421.
13. RFK, OH, JFK Library.
14. Stein and Plimpton, *American Journey*, p. 44.

7. McCarthyite

1. Cohn, *McCarthy*, pp. 45–46.
2. Ibid., p. 48.
3. Krock, *Memoirs*, p. 342.
4. Collier and Horowitz, *The Kennedys*, p. 202.

5. De Toledano, *RFK*, p. 51.
6. Nathan Borock, author interview.
7. Bobby's rush to the pay window was related to author by Willard Edwards, who, as correspondent for *The Chicago Tribune*, covered McCarthy from the beginning to his end. "The girls in the office were always astonished by that," he said.
8. Cohn, *McCarthy*, p. 66.
9. Sorensen, *Kennedy Legacy*, p. 36.
10. Author interview.
11. Ibid.
12. New York *Daily News*, June 17, 1984.
13. Rovere, *Senator Joe McCarthy*, p. 248.
14. Manchester, *Glory and the Dream*, p. 637.
15. Eugene J. McCarthy Papers, Box 47, Georgetown University Library, Washington, D.C. Quoted in Burner and West, *The Torch Is Passed*, p. 197.
16. Vidal, Gore, "The Best Man," *Esquire* (March 1963).
17. Kennedy, *The Enemy Within*, p. 176.
18. The exchange of letters was released to the press by McCarthy's office.
19. Author interview. Bayley is now dean of the Graduate School of Journalism, U.C. at Berkeley.
20. Kennedy, *The Enemy Within*, p. 172.
21. Thompson and Myers, *The Brothers Within*, p. 121.

8. First There Was Beck . . .

1. Author interview.
2. Dineen, *Kennedy Family*, p. 181.
3. Ibid., p. 182.
4. Author interview.
5. Collier and Horowitz, *The Kennedys*, p. 220.
6. Dineen, *Kennedy Family*, p. 216.
7. Lawford, *That Shining Hour*, p. 46.
8. Hooker, OH, JFK Library.
9. Ibid.

9. When Two Strong Men Meet Face to Face

1. James and James, *Hoffa and the Teamsters*, p. 37.
2. Mollenhoff, *Tentacles of Power*, p. 149; Sheridan, *Fall and Rise*, p. 32.
3. Schlesinger, *RFK*, p. 164, from RFK papers, May 3, 1957.
4. Pearson, *Diaries*, p. 378.
5. Mollenhoff, *Tentacles of Power*, p. 148.
6. Ibid., p. 149.

324

7. Ibid., pp. 154–55.
8. Ibid., pp. 198–99; Sheridan, *Fall and Rise,* p. 34.
9. Stein and Plimpton, *American Journey,* p. 57.
10. Sheridan, *Fall and Rise,* p. 300.
11. Moldea, *Hoffa Wars,* p. 185.
12. Burke, OH, JFK Library.
13. *The New York Times,* December 17, 1971.
14. Letter to RFK, February 17, 1960, in personal file, JFK Library.
15. Author interview.
16. Ibid.
17. *Time,* April 13, 1959.
18. Stein and Plimpton, *American Journey,* p. 53.
19. *The New Republic,* January 9, 1961.
20. Previant's "list" is in Proceedings of the Central Conference of Teamsters, Dept. 28, 1958, and is reprinted in *The California Law Review* 51 (1963): 297–98.

10. Electing Jack

1. Dolan, OH, JFK Library.
2. Ibid.
3. Lawford, *That Shining Hour,* p. 50.
4. Hooker, OH, JFK Library.
5. Author interview.
6. Salinger, *With Kennedy,* p. 46. Other versions, with similarities and differences, appear in White, *Making;* Sam Houston Johnson, Baker, *Wheeling;* Schlesinger, *RFK,* among others. Nobody knows, or is likely to know, the true story.
7. Conway, OH, JFK Library.
8. RFK, OH, JFK Library.
9. Halberstam, *Powers That Be,* p. 319.
10. Martin, *A Hero For Our Time,* p. 222.
11. Author interview.
12. Looking back on her life as a politician's wife, Pat Nixon said, "I've given up everything I've ever loved." For a full account of Mrs. Nixon's attitude toward politics, see Lester David, *The Lonely Lady of San Clemente* (New York: Thomas Y. Crowell, 1978), pp. 73–90.
13. Lisagor, OH, JFK Library.
14. Kennedy, *Times to Remember,* p. 221.
15. RFK, OH, JFK Library.
16. Author interview.
17. RFK, OH, JFK Library.
18. Ibid.
19. RFK address in Waterbury, Ct., November 6, 1960.
20. RFK, OH, JFK Library.
21. *Newsweek's* happy phrase, March 18, 1963. Fra Girolamo Savonarola, a fifteenth-century religious reformer, attacked moral laxity with burning zeal.

11. The AG—At Work

1. Guthman, *We Band of Brothers,* p. 82.
2. Sidey, *John F. Kennedy,* p. 145.
3. *Newsweek,* March 18, 1963.
4. Ibid.
5. Lawford, *That Shining Hour,* p. 78.
6. *The Boston Sunday Globe,* January 28, 1962.
7. Author interview.
8. Ibid.
9. *The New York Times,* August 11, 1962.
10. RFK, OH, JFK Library.
11. De Toledano, *J. Edgar Hoover,* p. 306.
12. RFK, OH, JFK Library.
13. Author interview.
14. Sullivan, *The Bureau,* p. 644.
15. Bradlee, *Conversations With Kennedy,* p. 33.
16. Sullivan, *The Bureau,* p. 50.
17. RFK, OH, JFK Library.

12. The AG—At Home

1. Smith, *Entertaining in the White House,* p. 240. Smith's excellent account includes favorite Kennedy recipes, table service, and many menus.
2. Author visit to Ted Kennedy's home.
3. *London Daily Mail,* March 23, 1968.
4. Author interview.
5. Ibid.
6. Edelman, OH, JFK Library.
7. Wofford, *Of Kennedys and Kings,* p. 409.
8. Author interview.
9. Dallas, *Kennedy Case,* p. 167.
10. Ibid., p. 110.

13. The Man to See

1. Sorensen, *Kennedy,* p. 301.
2. Day, *My Appointed Round,* p. 9.
3. RFK–JFK communication in Sorensen, *Kennedy,* p. 301; Dallas, *Kennedy Case,* p. 141.
4. Author interview.
5. Order to Harriman in Collier and Horowitz, *Kennedys,* p. 290; Harriman statement, OH, JFK Library.
6. Confidential source, former staff aide.
7. *Newsweek,* March 18, 1963.
8. Schlesinger, *A Thousand Days,* p. 574.
9. Anecdote told to author by Ramsey Clark.
10. For details of LBJ attitude toward RFK, see Sam Houston Johnson, *My Brother Lyndon,* pp. 159–81.

11. Dutton, OH, JFK Library.
12. Author interview.
13. Lisagor, OH, JFK Library.

14. Three Worst Foreign Crises

1. O'Donnell and Powers, *Johnny We Hardly Knew Ye*, p. 278.
2. RFK, OH, JFK Library.
3. Ibid.
4. Ibid.
5. Bowles, *Promises to Keep*, p. 332.
6. Author interview.
7. Marquis Childs, *Good Housekeeping*, May 1962.
8. Wofford, *Of Kennedys and Kings*, p. 351.
9. RFK, OH, JFK Library.
10. Childs, op. cit., p. 351.
11. Guthman, *We Band of Brothers*, p. 110.
12. Ibid., p. 113.
13. *Time*, February 1, 1963.
14. Talbot, *Khrushchev Remembers*, pp. 498–99.
15. Ibid., p. 505.
16. Ibid., p. 506.
17. Salinger, with Kennedy, p. 190.
18. O'Donnell and Powers, *Johnny We Hardly Knew Ye*, p. 303.
19. RFK, OH, JFK Library.
20. Author interview.
21. Salinger, who gave the authors more detailed information about the letters than has ever been revealed, said, "I am the key for them. I was the intermediary for their transmission." See also Salinger, *With Kennedy*, pp. 197–98.
22. RFK statements on Bolshakov from his OH, JFK Library.
23. Kennedy, *Thirteen Days*, p. 26.
24. Presidential recordings, Papers of John F. Kennedy, Presidential Papers, President's Office Files, Cuban Missile Crisis, October 16, 1962, pp. 14–31, JFK Library.
25. Kennedy, *Thirteen Days*, p. 31.
26. Sorensen, *Kennedy*, p. 765.
27. Ball, *The Past Has Another Pattern*, p. 290.
28. Cuban Missile Crisis recordings, op. cit., p. 24.
29. Martin, *A Hero for Our Time*, p. 461.
30. Ball, *The Past Has Another Pattern*, p. 291.
31. Lincoln, *My Twelve Years with John F. Kennedy*, p. 323.
32. Devine, *Cuban Missile Crisis*, p. 28.
33. Kennedy, *Thirteen Days*, p. 97.
34. Author interview.
35. Kennedy, *Thirteen Days*, p. 97.
36. Author interview with Salinger for this and

subsequent material on Khrushchev letters. See also Salinger, with Kennedy, passim, and Sorensen, *Kennedy*, pp. 621–25.
37. Taylor, *Swords and Plowshares*, p. 265.
38. Author interview with Donald Wilson.

15. Of Sex and Marilyn

1. Sullivan, *The Bureau*, p. 56.
2. Schoor files.
3. *Time*, June 1, 1962.
4. Martin, *Adlai Stevenson and the World*, p. 693.
5. Schlesinger, *RFK*, p. 637.
6. BBC Documentary, *The Last Days of Marilyn Monroe*.
7. Ibid.
8. *The New York Times*, October 5, 1985.
9. *The Los Angeles Herald-Examiner*, August 6, 1962.
10. Noguchi and DiMona, *Coroner*, pp. 67–8.
11. Author interview, all Guthman material.
12. *The New York Times*, November 23, 1985.
13. BBC Documentary, op. cit.
14. Author interview.
15. UPI, November 9, 1985.
16. *The New York Times*, November 23, 1985.
17. Noguchi and DiMona, *Coroner*, p. 84.
18. Pepitone and Stadiem, *Marilyn Monroe Confidential*, p. 236.
19. Here and subsequently, material from Hackett, Clark, Glass, O'Donnell, Torres, Adams, from author interviews. Schaap, *RFK*, p. 22.
20. This and preceding: RFK, OH, JFK Library.
21. For further details and documentation on Rometsch story, see *The New York Times*, October 29 and 30, 1963; *Time*, March 6, 1964; Baker, *Wheeling and Dealing*, p. 80; RFK, OH, JFK Library; *New York Post*, October 30, 1963.
22. Details in U.S. Congress. Senate. Select Committee to Study Governmental Activities with Respect to Intelligence Activities (Senator Frank Church, chairman), *Alleged Assassination Plots Involving Foreign Leaders*, Interim Report, 1975, pp. 129–30.
23. Ibid., p. 130.

16. Passage to Commitment

1. Author interview.
2. Newfield, *Robert Kennedy*, p. 46.
3. Author interview with Seigenthaler provided this detailed account of RFK reaction to King arrest.
4. Wofford, *Of Kennedys and Kings*, p. 21.

5. RFK's private visits to schools related to author by Guthman.
6. RFK, OH, JFK Library.
7. Author interview with Seigenthaler and Clark on blacks in Department of Justice.
8. Appearance before Senate Judiciary Committee hearings on his cabinet appointment, January 13, 1961.
9. Historic encounter betweeen RFK and King related to author by Seigenthaler.
10. Horne and Schickel, *Lena*, p. 277.
11. Ibid., pp. 279–80. See also, RFK, OH, JFK Library; Stein and Plimpton, *American Journey*, pp. 119–22; Guthman, *We Band of Brothers*, p. 219–21.
12. Ibid.
13. Author interview.

17. Quarterback for Civil Rights—1

1. Author interview.
2. Ibid.
3. Ibid.
4. RFK, OH, JFK Library.
5. Author interview provided Seigenthaler's graphic account of episode in Montgomery.
6. Guthman, *We Band of Brothers*, p. 178.
7. Ibid.

18. Quarterback for Civil Rights—2

Much of the material in this chapter comes from transcripts of recorded conversations newly released by the JFK Library. See Papers of John F. Kennedy, Presidential Papers, President's Office Files, Presidential Recordings, *Integration of the University of Mississippi*, 131 pp. Author interviews with Meredith provided additional information. See also Meredith, *Three Years in Mississippi; Time,* October 12, 1962; *Facts on File,* Vol. XXII, No. 1144, September 27–October 3, 1962; and Lincoln, *My Twelve Years with John F. Kennedy,* pp. 316–320. Other sources follow.

1. RFK, OH, JFK Library.
2. Schulberg, Budd, "Harbingers of Hope," *Esquire* (January 1969).
3. RFK, OH, JFK Library.
4. Clark, OH, JFK Library.
5. Author interview.
6. O'Donnell and Powers, *Johnny We Hardly Knew Ye,* pp. 254–55.
7. Guthman, *We Band of Brothers*, p. 205.
8. RFK, OH, JFK Library. For University of Alabama encounter, see Guthman, *We Band of Brothers,* pp. 207–23; *The New York Times,* June 12, 1963; *Time,* June 21, 1963.

9. Stein and Plimpton, *American Journey,* p. 125.

19. "Someone Turned Off His Switch"

1. The story of RFK birthday party and events at White House reception were related to author by Clark. See also Clark, OH, JFK Library.
2. Manchester, *Death of a President,* p. 33.
3. Clark, author interview.
4. Account of RFK trying to bar LBJ from Oval Office told to author by Smathers; see also LBJ, OH, JFK Library.
5. RFK, OH, JFK Library.
6. *Look,* 3/9/65.
7. Author interview.
8. Hooker, OH, JFK Library.
9. Kelley, *Jackie Oh!,* p. 236.
10. Author interviews.
11. Ibid.
12. Ibid.
13. Jackie reaction: chief sources: West, *Upstairs,* pp. 277–79; Kelley, *Jackie Oh!,* pp. 229–36; Martin, *A Hero for Our Time,* p. 571.
14. West, *Upstairs,* p. 281.
15. Salinger, author interview.
16. *Jet,* June 20, 1968.
17. *New York Post,* December 22, 1963.
18. Author interview.
19. Ibid.
20. *RFK* fatalism: author interviews with aides and friends. See also Newfield, *Robert Kennedy,* passim; Schlesinger, *RFK,* pp. 665–69.
21. Author interview.
22. Laing, *The Next Kennedy,* p. 257.
23. Guthman, Hackett: author interviews.
24. Schlesinger, *RFK,* p. 658.
25. Author interview.

20. For Love of a Brother—A Coverup

1. Wilson, OH, JFK Library.
2. *Look,* July 9, 1968. Cited in Salinger, *Honorable Professor,* p. 56.
3. Schlesinger, *RFK,* p. 662; Katzenbach, OH, JFK Library.
4. Church committee report, op. cit., pp. 17–19, 85–89.
5. Ibid., pp. 133–34; 332–33.
6. Ibid., p. 124.
7. Ibid., p. 135.
8. See Parmet, *JFK,* p. 219; Powers, The *Man Who Kept the Secrets,* p. 138; Wofford, *Of Kennedys and Kings,* p. 416 ff.
9. Amory, OH, JFK Library.
10. Church committee report, op. cit., p. 143.

11. Ibid., p. 149.
12. Ibid., p. 263.
13. Ibid., p. 333.
14. Ibid., p. 332.
15. Schlesinger, *RFK*, p. 532.
16. Church committee report, op. cit., p. 333.
17. *The Chicago Tribune*, June 17, 1975.
18. Ibid., June 16, 1975.
19. Janis, Leon, "The Last Days of the President," *Atlantic* (July 1973).
20. Sheridan, OH, JFK Library.

21. Indecision

1. English, OH, JFK Library.
2. Author interviews.
3. Ibid.
4. *Time*, October 30, 1964.
5. Lisagor, Peter, "Portrait of a Man Emerging from the Shadows," *The New York Times Magazine*, July 19, 1964. Lisagor interviewed RFK in June.
6. Johnson, *My Brother Lyndon*. Sam Houston discusses the "Bobby problem" on pp. 159–81.
7. Account of air crash and RFK at hospital from *The New York Herald-Tribune, The Boston Globe*, and *The Springfield Republican*, June 20, 1964; also author interviews with Birch Bayh and hospital personnel.
8. Kennedy, *Times to Remember*, p. 457.
9. *The New York Times*, June 30, 1964.
10. Vanden Heuvel and Gwirtzman, *On His Own*, p. 44.
11. Guthman, *We Band of Brothers*, p. 280.
12. Johnson, *My Brother Lyndon*, p. 167.
13. RFK–LBJ interview and subsequent details from author interviews with Clark and other aides, supplemented by Guthman, *We Band of Brothers;* Vanden Heuvel and Gwirtzman, *On His Own;* and Sam Houston Johnson, *My Brother Lyndon*.
14. Evans and Novak, *Lyndon B. Johnson and the Exercise of Power*, p. 446.
15. McGovern, OH, JFK Library.
16. Thimmesch and Johnson, *Robert Kennedy at 40*, p. 173.
17. Schlesinger, *RFK*, p. 721.

22. "Ich Bin Ein New Yorker"

1. Gardner, *Robert Kennedy in New York*, p. 19.
2. *The New York Times*, September 4, 1964.
3. Gardner, *Robert Kennedy in New York*, p. 8.
4. Ibid., p. 36.
5. *The New York Times*, October 9, 1964.
6. Upstate tour from author interviews with Burns, Guthman; Burns, OH, JFK Library.
7. Author interview with Sol Handwerker, Jay Cohen.
8. Felknor, *Dirty Politics*, p. 192.
9. The Gardner, Thimmesch and Johnson, and Guthman books provided much campaign material; so did the files of *The New York Times, The New York Herald-Tribune, The Boston Globe, The Worcester Sunday-Telegram*.
10. Nickerson, OH, JFK Library.

23. The Freshman Senator

1. Harris, *Potomac*, p. 53.
2. Barthelmes, OH, JFK Library.
3. Laing, *The Next Kennedy*, p. 37.
4. Barthelmes, OH, JFK Library.
5. Edelman, OH, JFK Library.
6. RFK dealings with media; Javits story: Barthelmes, OH, JFK Library.
7. Harris recollections, author interview.
8. Javits, OH, JFK Library.
9. Barthelmes, OH, JFK Library.
10. David, *Ted Kennedy*, p. 163.
11. Edelman, OH, JFK Library.
12. Kupferman, OH, JFK Library.
13. RFK personal characteristics, Barthelmes, OH, JFK Library; English, Burns, Salinger, Guthman, Harris, author interviews.
14. Newburg, OH, JFK Library.
15. Littlefield, Burns recollections, author interviews.
16. Barthelmes OH, JFK Library.
17. Harris, *Potomac*, p. 146.

24. Catharsis

1. Spalding, OH, JFK Library.
2. *Life*, April 9, 1965.
3. Stein and Plimpton, *American Journey*, p. 171.
4. *Life*, April 9, 1975.
5. Author interview.
6. Confidential source.
7. Laing, *The Next Kennedy*, p. 305.
8. Wilson, author interview and OH, JFK Library.
9. *Redbook* episode: RFK Papers, Attorney General's Correspondence, Personal File, Box 14, 1961–1964, JFK Library. Story of Carey prank detailed in David, *Ted Kennedy*, pp. 56–57.
10. The "book" episode has been discussed extensively by Lasky, Newfield, Shannon, De Toledano, and Schlesinger. See also John

Corry, *The Manchester Affair* (New York: Putnam, 1967), and Manchester's own story of the controversy in *Look*, April 4, 1967.

11. Stein and Plimpton, *American Journey*, p. 215.

12. Hamill, Pete, "Why, God, Why?" *Good Housekeeping*.

13. Johnston, OH, JFK Library.

14. Schmidt, OH, JFK Library for this and subsequent statements.

15. Bedford-Stuyvesant Restoration Corp., Brooklyn, N.Y. provided much information on the project.

16. Chavez episode: author interview, supplemented by his OH, JFK Library.

17. Insights into RFK and Indians provided by Mrs. Fred Harris.

18. Author interview, Burns.

25. "What Shall I Do?"

1. English, *Divided They Stand*, p. 57.

2. Jenny Littlefield was major source for Lowenstein–RFK material, supplemented by Harris, *Dreams Die Hard;* English, *Divided They Stand;* Newfield, *Robert Kennedy;* and Witcover, *85 Days.*

3. Krock, *Memoirs*, p. 328.

4. Author interview.

5. Collier and Horowitz, *The Kennedys*, pp. 291–92.

6. Author interview.

7. Ibid.

8. *Village Voice*, December 28, 1967.

9. Author interview, Newfield.

10. Ibid, Salinger.

11. Witcover, *85 Days*, p. 28.

12. White, *Making of the President–1968*, p. 85.

13. Story of January 20–21 meeting: Frank J. Burns, OH, JFK Library.

14. Newfield, *Robert Kennedy*, p. 204.

15. Vanden Heuvel and Gwirtzman, *On His Own*, pp. 260–61.

26. "I Am Announcing My Candidacy"

1. Author interview, Hamill's account.

2. Schmidt, OH, JFK Library.

3. Author interview with Chavez and his OH at JFK Library were major sources for events and statements at Delano.

4. *The Washington Star,* March 18, 1968.

5. Account of publishers' dinner at Hickory Hill was related to author by Mr. and Mrs. Laursen. Laursen and Grunfeld published stories of their visit in *Merrick Life*, June 13, 1968, and *The Marathon Independent*, March 21, 1968.

6. Harris, author interview. Senator Harris was a guest at the dinner.

7. Greenfield, OH, JFK Library.

8. AP, March 16, 1968, in *Newsday*.

9. Burke, OH, JFK Library.

10. Author interview with Hamill.

11. McCarthy statements from author interview.

12. Ibid.

13. Jennie Littlefield, author interview. See also Newfield, *Robert Kennedy*, p. 237.

14. English, *Divided They Stand*, p. 110.

27. March 16 to June 4

1. Salinger, *Honorable Profession*, p. 23.

2. Greenfield, OH, JFK Library.

3. Dutton, OH, JFK Library.

4. Ibid.

5. Ibid.

6. Newburg, OH, JFK Library.

7. The account of how RFK learned of Johnson's decision is from author interviews with Burns and English, and from Burns, OH, JFK Library.

8. Salinger, who was traveling with Bobby, reported the scene at the airport to the authors.

9. Scene at outdoor rally from Dutton, OH, JFK Library, and many media people present.

10. Greenfield, OH, JFK Library.

11. English, *Divided They Stand*, p. 131.

12. Stein and Plimpton, *American Journey*, pp. 285–86.

13. Steve Bell, Perspective Radio Network, June 9, 1968, reprinted in Salinger, *Honorable Profession*, p. 135.

14. Greenfield, OH, JFK Library.

15. Salinger, *With Kennedy*, p. 90.

16. Confidential source.

17. Wilson, OH, JFK Library. See also Witcover, *85 Days*, pp. 213–15.

18. Newfield, *Robert Kennedy*, p. 282.

19. Gary, *White Dog*, p. 192.

20. Author interview.

21. Gary, *White Dog*, p. 194.

22. Author interview.

BIBLIOGRAPHY

Baker, Bobby. *Wheeling and Dealing: Confessions of a Capitol Hill Operator.* New York: W.W. Norton & Co., 1978.

Ball, George W. *The Past Has Another Pattern: Memoirs.* New York, London: W.W. Norton & Co., 1982.

Blair, Joan and Clay Blair, Jr. *The Search for JFK.* New York: Berkley Publishing Corp., 1976.

Bowles, Chester. *Promises to Keep: My Years in Public Life (1941–1969).* New York: Harper & Row, 1971.

✓ Bradlee, Benjamin C. *Conversations With Kennedy.* New York: W.W. Norton & Co., 1975.

Bruno, Jerry and Jeff Greenfield. *The Advance Man.* New York: William Morrow and Co., 1971.

Burner, David and Thomas R. West. *The Torch Is Passed: The Kennedy Brothers and American Liberalism.* New York: Atheneum, 1984.

Cameron, Gail. *Rose.* New York: G.P. Putnam's Sons, 1971.

Collier, Peter and David Horowitz. *The Kennedys: An American Drama.* New York: Summit Books, 1984.

Cohn, Roy. *McCarthy.* New York: New American Library, 1968.

Dallas, Rita. *The Kennedy Case.* G.P. Putnam's Sons, 1973.

David, Lester. *Ted Kennedy: Triumphs and Tragedies.* New York: Grosset & Dunlap, 1971, 1972.

Day, J. Edward. *My Appointed Round: 929 Days as Postmaster General.* New York, Chicago, San Francisco: Holt, Rinehart and Winston, 1965.

De Toledano, Ralph. *J. Edgar Hoover: The Man In His Time.* New Rochelle, N.Y.: Arlington House, 1973.

————. *RFK: The Man Who Would Be President.* New York: G.P. Putnam's Sons, 1967.

Detzer, David. *The Brink: Cuban Missile Crisis, 1962.* New York: Thomas Y. Crowell, 1979.

Devine, Robert A., ed. *Cuban Missile Crisis.* Chicago: Quadrangle Books, 1971.

Dineen, Joseph F. *The Kennedy Family.* Boston, Toronto: Little, Brown & Co., 1959.

English, David and the staff of *The London Daily Express. Divided They Stand.* Englewood Cliffs, N.J.: Prentice-Hall, 1969.

Evans, Rowland and Robert Novak. *Lyndon B. Johnson and the Exercise of Power.* New York: New American Library, 1966.

Gunther, John. *Inside USA.* New York and London: Harper & Brothers, 1947.

Guthman, Edwin G. *We Band of Brothers.* New York: Harper & Row, 1971.

Gager, Nancy. *Kennedy Wives, Kennedy Women.* New York: Dell, 1976.

Gardner, Gerald. *Robert Kennedy in New York.* New York: Random House, 1965.

Gary, Romain. *White Dog.* New York: World Publishing Co., 1970.

Halberstam, David. *The Unfinished Odyssey of Robert Kennedy.* New York: Random House, 1968.

————. *The Powers That Be.* New York: Alfred A. Knopf, 1979.

Harris, David. *Dreams Die Hard.* New York: St. Martin's/Marek, 1982.

Harris, Fred R. *Potomac Fever.* New York: W.W. Norton & Co., 1977.

Harwood, Richard and Haynes Johnson. *Lyndon.* New York, Washington, London: Praeger Publishers, 1973.

Horne, Lena and Richard Schickel. *Lena.* Garden City, N.Y.: Doubleday & Co., 1965.

Humphrey, Hubert H. *The Education of a Public Man: My Life and Politics*. New York: Doubleday & Co., 1976.

Ickes, Harold L. *The Secret Diary of Harold L. Ickes,* Vol. III. New York: Simon and Schuster, 1953–4.

James, Ralph and Estelle James. *Hoffa and the Teamsters: A Study of Union Power*. Princeton, N.J., New York, Toronto, London: D. Van Nostrand Co., 1965.

Javits, Jacob K. *Javits: The Autobiography of a Public Man*. Boston: Houghton Mifflin Co., 1981.

Kelley, Kitty. *Jackie Oh!* Secaucus, N.J.: Lyle Stuart, 1978.

Kennedy, Robert F. *The Enemy Within*. New York and Evanston: Harper & Row, 1960.

————. *Thirteen Days: A Memoir of the Cuban Missile Crisis*. New York: W.W. Norton & Company, 1969.

Kennedy, Rose Fitzgerald. *Times to Remember*. Garden City, N.Y.: Doubleday & Co., 1974.

King, Coretta Scott. *My Life with Martin Luther King, Jr*. New York, Chicago, San Francisco: Holt, Rinehart and Winston, 1969.

Krock, Arthur. *Memoirs: Sixty Years on the Firing Line*. New York: Funk & Wagnalls, 1968.

Koskoff, David E. *Joseph P. Kennedy: A Life and Times*. Englewood Cliffs, N.J.: Prentice-Hall, 1974.

Laing, Margaret. *The Next Kennedy*. New York: Coward-McCann, 1968.

Lawford, Patricia Kennedy, ed. *That Shining Hour*. Privately published.

Lincoln, Evelyn. *My Twelve Years with John F. Kennedy*. New York: David McKay Co., 1965.

Lord, Walter. *The Past That Would Not Die*. New York, Evanston and London: Harper & Row, 1965.

Mailer, Norman. *Marilyn*. New York: Grosset & Dunlap, 1973.

Manchester, William. *The Glory and the Dream*. Boston, Toronto: Little, Brown and Co., 1973–4.

Martin, John Bartlow. *Adlai Stevenson and the World*. Garden City, N.Y.: Doubleday & Co., 1977.

Martin, Ralph G. *A Hero for Our Time: An Intimate Story of the Kennedy Years*. New York: Macmillan Publishing Co., 1983.

McCarthy, Eugene J. *The Year of the People*. Garden City, N.Y.: Doubleday & Co., 1969.

McTaggart, Lynne. *Kathleen Kennedy: Her Life and Times*. Garden City, N.Y.: The Dial Press, 1983.

Meredith, James. *Three Years in Mississippi*. Bloomington, London: Indiana University Press, 1965.

Messick, Hank. *John Edgar Hoover*. New York. David McKay Co., 1972.

Moldea, Dan E. *The Hoffa Wars; Teamsters, Rebels, Politicians and the Mob*. New York. Paddington Press, 1978.

Mollenhoff, Clark R. *Tentacles of Power: The Story of Jimmy Hoffa*. World Publishing Co., 1965.

Newfield, Jack. *Robert Kennedy: A Memoir*. New York: E.P. Dutton & Co., 1969.

Noguchi, Thomas T. and Joseph DiMona. *Coroner*. New York: Pocket Books, 1983.

O'Donnell, Kenneth P. and David F. Powers. *Johnny We Hardly Knew Ye*. Boston, Toronto: Little, Brown and Co., 1970, 1972.

Paar, Jack. *My Saber Is Bent*. New York: Trident Press, Simon and Schuster, 1961.

Parmet, Herbert S. *Jack, The Struggles of John Kennedy*. Garden City, N.Y.: The Dial Press, 1980.

———. *JFK: The Presidency of John F. Kennedy.* Garden City, N.Y.: The Dial Press, 1983.

Pearson, Drew. *Diaries, 1949–1959,* ed. Tyler Abell. New York: Holt, Rinehart and Winston, 1974.

Pepitone, Lena and William Stadiem. *Marilyn Monroe Confidential: An Intimate Personal Account.* New York: Simon and Schuster, 1979.

Ross, Douglas. *Robert F. Kennedy: Apostle of Change.* New York: Trident Press, Simon and Schuster, 1968.

Rovere, Richard. *Senator Joe McCarthy.* New York: Harcourt, Brace and Co., 1959.

Salinger, Pierre. *With Kennedy.* Garden City, N.Y.: Doubleday and Co., 1966.

———, ed. *An Honorable Profession: A Tribute to Robert Kennedy.* Garden City, N.Y.: Doubleday and Co., 1968.

Schlesinger, Arthur M., Jr. *A Thousand Days: John F. Kennedy in the White House.* Boston: Houghton Mifflin Co.; Cambridge: The Riverside Press, 1965.

———. *Robert Kennedy and His Times.* New York: Ballantine Books, 1979.

Schoor, Gene. *Young Robert Kennedy.* New York: McGraw-Hill Book Co., 1969.

Searls, Hank. *The Lost Prince: Young Joe, The Forgotten Kennedy.* New York and Cleveland: World Publishing Co., 1969.

Shannon, William J. *The Heir Apparent: Robert Kennedy and the Struggle for Power.* New York: The Macmillan Co., 1967.

Sheridan, Walter. *The Fall and Rise of Jimmy Hoffa.* New York: Saturday Review Press, 1972.

Sidey, Hugh. *John F. Kennedy: A Reporter's Inside Story.* New York: Atheneum, 1963.

Smith, Marie. *Entertaining in the White House.* New York: MacFadden Bartell Corp., 1970.

Stein, Jean and George Plimpton. *American Journey: The Times of Robert Kennedy.* New York: Harcourt Brace Jovanovich, 1970.

Sorensen, Theodore C. *Kennedy.* New York: Bantam, 1966.

———. *The Kennedy Legacy: A Peaceful Revolution for the Seventies.* New York: The Macmillan Co., 1969.

Sullivan, William C. *The Bureau: My 30 Years in Hoover's FBI.* New York, London: W.W. Norton & Company, 1979.

Summers, Anthony. *Goddess: The Secret Lives of Marilyn Monroe.* New York: Macmillan Publishing Co., 1985.

Talbot, Strobe, ed. *Khrushchev Remembers.* Boston, Toronto: Little, Brown and Co., 1974.

Taylor, Gen. Maxwell D. *Swords and Plowshares.* New York: W.W. Norton & Co., 1972.

Thimmesch, Nick, and William Johnson. *Robert Kennedy at 40.* New York: W.W. Norton & Co., 1965.

Thompson, Robert E., and Hortense Myers. *Robert F. Kennedy: The Brother Within.* New York: The Macmillan Company, 1972.

Vanden Heuvel, William and Milton Gwirtzman. *On His Own: RFK 1964–68.* Garden City, N.Y.: Doubleday & Co., 1970.

West, J.B. *Upstairs at the White House.* New York: Coward, McCann & Geoghegan, 1973.

✓ Whalen, Richard J. *The Founding Father: The Story of Joseph P. Kennedy.* New York: New American Library, 1964.

✓ White, Theodore H. *The Making of the President—1968.* New York: Atheneum, 1969.

Witcover, Jules. *85 Days: The Last Campaign of Robert F. Kennedy.* New York: Ace Publishing Corp., 1969.

Wofford, Harris. *Of Kennedys and Kings.* New York: Farrar, Straus & Giroux, 1980.

Wyden, Peter. *Bay of Pigs: The Untold Story,* New York: Simon & Schuster, 1979.

Index